To my parents

Paul
Up North

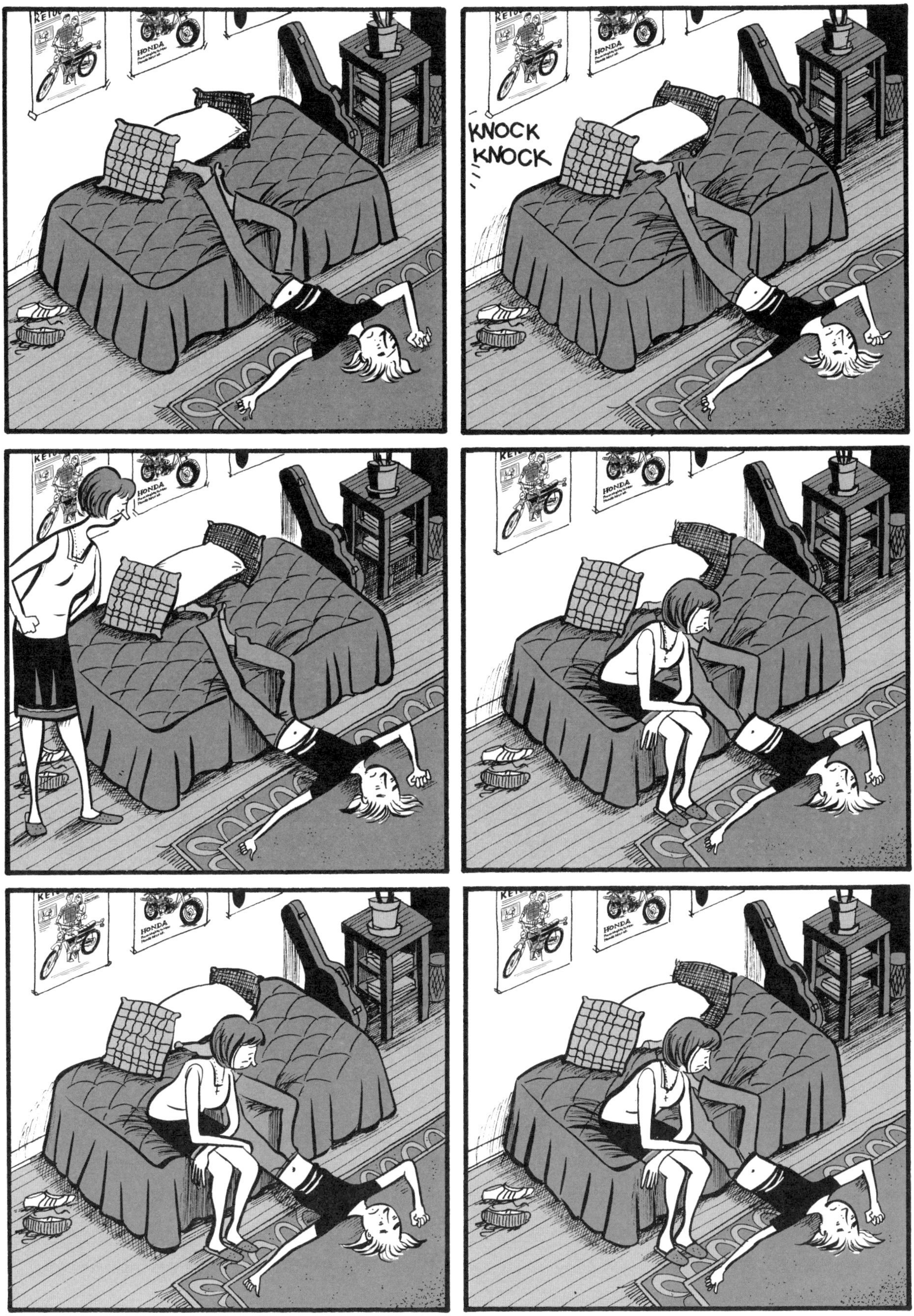
HONDA
KNOCK
KNOCK

Paul Up North © Michel Rabagliati, 2016

Originally published as *Paul dans le Nord* by Les Éditions de la Pastèque, © 2015

Translation by Helge Dascher
Thanks to Rob Aspinall, Dag Dascher, John Kadlecek, Mark Lang, and Paul "2 Dice" Paradis.

BDANG logo by Billy Mavreas
BDANG Imprint edited by Andy Brown

Library and Archives Canada Cataloguing in Publication

Rabagliati, Michel
[Paul dans le Nord. English]
     Paul up North / Michel Rabagliati.

 Translation of: Paul dans le Nord.
ISBN 978-1-77262-001-6 (paperback)

     1. Graphic novels. I. Title. II. Title: Paul dans le
Nord. English

PN6734.P38628R3213 2016   741.5'971   C2016-900436-8

 |7

First English Edition
Printed by Gauvin Press in Gatineau, Quebec, Canada

Conundrum Press
Wolfville, NS, Canada
www.conundrumpress.com

Conundrum Press acknowledges the financial support of the Canada Council for the Arts and the Government of Canada through the Canada Book Fund toward its publishing activities.

We acknowledge the financial support of the Government of Canada through the National Translation Program for Book Publishing, an initiative of the Roadmap for Canada's Official Languages 2013-2018 : Education, Immigration, Communities, for our translation activities.

 Canada Council for the Arts   Conseil des Arts du Canada

 Canada

Michel Rabagliati

Paul Up North

Conundrum

Saint-Sauveur

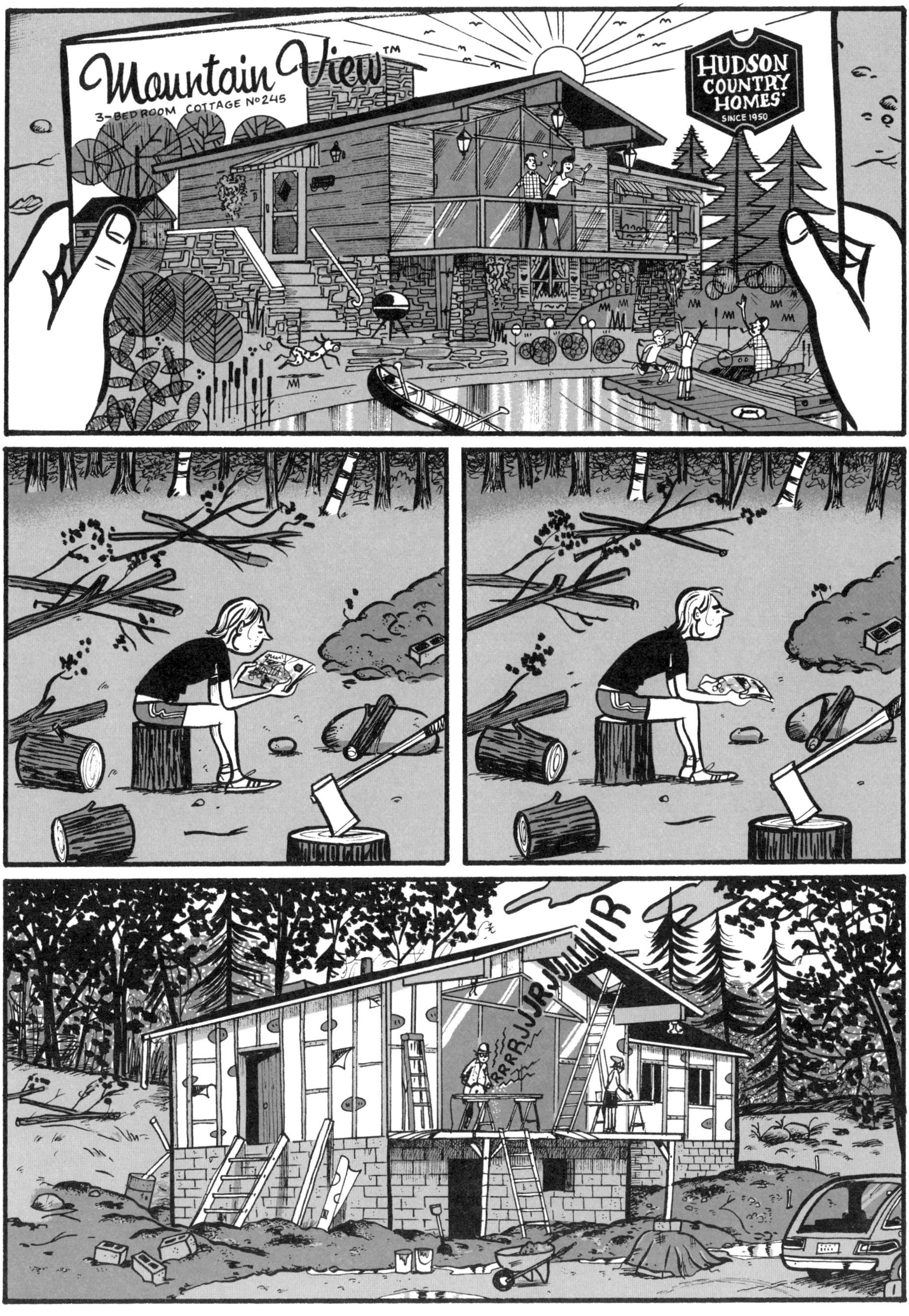
Mountain View™
3-BEDROOM COTTAGE No245
HUDSON COUNTRY HOMES
SINCE 1950
RRRRJJJJRJJJJJJIR

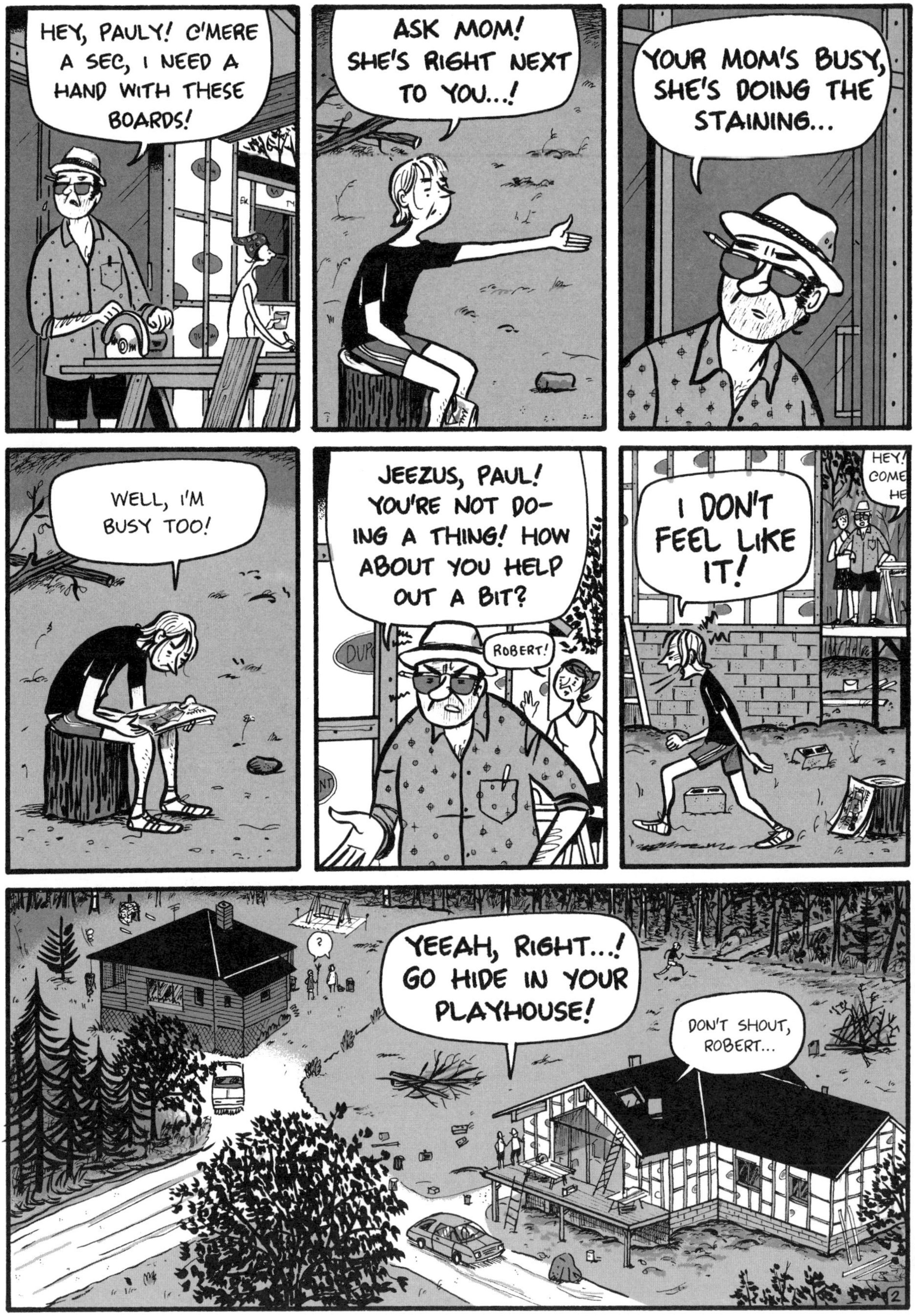
HEY, PAULY! C'MERE A SEC, I NEED A HAND WITH THESE BOARDS!
ASK MOM! SHE'S RIGHT NEXT TO YOU...!
YOUR MOM'S BUSY, SHE'S DOING THE STAINING...
WELL, I'M BUSY TOO!
JEEZUS, PAUL! YOU'RE NOT DOING A THING! HOW ABOUT YOU HELP OUT A BIT?
ROBERT!
I DON'T FEEL LIKE IT!
YEEAH, RIGHT...! GO HIDE IN YOUR PLAYHOUSE!
DON'T SHOUT, ROBERT...
?
2

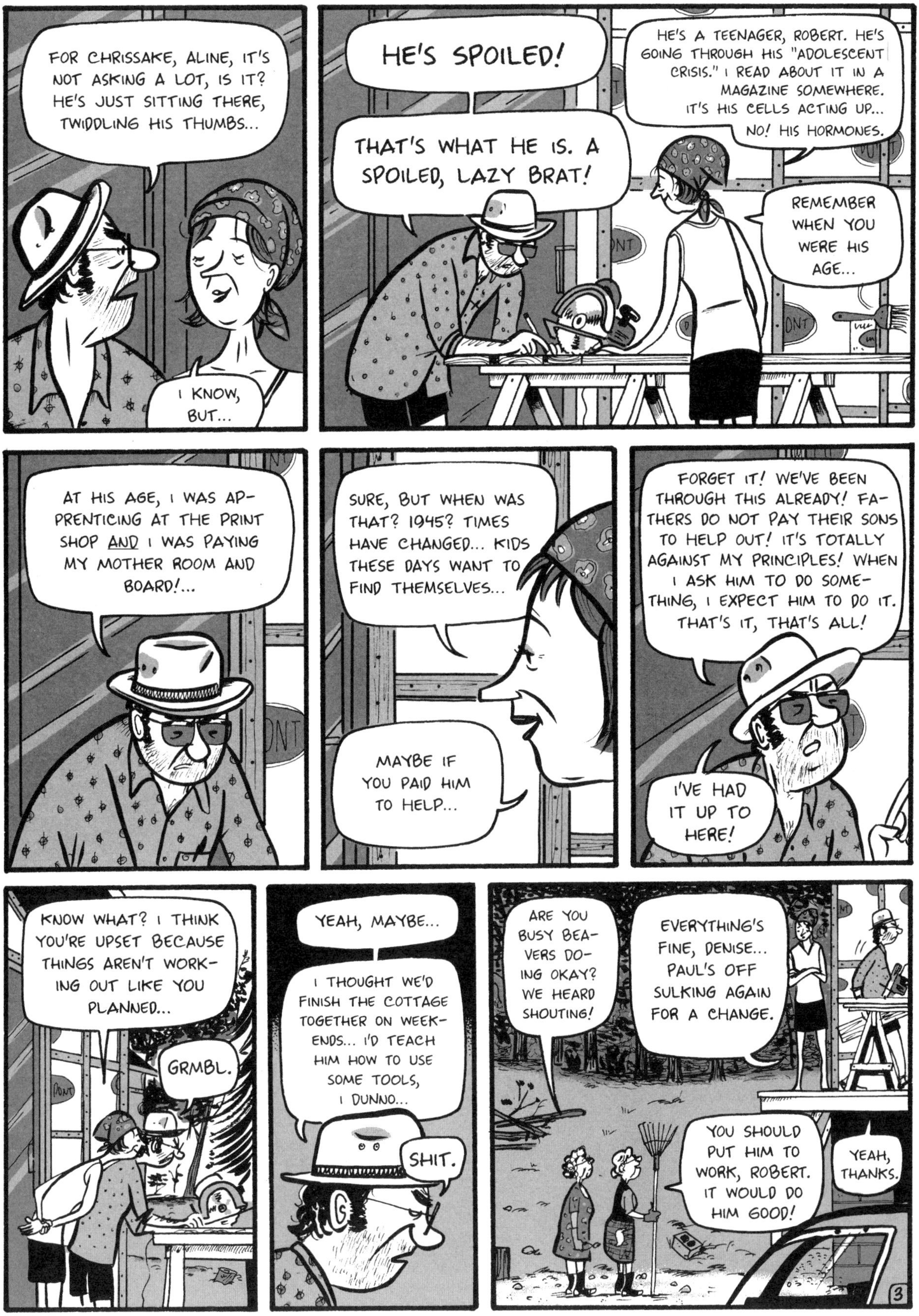
FOR CHRISSAKE, ALINE, IT'S NOT ASKING A LOT, IS IT? HE'S JUST SITTING THERE, TWIDDLING HIS THUMBS...
I KNOW, BUT...
HE'S SPOILED!
THAT'S WHAT HE IS. A SPOILED, LAZY BRAT!
HE'S A TEENAGER, ROBERT. HE'S GOING THROUGH HIS "ADOLESCENT CRISIS." I READ ABOUT IT IN A MAGAZINE SOMEWHERE. IT'S HIS CELLS ACTING UP... NO! HIS HORMONES.
REMEMBER WHEN YOU WERE HIS AGE...
AT HIS AGE, I WAS APPRENTICING AT THE PRINT SHOP AND I WAS PAYING MY MOTHER ROOM AND BOARD!...
SURE, BUT WHEN WAS THAT? 1945? TIMES HAVE CHANGED... KIDS THESE DAYS WANT TO FIND THEMSELVES...
MAYBE IF YOU PAID HIM TO HELP...
FORGET IT! WE'VE BEEN THROUGH THIS ALREADY! FATHERS DO NOT PAY THEIR SONS TO HELP OUT! IT'S TOTALLY AGAINST MY PRINCIPLES! WHEN I ASK HIM TO DO SOMETHING, I EXPECT HIM TO DO IT. THAT'S IT, THAT'S ALL!
I'VE HAD IT UP TO HERE!
KNOW WHAT? I THINK YOU'RE UPSET BECAUSE THINGS AREN'T WORKING OUT LIKE YOU PLANNED...
GRMBL.
YEAH, MAYBE...
I THOUGHT WE'D FINISH THE COTTAGE TOGETHER ON WEEKENDS... I'D TEACH HIM HOW TO USE SOME TOOLS, I DUNNO...
SHIT.
ARE YOU BUSY BEAVERS DOING OKAY? WE HEARD SHOUTING!
EVERYTHING'S FINE, DENISE... PAUL'S OFF SULKING AGAIN FOR A CHANGE.
YOU SHOULD PUT HIM TO WORK, ROBERT. IT WOULD DO HIM GOOD!
YEAH, THANKS.
3

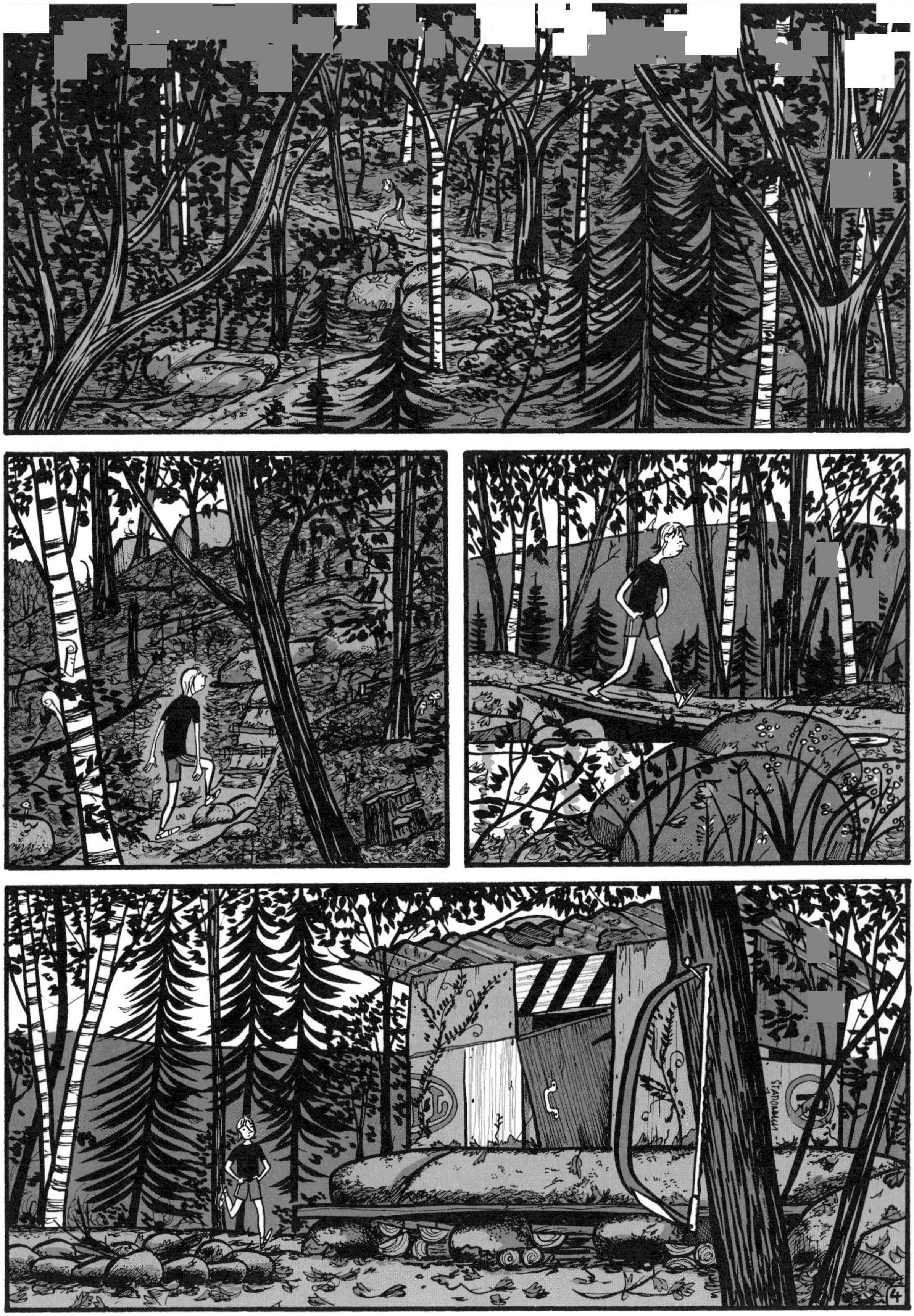

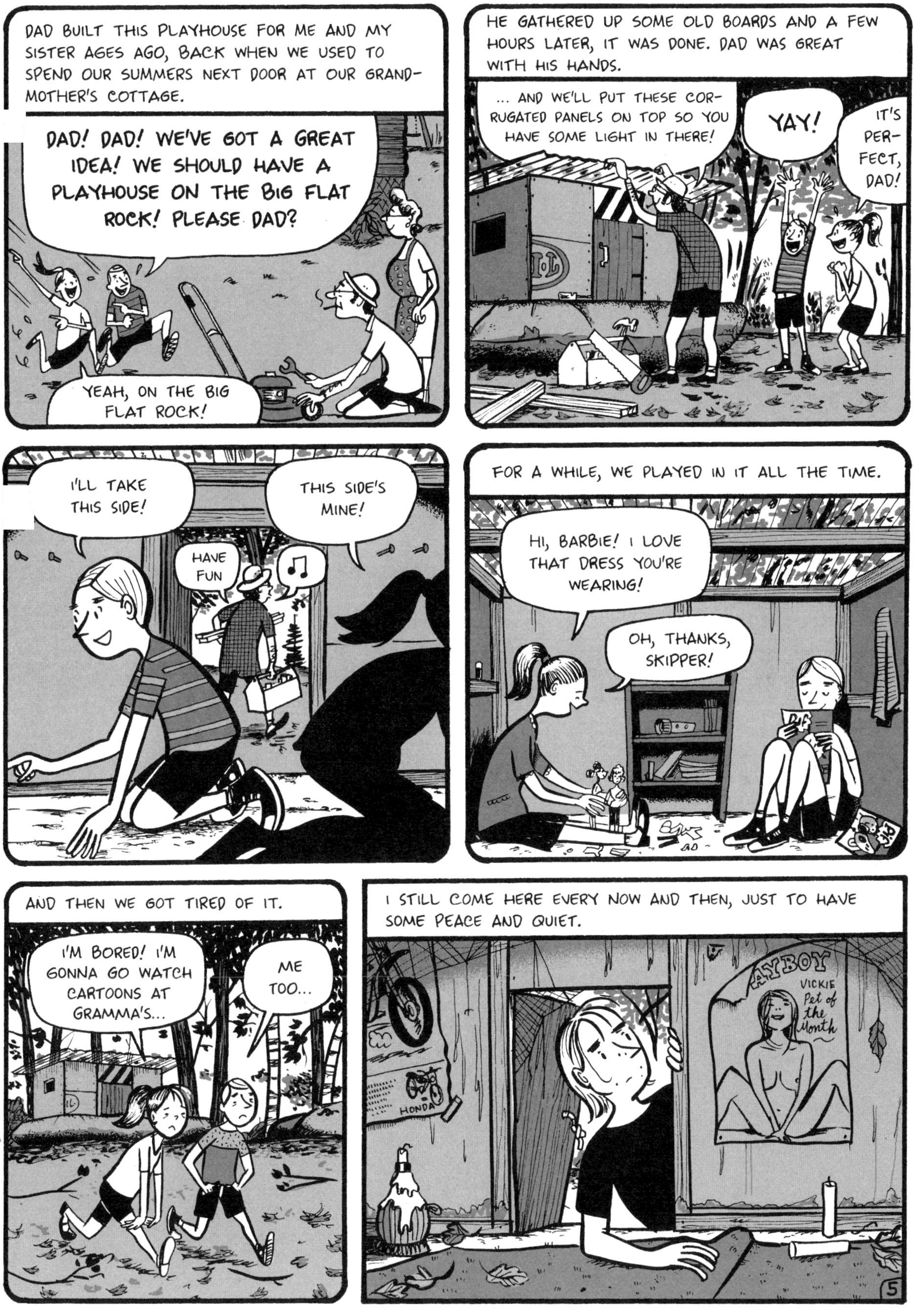
DAD BUILT THIS PLAYHOUSE FOR ME AND MY SISTER AGES AGO, BACK WHEN WE USED TO SPEND OUR SUMMERS NEXT DOOR AT OUR GRAND-MOTHER'S COTTAGE.
DAD! DAD! WE'VE GOT A GREAT IDEA! WE SHOULD HAVE A PLAYHOUSE ON THE BIG FLAT ROCK! PLEASE DAD?
YEAH, ON THE BIG FLAT ROCK!
HE GATHERED UP SOME OLD BOARDS AND A FEW HOURS LATER, IT WAS DONE. DAD WAS GREAT WITH HIS HANDS.
... AND WE'LL PUT THESE COR-RUGATED PANELS ON TOP SO YOU HAVE SOME LIGHT IN THERE!
YAY!
IT'S PER-FECT, DAD!
I'LL TAKE THIS SIDE!
THIS SIDE'S MINE!
HAVE FUN
♫
FOR A WHILE, WE PLAYED IN IT ALL THE TIME.
HI, BARBIE! I LOVE THAT DRESS YOU'RE WEARING!
OH, THANKS, SKIPPER!
AND THEN WE GOT TIRED OF IT.
I'M BORED! I'M GONNA GO WATCH CARTOONS AT GRAMMA'S...
ME TOO...
I STILL COME HERE EVERY NOW AND THEN, JUST TO HAVE SOME PEACE AND QUIET.
AYBOY
VICKIE Pet of the Month
HONDA
5

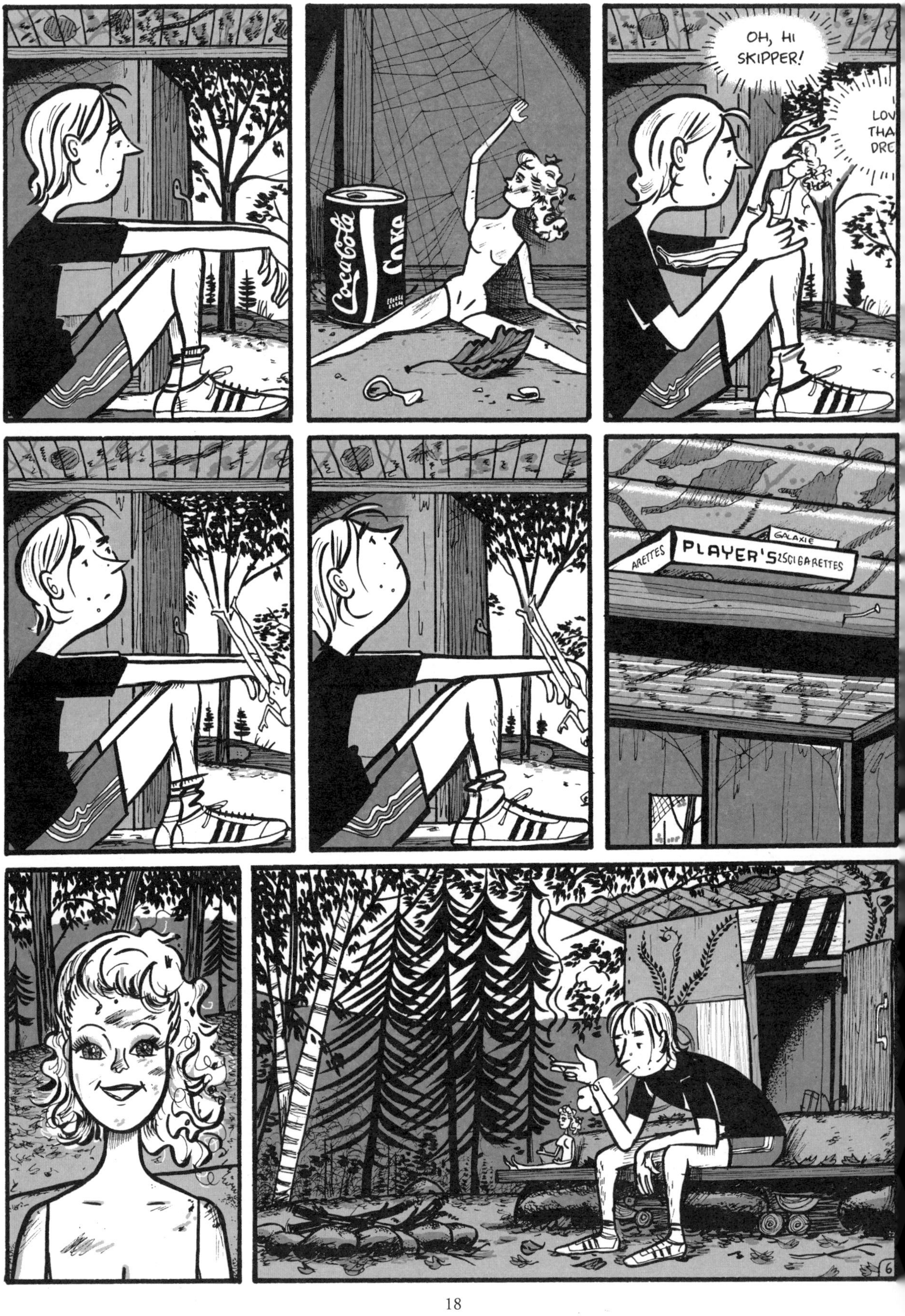

Coca-Cola
Coke
OH, HI SKIPPER!
LOV
THA
DRE
ARETTES
PLAYER'S 25 CIGARETTES
GALAXIE

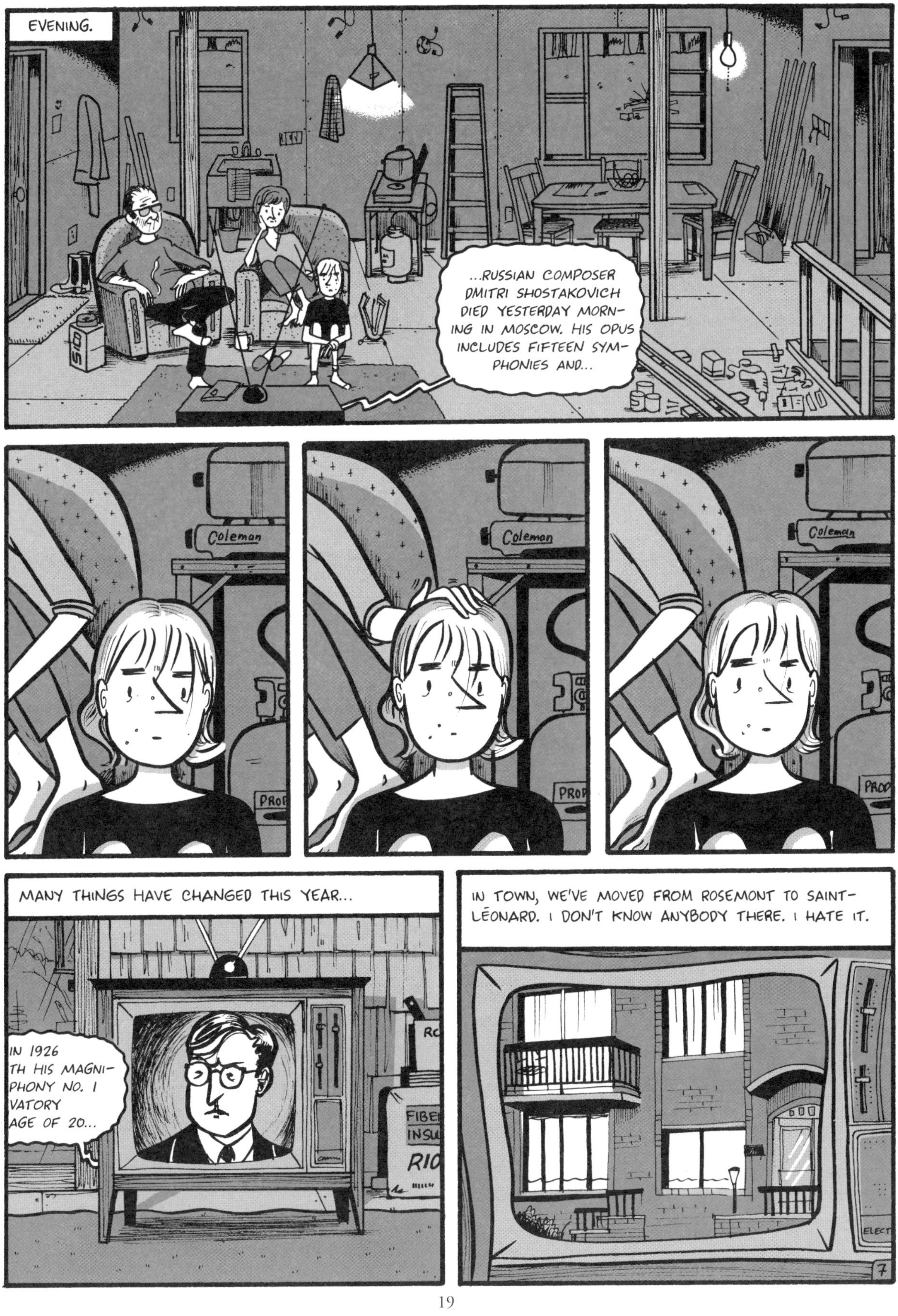
EVENING.
...RUSSIAN COMPOSER DMITRI SHOSTAKOVICH DIED YESTERDAY MORNING IN MOSCOW. HIS OPUS INCLUDES FIFTEEN SYMPHONIES AND...
Coleman
Coleman
Coleman
MANY THINGS HAVE CHANGED THIS YEAR...
IN 1926
TH HIS MAGNI-
PHONY NO. 1
VATORY
AGE OF 20...
IN TOWN, WE'VE MOVED FROM ROSEMONT TO SAINT-LÉONARD. I DON'T KNOW ANYBODY THERE. I HATE IT.
7

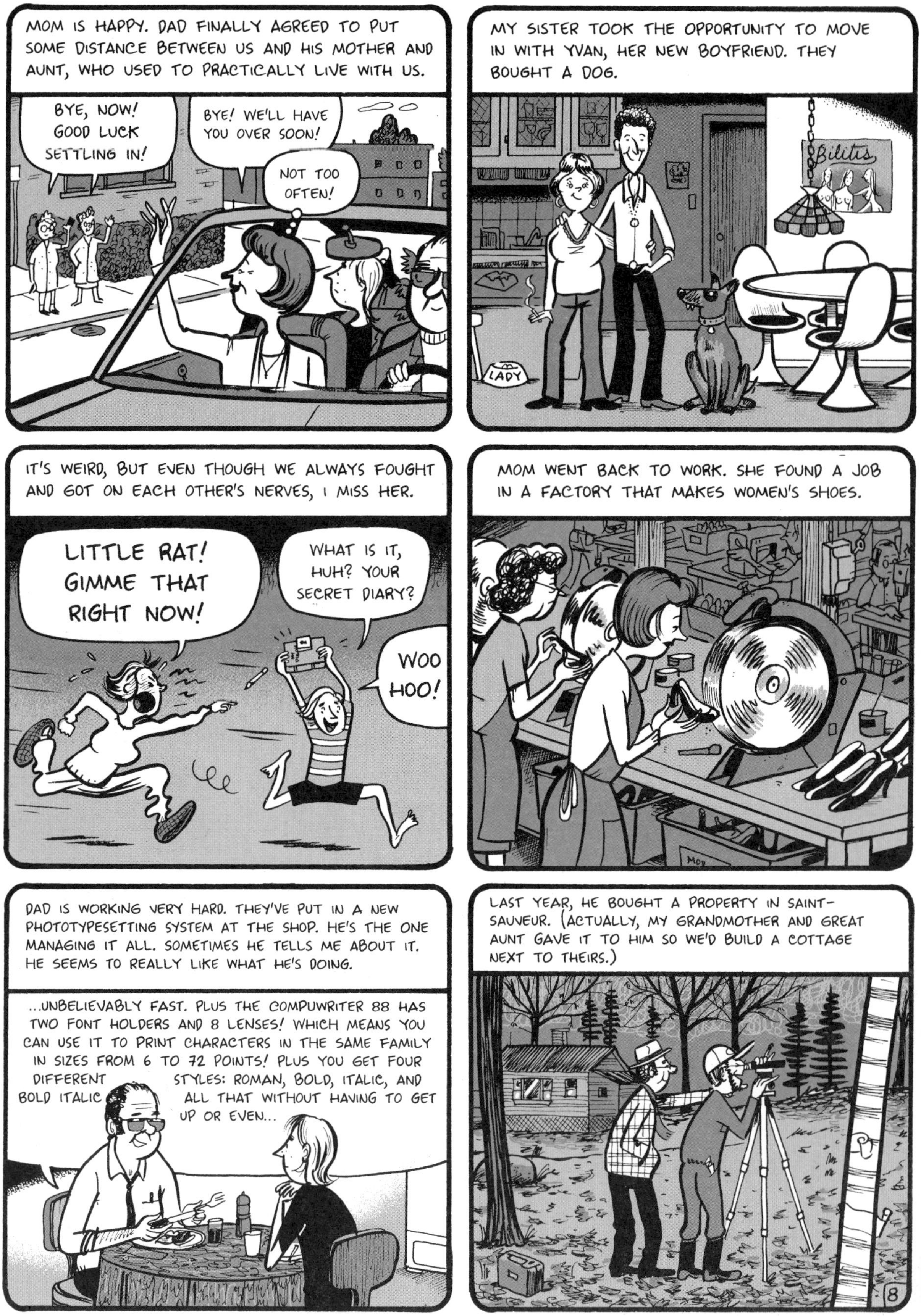
MOM IS HAPPY. DAD FINALLY AGREED TO PUT SOME DISTANCE BETWEEN US AND HIS MOTHER AND AUNT, WHO USED TO PRACTICALLY LIVE WITH US.
BYE, NOW! GOOD LUCK SETTLING IN!
BYE! WE'LL HAVE YOU OVER SOON!
NOT TOO OFTEN!
MY SISTER TOOK THE OPPORTUNITY TO MOVE IN WITH YVAN, HER NEW BOYFRIEND. THEY BOUGHT A DOG.
Bilitis
LADY
IT'S WEIRD, BUT EVEN THOUGH WE ALWAYS FOUGHT AND GOT ON EACH OTHER'S NERVES, I MISS HER.
LITTLE RAT! GIMME THAT RIGHT NOW!
WHAT IS IT, HUH? YOUR SECRET DIARY?
WOO HOO!
MOM WENT BACK TO WORK. SHE FOUND A JOB IN A FACTORY THAT MAKES WOMEN'S SHOES.
DAD IS WORKING VERY HARD. THEY'VE PUT IN A NEW PHOTOTYPESETTING SYSTEM AT THE SHOP. HE'S THE ONE MANAGING IT ALL. SOMETIMES HE TELLS ME ABOUT IT. HE SEEMS TO REALLY LIKE WHAT HE'S DOING.
...UNBELIEVABLY FAST. PLUS THE COMPUWRITER 88 HAS TWO FONT HOLDERS AND 8 LENSES! WHICH MEANS YOU CAN USE IT TO PRINT CHARACTERS IN THE SAME FAMILY IN SIZES FROM 6 TO 72 POINTS! PLUS YOU GET FOUR DIFFERENT STYLES: ROMAN, BOLD, ITALIC, AND BOLD ITALIC. ALL THAT WITHOUT HAVING TO GET UP OR EVEN...
LAST YEAR, HE BOUGHT A PROPERTY IN SAINT-SAUVEUR. (ACTUALLY, MY GRANDMOTHER AND GREAT AUNT GAVE IT TO HIM SO WE'D BUILD A COTTAGE NEXT TO THEIRS.)
8

MOM WASN'T TOO HAPPY ABOUT IT, BUT SINCE DAD HAD DONE HIS PART IN TOWN, SHE FINALLY GAVE IN AND AGREED TO THE COTTAGE IDEA.

...AND WE'LL SEE THEM ONLY ON WEEKENDS. THEY HAVE THEIR PLACE, SO IT WON'T BE LIKE LIVING TOGETHER.

ALL RIGHT, ROBERT, FINE! BUT IT'S THE SAME OLD STORY EVERY TIME: THEY ALWAYS MANAGE TO GET THEIR WAY IN THE END!

I JUST HOPE WE DON'T REGRET IT.

AS FOR ME, UNTIL SCHOOL STARTS, I'M WORKING WEEKDAYS WITH MY UNCLE RAYNALD, WHO HAS A COUPLE OF LANDSCAPING CONTRACTS.

AIR LIQUIDE CANADA

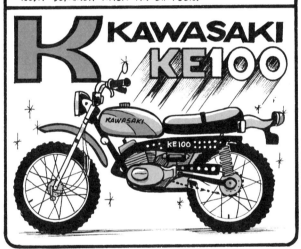

I'M TRYING TO SAVE UP TO BUY A MOTORCYCLE NEXT SUMMER WHEN I'M SIXTEEN.

KAWASAKI KE100

KAWASAKI

KE100

I'VE GOT A LONG WAY TO GO. DAD'S REFUSING TO CONTRIBUTE A SINGLE PENNY. HE KEEPS SAYING, "IF YOU WANT IT, YOU'VE GOT TO WORK FOR IT."

PROPANE

...CONSTRUCTION DELAYS DUE TO STRIKES, VANDALISM, AND DESIGN PROBLEMS. THE EXECUTIVE COMMITTEE ACKNOWLEDGES SERIOUS CONCERNS OVER WHETHER THE FACILITIES WILL BE READY IN TIME FOR THE GAMES...

BREAKING NEWS

RON

FIBERG INSULAT

RIO

WAY TO GO, UNIONS!..

BUNCHA INCOMPETENTS!

MAKIN' US PROUD!

WOW!

CLAP CLAP

9

Gogo Bar

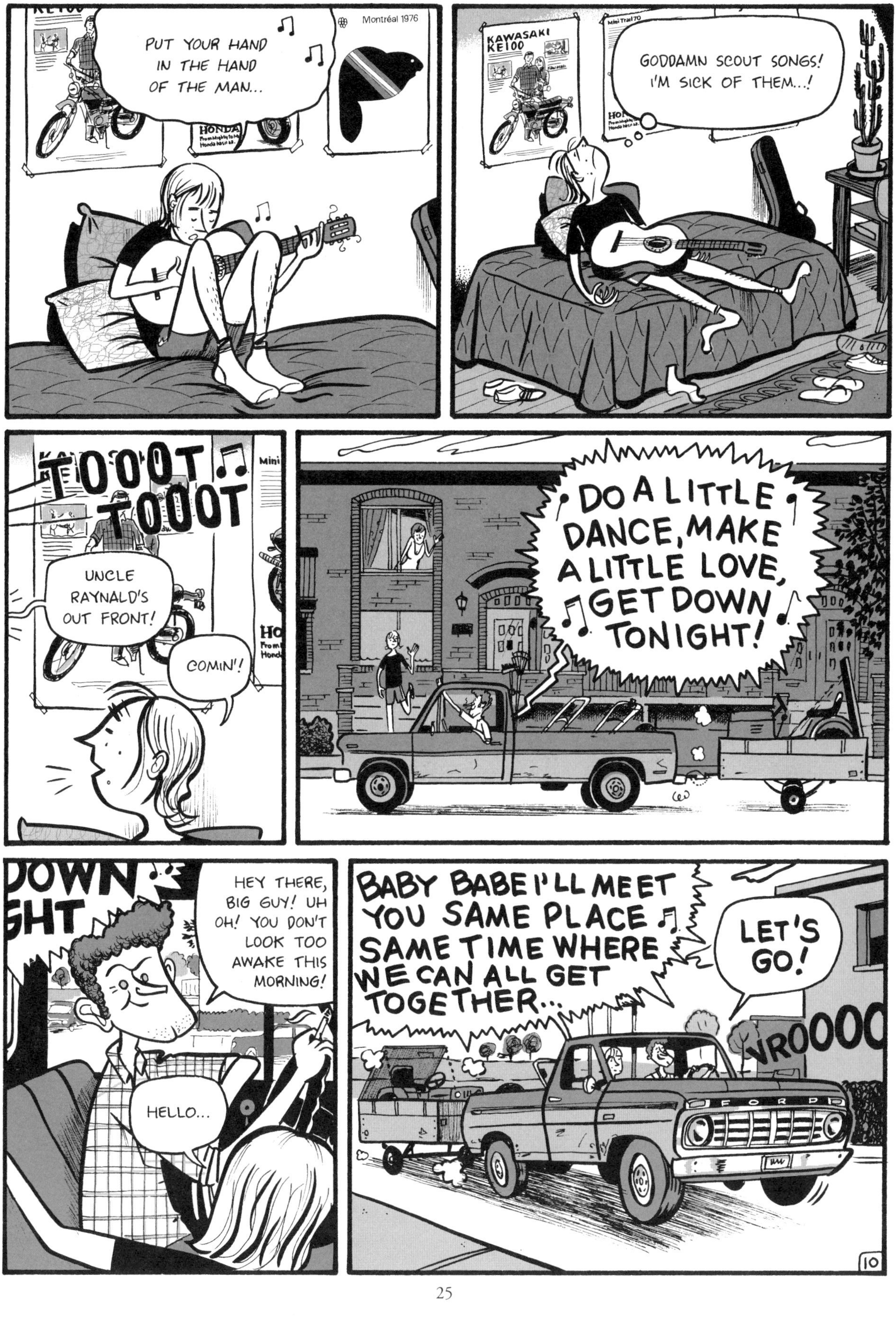
Montréal 1976
PUT YOUR HAND IN THE HAND OF THE MAN...
KAWASAKI KE100
HONDA
Mini Trail 70
GODDAMN SCOUT SONGS! I'M SICK OF THEM...!
TOOOT TOOOT
UNCLE RAYNALD'S OUT FRONT!
COMIN'!
DO A LITTLE DANCE, MAKE A LITTLE LOVE, GET DOWN TONIGHT!
HEY THERE, BIG GUY! UH OH! YOU DON'T LOOK TOO AWAKE THIS MORNING!
HELLO...
BABY BABE I'LL MEET YOU SAME PLACE SAME TIME WHERE WE CAN ALL GET TOGETHER...
LET'S GO!
VROOOO
FORD
10

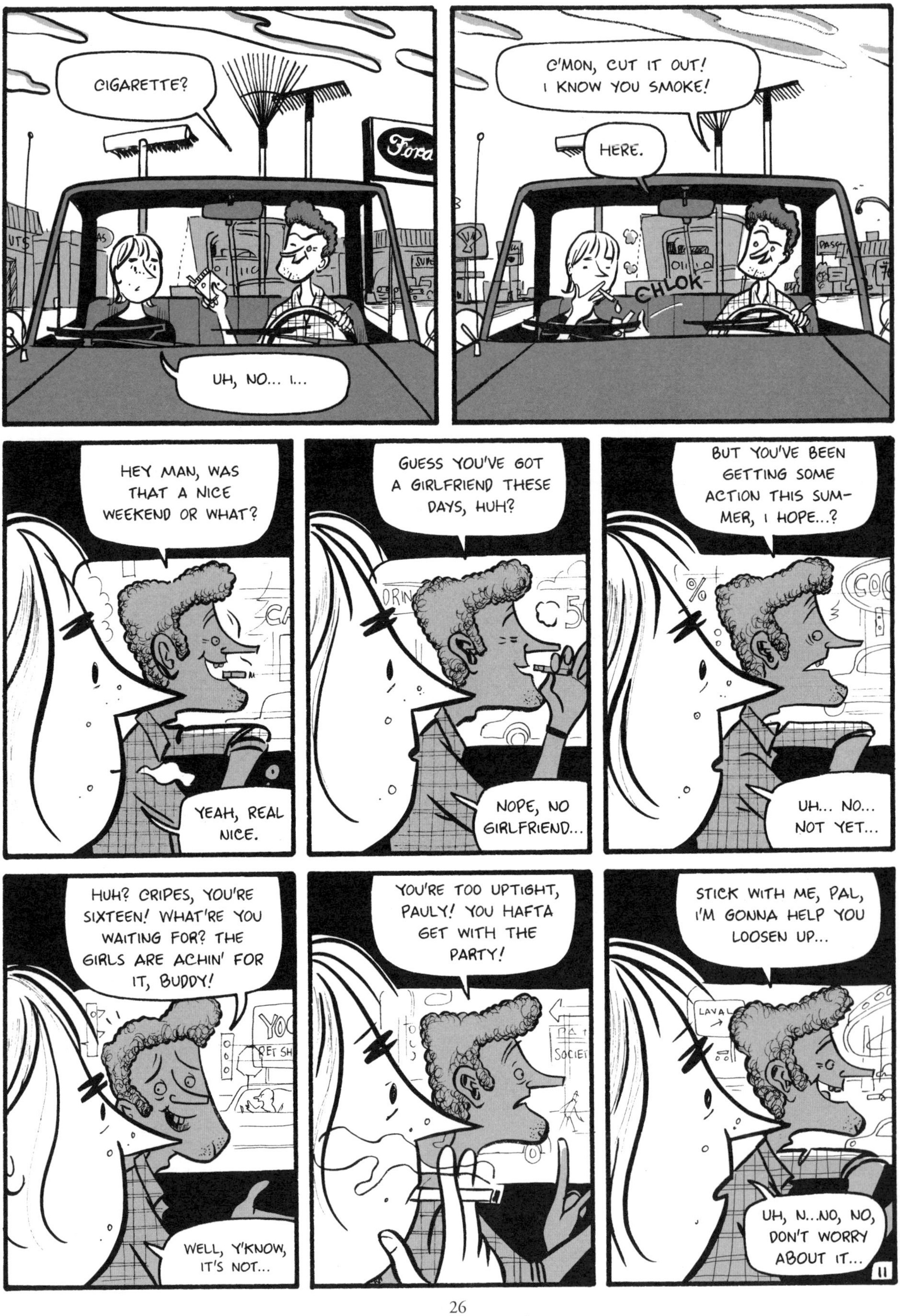
CIGARETTE?
UH, NO... I...
Ford
C'MON, CUT IT OUT! I KNOW YOU SMOKE!
HERE.
CHLOK
HEY MAN, WAS THAT A NICE WEEKEND OR WHAT?
YEAH, REAL NICE.
GUESS YOU'VE GOT A GIRLFRIEND THESE DAYS, HUH?
NOPE, NO GIRLFRIEND...
BUT YOU'VE BEEN GETTING SOME ACTION THIS SUM-MER, I HOPE...?
UH... NO... NOT YET...
HUH? CRIPES, YOU'RE SIXTEEN! WHAT'RE YOU WAITING FOR? THE GIRLS ARE ACHIN' FOR IT, BUDDY!
WELL, Y'KNOW, IT'S NOT...
YOU'RE TOO UPTIGHT, PAULY! YOU HAFTA GET WITH THE PARTY!
STICK WITH ME, PAL, I'M GONNA HELP YOU LOOSEN UP...
LAVAL
UH, N...NO, NO, DON'T WORRY ABOUT IT...
11

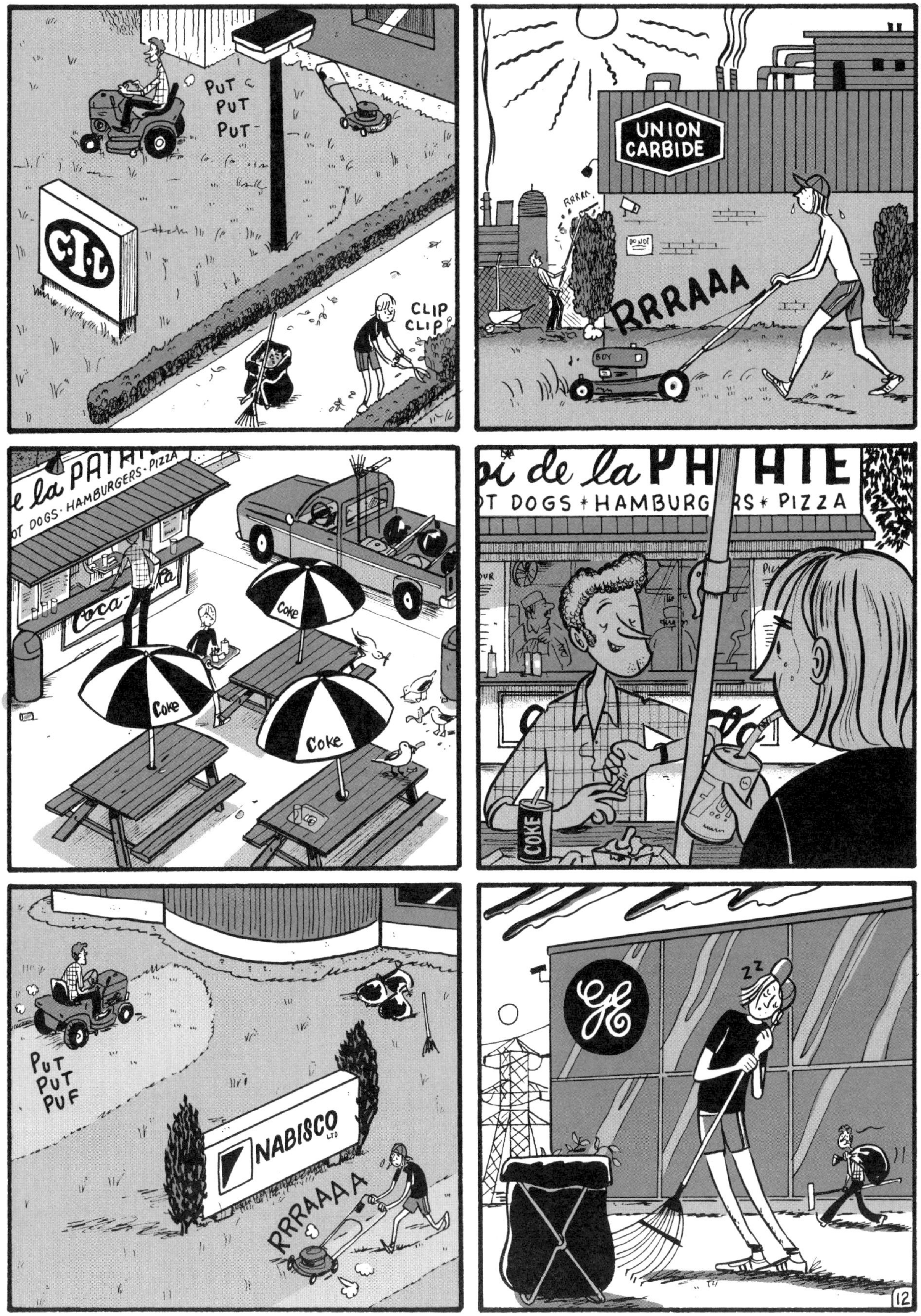
PUT
PUT
PUT
C·I·L
CLIP
CLIP
UNION
CARBIDE
DO NOT
RRRAAA
BOY
la PATATE
DOGS · HAMBURGERS · PIZZA
Coke
Coke
Coke
i de la PATATE
OT DOGS * HAMBURG RS * PIZZA
COKE
PUT
PUT
PUF
NABISCO
LTD
RRRAAAA
i de la PATATE
Z Z
12

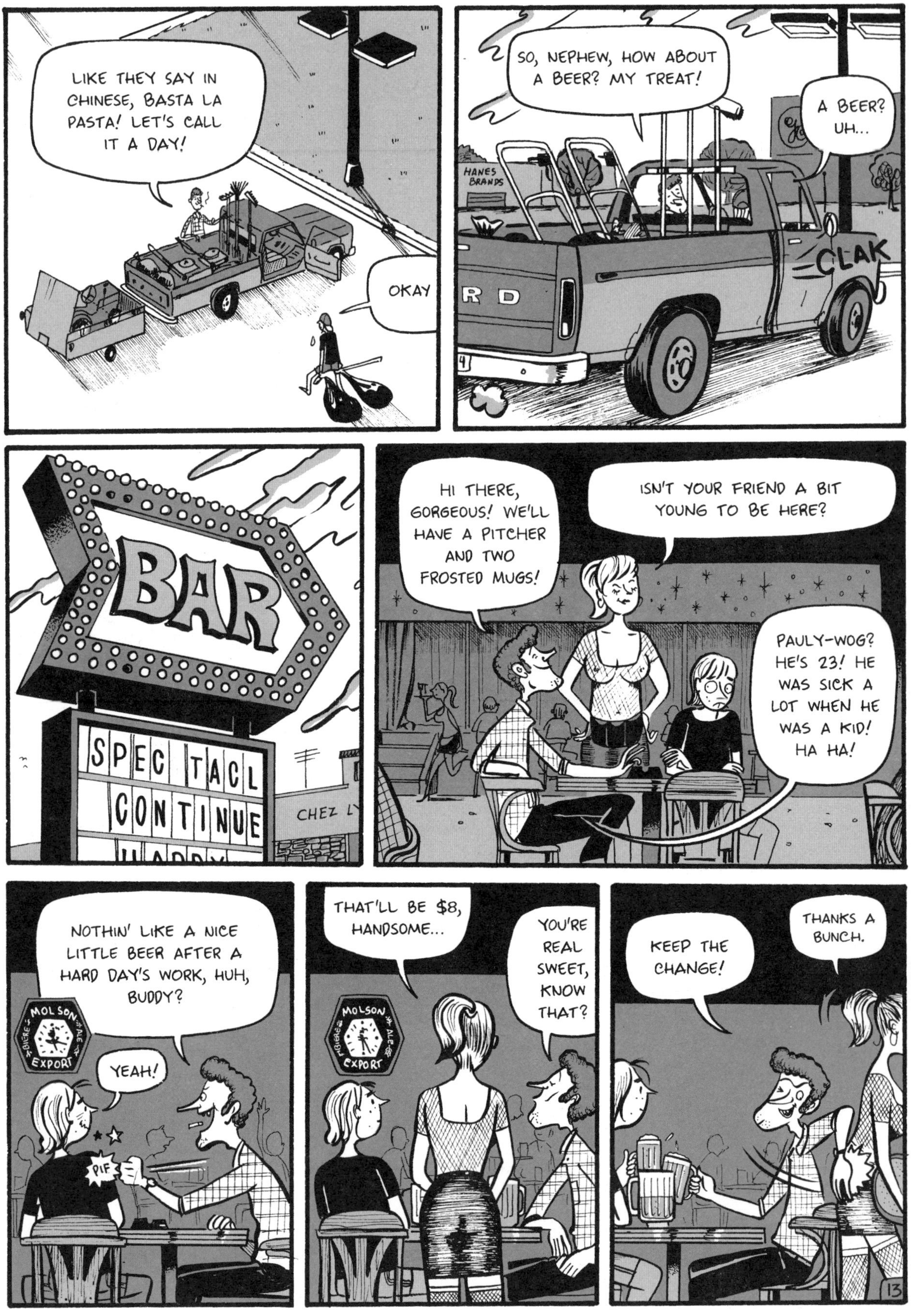

LIKE THEY SAY IN CHINESE, BASTA LA PASTA! LET'S CALL IT A DAY!
OKAY
SO, NEPHEW, HOW ABOUT A BEER? MY TREAT!
A BEER? UH...
HANES BRANDS
CLAK
RD
BAR
SPEC TACL
CONTINUE
CHEZ L
HI THERE, GORGEOUS! WE'LL HAVE A PITCHER AND TWO FROSTED MUGS!
ISN'T YOUR FRIEND A BIT YOUNG TO BE HERE?
PAULY-WOG? HE'S 23! HE WAS SICK A LOT WHEN HE WAS A KID! HA HA!
NOTHIN' LIKE A NICE LITTLE BEER AFTER A HARD DAY'S WORK, HUH, BUDDY?
MOLSON EXPORT
YEAH!
PIF
THAT'LL BE $8, HANDSOME...
YOU'RE REAL SWEET, KNOW THAT?
KEEP THE CHANGE!
THANKS A BUNCH.
13

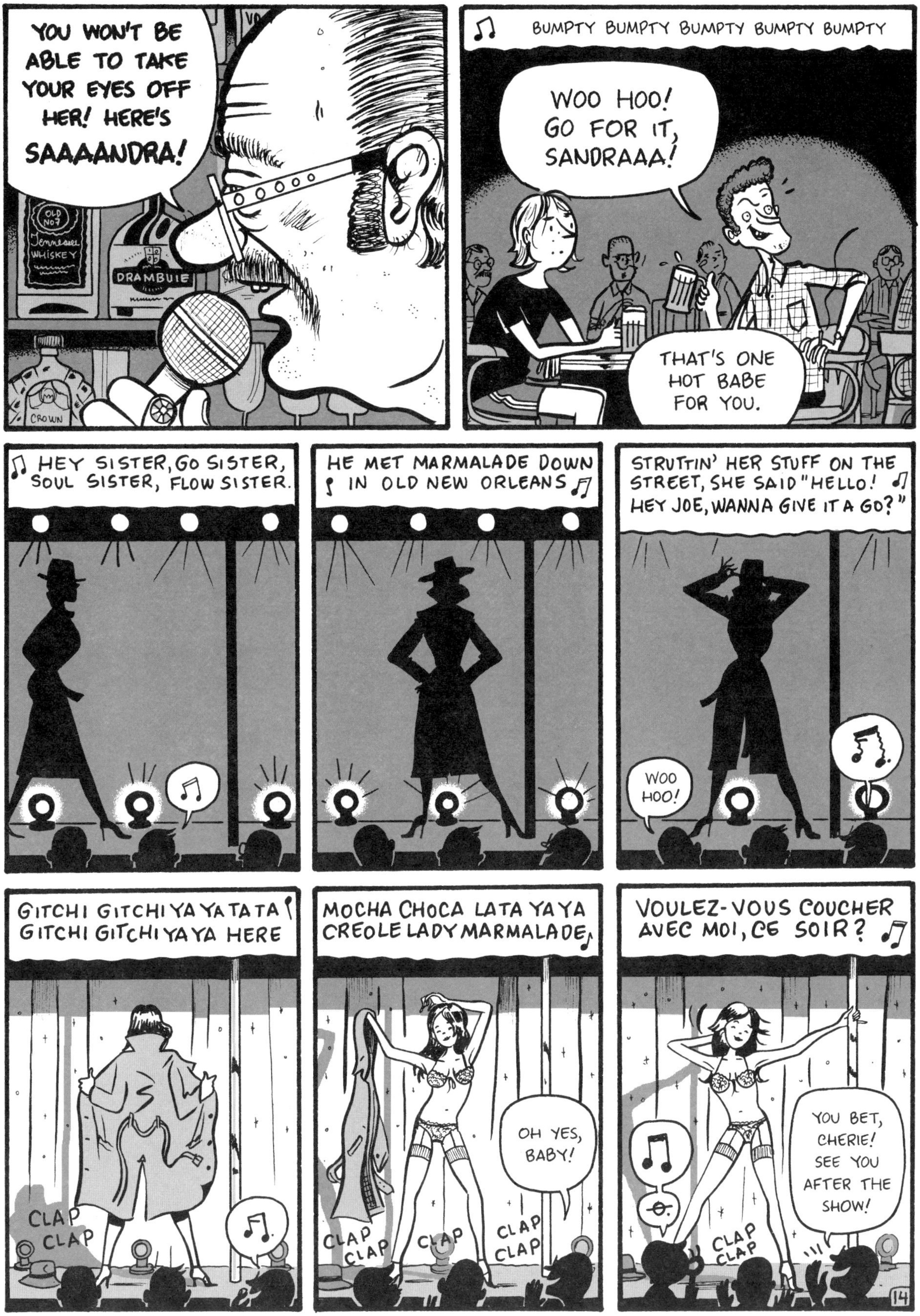
YOU WON'T BE ABLE TO TAKE YOUR EYES OFF HER! HERE'S SAAAANDRA!
OLD No7 Tennessee WHISKEY
DRAMBUIE
CROWN
BUMPTY BUMPTY BUMPTY BUMPTY BUMPTY
WOO HOO! GO FOR IT, SANDRAAA!
THAT'S ONE HOT BABE FOR YOU.
HEY SISTER, GO SISTER, SOUL SISTER, FLOW SISTER.
HE MET MARMALADE DOWN IN OLD NEW ORLEANS
STRUTTIN' HER STUFF ON THE STREET, SHE SAID "HELLO! HEY JOE, WANNA GIVE IT A GO?"
WOO HOO!
GITCHI GITCHI YA YA TA TA GITCHI GITCHI YA YA HERE
CLAP CLAP
MOCHA CHOCA LATA YA YA CREOLE LADY MARMALADE
OH YES, BABY!
CLAP CLAP
CLAP CLAP
CLAP CLAP
VOULEZ-VOUS COUCHER AVEC MOI, CE SOIR?
YOU BET, CHERIE! SEE YOU AFTER THE SHOW!
CLAP CLAP
14

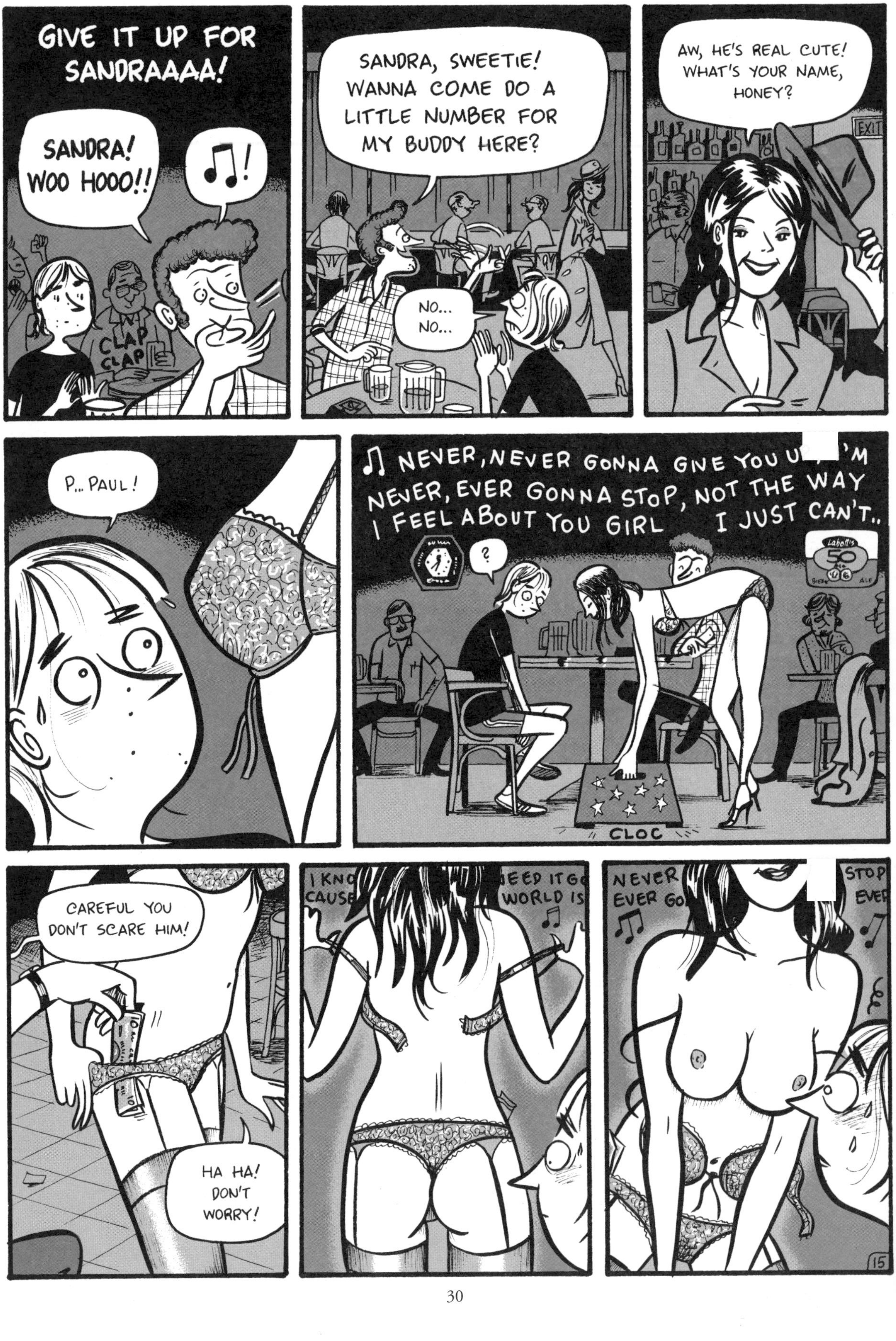
GIVE IT UP FOR SANDRAAAA!
SANDRA! WOO HOOO!!
♫!
CLAP CLAP
SANDRA, SWEETIE! WANNA COME DO A LITTLE NUMBER FOR MY BUDDY HERE?
NO... NO...
AW, HE'S REAL CUTE! WHAT'S YOUR NAME, HONEY?
EXIT
P... PAUL!
♫ NEVER, NEVER GONNA GIVE YOU U
'M
NEVER, EVER GONNA STOP, NOT THE WAY
I FEEL ABOUT YOU GIRL I JUST CAN'T..
?
Labatt's 50
CLOC
CAREFUL YOU DON'T SCARE HIM!
HA HA! DON'T WORRY!
I KNO
CAUSE
NEED IT GO
WORLD IS
NEVER
EVER GO
STOP
EVER
15

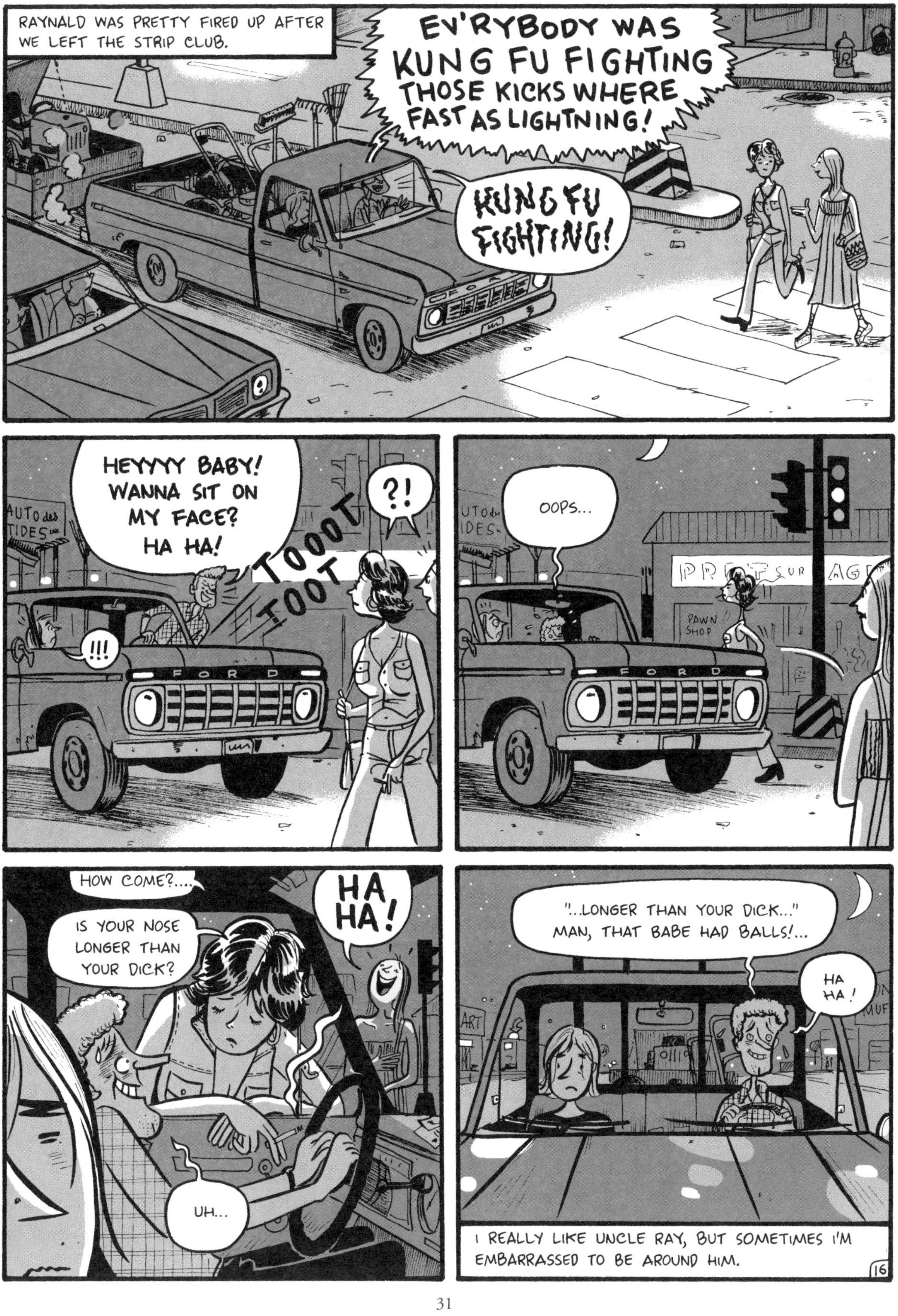
RAYNALD WAS PRETTY FIRED UP AFTER WE LEFT THE STRIP CLUB.
EV'RYBODY WAS KUNG FU FIGHTING THOSE KICKS WHERE FAST AS LIGHTNING!
KUNG FU FIGHTING!
HEYYYY BABY! WANNA SIT ON MY FACE? HA HA!
TOOOT TOOOT
?!
!!!
OOPS...
PAWN SHOP
HOW COME?....
IS YOUR NOSE LONGER THAN YOUR DICK?
HA HA!
UH...
"...LONGER THAN YOUR DICK..." MAN, THAT BABE HAD BALLS!...
HA HA!
I REALLY LIKE UNCLE RAY, BUT SOMETIMES I'M EMBARRASSED TO BE AROUND HIM.
16

Sveight

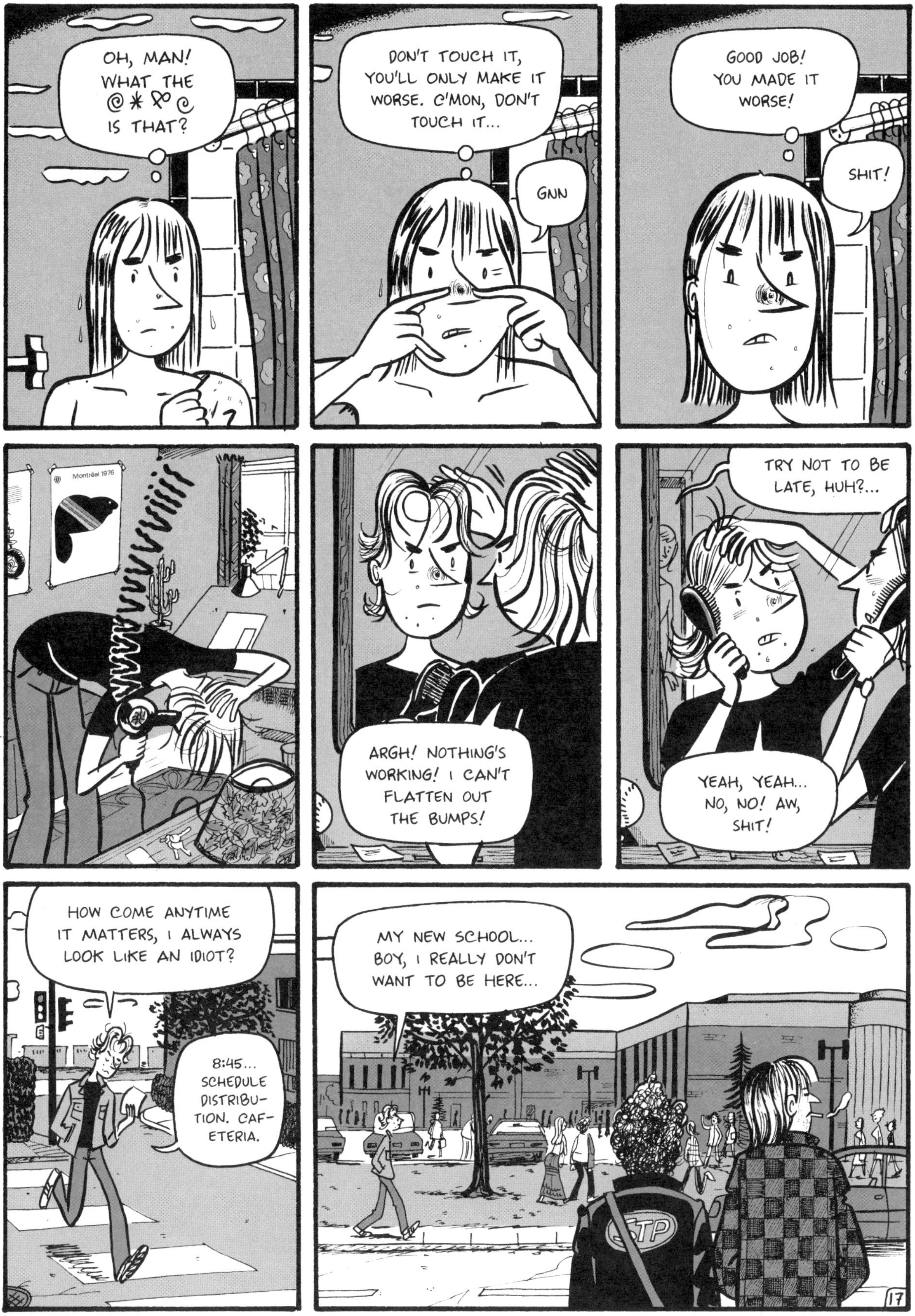
OH, MAN! WHAT THE @*&%@ IS THAT?
DON'T TOUCH IT, YOU'LL ONLY MAKE IT WORSE. C'MON, DON'T TOUCH IT...
GNN
GOOD JOB! YOU MADE IT WORSE!
SHIT!
Montréal 1976
ARGH! NOTHING'S WORKING! I CAN'T FLATTEN OUT THE BUMPS!
TRY NOT TO BE LATE, HUH?...
YEAH, YEAH... NO, NO! AW, SHIT!
HOW COME ANYTIME IT MATTERS, I ALWAYS LOOK LIKE AN IDIOT?
8:45... SCHEDULE DISTRIBU-TION. CAF-ETERIA.
MY NEW SCHOOL... BOY, I REALLY DON'T WANT TO BE HERE...
STP
17

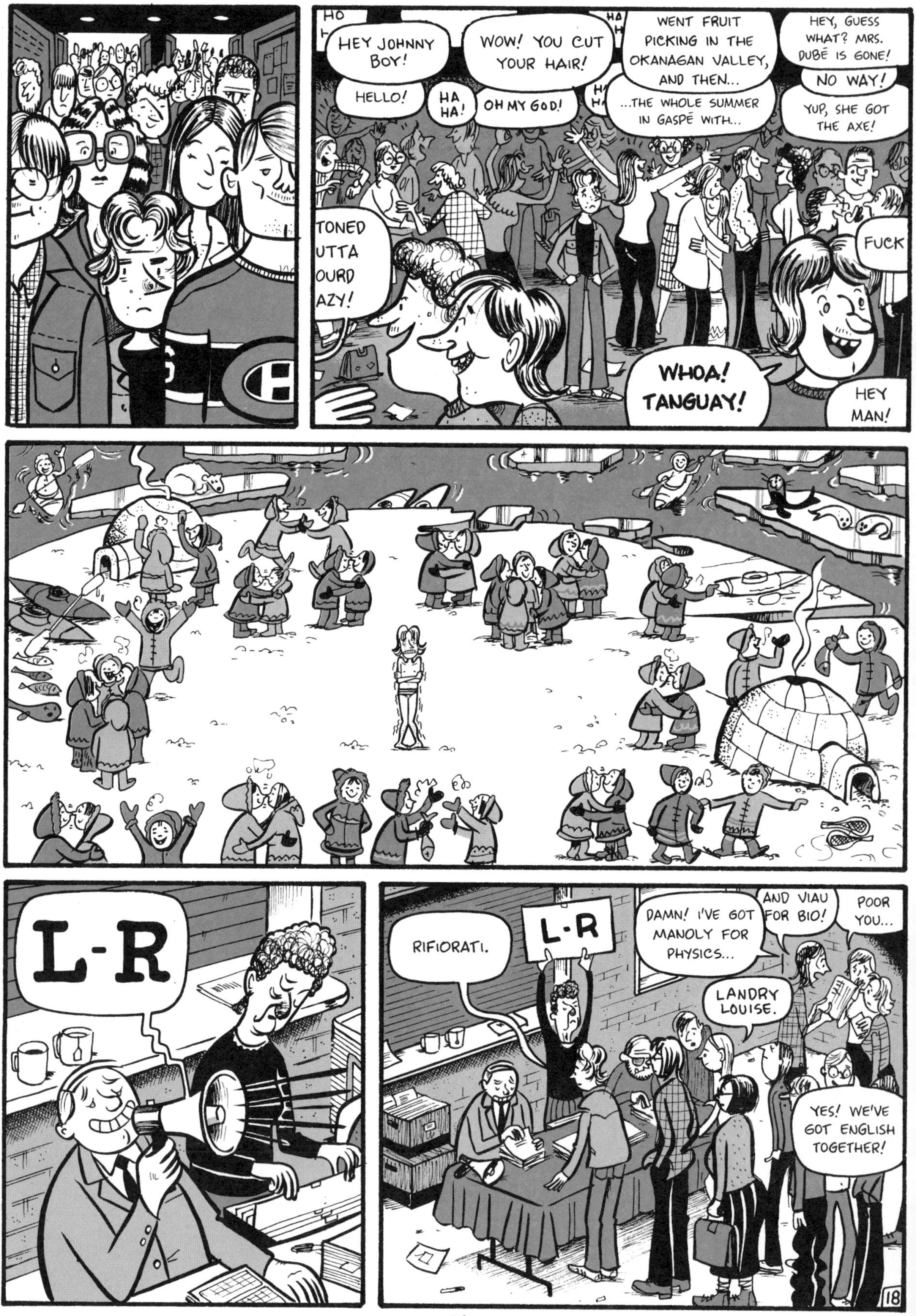
HO
HEY JOHNNY BOY!
HELLO!
HA HA!
WOW! YOU CUT YOUR HAIR!
OH MY GOD!
HA
WENT FRUIT PICKING IN THE OKANAGAN VALLEY, AND THEN...
...THE WHOLE SUMMER IN GASPÉ WITH...
HEY, GUESS WHAT? MRS. DUBÉ IS GONE!
NO WAY!
YUP, SHE GOT THE AXE!
TONED UTTA OURD AZY!
FUCK
WHOA! TANGUAY!
HEY MAN!
L-R
RIFIORATI.
L-R
DAMN! I'VE GOT MANOLY FOR PHYSICS...
AND VIAU FOR BIO!
POOR YOU...
LANDRY LOUISE.
YES! WE'VE GOT ENGLISH TOGETHER!
18

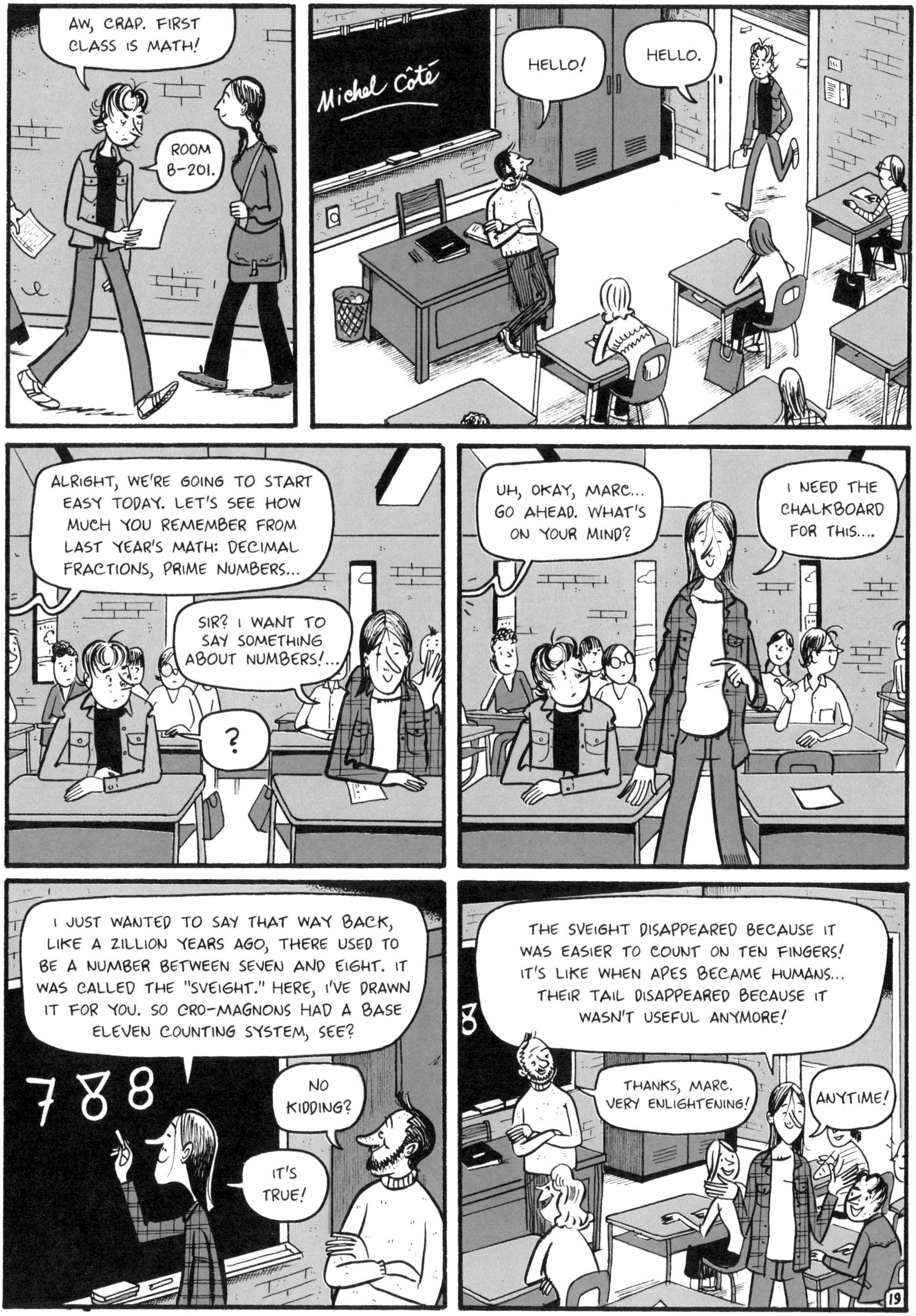
AW, CRAP. FIRST CLASS IS MATH!
ROOM B-201.
Michel Côté
HELLO!
HELLO.
ALRIGHT, WE'RE GOING TO START EASY TODAY. LET'S SEE HOW MUCH YOU REMEMBER FROM LAST YEAR'S MATH: DECIMAL FRACTIONS, PRIME NUMBERS...
SIR? I WANT TO SAY SOMETHING ABOUT NUMBERS!...
?
UH, OKAY, MARC... GO AHEAD. WHAT'S ON YOUR MIND?
I NEED THE CHALKBOARD FOR THIS....
I JUST WANTED TO SAY THAT WAY BACK, LIKE A ZILLION YEARS AGO, THERE USED TO BE A NUMBER BETWEEN SEVEN AND EIGHT. IT WAS CALLED THE "SVEIGHT." HERE, I'VE DRAWN IT FOR YOU. SO CRO-MAGNONS HAD A BASE ELEVEN COUNTING SYSTEM, SEE?
7 8 8
NO KIDDING?
IT'S TRUE!
THE SVEIGHT DISAPPEARED BECAUSE IT WAS EASIER TO COUNT ON TEN FINGERS! IT'S LIKE WHEN APES BECAME HUMANS... THEIR TAIL DISAPPEARED BECAUSE IT WASN'T USEFUL ANYMORE!
THANKS, MARC. VERY ENLIGHTENING!
ANYTIME!
19

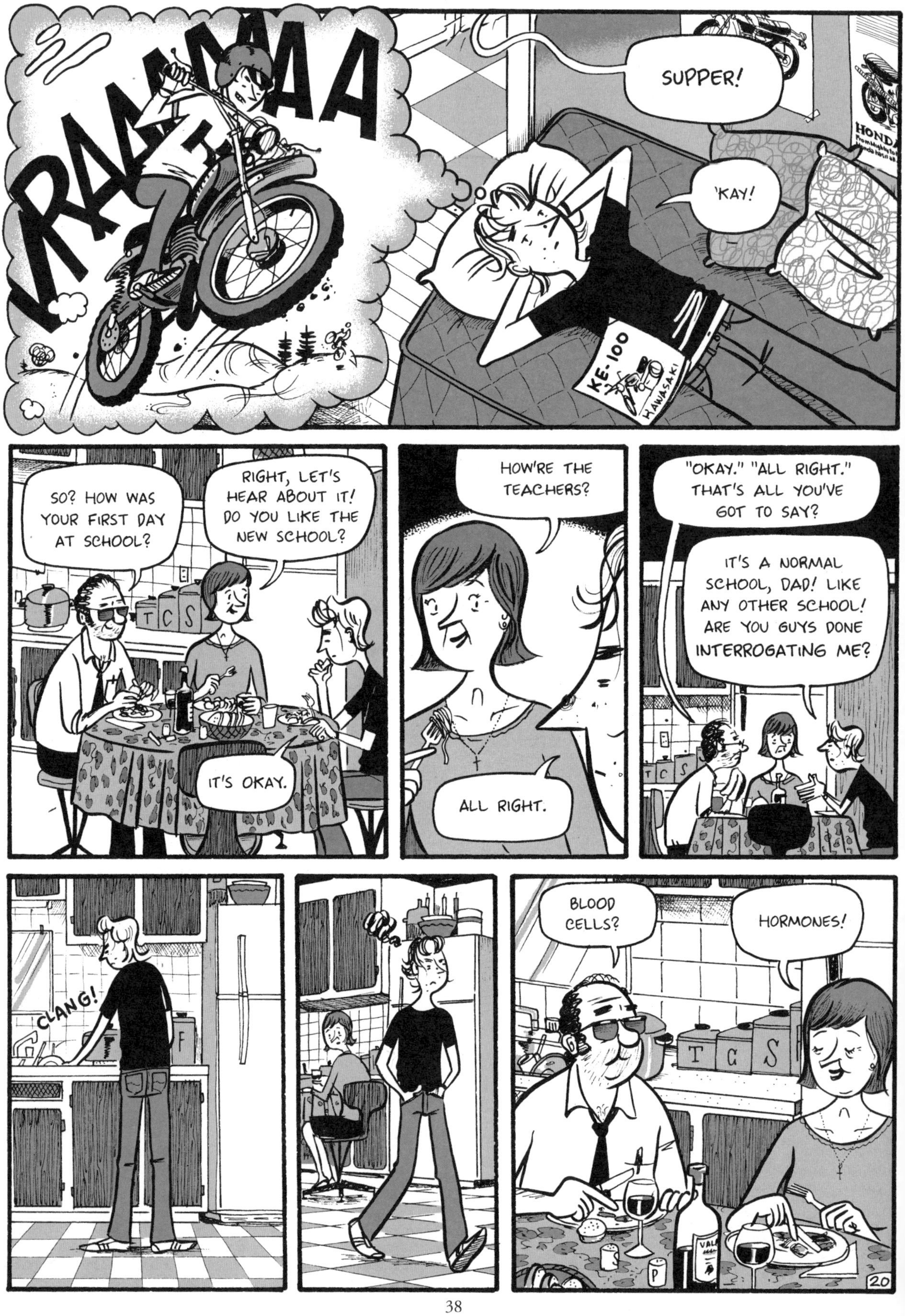
RAAAMMAA
SUPPER!
'KAY!
HONDA
KE-100
KAWASAKI
SO? HOW WAS YOUR FIRST DAY AT SCHOOL?
RIGHT, LET'S HEAR ABOUT IT! DO YOU LIKE THE NEW SCHOOL?
IT'S OKAY.
HOW'RE THE TEACHERS?
ALL RIGHT.
"OKAY." "ALL RIGHT." THAT'S ALL YOU'VE GOT TO SAY?
IT'S A NORMAL SCHOOL, DAD! LIKE ANY OTHER SCHOOL! ARE YOU GUYS DONE INTERROGATING ME?
CLANG!
BLOOD CELLS?
HORMONES!
20

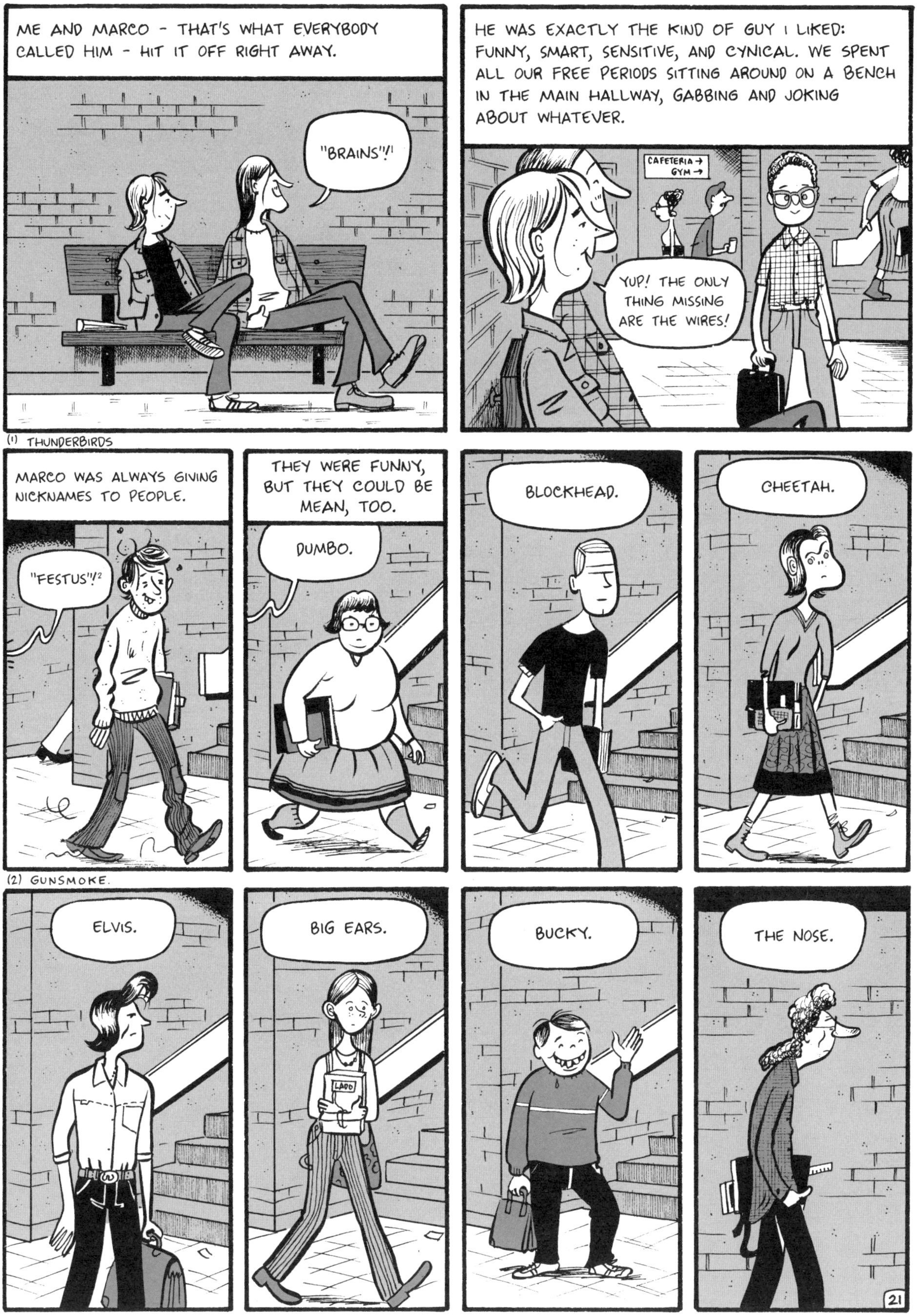
ME AND MARCO - THAT'S WHAT EVERYBODY CALLED HIM - HIT IT OFF RIGHT AWAY.
"BRAINS"!1
HE WAS EXACTLY THE KIND OF GUY I LIKED: FUNNY, SMART, SENSITIVE, AND CYNICAL. WE SPENT ALL OUR FREE PERIODS SITTING AROUND ON A BENCH IN THE MAIN HALLWAY, GABBING AND JOKING ABOUT WHATEVER.
CAFETERIA →
GYM →
YUP! THE ONLY THING MISSING ARE THE WIRES!
(1) THUNDERBIRDS
MARCO WAS ALWAYS GIVING NICKNAMES TO PEOPLE.
"FESTUS"!2
THEY WERE FUNNY, BUT THEY COULD BE MEAN, TOO.
DUMBO.
BLOCKHEAD.
CHEETAH.
(2) GUNSMOKE.
ELVIS.
BIG EARS.
LADD
BUCKY.
THE NOSE.
21

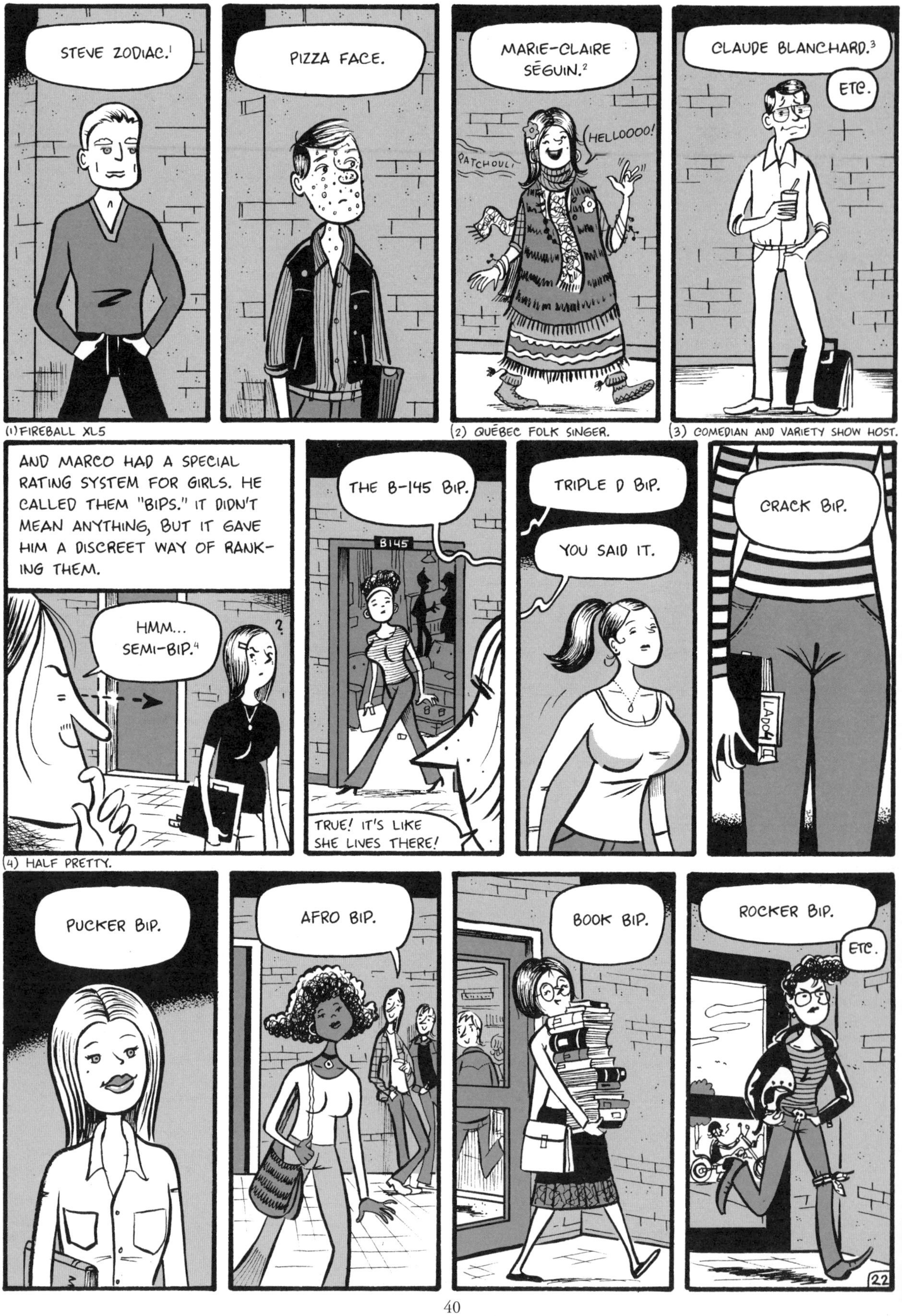

STEVE ZODIAC.[1]
PIZZA FACE.
MARIE-CLAIRE SÉGUIN.[2]
PATCHOULI
HELLOOOO!
CLAUDE BLANCHARD.[3]
ETC.
(1) FIREBALL XL5
(2) QUÉBEC FOLK SINGER.
(3) COMEDIAN AND VARIETY SHOW HOST.
AND MARCO HAD A SPECIAL RATING SYSTEM FOR GIRLS. HE CALLED THEM "BIPS." IT DIDN'T MEAN ANYTHING, BUT IT GAVE HIM A DISCREET WAY OF RANKING THEM.
HMM... SEMI-BIP.[4]
?
THE B-145 BIP.
B145
TRUE! IT'S LIKE SHE LIVES THERE!
TRIPLE D BIP.
YOU SAID IT.
CRACK BIP.
(4) HALF PRETTY.
PUCKER BIP.
AFRO BIP.
BOOK BIP.
ROCKER BIP.
ETC.
22

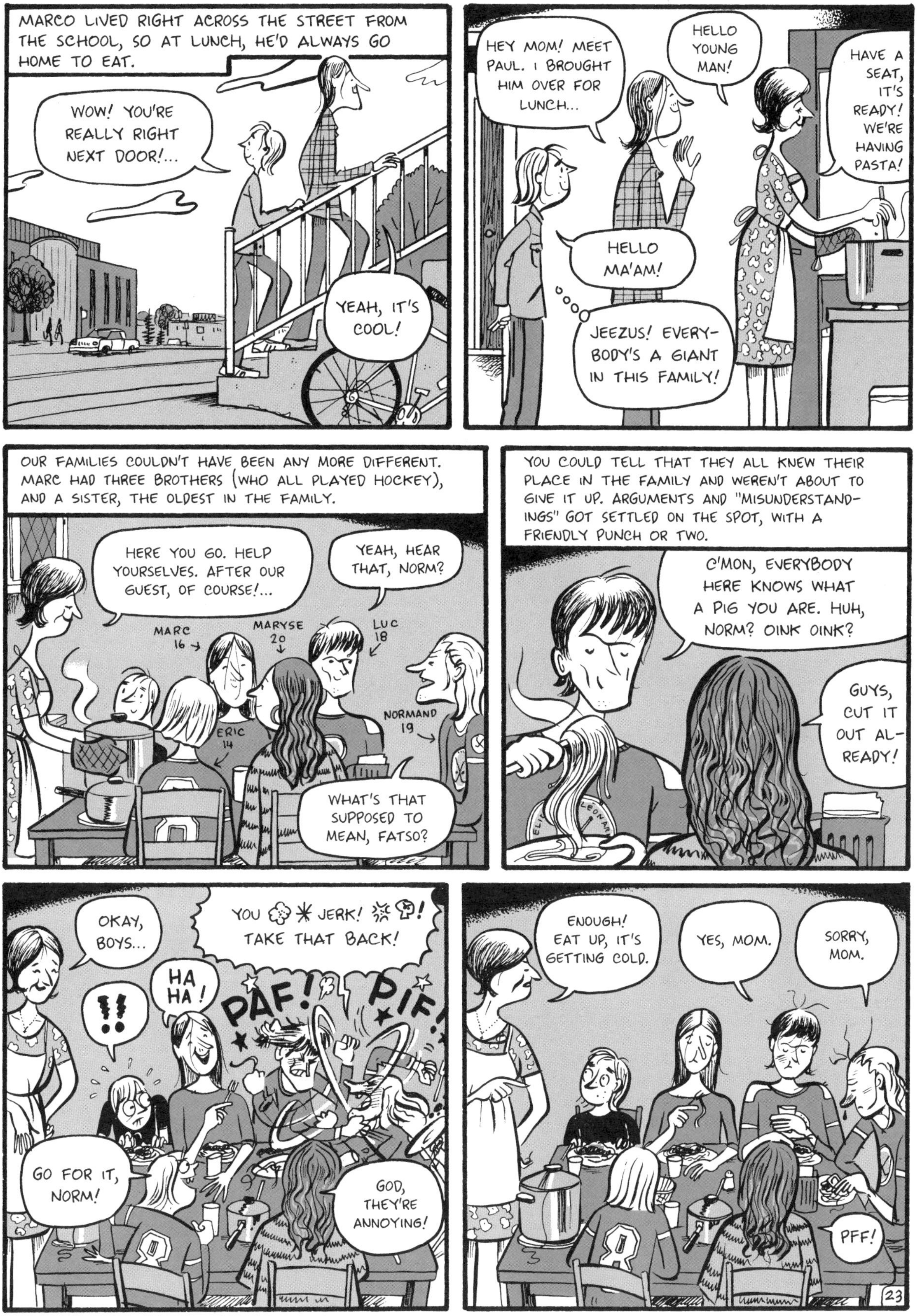
MARCO LIVED RIGHT ACROSS THE STREET FROM THE SCHOOL, SO AT LUNCH, HE'D ALWAYS GO HOME TO EAT.
WOW! YOU'RE REALLY RIGHT NEXT DOOR!...
YEAH, IT'S COOL!
HEY MOM! MEET PAUL. I BROUGHT HIM OVER FOR LUNCH...
HELLO YOUNG MAN!
HAVE A SEAT, IT'S READY! WE'RE HAVING PASTA!
HELLO MA'AM!
JEEZUS! EVERYBODY'S A GIANT IN THIS FAMILY!
OUR FAMILIES COULDN'T HAVE BEEN ANY MORE DIFFERENT. MARC HAD THREE BROTHERS (WHO ALL PLAYED HOCKEY), AND A SISTER, THE OLDEST IN THE FAMILY.
HERE YOU GO. HELP YOURSELVES. AFTER OUR GUEST, OF COURSE!...
YEAH, HEAR THAT, NORM?
MARC 16
MARYSE 20
LUC 18
ERIC 14
NORMAND 19
WHAT'S THAT SUPPOSED TO MEAN, FATSO?
YOU COULD TELL THAT THEY ALL KNEW THEIR PLACE IN THE FAMILY AND WEREN'T ABOUT TO GIVE IT UP. ARGUMENTS AND "MISUNDERSTANDINGS" GOT SETTLED ON THE SPOT, WITH A FRIENDLY PUNCH OR TWO.
C'MON, EVERYBODY HERE KNOWS WHAT A PIG YOU ARE. HUH, NORM? OINK OINK?
GUYS, CUT IT OUT ALREADY!
OKAY, BOYS...
YOU JERK! TAKE THAT BACK!
!!
HA HA!
PAF!
PIF!
GO FOR IT, NORM!
GOD, THEY'RE ANNOYING!
ENOUGH! EAT UP, IT'S GETTING COLD.
YES, MOM.
SORRY, MOM.
PFF!
23

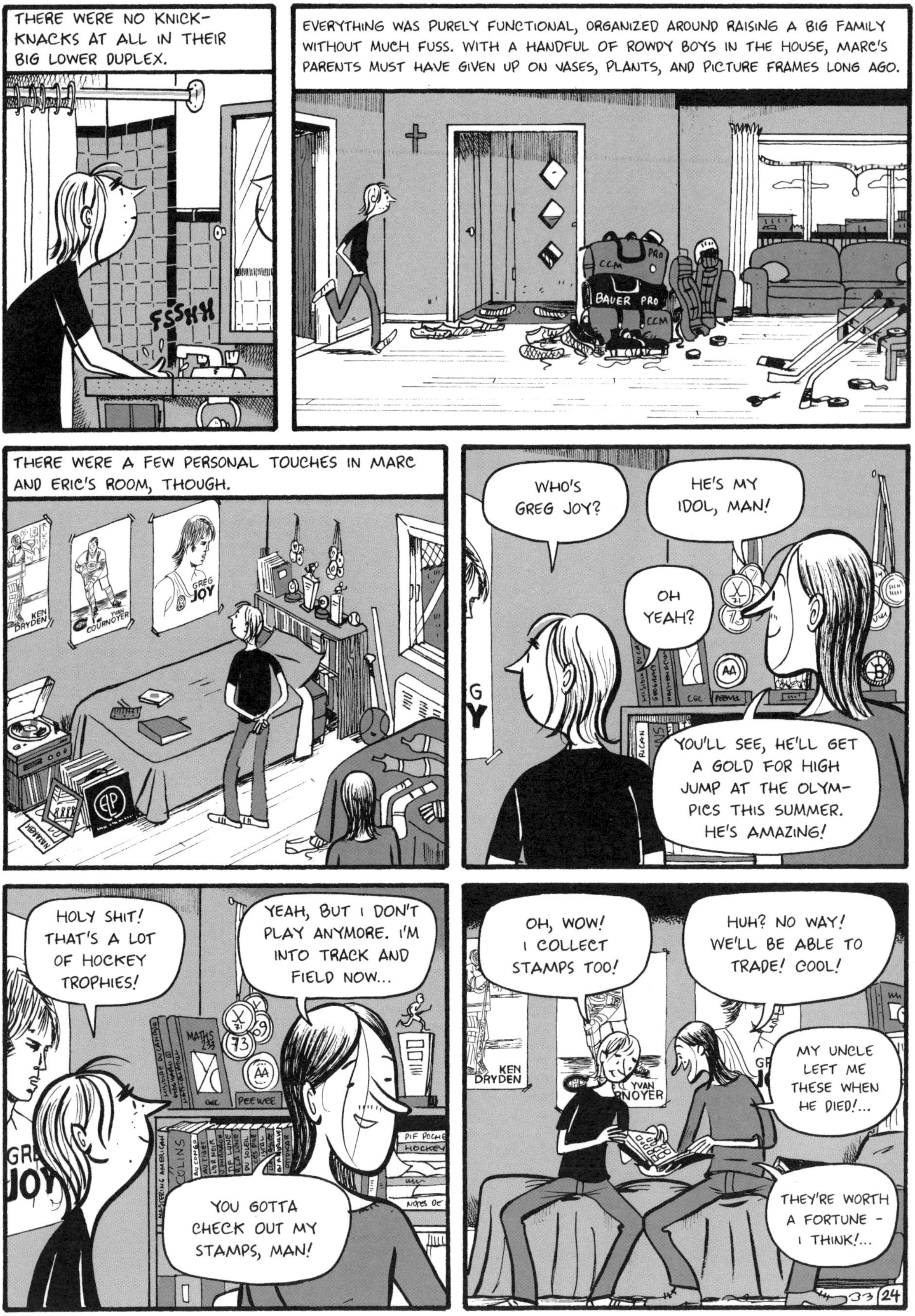
THERE WERE NO KNICK-KNACKS AT ALL IN THEIR BIG LOWER DUPLEX.
FSSHH
EVERYTHING WAS PURELY FUNCTIONAL, ORGANIZED AROUND RAISING A BIG FAMILY WITHOUT MUCH FUSS. WITH A HANDFUL OF ROWDY BOYS IN THE HOUSE, MARC'S PARENTS MUST HAVE GIVEN UP ON VASES, PLANTS, AND PICTURE FRAMES LONG AGO.
CCM
PRO
BAUER PRO
CCM
THERE WERE A FEW PERSONAL TOUCHES IN MARC AND ERIC'S ROOM, THOUGH.
KEN DRYDEN
YVAN COURNOYER
GREG JOY
WHO'S GREG JOY?
HE'S MY IDOL, MAN!
OH YEAH?
YOU'LL SEE, HE'LL GET A GOLD FOR HIGH JUMP AT THE OLYMPICS THIS SUMMER. HE'S AMAZING!
HOLY SHIT! THAT'S A LOT OF HOCKEY TROPHIES!
YEAH, BUT I DON'T PLAY ANYMORE. I'M INTO TRACK AND FIELD NOW...
MATHS
PEEWEE
YOU GOTTA CHECK OUT MY STAMPS, MAN!
OH, WOW! I COLLECT STAMPS TOO!
HUH? NO WAY! WE'LL BE ABLE TO TRADE! COOL!
KEN DRYDEN
YVAN COURNOYER
MY UNCLE LEFT ME THESE WHEN HE DIED!...
THEY'RE WORTH A FORTUNE - I THINK!...

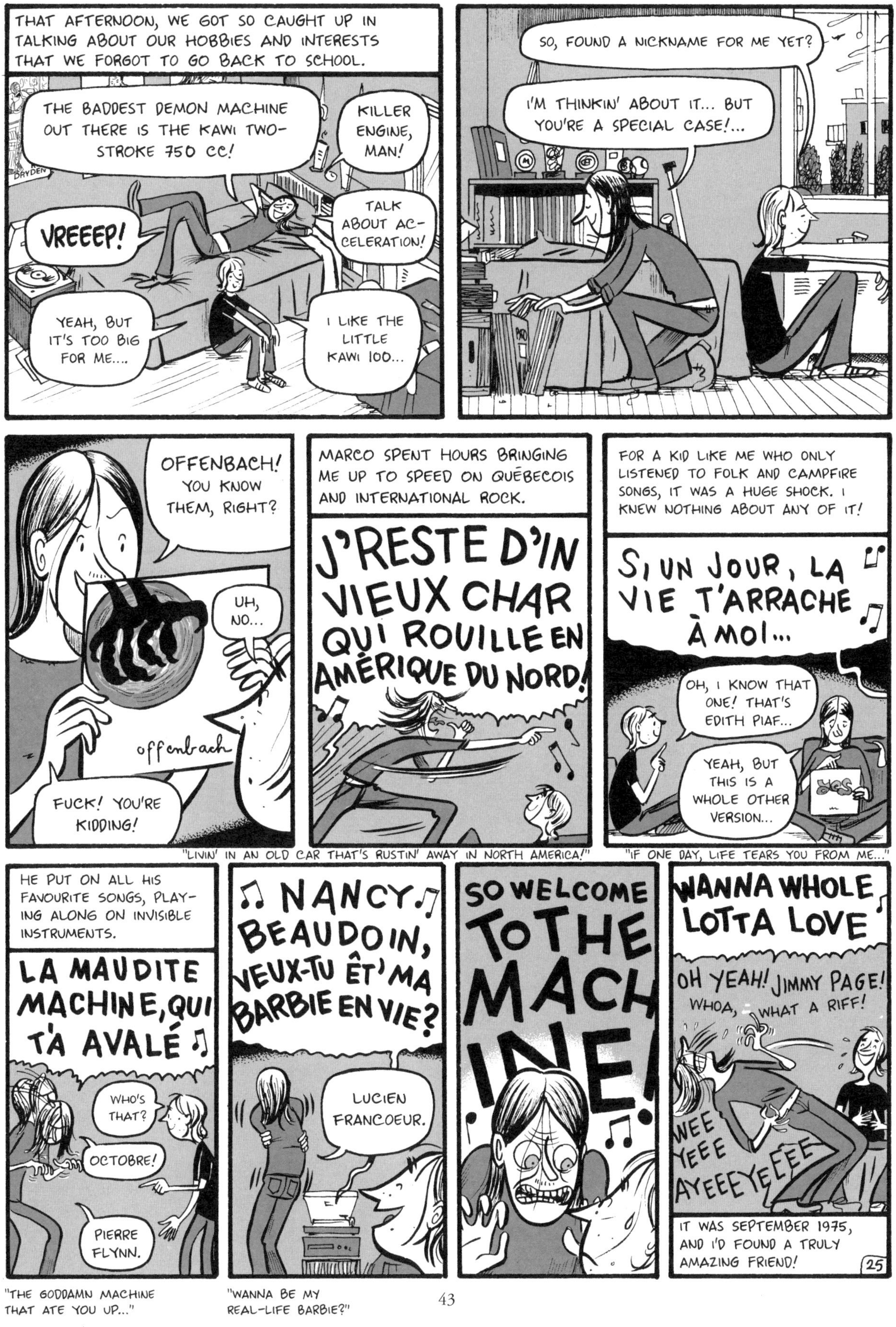
THAT AFTERNOON, WE GOT SO CAUGHT UP IN TALKING ABOUT OUR HOBBIES AND INTERESTS THAT WE FORGOT TO GO BACK TO SCHOOL.
THE BADDEST DEMON MACHINE OUT THERE IS THE KAWI TWO-STROKE 750 CC!
KILLER ENGINE, MAN!
VREEEP!
TALK ABOUT ACCELERATION!
YEAH, BUT IT'S TOO BIG FOR ME....
I LIKE THE LITTLE KAWI 100...
SO, FOUND A NICKNAME FOR ME YET?
I'M THINKIN' ABOUT IT... BUT YOU'RE A SPECIAL CASE!...
OFFENBACH! YOU KNOW THEM, RIGHT?
UH, NO...
offenbach
FUCK! YOU'RE KIDDING!
MARCO SPENT HOURS BRINGING ME UP TO SPEED ON QUÉBECOIS AND INTERNATIONAL ROCK.
J'RESTE D'IN VIEUX CHAR QUI ROUILLE EN AMÉRIQUE DU NORD!
"LIVIN' IN AN OLD CAR THAT'S RUSTIN' AWAY IN NORTH AMERICA!"
FOR A KID LIKE ME WHO ONLY LISTENED TO FOLK AND CAMPFIRE SONGS, IT WAS A HUGE SHOCK. I KNEW NOTHING ABOUT ANY OF IT!
SI UN JOUR, LA VIE T'ARRACHE À MOI...
OH, I KNOW THAT ONE! THAT'S EDITH PIAF...
YEAH, BUT THIS IS A WHOLE OTHER VERSION...
"IF ONE DAY, LIFE TEARS YOU FROM ME..."
HE PUT ON ALL HIS FAVOURITE SONGS, PLAYING ALONG ON INVISIBLE INSTRUMENTS.
LA MAUDITE MACHINE, QUI T'A AVALÉ
WHO'S THAT?
OCTOBRE!
PIERRE FLYNN.
"THE GODDAMN MACHINE THAT ATE YOU UP..."
NANCY BEAUDOIN, VEUX-TU ÊT' MA BARBIE EN VIE?
LUCIEN FRANCOEUR.
"WANNA BE MY REAL-LIFE BARBIE?"
SO WELCOME TO THE MACHINE!
WANNA WHOLE LOTTA LOVE
OH YEAH! JIMMY PAGE! WHOA, WHAT A RIFF!
WEE YEEE AYEEEYEEEE
IT WAS SEPTEMBER 1975, AND I'D FOUND A TRULY AMAZING FRIEND!
25

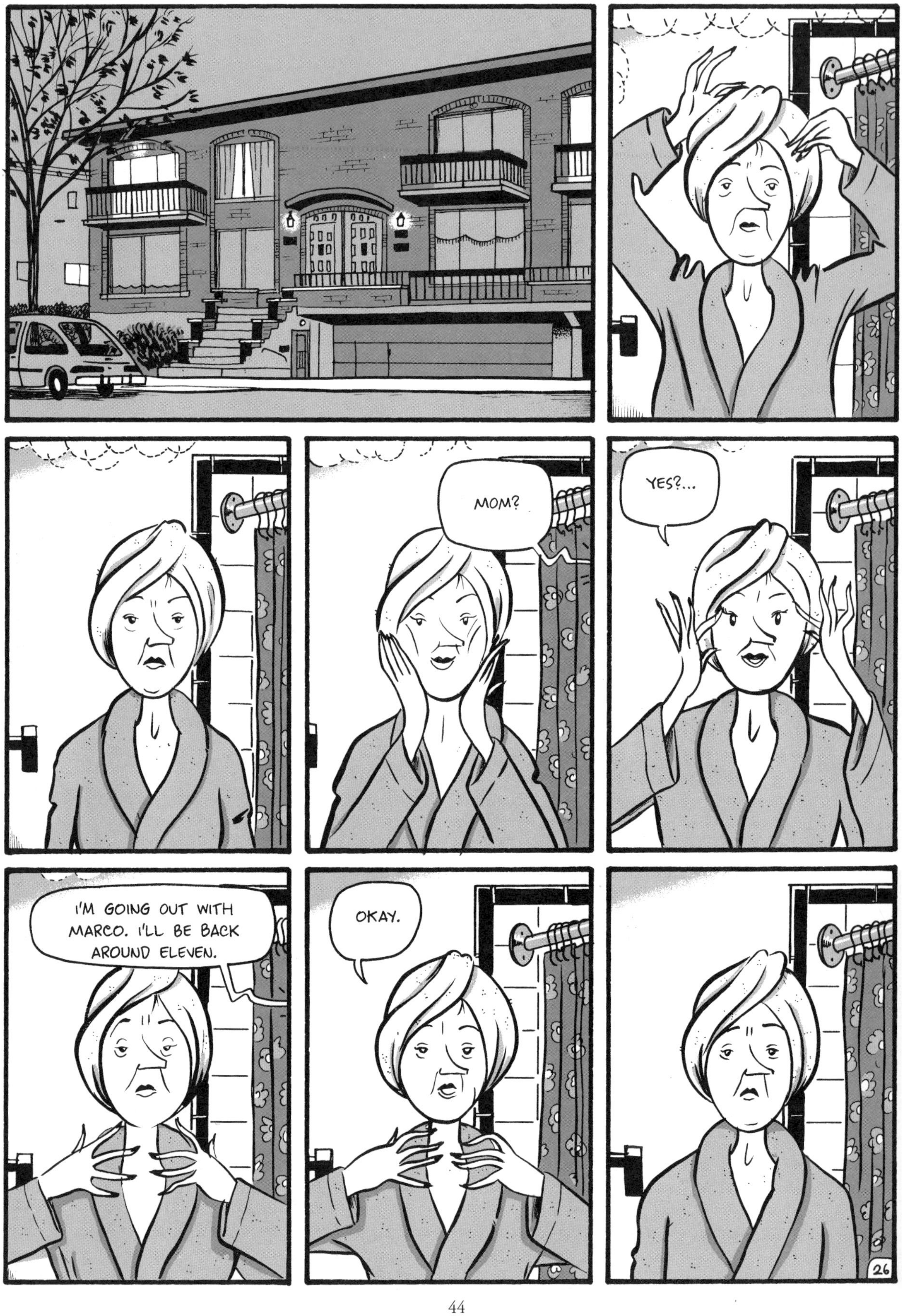
MOM?
YES?...
I'M GOING OUT WITH MARCO. I'LL BE BACK AROUND ELEVEN.
OKAY.
26

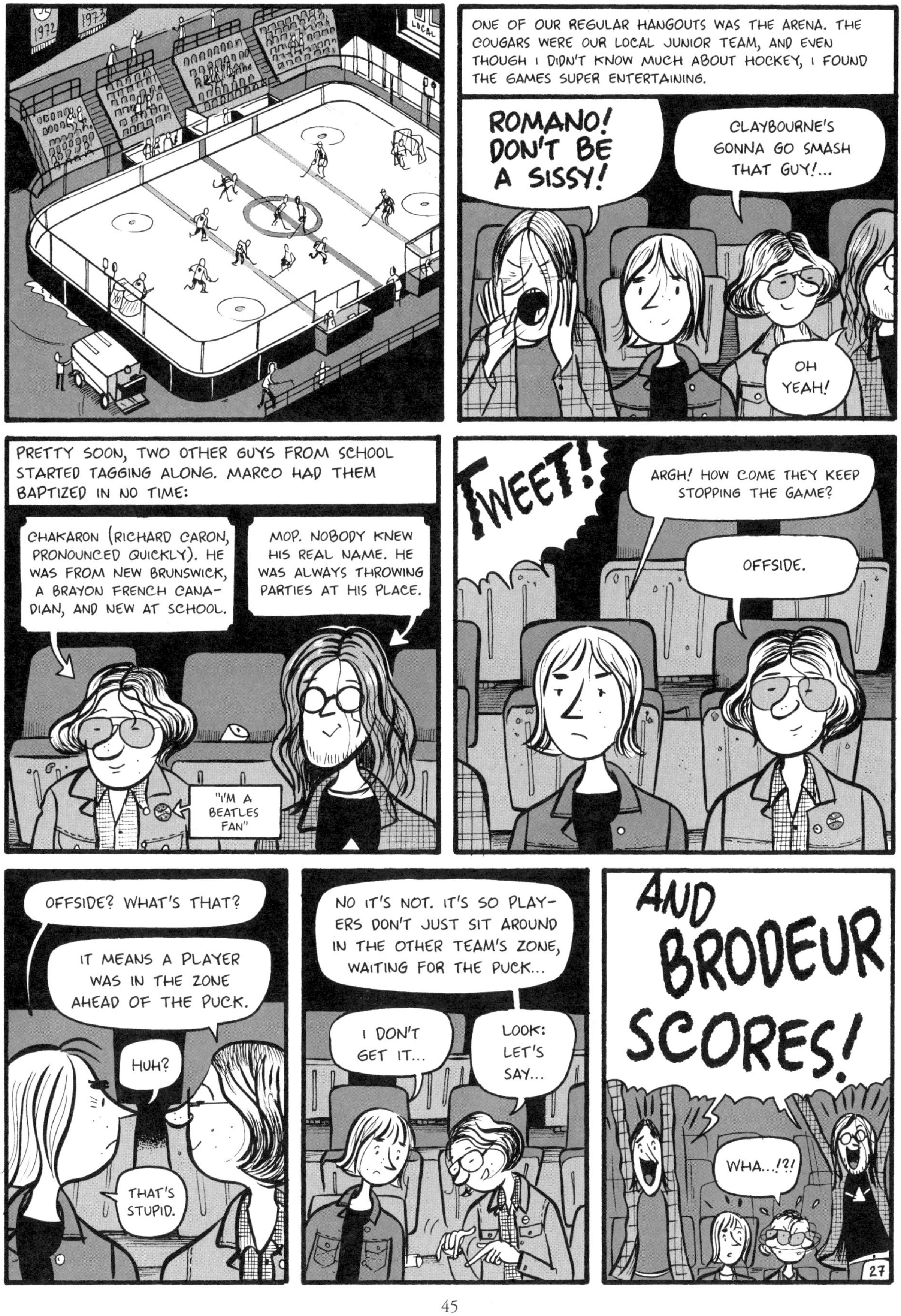
1972
1973
LOCAL
ONE OF OUR REGULAR HANGOUTS WAS THE ARENA. THE COUGARS WERE OUR LOCAL JUNIOR TEAM, AND EVEN THOUGH I DIDN'T KNOW MUCH ABOUT HOCKEY, I FOUND THE GAMES SUPER ENTERTAINING.
ROMANO! DON'T BE A SISSY!
CLAYBOURNE'S GONNA GO SMASH THAT GUY!...
OH YEAH!
PRETTY SOON, TWO OTHER GUYS FROM SCHOOL STARTED TAGGING ALONG. MARCO HAD THEM BAPTIZED IN NO TIME:
CHAKARON (RICHARD CARON, PRONOUNCED QUICKLY). HE WAS FROM NEW BRUNSWICK, A BRAYON FRENCH CANADIAN, AND NEW AT SCHOOL.
MOP. NOBODY KNEW HIS REAL NAME. HE WAS ALWAYS THROWING PARTIES AT HIS PLACE.
"I'M A BEATLES FAN"
TWEET!
ARGH! HOW COME THEY KEEP STOPPING THE GAME?
OFFSIDE.
OFFSIDE? WHAT'S THAT?
IT MEANS A PLAYER WAS IN THE ZONE AHEAD OF THE PUCK.
HUH?
THAT'S STUPID.
NO IT'S NOT. IT'S SO PLAYERS DON'T JUST SIT AROUND IN THE OTHER TEAM'S ZONE, WAITING FOR THE PUCK...
I DON'T GET IT...
LOOK: LET'S SAY...
AND BRODEUR SCORES!
WHA...!?!
27

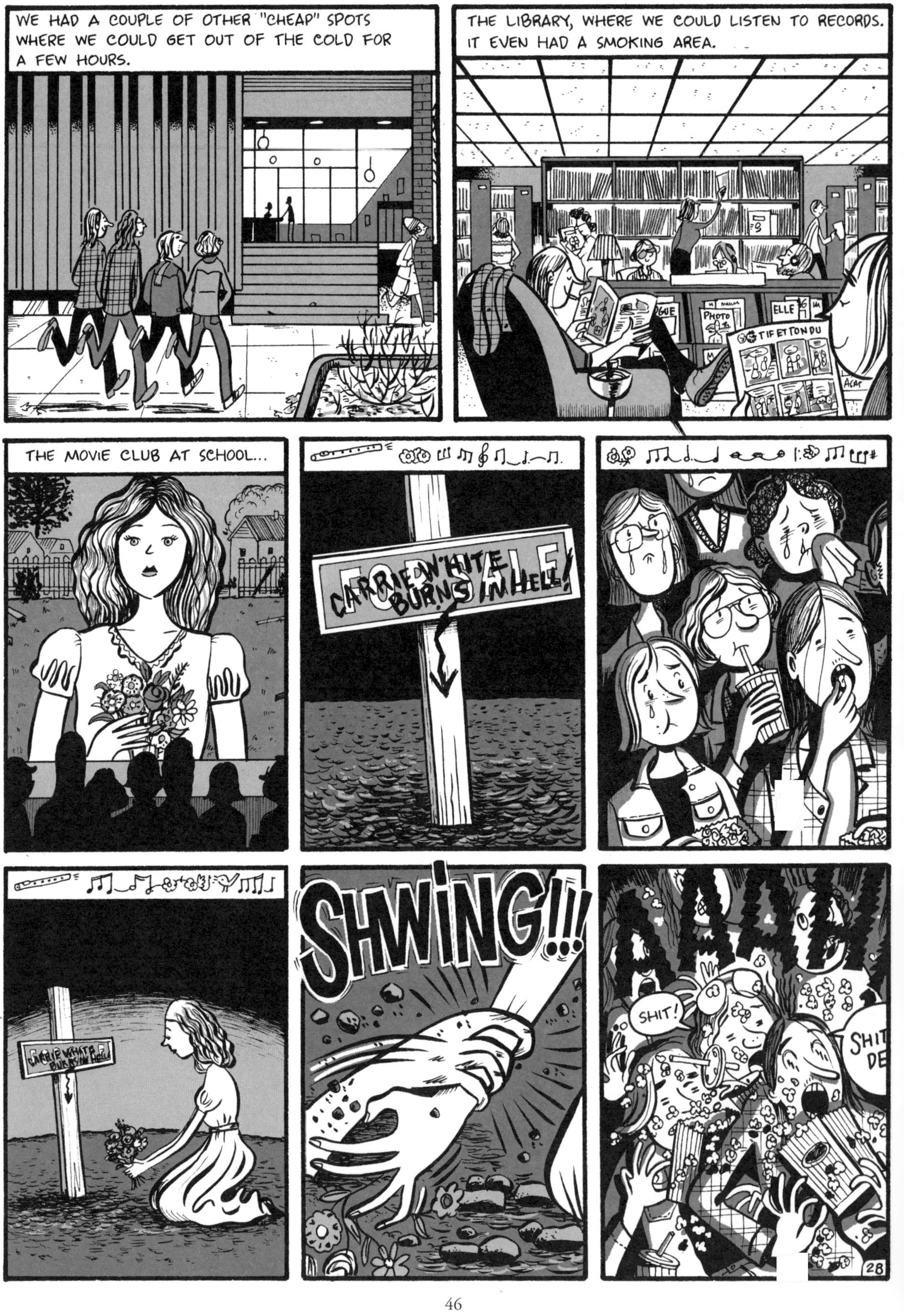
WE HAD A COUPLE OF OTHER "CHEAP" SPOTS WHERE WE COULD GET OUT OF THE COLD FOR A FEW HOURS.
THE LIBRARY, WHERE WE COULD LISTEN TO RECORDS. IT EVEN HAD A SMOKING AREA.
PHOTO
ELLE
TIF ET TONDU
THE MOVIE CLUB AT SCHOOL...
CARRIE WHITE BURNS IN HELL!
SHWING!!!
SHIT!
28

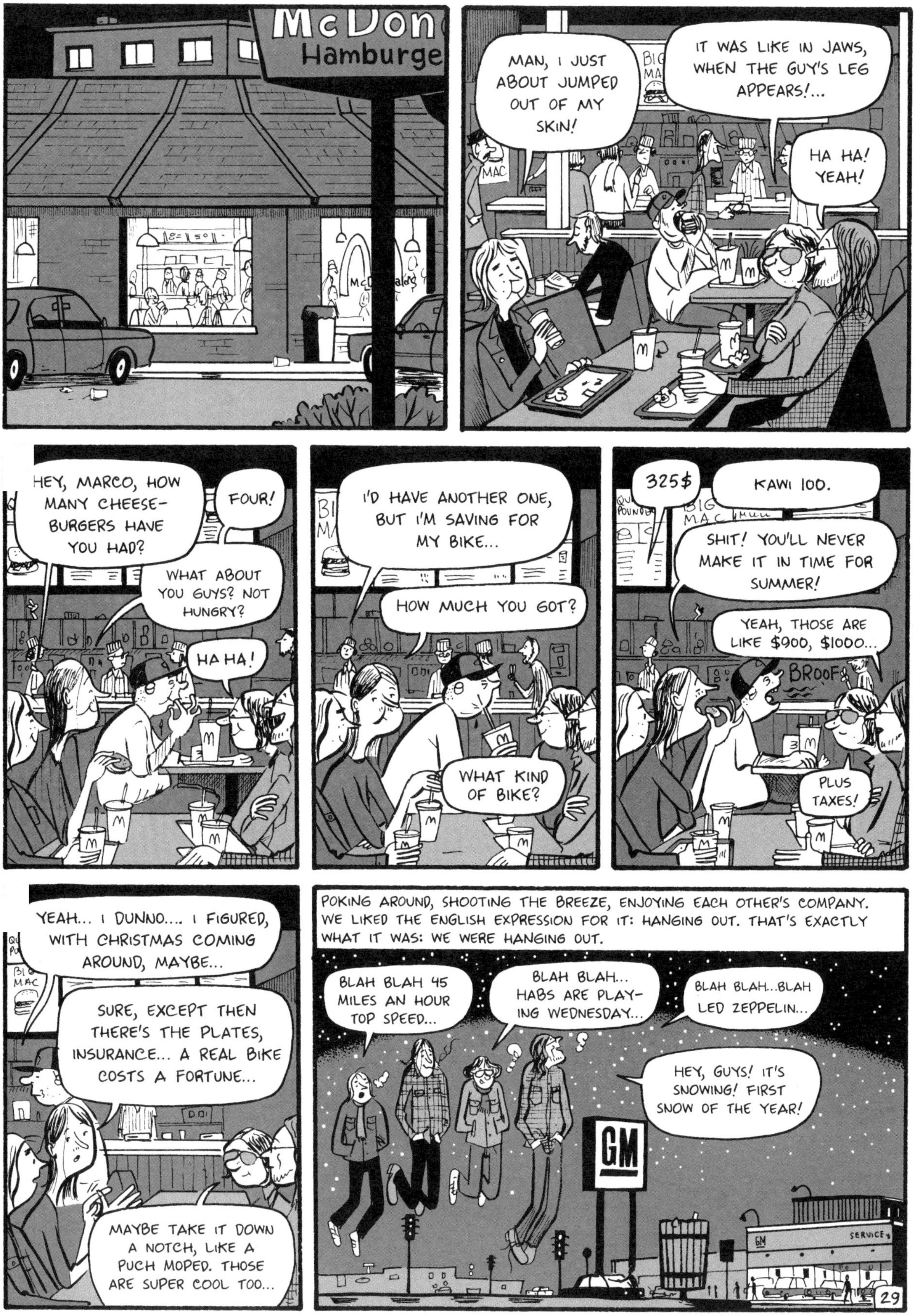
McDon
Hamburge
MAN, I JUST ABOUT JUMPED OUT OF MY SKIN!
IT WAS LIKE IN JAWS, WHEN THE GUY'S LEG APPEARS!...
HA HA! YEAH!
HEY, MARCO, HOW MANY CHEESE-BURGERS HAVE YOU HAD?
FOUR!
WHAT ABOUT YOU GUYS? NOT HUNGRY?
HA HA!
I'D HAVE ANOTHER ONE, BUT I'M SAVING FOR MY BIKE...
HOW MUCH YOU GOT?
WHAT KIND OF BIKE?
325$
KAWI 100.
SHIT! YOU'LL NEVER MAKE IT IN TIME FOR SUMMER!
YEAH, THOSE ARE LIKE $900, $1000...
BROOF
PLUS TAXES!
YEAH... I DUNNO.... I FIGURED, WITH CHRISTMAS COMING AROUND, MAYBE...
SURE, EXCEPT THEN THERE'S THE PLATES, INSURANCE... A REAL BIKE COSTS A FORTUNE...
MAYBE TAKE IT DOWN A NOTCH, LIKE A PUCH MOPED. THOSE ARE SUPER COOL TOO...
POKING AROUND, SHOOTING THE BREEZE, ENJOYING EACH OTHER'S COMPANY. WE LIKED THE ENGLISH EXPRESSION FOR IT: HANGING OUT. THAT'S EXACTLY WHAT IT WAS: WE WERE HANGING OUT.
BLAH BLAH 45 MILES AN HOUR TOP SPEED...
BLAH BLAH... HABS ARE PLAY-ING WEDNESDAY...
BLAH BLAH...BLAH LED ZEPPELIN...
HEY, GUYS! IT'S SNOWING! FIRST SNOW OF THE YEAR!
GM
SERVICE
29

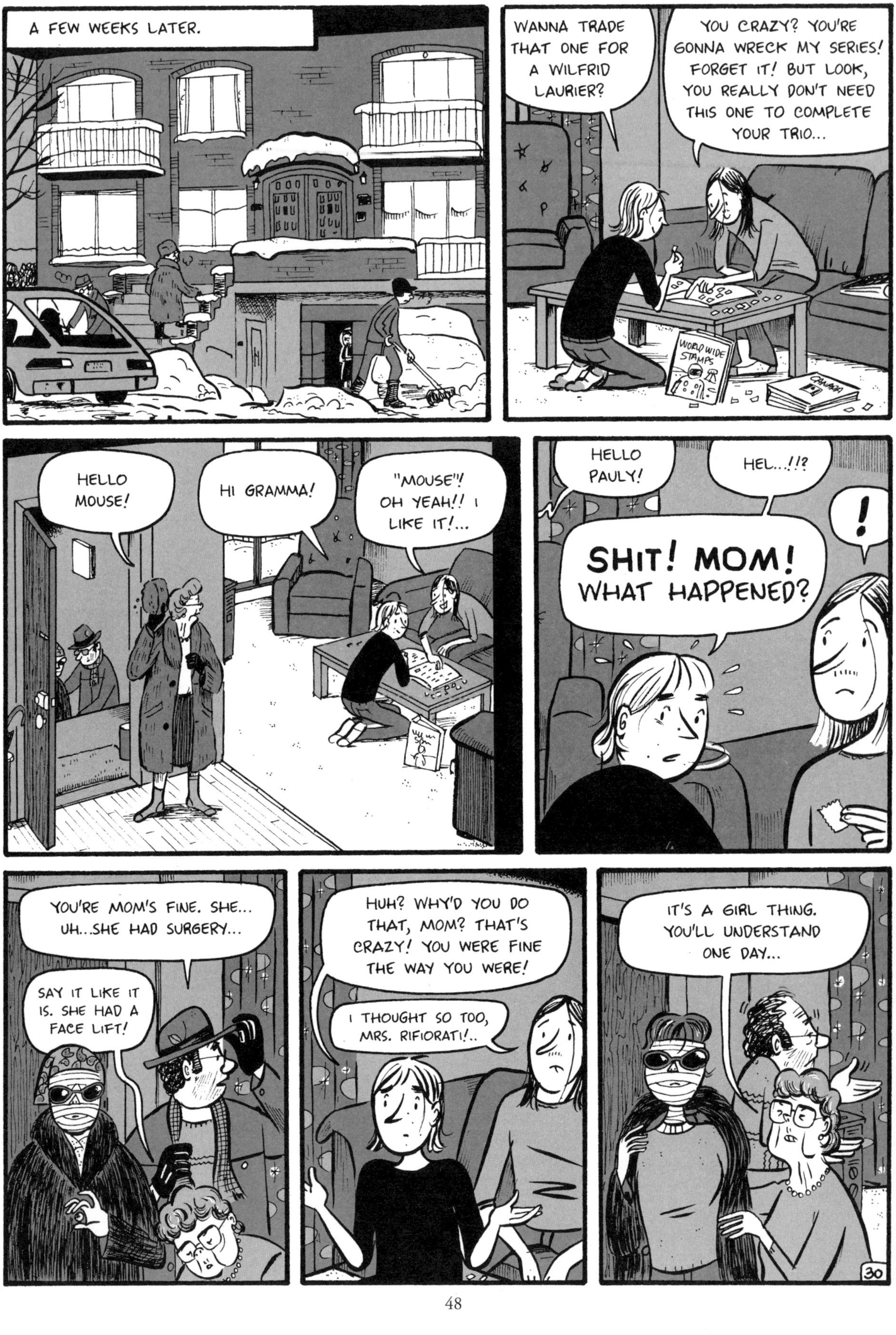
A FEW WEEKS LATER.
WANNA TRADE THAT ONE FOR A WILFRID LAURIER?
YOU CRAZY? YOU'RE GONNA WRECK MY SERIES! FORGET IT! BUT LOOK, YOU REALLY DON'T NEED THIS ONE TO COMPLETE YOUR TRIO...
WORLD WIDE STAMPS
CANADA
HELLO MOUSE!
HI GRAMMA!
"MOUSE"! OH YEAH!! I LIKE IT!...
HELLO PAULY!
HEL...!!?
!
SHIT! MOM! WHAT HAPPENED?
YOU'RE MOM'S FINE. SHE... UH...SHE HAD SURGERY...
SAY IT LIKE IT IS. SHE HAD A FACE LIFT!
HUH? WHY'D YOU DO THAT, MOM? THAT'S CRAZY! YOU WERE FINE THE WAY YOU WERE!
I THOUGHT SO TOO, MRS. RIFIORATI!..
IT'S A GIRL THING. YOU'LL UNDERSTAND ONE DAY...
30

CHRISTMAS.

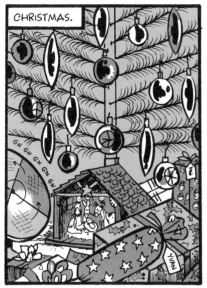

...HERE, KIDDO. THIS IS FROM ME. BET YOU CAN'T GUESS WHAT IT IS, HUH?

AND THIS ONE'S FROM US!

GOODNESS, MOUSE! YOU SURE ARE SPOILED THIS YEAR!

WHOA, GUYS! STOP! I'M NOT THE ONLY ONE HERE!

THAT CHRISTMAS, BESIDES THE USUAL SWEATERS AND SOCKS, I GOT: A BEAU DOMMAGE ALBUM...

$50 FROM MY GRANDMOTHER AND MY GREAT AUNT...

F...FIFTY! A FIFTY DOLLAR BILL!

A SET OF STABILO MARKERS...

NO WAY! AND IT'S THE 48-COLOUR SET!

AND THE USUAL SPIROU ALMANAC.

MOM'S BANDAGES WERE OFF. HER FACE WAS STILL A BIT PUFFY AND BRUISED, BUT SHE WAS IN A GOOD MOOD.

HA!... IT WOULDN'T BE CHRISTMAS WITHOUT SPIROU, HUH, PAULY?

MORE BAKED BEANS, ANYBODY?

I WON'T SAY NO, MOM...

GOT ANY MEAT LEFT, ALINE?

OOF! NOT FOR ME! I'M STUFFED!

MLOP GLOP MYUM...

31

Elohim

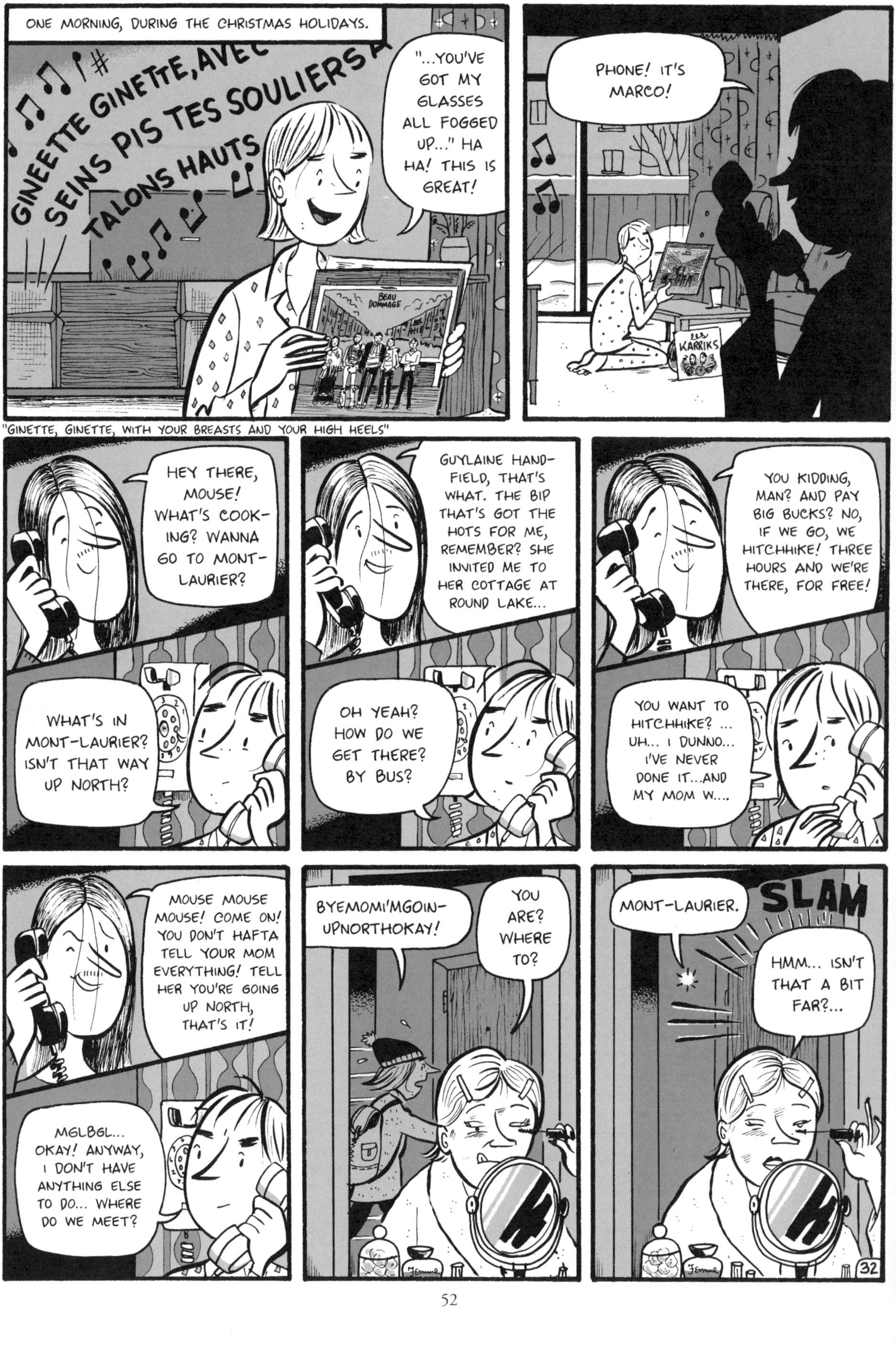

ONE MORNING, DURING THE CHRISTMAS HOLIDAYS.
GINEETTE GINETTE, AVEC SEINS PIS TES SOULIERS À TALONS HAUTS
BEAU DOMMAGE
"...YOU'VE GOT MY GLASSES ALL FOGGED UP..." HA HA! THIS IS GREAT!
"GINETTE, GINETTE, WITH YOUR BREASTS AND YOUR HIGH HEELS"
PHONE! IT'S MARCO!
LES KARRIKS
HEY THERE, MOUSE! WHAT'S COOK-ING? WANNA GO TO MONT-LAURIER?
WHAT'S IN MONT-LAURIER? ISN'T THAT WAY UP NORTH?
GUYLAINE HAND-FIELD, THAT'S WHAT. THE BIP THAT'S GOT THE HOTS FOR ME, REMEMBER? SHE INVITED ME TO HER COTTAGE AT ROUND LAKE...
OH YEAH? HOW DO WE GET THERE? BY BUS?
YOU KIDDING, MAN? AND PAY BIG BUCKS? NO, IF WE GO, WE HITCHHIKE! THREE HOURS AND WE'RE THERE, FOR FREE!
YOU WANT TO HITCHHIKE? ... UH... I DUNNO... I'VE NEVER DONE IT...AND MY MOM W....
MOUSE MOUSE MOUSE! COME ON! YOU DON'T HAFTA TELL YOUR MOM EVERYTHING! TELL HER YOU'RE GOING UP NORTH, THAT'S IT!
MGLBGL... OKAY! ANYWAY, I DON'T HAVE ANYTHING ELSE TO DO... WHERE DO WE MEET?
BYEMOMI'MGOIN-UPNORTHOKAY!
YOU ARE? WHERE TO?
MONT-LAURIER.
SLAM
HMM... ISN'T THAT A BIT FAR?...
32

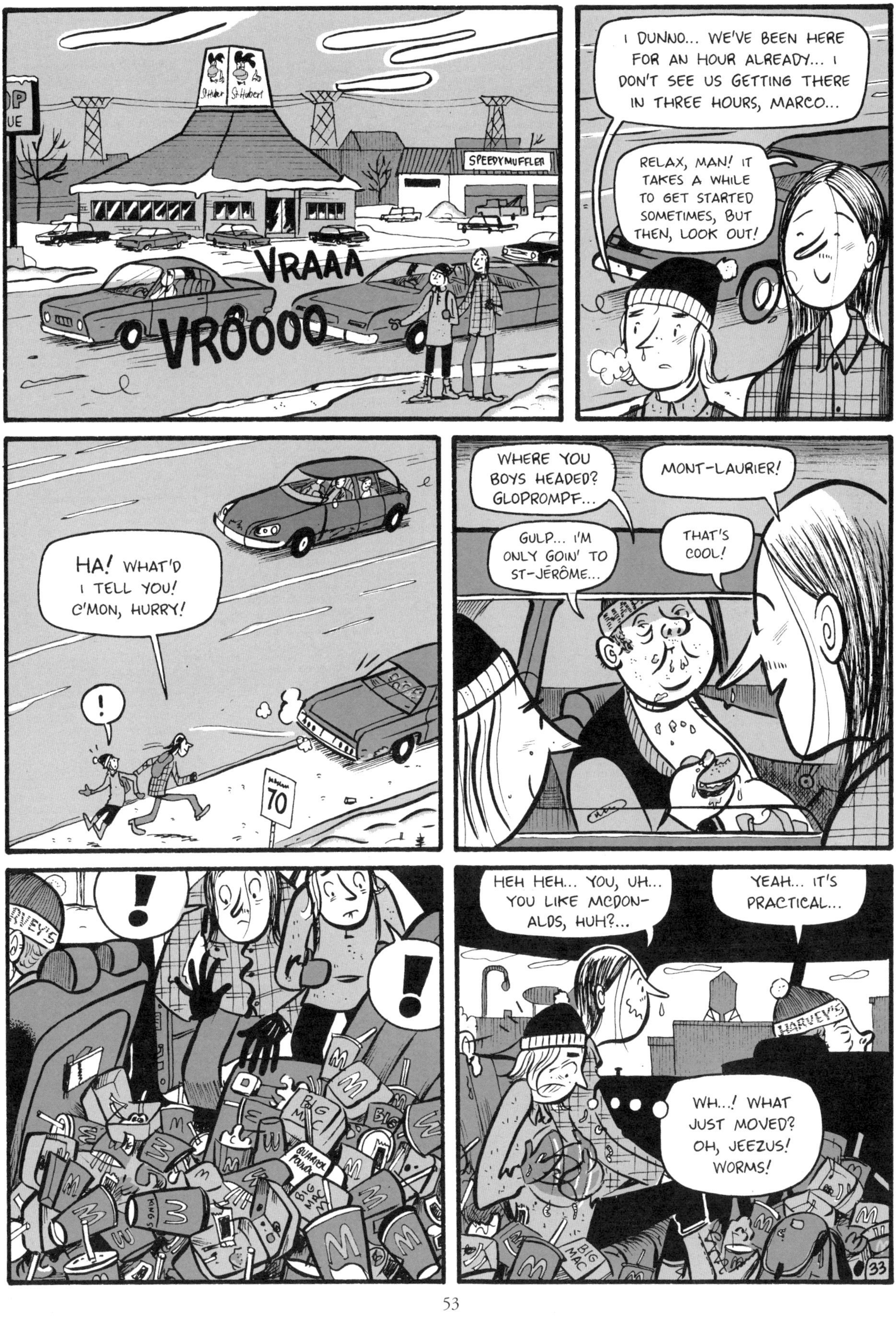
St-Hubert
St-Hubert
SPEEDYMUFFLER
VRAAA
VROOOO
I DUNNO... WE'VE BEEN HERE FOR AN HOUR ALREADY... I DON'T SEE US GETTING THERE IN THREE HOURS, MARCO...
RELAX, MAN! IT TAKES A WHILE TO GET STARTED SOMETIMES, BUT THEN, LOOK OUT!
HA! WHAT'D I TELL YOU! C'MON, HURRY!
!
70
WHERE YOU BOYS HEADED? GLOPROMPF...
MONT-LAURIER!
GULP... I'M ONLY GOIN' TO ST-JÉRÔME...
THAT'S COOL!
!
!
BIG MAC
QUARTER POUNDER
BIG MAC
HEH HEH... YOU, UH... YOU LIKE MCDON-ALDS, HUH?...
YEAH... IT'S PRACTICAL...
HARVEY'S
WH...! WHAT JUST MOVED? OH, JEEZUS! WORMS!
BIG MAC
33

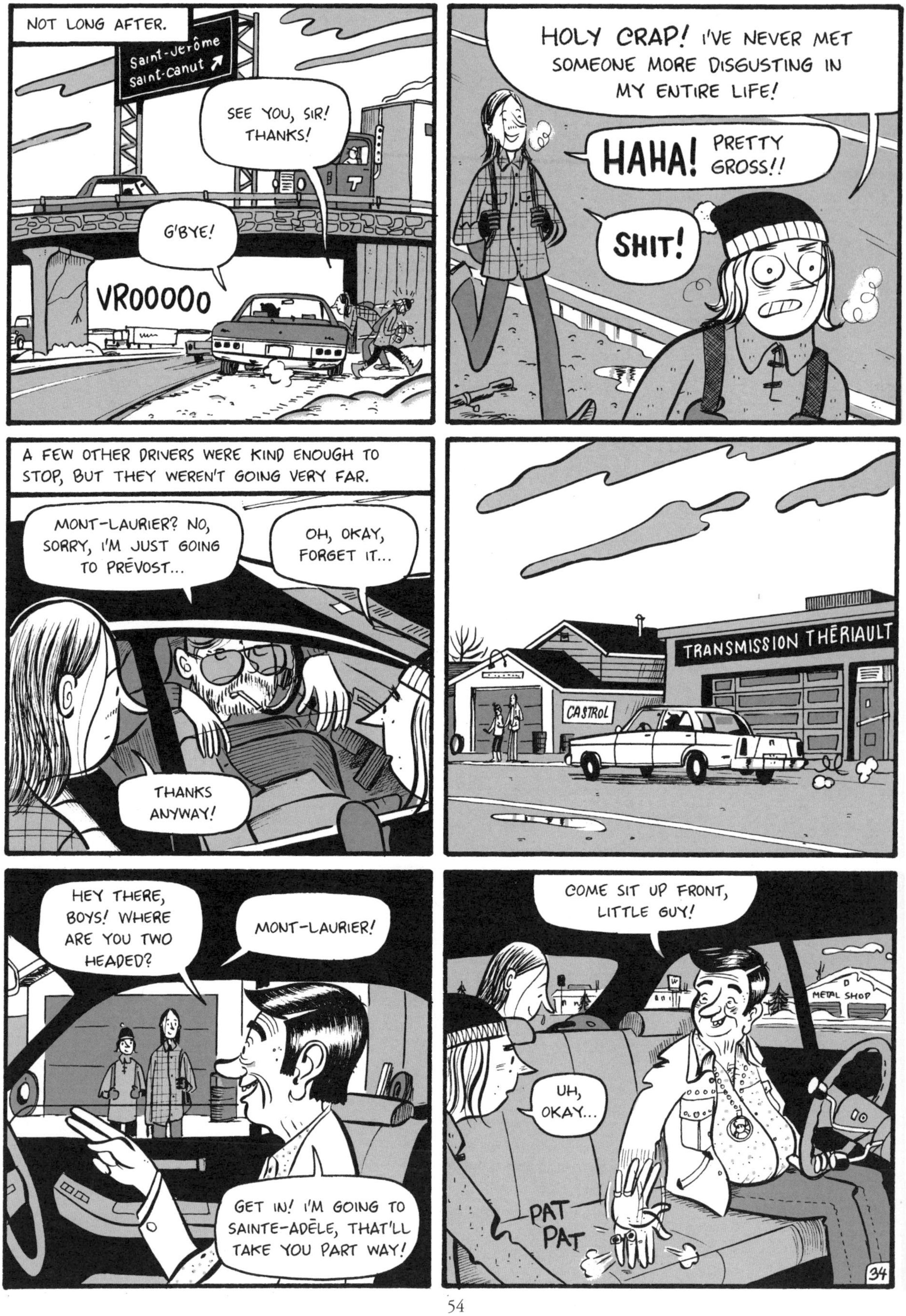
NOT LONG AFTER.
Saint-Jérôme
Saint-Canut
SEE YOU, SIR! THANKS!
G'BYE!
VROOOOO
HOLY CRAP! I'VE NEVER MET SOMEONE MORE DISGUSTING IN MY ENTIRE LIFE!
HAHA! PRETTY GROSS!!
SHIT!
A FEW OTHER DRIVERS WERE KIND ENOUGH TO STOP, BUT THEY WEREN'T GOING VERY FAR.
MONT-LAURIER? NO, SORRY, I'M JUST GOING TO PRÉVOST...
OH, OKAY, FORGET IT...
THANKS ANYWAY!
TRANSMISSION THÉRIAULT
CASTROL
HEY THERE, BOYS! WHERE ARE YOU TWO HEADED?
MONT-LAURIER!
GET IN! I'M GOING TO SAINTE-ADÈLE, THAT'LL TAKE YOU PART WAY!
COME SIT UP FRONT, LITTLE GUY!
METAL SHOP
UH, OKAY...
PAT PAT
34

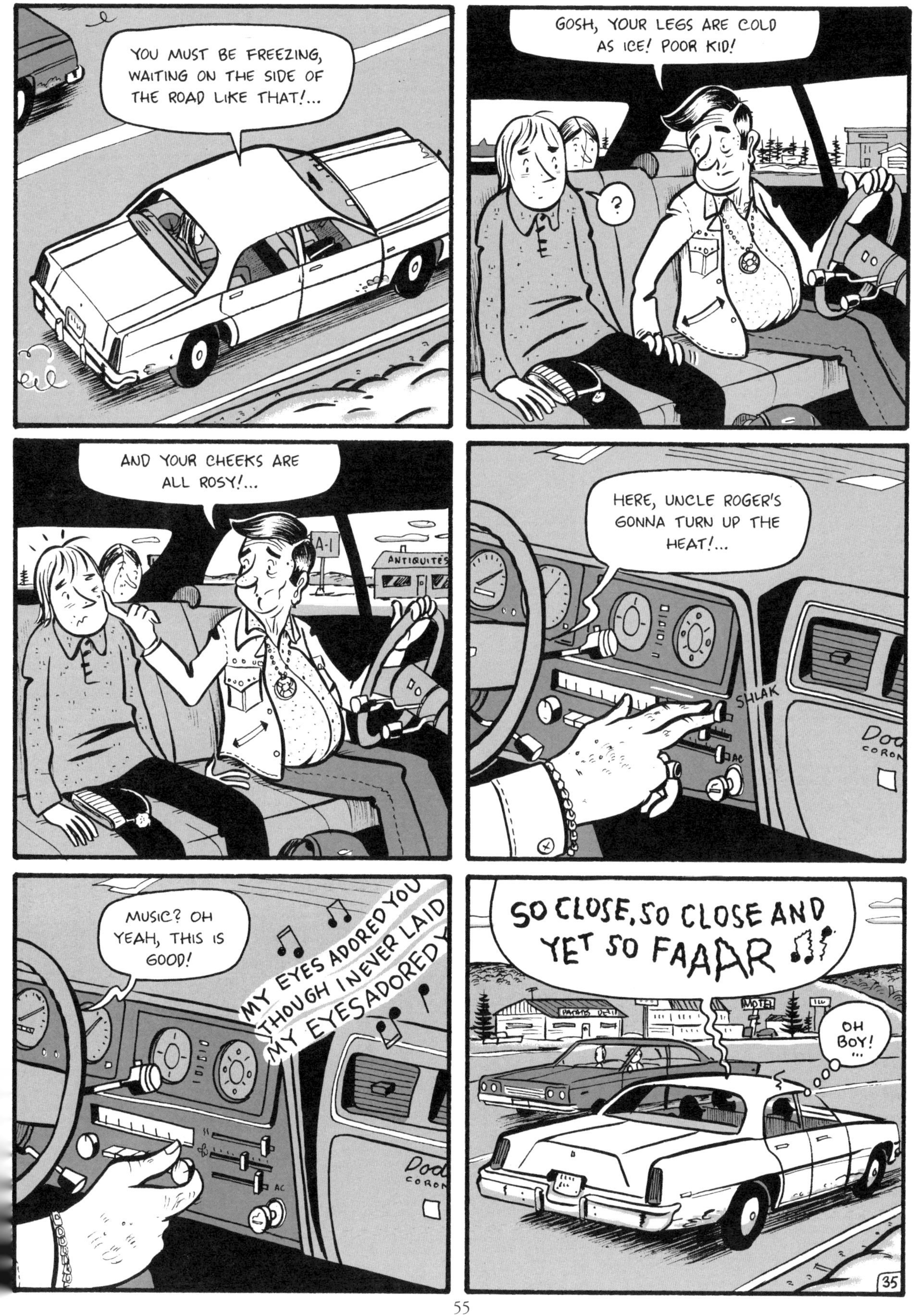
YOU MUST BE FREEZING, WAITING ON THE SIDE OF THE ROAD LIKE THAT!...
GOSH, YOUR LEGS ARE COLD AS ICE! POOR KID!
?
AND YOUR CHEEKS ARE ALL ROSY!...
A-1
ANTIQUITÉS
HERE, UNCLE ROGER'S GONNA TURN UP THE HEAT!...
SHLAK
AC
MUSIC? OH YEAH, THIS IS GOOD!
MY EYES ADORED YOU
THOUGH I NEVER LAID
MY EYESADOREDY
SO CLOSE, SO CLOSE AND YET SO FAAAR
MOTEL
OH BOY! ...
35

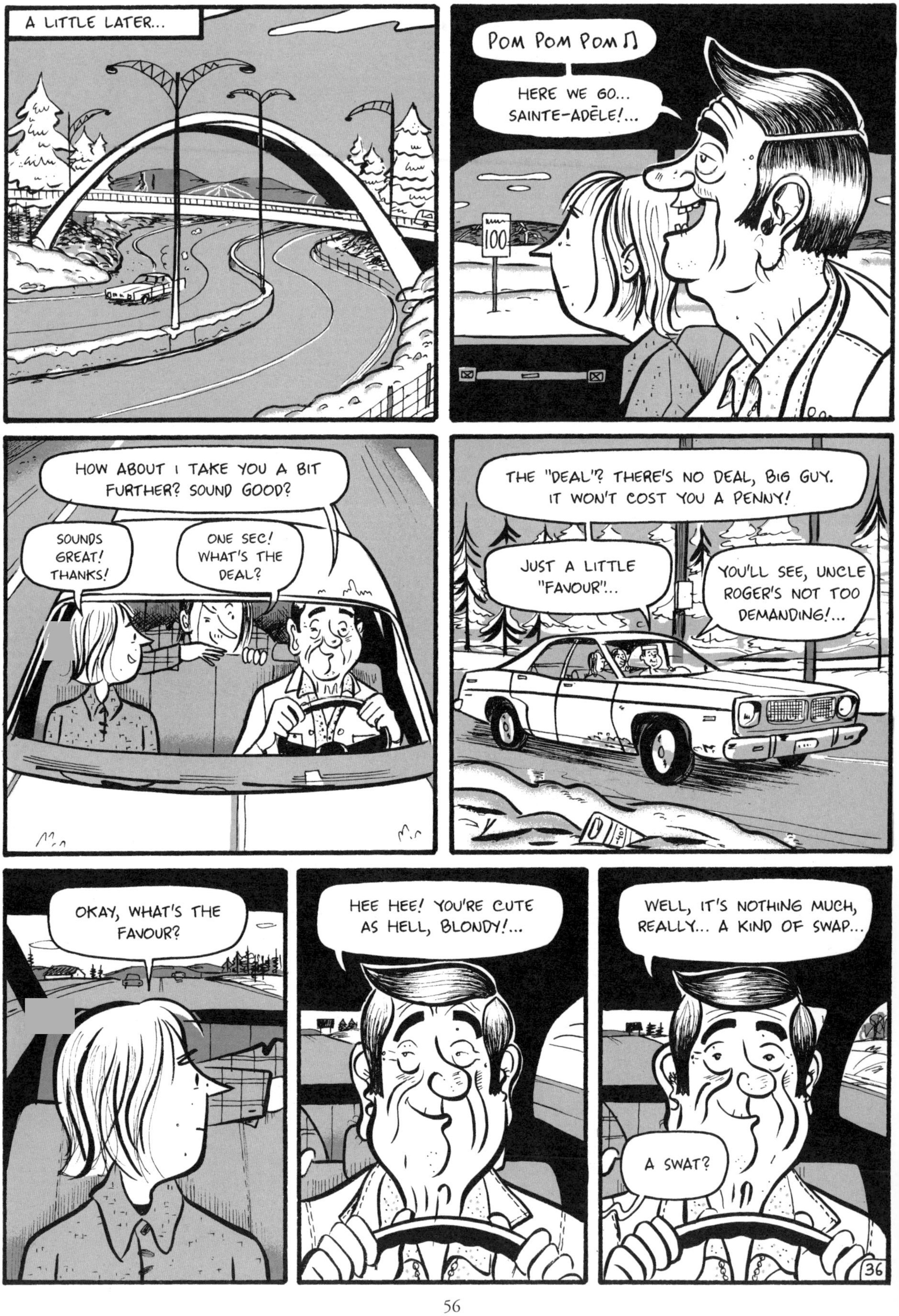
A LITTLE LATER...
POM POM POM ♫
HERE WE GO... SAINTE-ADÈLE!...
100
HOW ABOUT I TAKE YOU A BIT FURTHER? SOUND GOOD?
SOUNDS GREAT! THANKS!
ONE SEC! WHAT'S THE DEAL?
THE "DEAL"? THERE'S NO DEAL, BIG GUY. IT WON'T COST YOU A PENNY!
JUST A LITTLE "FAVOUR"...
YOU'LL SEE, UNCLE ROGER'S NOT TOO DEMANDING!...
OKAY, WHAT'S THE FAVOUR?
HEE HEE! YOU'RE CUTE AS HELL, BLONDY!...
WELL, IT'S NOTHING MUCH, REALLY... A KIND OF SWAP...
A SWAT?
36

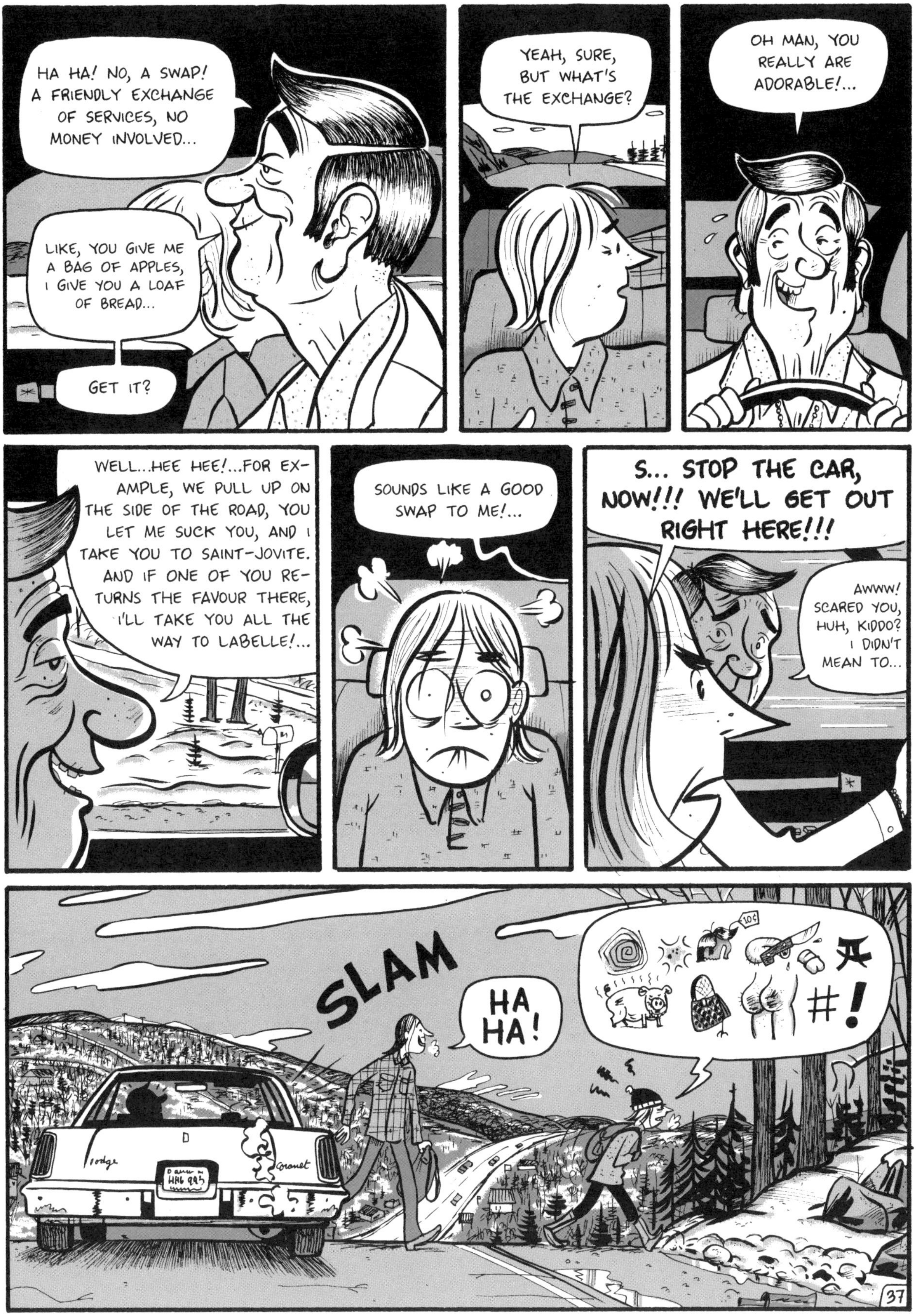
HA HA! NO, A SWAP! A FRIENDLY EXCHANGE OF SERVICES, NO MONEY INVOLVED...
LIKE, YOU GIVE ME A BAG OF APPLES, I GIVE YOU A LOAF OF BREAD...
GET IT?
YEAH, SURE, BUT WHAT'S THE EXCHANGE?
OH MAN, YOU REALLY ARE ADORABLE!...
WELL...HEE HEE!...FOR EXAMPLE, WE PULL UP ON THE SIDE OF THE ROAD, YOU LET ME SUCK YOU, AND I TAKE YOU TO SAINT-JOVITE. AND IF ONE OF YOU RETURNS THE FAVOUR THERE, I'LL TAKE YOU ALL THE WAY TO LABELLE!...
SOUNDS LIKE A GOOD SWAP TO ME!...
S... STOP THE CAR, NOW!!! WE'LL GET OUT RIGHT HERE!!!
AWWW! SCARED YOU, HUH, KIDDO? I DIDN'T MEAN TO...
SLAM
HA HA!
#!
37

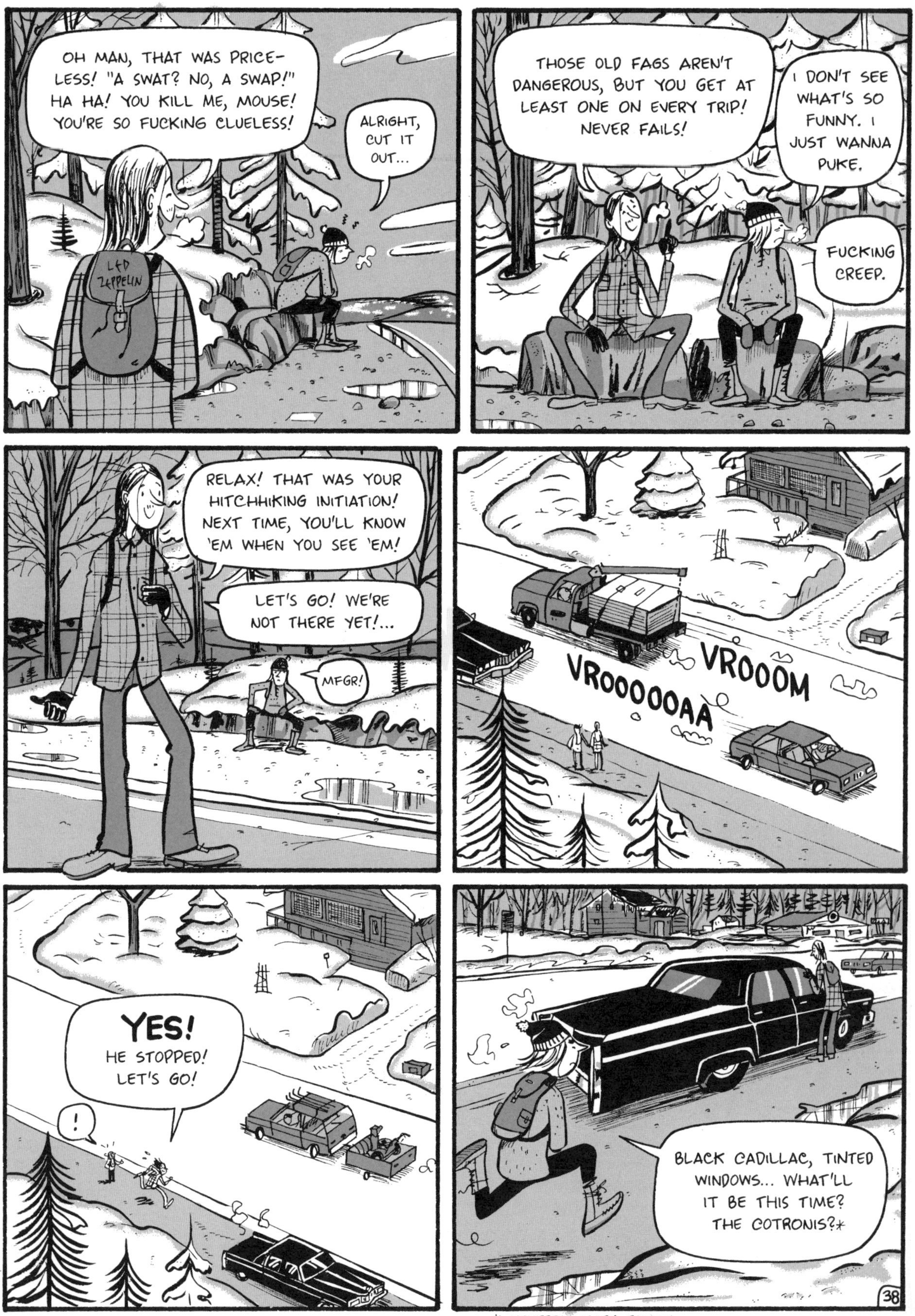
OH MAN, THAT WAS PRICE-LESS! "A SWAT? NO, A SWAP!" HA HA! YOU KILL ME, MOUSE! YOU'RE SO FUCKING CLUELESS!
ALRIGHT, CUT IT OUT...
LED ZEPPELIN
THOSE OLD FAGS AREN'T DANGEROUS, BUT YOU GET AT LEAST ONE ON EVERY TRIP! NEVER FAILS!
I DON'T SEE WHAT'S SO FUNNY. I JUST WANNA PUKE.
FUCKING CREEP.
RELAX! THAT WAS YOUR HITCHHIKING INITIATION! NEXT TIME, YOU'LL KNOW 'EM WHEN YOU SEE 'EM!
LET'S GO! WE'RE NOT THERE YET!...
MFGR!
VROOOM
VROOOOOAA
YES! HE STOPPED! LET'S GO!
!
BLACK CADILLAC, TINTED WINDOWS... WHAT'LL IT BE THIS TIME? THE COTRONIS?*
38

* MONTREAL MAFIA FAMILY.

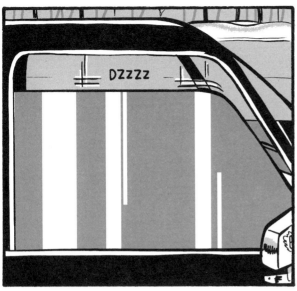

GOT ANY MONEY?

WELL...UH...HEH HEH! NOT EXACTLY. THAT'S WHY WE'RE HITCHHIKING...

I NEED TO FILL UP! IT'S AN EMERGENCY! I'LL GIVE YOU A LIFT IF YOU PAY FOR THE GAS!

WELL, IT'S JUST THAT...

FORGET IT, MARYSE! YOU CAN SEE THEY'RE POOR AS SHIT! LET'S GO!

TOOOOO

VROOOR

39

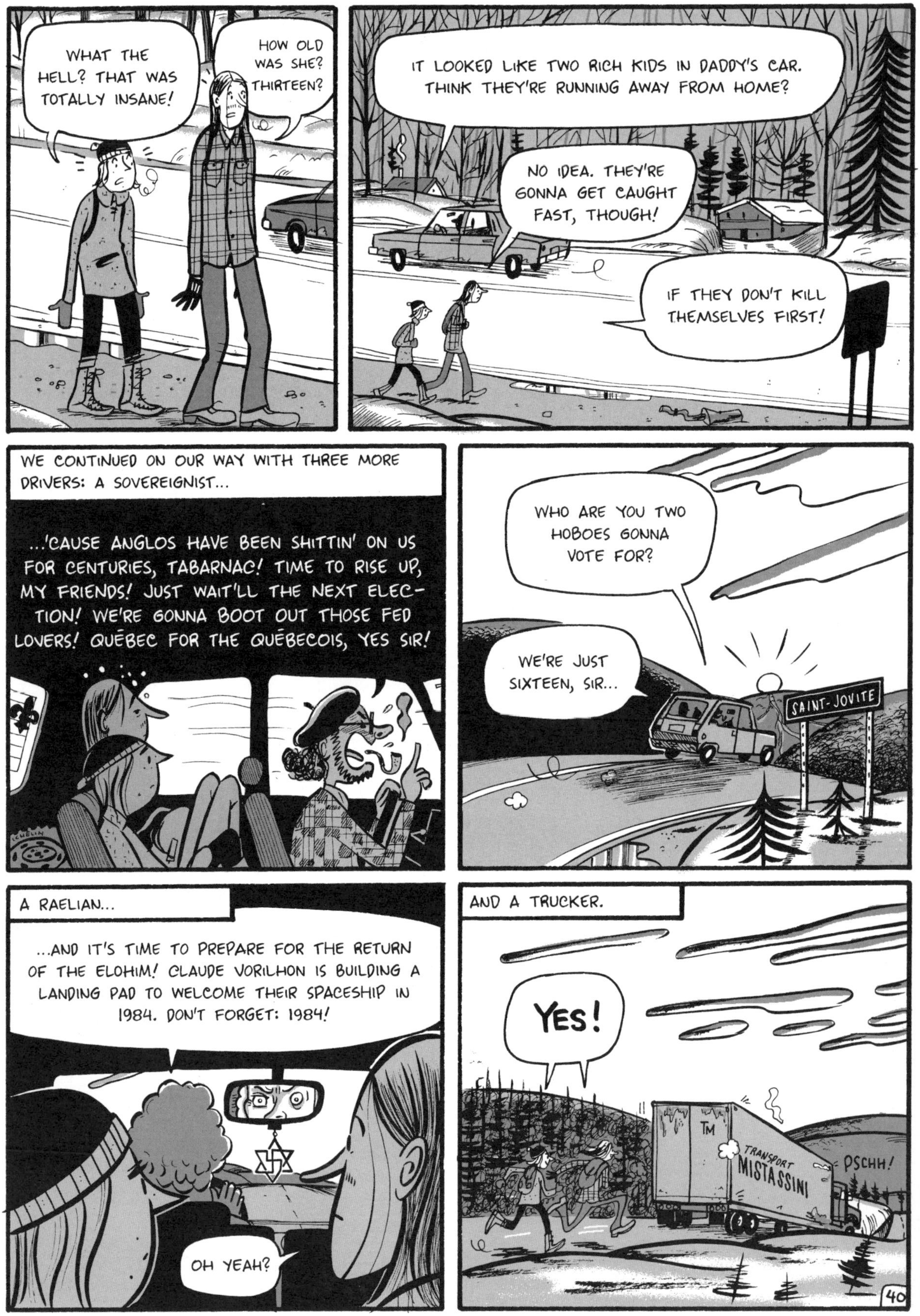
WHAT THE HELL? THAT WAS TOTALLY INSANE!
HOW OLD WAS SHE? THIRTEEN?
IT LOOKED LIKE TWO RICH KIDS IN DADDY'S CAR. THINK THEY'RE RUNNING AWAY FROM HOME?
NO IDEA. THEY'RE GONNA GET CAUGHT FAST, THOUGH!
IF THEY DON'T KILL THEMSELVES FIRST!
WE CONTINUED ON OUR WAY WITH THREE MORE DRIVERS: A SOVEREIGNIST...
...'CAUSE ANGLOS HAVE BEEN SHITTIN' ON US FOR CENTURIES, TABARNAC! TIME TO RISE UP, MY FRIENDS! JUST WAIT'LL THE NEXT ELECTION! WE'RE GONNA BOOT OUT THOSE FED LOVERS! QUÉBEC FOR THE QUÉBECOIS, YES SIR!
WHO ARE YOU TWO HOBOES GONNA VOTE FOR?
WE'RE JUST SIXTEEN, SIR...
SAINT-JOVITE
A RAELIAN...
...AND IT'S TIME TO PREPARE FOR THE RETURN OF THE ELOHIM! CLAUDE VORILHON IS BUILDING A LANDING PAD TO WELCOME THEIR SPACESHIP IN 1984. DON'T FORGET: 1984!
OH YEAH?
AND A TRUCKER.
YES!
TM
TRANSPORT MISTASSINI
PSCHH!
40

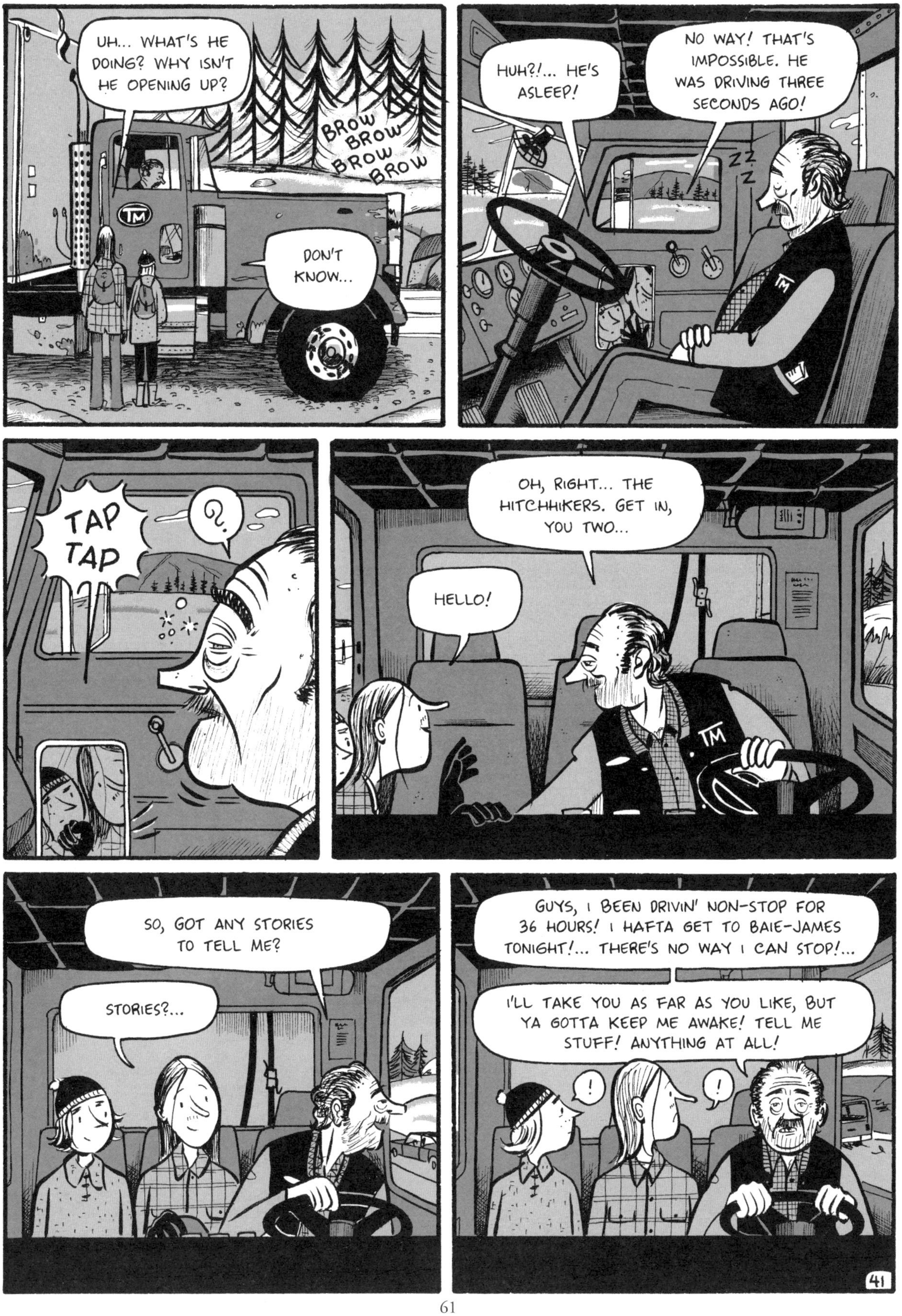
UH... WHAT'S HE DOING? WHY ISN'T HE OPENING UP?
BROW BROW BROW BROW
DON'T KNOW...
HUH?!... HE'S ASLEEP!
NO WAY! THAT'S IMPOSSIBLE. HE WAS DRIVING THREE SECONDS AGO!
ZZZ
TAP TAP
?
OH, RIGHT... THE HITCHHIKERS. GET IN, YOU TWO...
HELLO!
SO, GOT ANY STORIES TO TELL ME?
STORIES?...
GUYS, I BEEN DRIVIN' NON-STOP FOR 36 HOURS! I HAFTA GET TO BAIE-JAMES TONIGHT!... THERE'S NO WAY I CAN STOP!...
I'LL TAKE YOU AS FAR AS YOU LIKE, BUT YA GOTTA KEEP ME AWAKE! TELL ME STUFF! ANYTHING AT ALL!
!
!
41

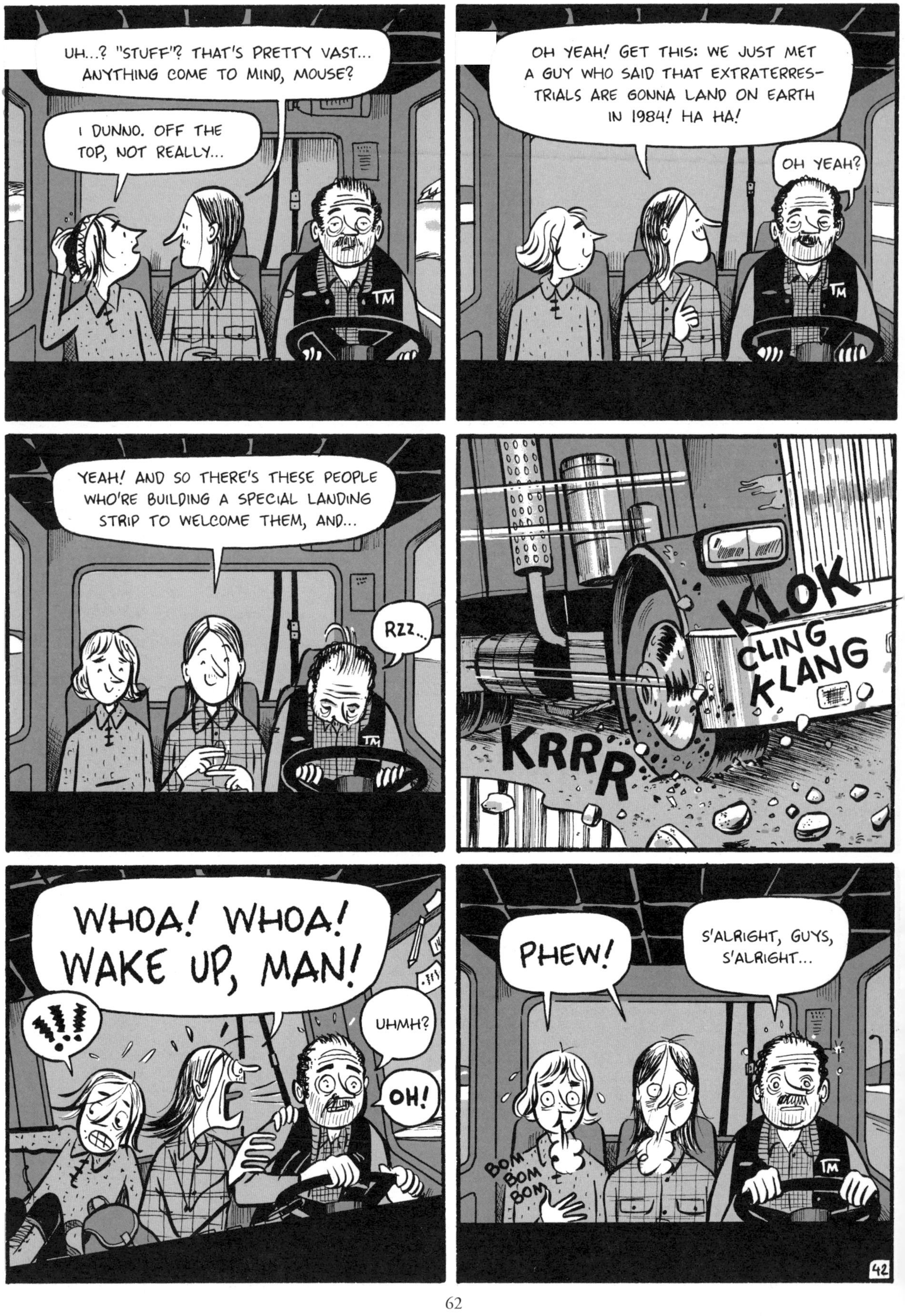
UH...? "STUFF"? THAT'S PRETTY VAST... ANYTHING COME TO MIND, MOUSE?
I DUNNO. OFF THE TOP, NOT REALLY...
OH YEAH! GET THIS: WE JUST MET A GUY WHO SAID THAT EXTRATERRES-TRIALS ARE GONNA LAND ON EARTH IN 1984! HA HA!
OH YEAH?
YEAH! AND SO THERE'S THESE PEOPLE WHO'RE BUILDING A SPECIAL LANDING STRIP TO WELCOME THEM, AND...
RZZ...
KLOK
CLING
KLANG
KRRR
WHOA! WHOA! WAKE UP, MAN!
!!!
UHMH?
OH!
PHEW!
S'ALRIGHT, GUYS, S'ALRIGHT...
BOM BOM BOM
42

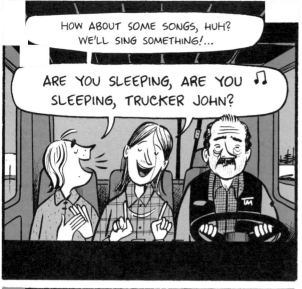

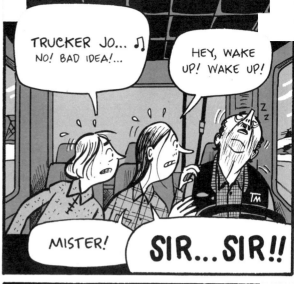

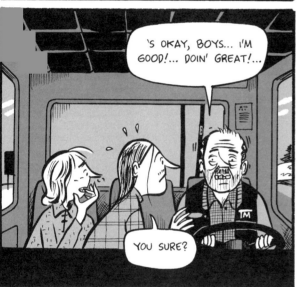

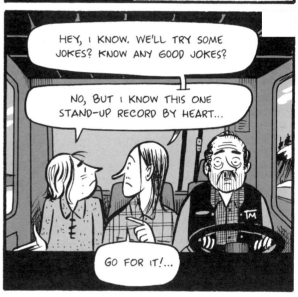

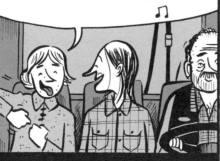

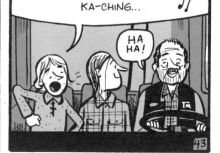

63

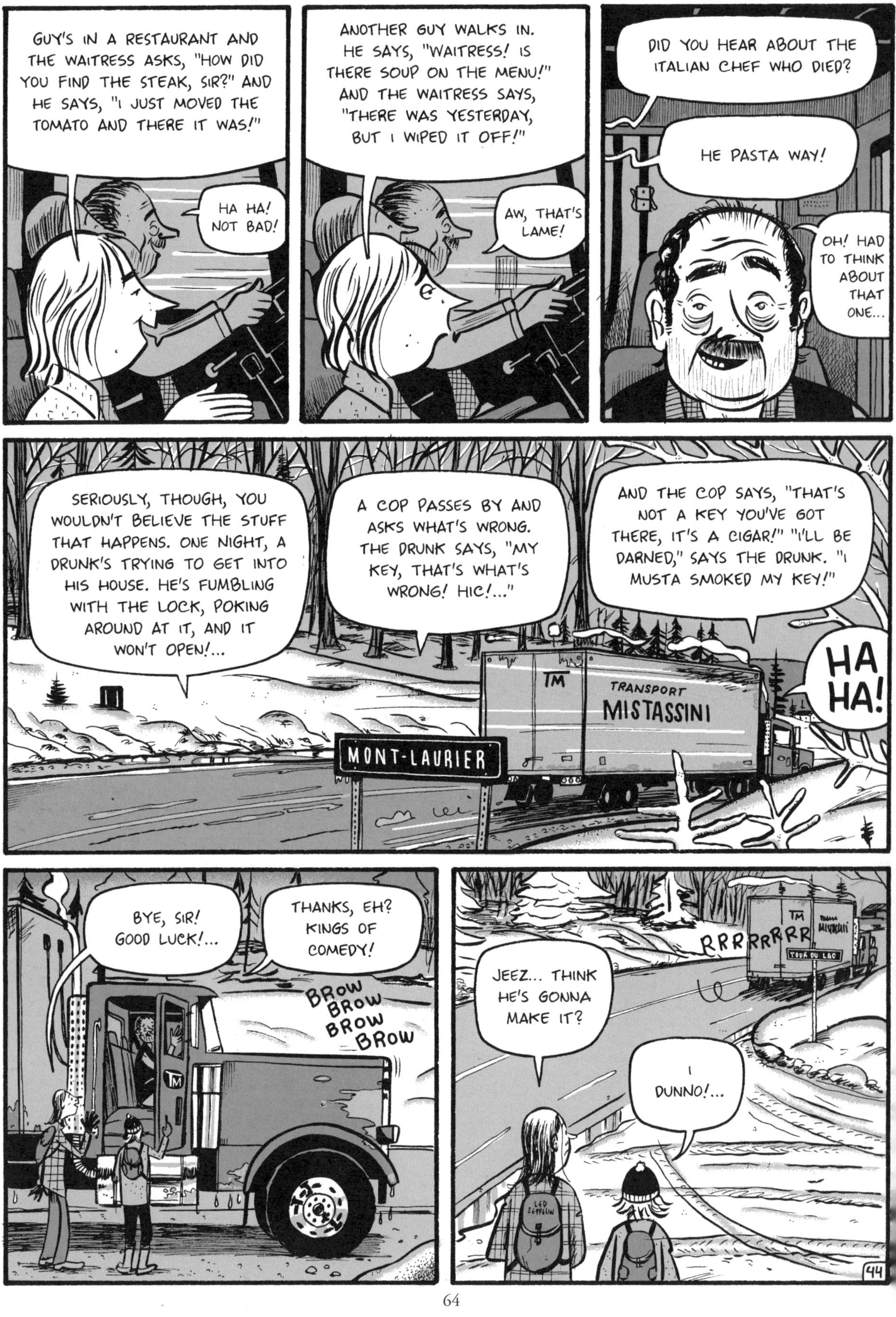
GUY'S IN A RESTAURANT AND THE WAITRESS ASKS, "HOW DID YOU FIND THE STEAK, SIR?" AND HE SAYS, "I JUST MOVED THE TOMATO AND THERE IT WAS!"
HA HA! NOT BAD!
ANOTHER GUY WALKS IN. HE SAYS, "WAITRESS! IS THERE SOUP ON THE MENU!" AND THE WAITRESS SAYS, "THERE WAS YESTERDAY, BUT I WIPED IT OFF!"
AW, THAT'S LAME!
DID YOU HEAR ABOUT THE ITALIAN CHEF WHO DIED?
HE PASTA WAY!
OH! HAD TO THINK ABOUT THAT ONE...
SERIOUSLY, THOUGH, YOU WOULDN'T BELIEVE THE STUFF THAT HAPPENS. ONE NIGHT, A DRUNK'S TRYING TO GET INTO HIS HOUSE. HE'S FUMBLING WITH THE LOCK, POKING AROUND AT IT, AND IT WON'T OPEN!...
A COP PASSES BY AND ASKS WHAT'S WRONG. THE DRUNK SAYS, "MY KEY, THAT'S WHAT'S WRONG! HIC!..."
AND THE COP SAYS, "THAT'S NOT A KEY YOU'VE GOT THERE, IT'S A CIGAR!" "I'LL BE DARNED," SAYS THE DRUNK. "I MUSTA SMOKED MY KEY!"
HA HA!
TM
TRANSPORT MISTASSINI
MONT-LAURIER
BYE, SIR! GOOD LUCK!...
THANKS, EH? KINGS OF COMEDY!
BROW BROW BROW BROW
TM
RRRRRRRR
TOUR DU LAC
JEEZ... THINK HE'S GONNA MAKE IT?
I DUNNO!...
LED ZEPPELIN
44

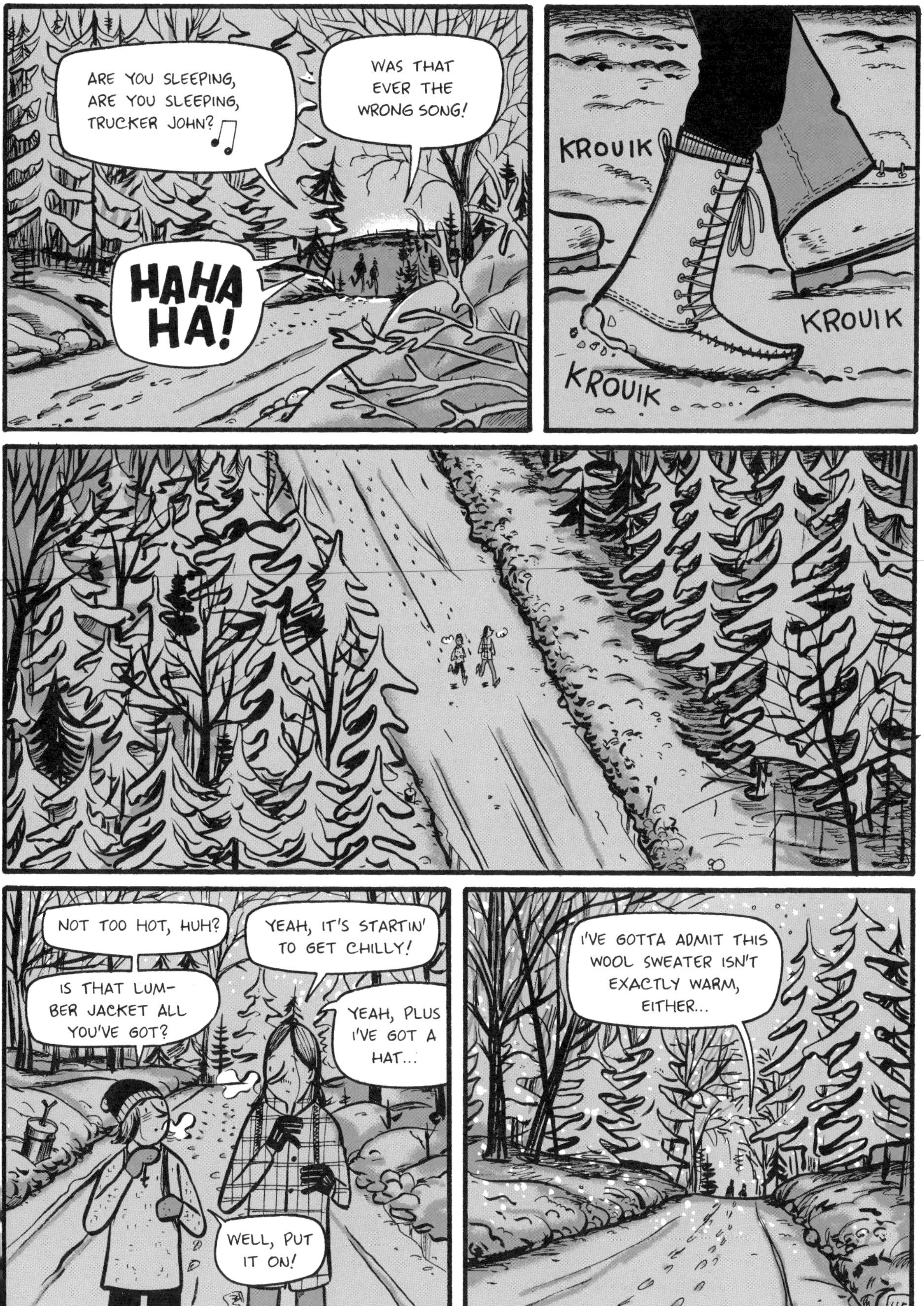
ARE YOU SLEEPING, ARE YOU SLEEPING, TRUCKER JOHN?
WAS THAT EVER THE WRONG SONG!
HAHA HA!
KROUIK
KROUIK
KROUIK
NOT TOO HOT, HUH?
IS THAT LUMBER JACKET ALL YOU'VE GOT?
YEAH, IT'S STARTIN' TO GET CHILLY!
YEAH, PLUS I'VE GOT A HAT...
WELL, PUT IT ON!
I'VE GOTTA ADMIT THIS WOOL SWEATER ISN'T EXACTLY WARM, EITHER...
45

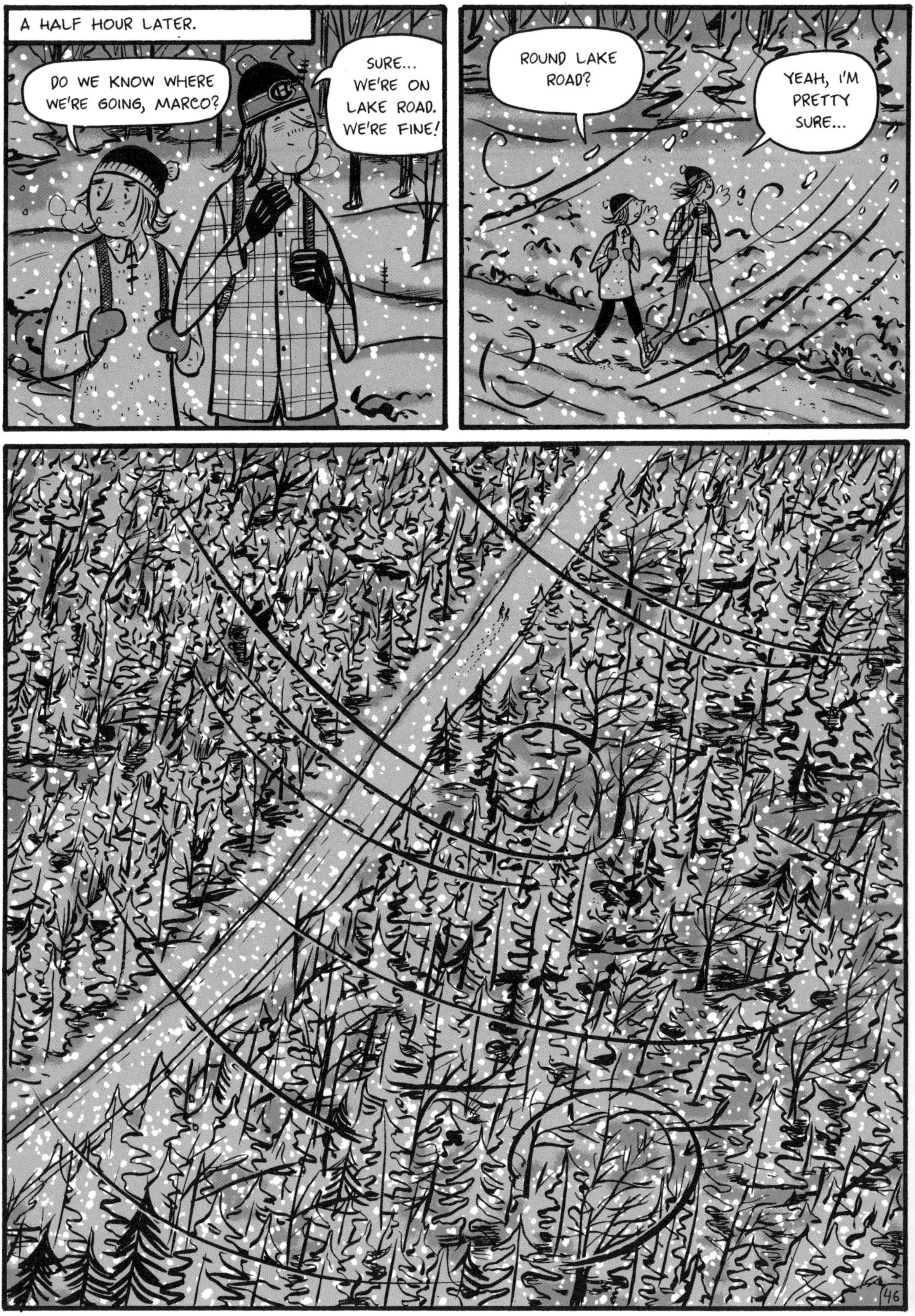
A HALF HOUR LATER.
DO WE KNOW WHERE WE'RE GOING, MARCO?
SURE... WE'RE ON LAKE ROAD. WE'RE FINE!
ROUND LAKE ROAD?
YEAH, I'M PRETTY SURE...
46

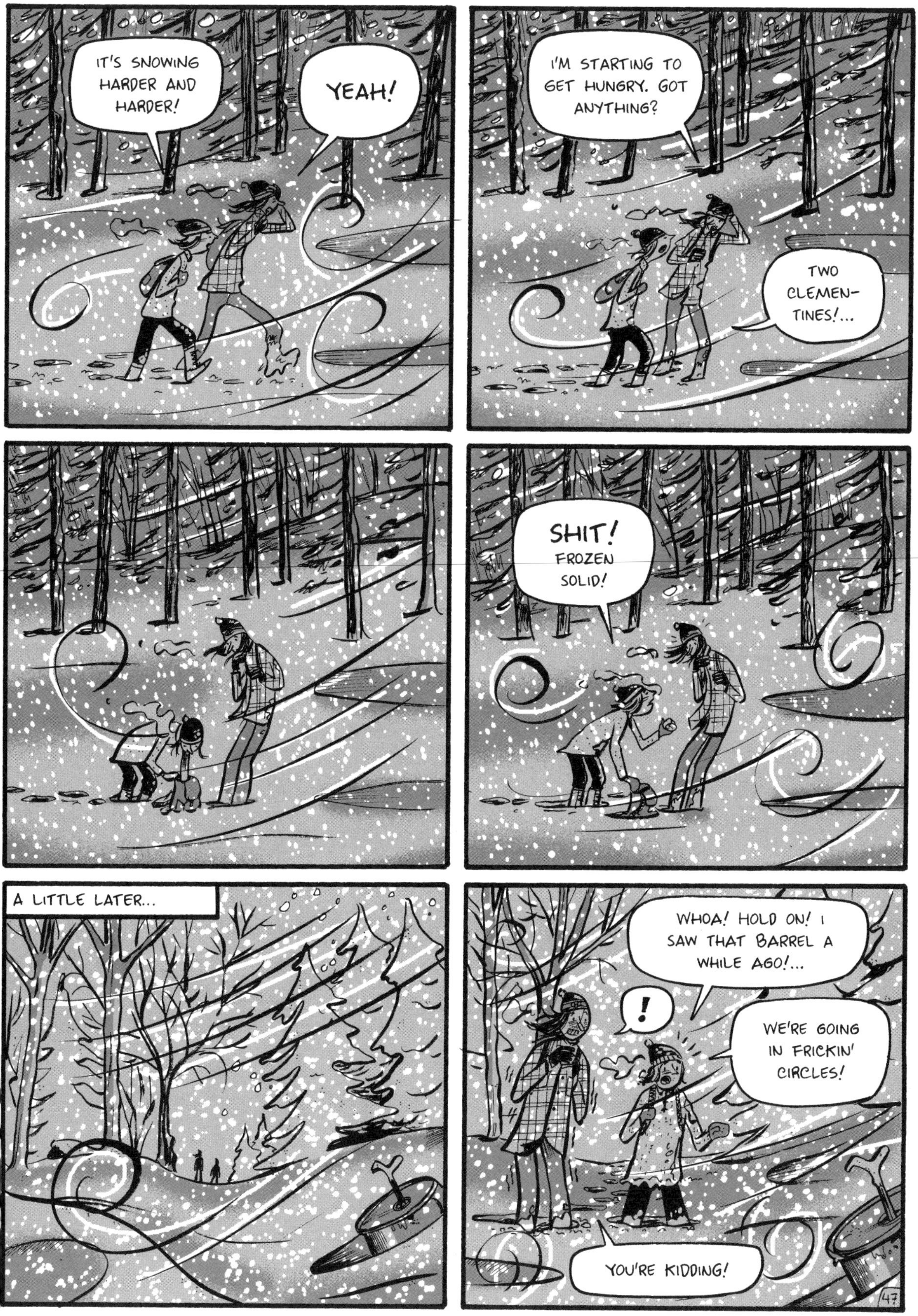
IT'S SNOWING HARDER AND HARDER!
YEAH!
I'M STARTING TO GET HUNGRY. GOT ANYTHING?
TWO CLEMEN-TINES!...
SHIT! FROZEN SOLID!
A LITTLE LATER...
WHOA! HOLD ON! I SAW THAT BARREL A WHILE AGO!...
!
WE'RE GOING IN FRICKIN' CIRCLES!
YOU'RE KIDDING!
47

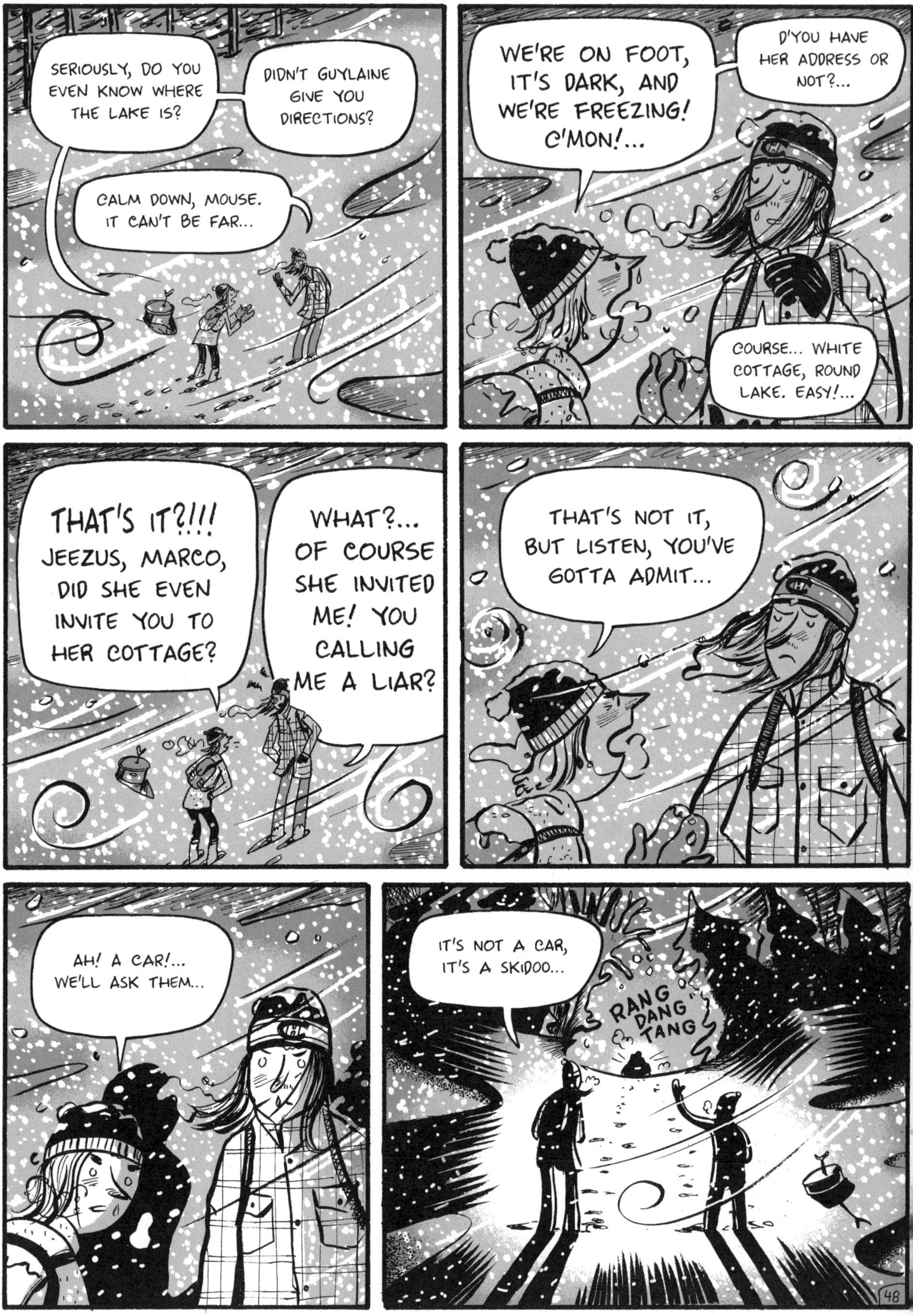
SERIOUSLY, DO YOU EVEN KNOW WHERE THE LAKE IS?
DIDN'T GUYLAINE GIVE YOU DIRECTIONS?
CALM DOWN, MOUSE. IT CAN'T BE FAR...
WE'RE ON FOOT, IT'S DARK, AND WE'RE FREEZING! C'MON!...
D'YOU HAVE HER ADDRESS OR NOT?...
COURSE... WHITE COTTAGE, ROUND LAKE. EASY!...
THAT'S IT?!!! JEEZUS, MARCO, DID SHE EVEN INVITE YOU TO HER COTTAGE?
WHAT?... OF COURSE SHE INVITED ME! YOU CALLING ME A LIAR?
THAT'S NOT IT, BUT LISTEN, YOU'VE GOTTA ADMIT...
AH! A CAR!... WE'LL ASK THEM...
IT'S NOT A CAR, IT'S A SKIDOO...
RANG DANG TANG
48

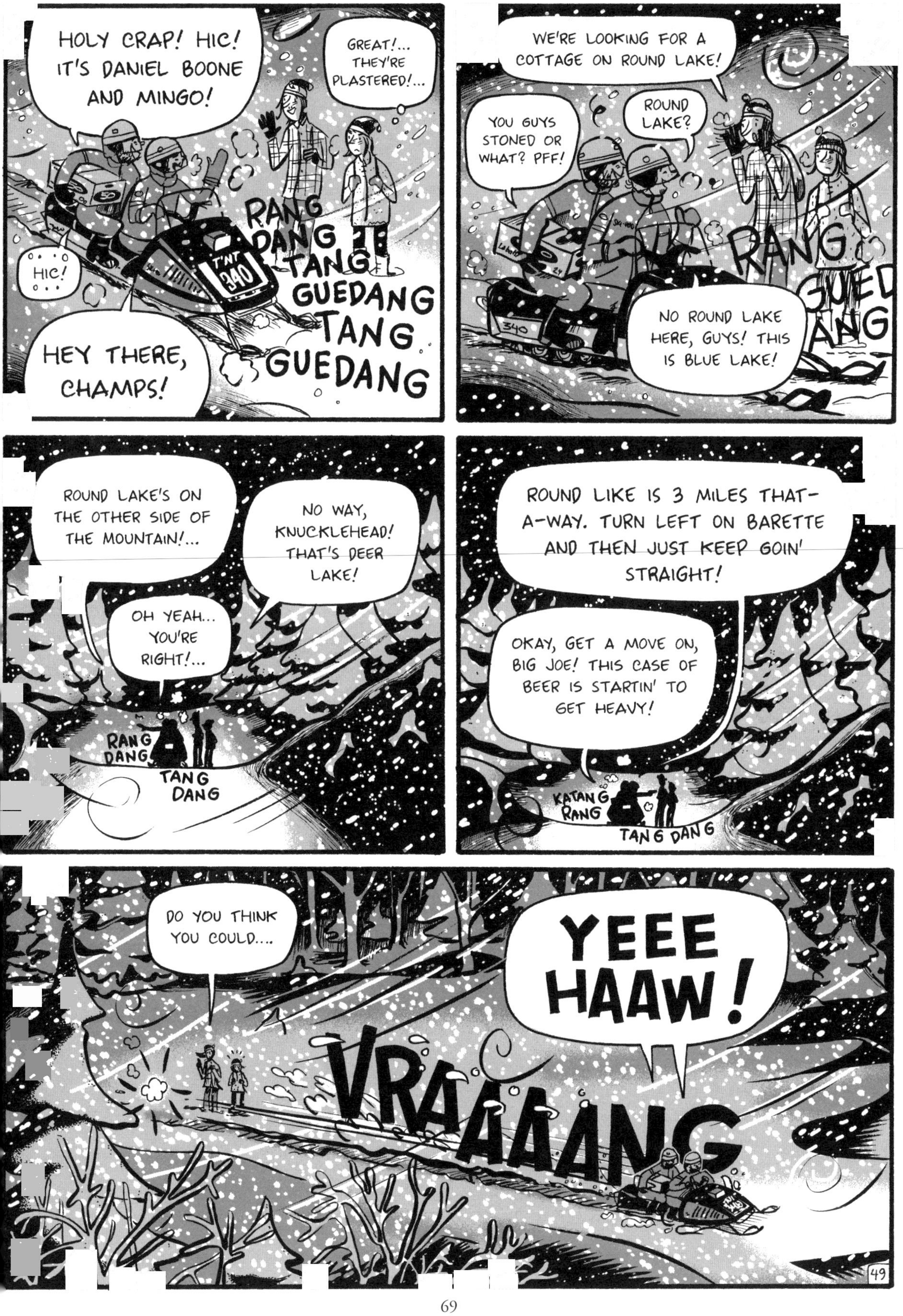
HOLY CRAP! HIC! IT'S DANIEL BOONE AND MINGO!
GREAT!... THEY'RE PLASTERED!...
HIC!
HEY THERE, CHAMPS!
RANG DANG TANG GUEDANG TANG GUEDANG
T'NT 340
WE'RE LOOKING FOR A COTTAGE ON ROUND LAKE!
YOU GUYS STONED OR WHAT? PFF!
ROUND LAKE?
RANG GUED ANG
NO ROUND LAKE HERE, GUYS! THIS IS BLUE LAKE!
ROUND LAKE'S ON THE OTHER SIDE OF THE MOUNTAIN!...
NO WAY, KNUCKLEHEAD! THAT'S DEER LAKE!
OH YEAH... YOU'RE RIGHT!...
RANG DANG
TANG DANG
ROUND LIKE IS 3 MILES THAT-A-WAY. TURN LEFT ON BARETTE AND THEN JUST KEEP GOIN' STRAIGHT!
OKAY, GET A MOVE ON, BIG JOE! THIS CASE OF BEER IS STARTIN' TO GET HEAVY!
KATANG RANG
TANG DANG
DO YOU THINK YOU COULD....
YEEE HAAW!
VRAAAANG
49

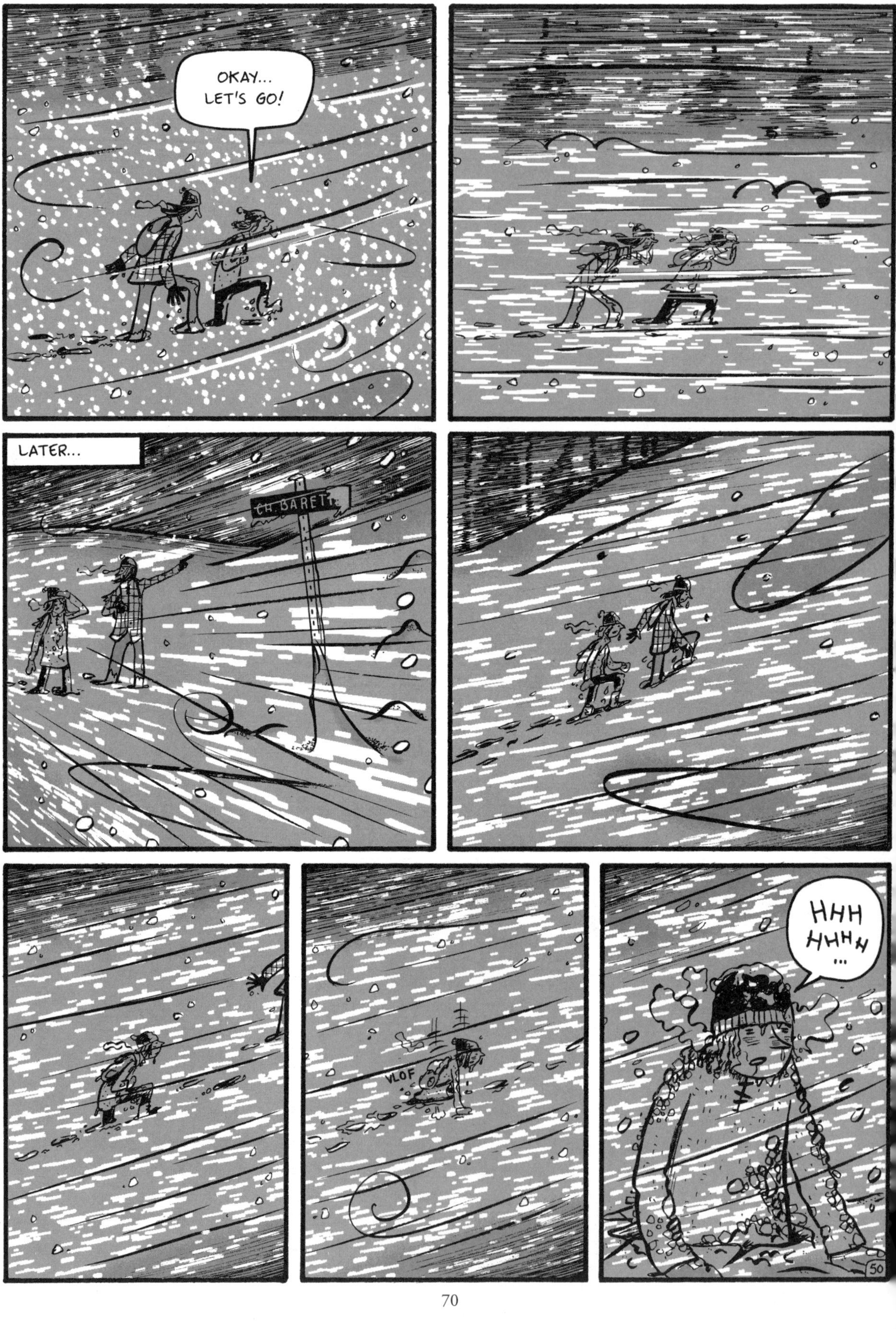
OKAY...
LET'S GO!
LATER...
CH. BARET
VLOF
HHH
HHHH
...
50

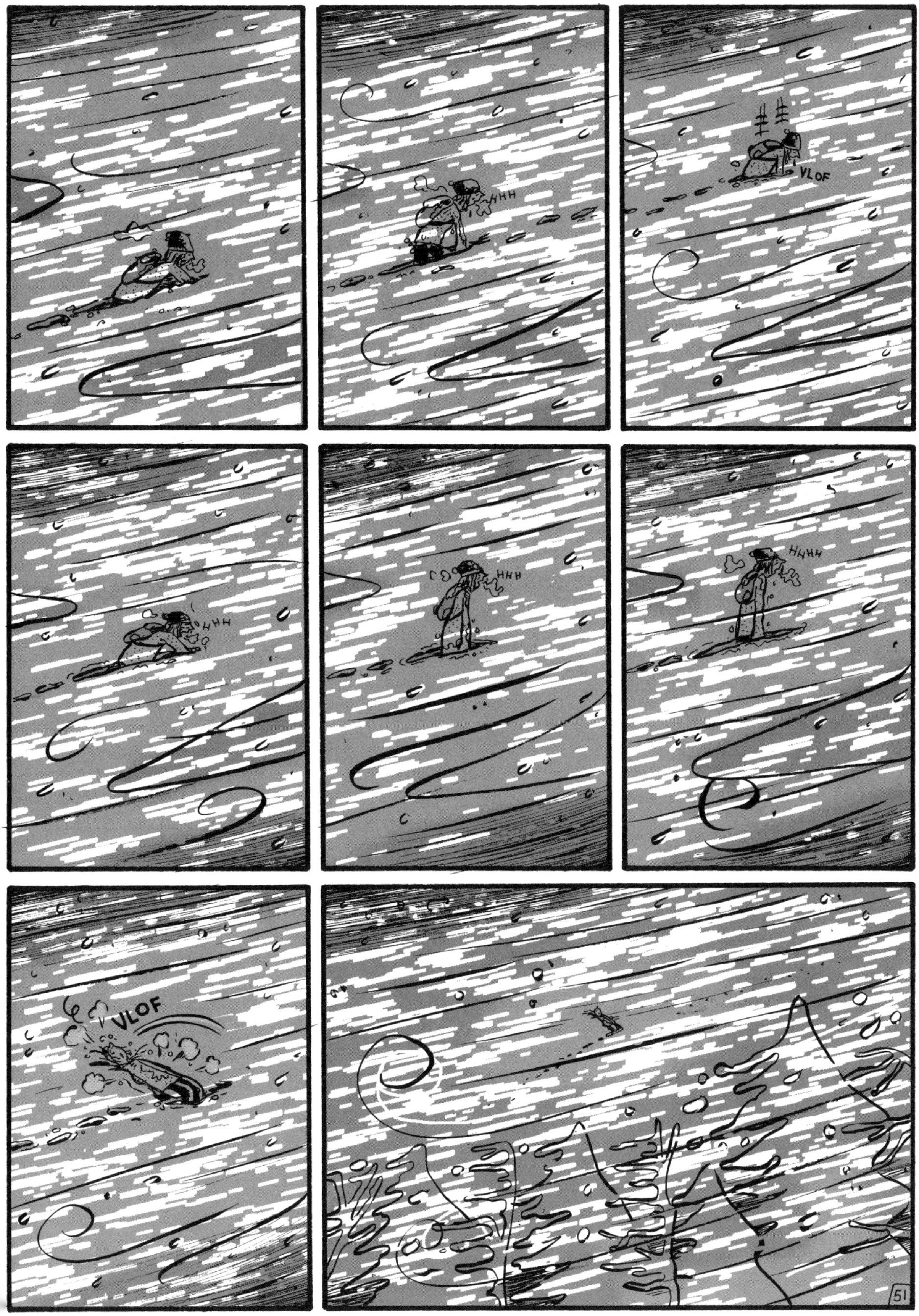
HHH
VLOF
HHH
HHH
HHHH
VLOF
51

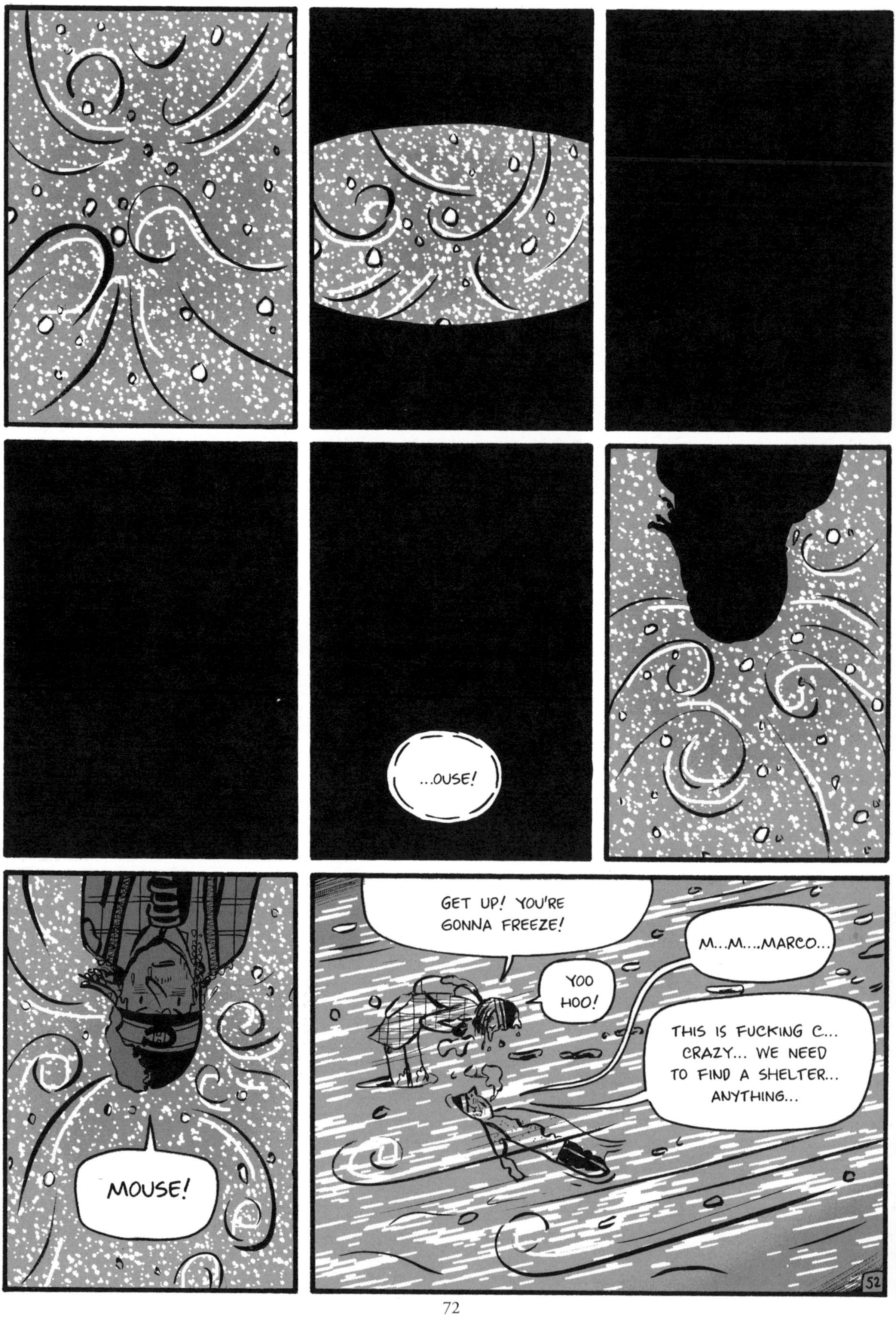
...OUSE!
MOUSE!
GET UP! YOU'RE GONNA FREEZE!
YOO HOO!
M...M....MARCO...
THIS IS FUCKING C... CRAZY... WE NEED TO FIND A SHELTER... ANYTHING...
52

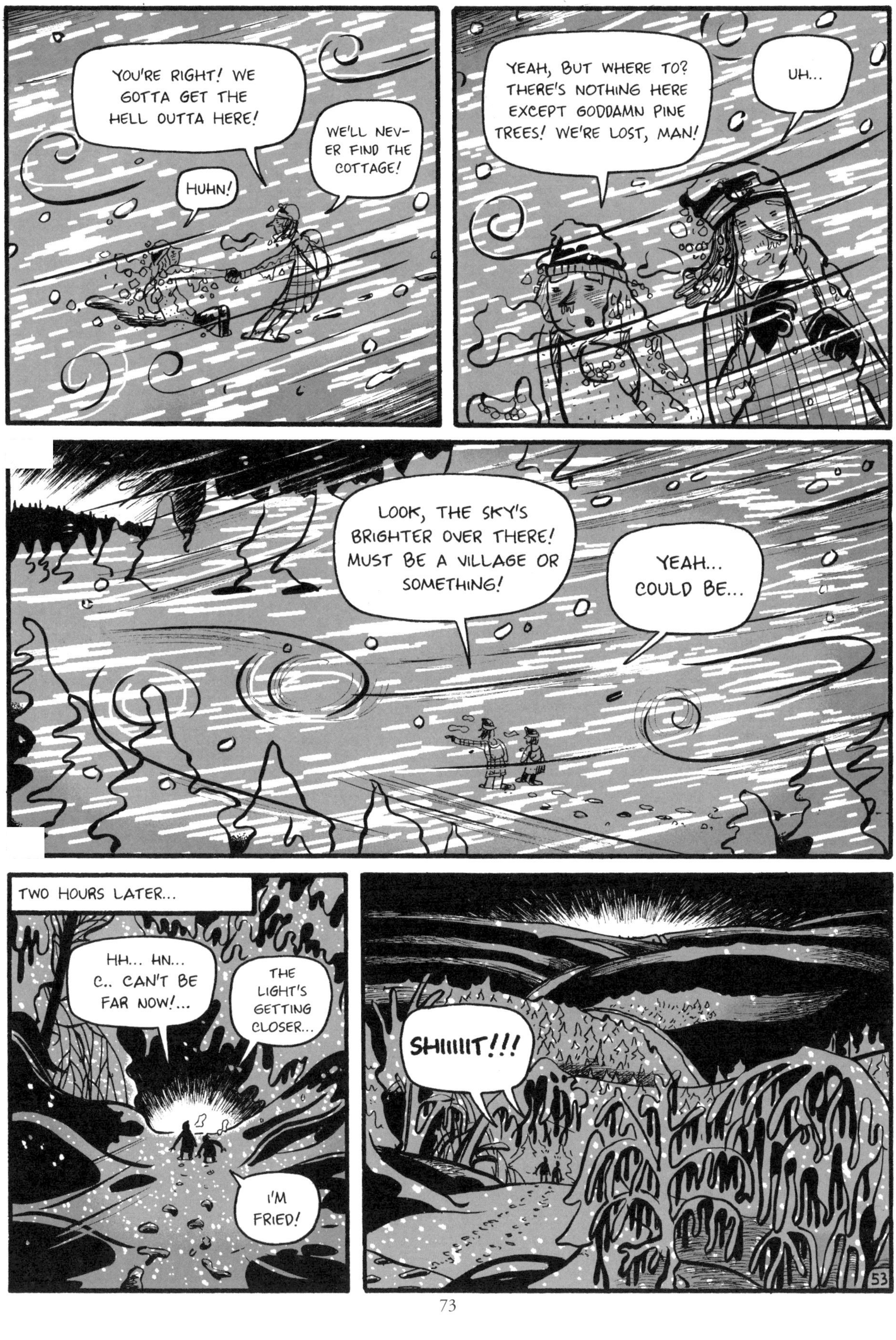
YOU'RE RIGHT! WE GOTTA GET THE HELL OUTTA HERE!
HUHN!
WE'LL NEV-ER FIND THE COTTAGE!
YEAH, BUT WHERE TO? THERE'S NOTHING HERE EXCEPT GODDAMN PINE TREES! WE'RE LOST, MAN!
UH...
LOOK, THE SKY'S BRIGHTER OVER THERE! MUST BE A VILLAGE OR SOMETHING!
YEAH... COULD BE...
TWO HOURS LATER...
HH... HN... C.. CAN'T BE FAR NOW!...
THE LIGHT'S GETTING CLOSER...
I'M FRIED!
SHIIIIIT!!!
53

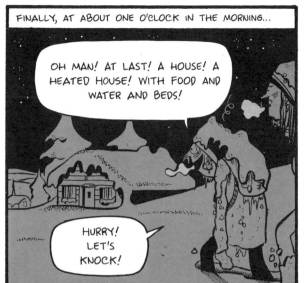

FINALLY, AT ABOUT ONE O'CLOCK IN THE MORNING...

OH MAN! AT LAST! A HOUSE! A HEATED HOUSE! WITH FOOD AND WATER AND BEDS!

HURRY! LET'S KNOCK!

YOU CRAZY, MOUSE? IT'S PAST MIDNIGHT! WE'LL BE LOOKING DOWN THE BARREL OF A GUN! LET'S FIND THE CHURCH. IN BOOKS AND MOVIES, PRIESTS ARE ALWAYS HELPING OUT TRAVELLERS IN NEED...

G...G...GOOD IDEA... LET'S W...WALK SOME MORE!...

THERE'S A CAR... THAT'S A GOOD SIGN! LET'S TRY THE PRESBYTERY!...

I'M TOTALLY WIPED!...

KNOCK KNOCK

ZZZ

RZZ

BANG BANG BANG

ZZZ

54

74

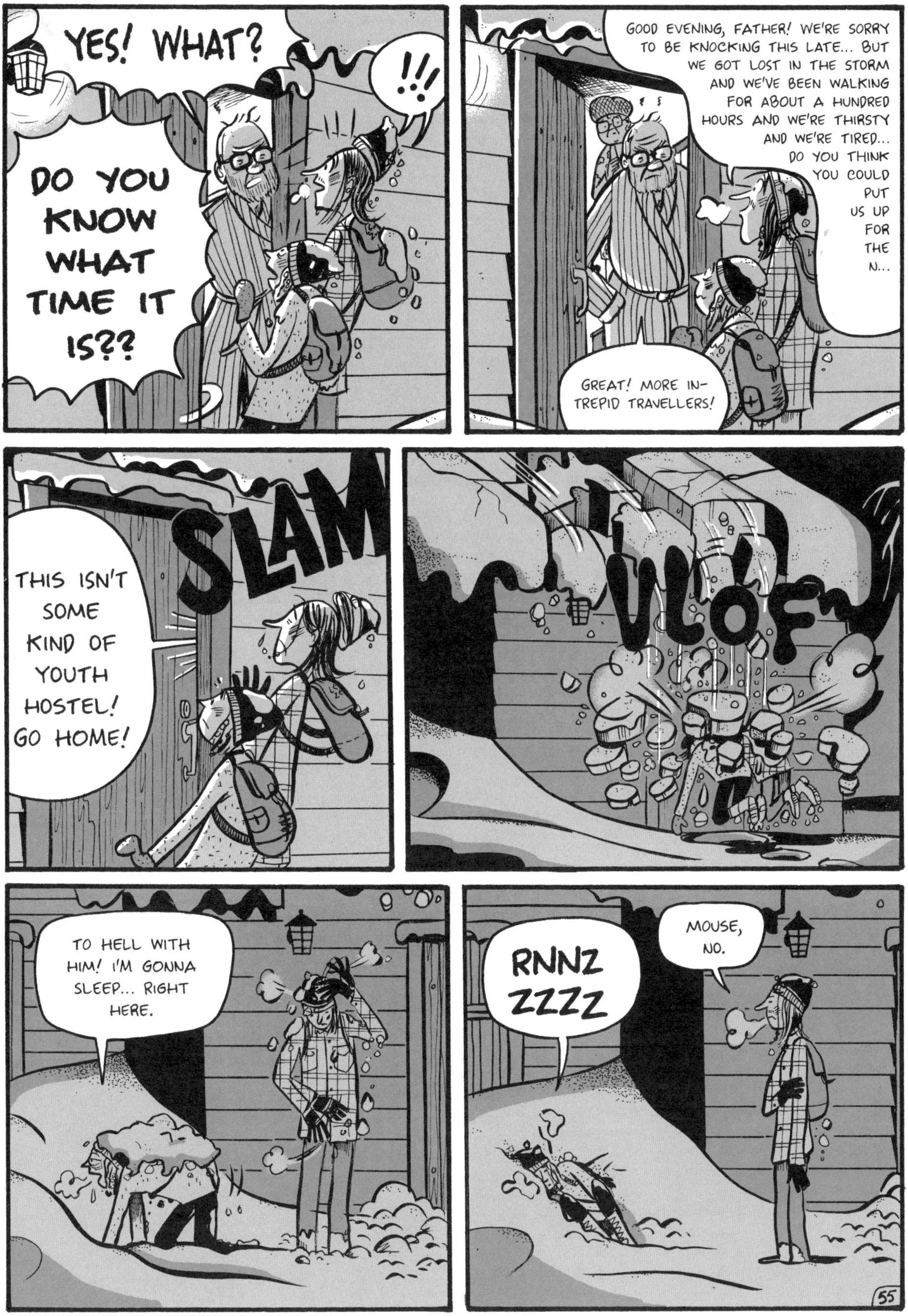
YES! WHAT?
!!!
DO YOU KNOW WHAT TIME IT IS??
GOOD EVENING, FATHER! WE'RE SORRY TO BE KNOCKING THIS LATE... BUT WE GOT LOST IN THE STORM AND WE'VE BEEN WALKING FOR ABOUT A HUNDRED HOURS AND WE'RE THIRSTY AND WE'RE TIRED... DO YOU THINK YOU COULD PUT US UP FOR THE N...
GREAT! MORE IN-TREPID TRAVELLERS!
SLAM
THIS ISN'T SOME KIND OF YOUTH HOSTEL! GO HOME!
VLOF
TO HELL WITH HIM! I'M GONNA SLEEP... RIGHT HERE.
RNNZ ZZZZ
MOUSE, NO.
55

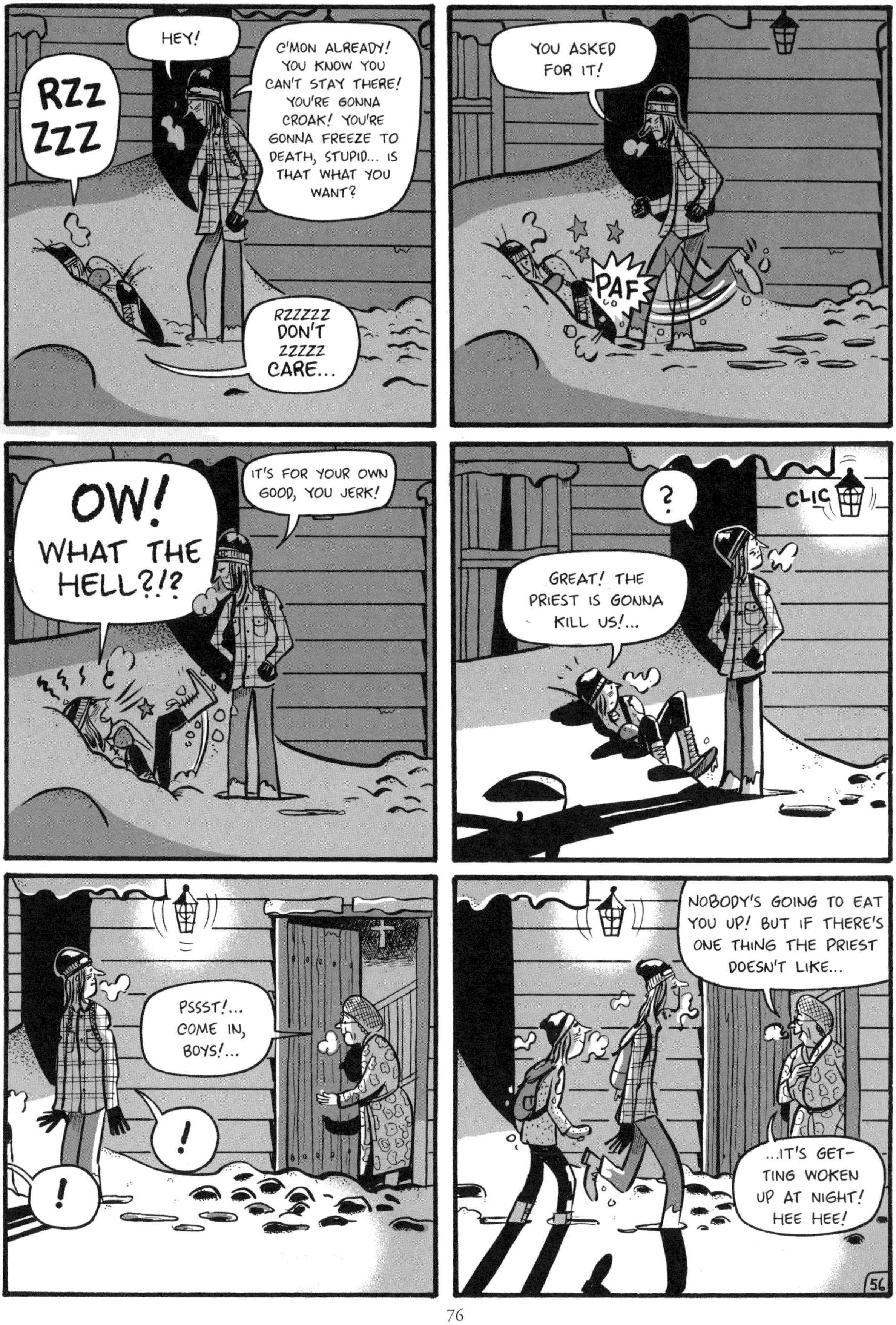
RZZ ZZZ
HEY!
C'MON ALREADY! YOU KNOW YOU CAN'T STAY THERE! YOU'RE GONNA CROAK! YOU'RE GONNA FREEZE TO DEATH, STUPID... IS THAT WHAT YOU WANT?
RZZZZZ DON'T ZZZZZ CARE...
YOU ASKED FOR IT!
PAF
OW! WHAT THE HELL?!?
IT'S FOR YOUR OWN GOOD, YOU JERK!
?
CLIC
GREAT! THE PRIEST IS GONNA KILL US!...
PSSST!... COME IN, BOYS!...
!
!
NOBODY'S GOING TO EAT YOU UP! BUT IF THERE'S ONE THING THE PRIEST DOESN'T LIKE...
...IT'S GETTING WOKEN UP AT NIGHT! HEE HEE!
56

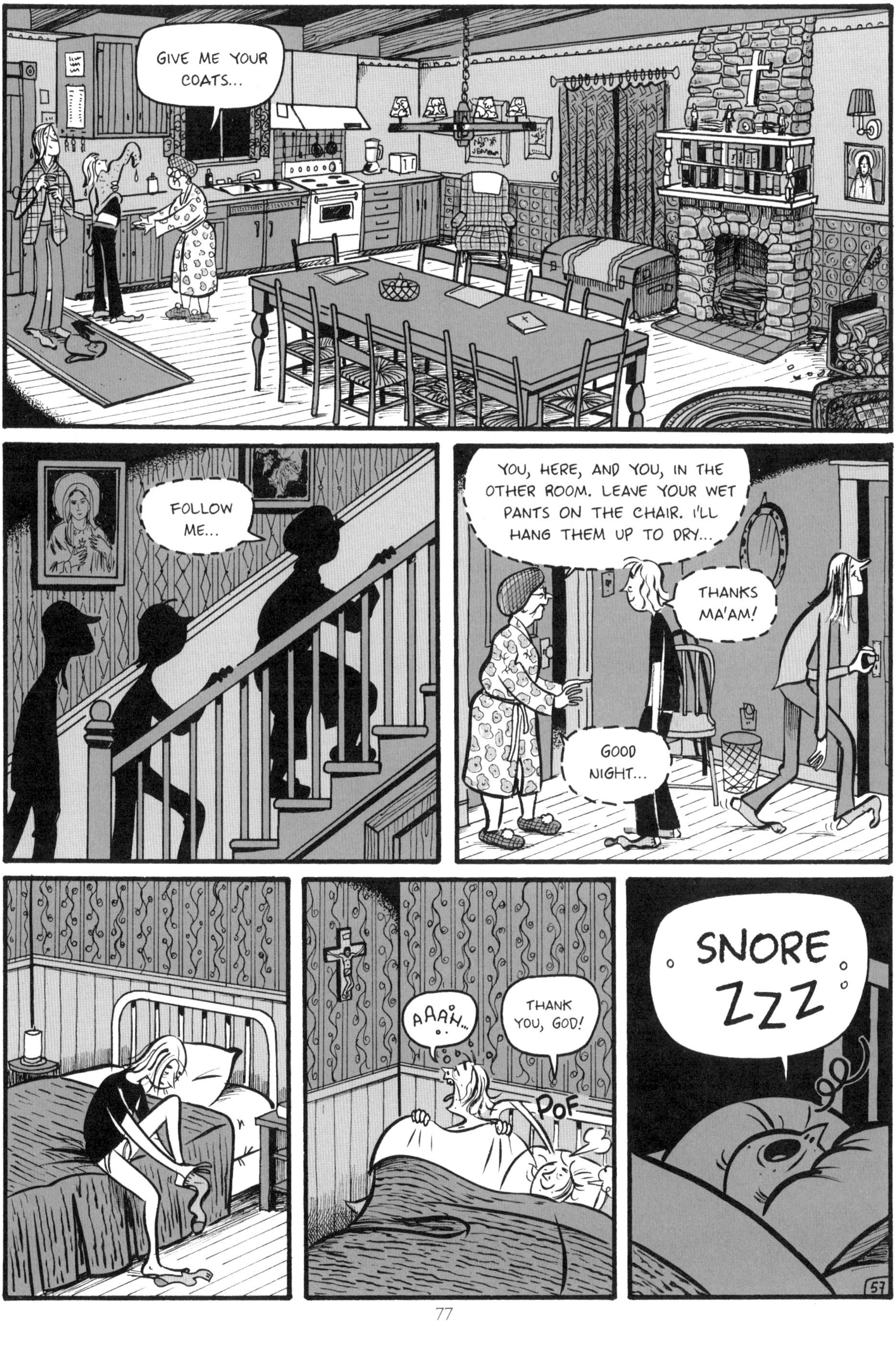
GIVE ME YOUR COATS...
FOLLOW ME...
YOU, HERE, AND YOU, IN THE OTHER ROOM. LEAVE YOUR WET PANTS ON THE CHAIR. I'LL HANG THEM UP TO DRY...
THANKS MA'AM!
GOOD NIGHT...
AAAH...
THANK YOU, GOD!
POF
SNORE
ZZZ
57

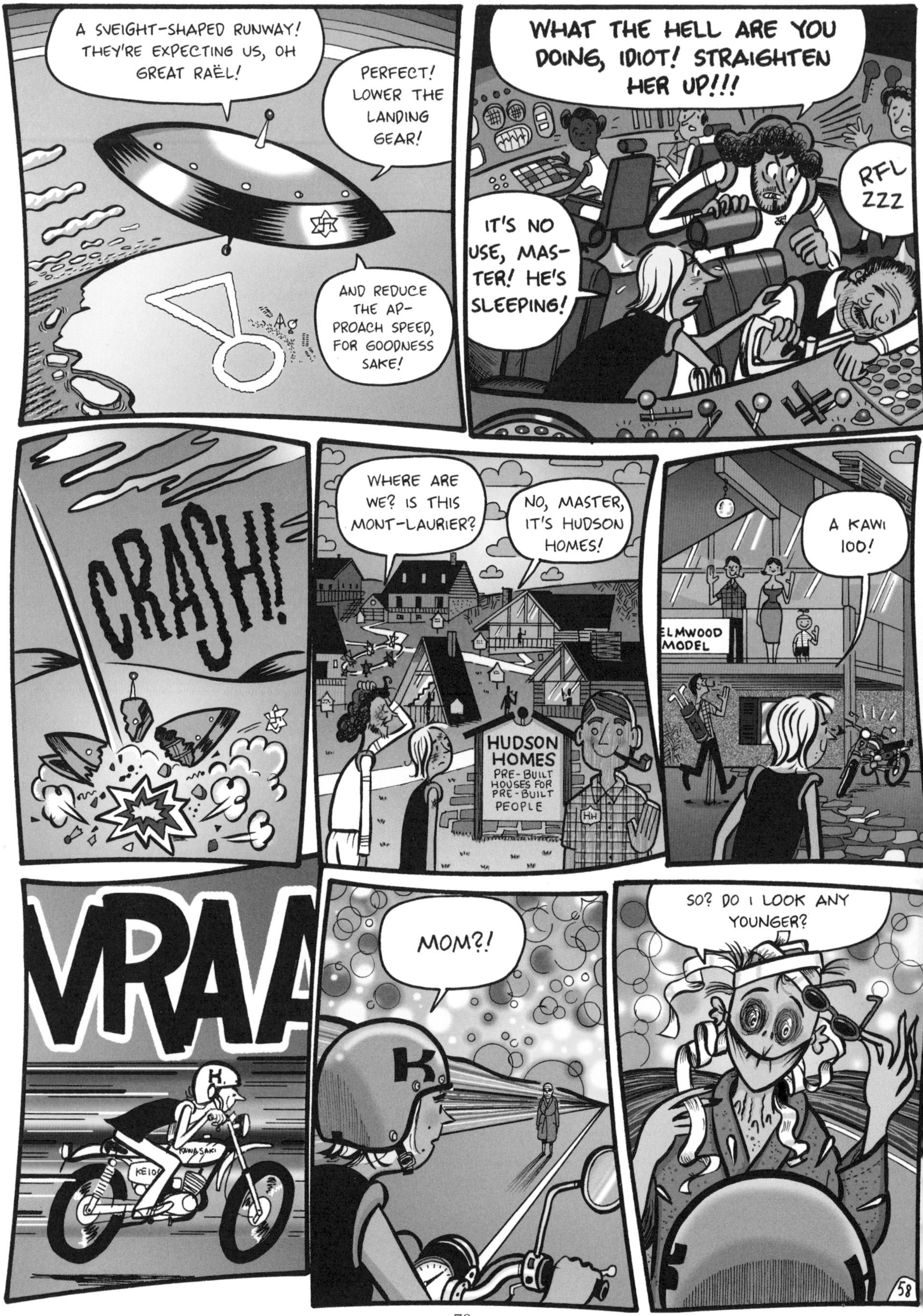
A SVEIGHT-SHAPED RUNWAY! THEY'RE EXPECTING US, OH GREAT RAËL!
PERFECT! LOWER THE LANDING GEAR!
AND REDUCE THE AP-PROACH SPEED, FOR GOODNESS SAKE!
WHAT THE HELL ARE YOU DOING, IDIOT! STRAIGHTEN HER UP!!!
IT'S NO USE, MAS-TER! HE'S SLEEPING!
RFL ZZZ
CRASH!
WHERE ARE WE? IS THIS MONT-LAURIER?
NO, MASTER, IT'S HUDSON HOMES!
HUDSON HOMES PRE-BUILT HOUSES FOR PRE-BUILT PEOPLE
ELMWOOD MODEL
A KAWI 100!
VRAA
KAWASAKI
KE100
MOM?!
SO? DO I LOOK ANY YOUNGER?
58

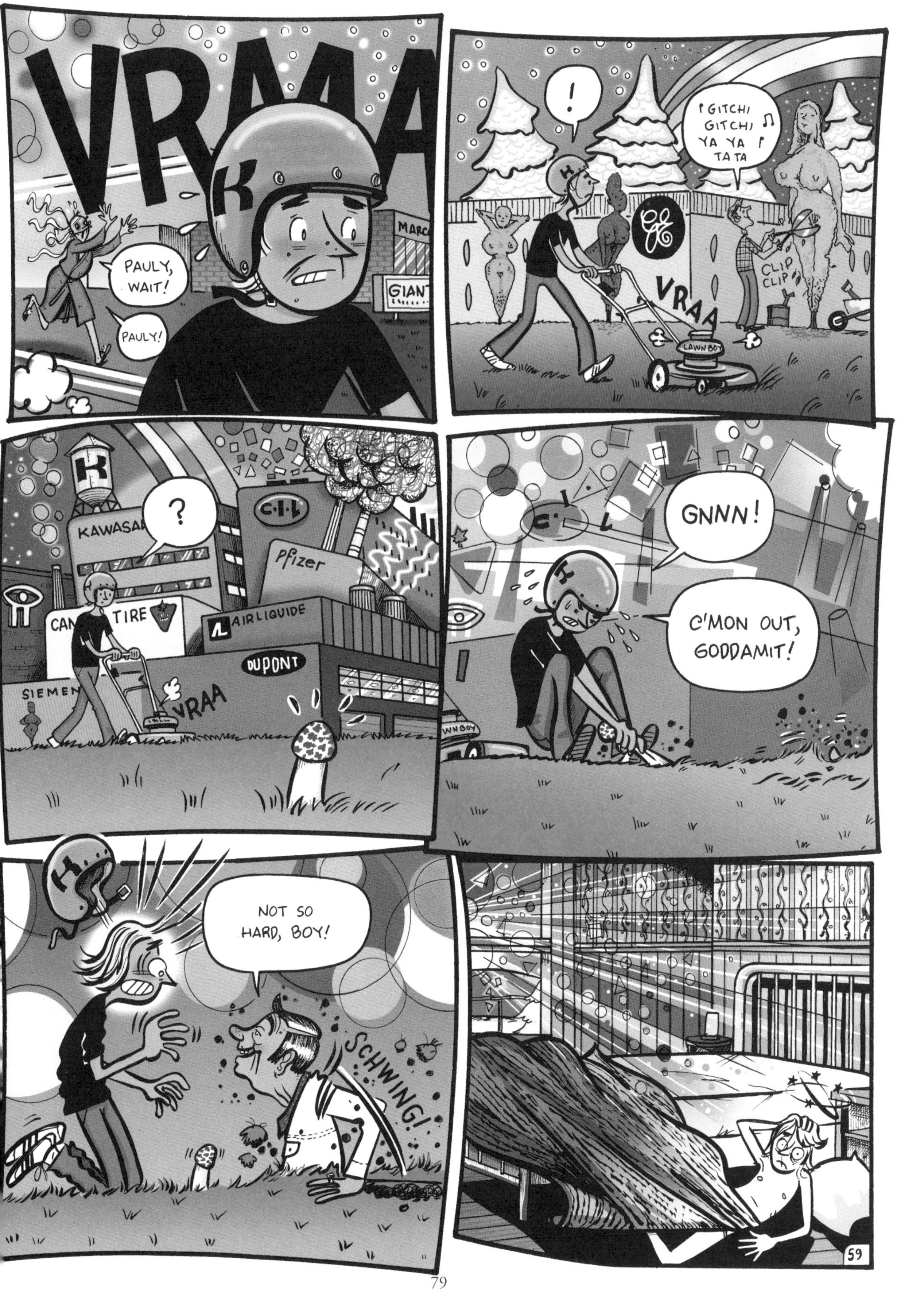
VRAAA
MARC
GIANT
PAULY, WAIT!
PAULY!
!
GITCHI GITCHI YA YA TA TA
CLIP CLIP
VRAA
LAWNBOY
?
KAWASA
C·I·L
pfizer
CAN TIRE
AIRLIQUIDE
DUPONT
SIEMEN
VRAA
GNNN!
C'MON OUT, GODDAMIT!
WNBOY
NOT SO HARD, BOY!
SCHWING!
59

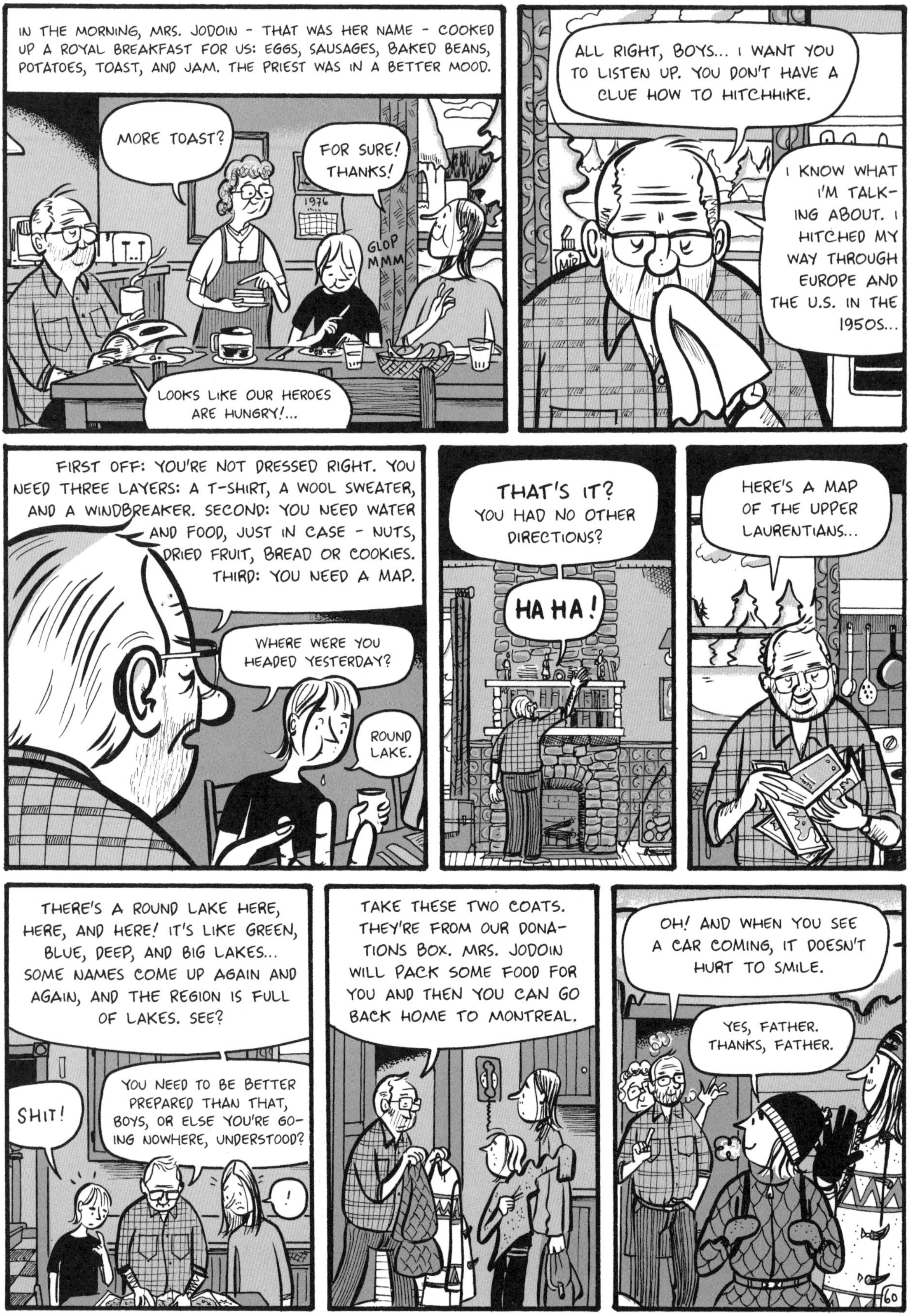
IN THE MORNING, MRS. JODOIN - THAT WAS HER NAME - COOKED UP A ROYAL BREAKFAST FOR US: EGGS, SAUSAGES, BAKED BEANS, POTATOES, TOAST, AND JAM. THE PRIEST WAS IN A BETTER MOOD.
MORE TOAST?
FOR SURE! THANKS!
1976
GLOP
MMM
LOOKS LIKE OUR HEROES ARE HUNGRY!...
ALL RIGHT, BOYS... I WANT YOU TO LISTEN UP. YOU DON'T HAVE A CLUE HOW TO HITCHHIKE.
I KNOW WHAT I'M TALKING ABOUT. I HITCHED MY WAY THROUGH EUROPE AND THE U.S. IN THE 1950S...
FIRST OFF: YOU'RE NOT DRESSED RIGHT. YOU NEED THREE LAYERS: A T-SHIRT, A WOOL SWEATER, AND A WINDBREAKER. SECOND: YOU NEED WATER AND FOOD, JUST IN CASE - NUTS, DRIED FRUIT, BREAD OR COOKIES. THIRD: YOU NEED A MAP.
WHERE WERE YOU HEADED YESTERDAY?
ROUND LAKE.
THAT'S IT? YOU HAD NO OTHER DIRECTIONS?
HA HA!
HERE'S A MAP OF THE UPPER LAURENTIANS...
THERE'S A ROUND LAKE HERE, HERE, AND HERE! IT'S LIKE GREEN, BLUE, DEEP, AND BIG LAKES... SOME NAMES COME UP AGAIN AND AGAIN, AND THE REGION IS FULL OF LAKES. SEE?
SHIT!
YOU NEED TO BE BETTER PREPARED THAN THAT, BOYS, OR ELSE YOU'RE GOING NOWHERE, UNDERSTOOD?
!
TAKE THESE TWO COATS. THEY'RE FROM OUR DONATIONS BOX. MRS. JODOIN WILL PACK SOME FOOD FOR YOU AND THEN YOU CAN GO BACK HOME TO MONTREAL.
OH! AND WHEN YOU SEE A CAR COMING, IT DOESN'T HURT TO SMILE.
YES, FATHER. THANKS, FATHER.
60

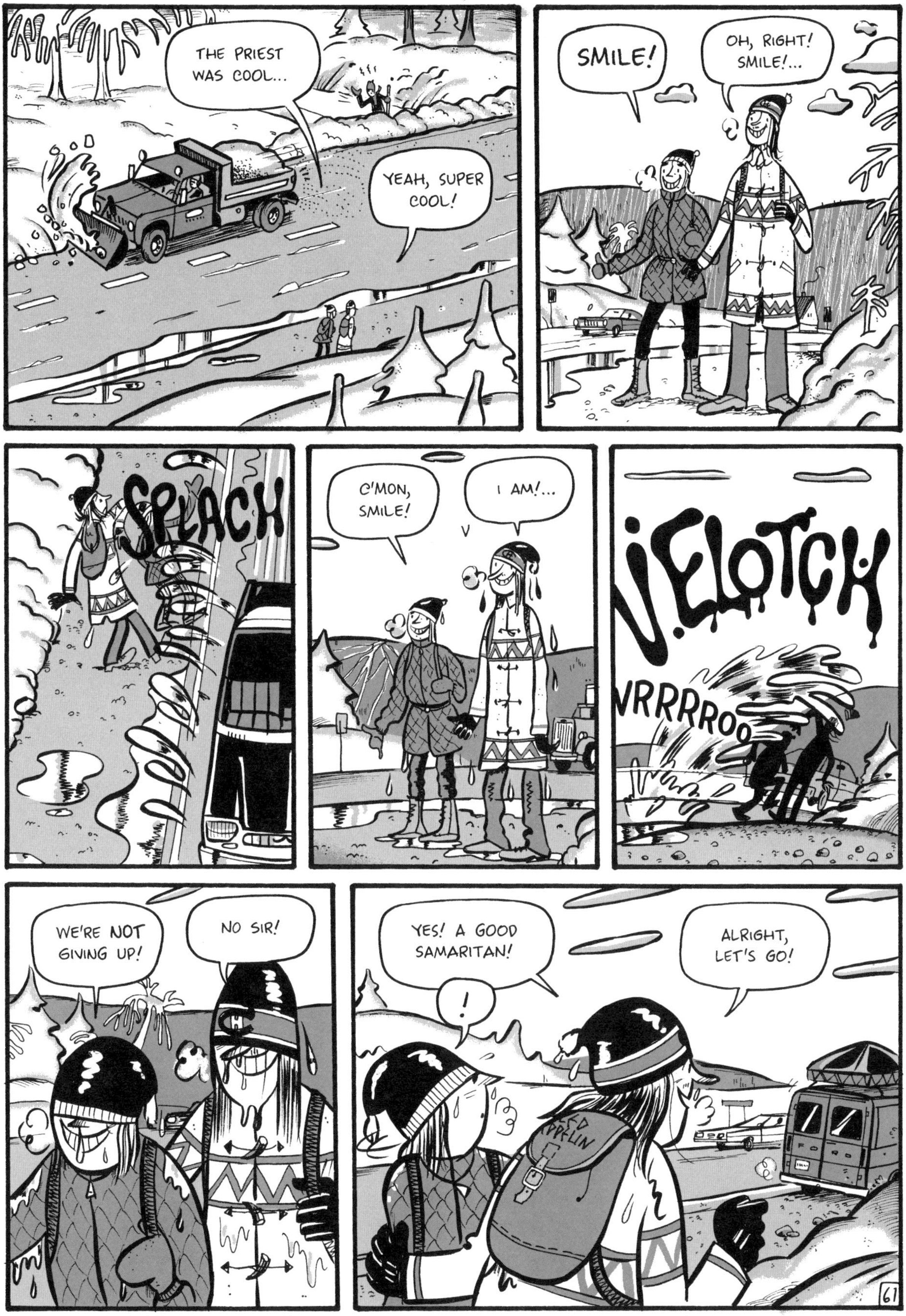
THE PRIEST WAS COOL...
YEAH, SUPER COOL!
SMILE!
OH, RIGHT! SMILE!...
SPLACH
C'MON, SMILE!
I AM!...
V
VELOTCH
VRRRROO
WE'RE NOT GIVING UP!
NO SIR!
YES! A GOOD SAMARITAN!
!
ALRIGHT, LET'S GO!
LED ZEPPELIN
61

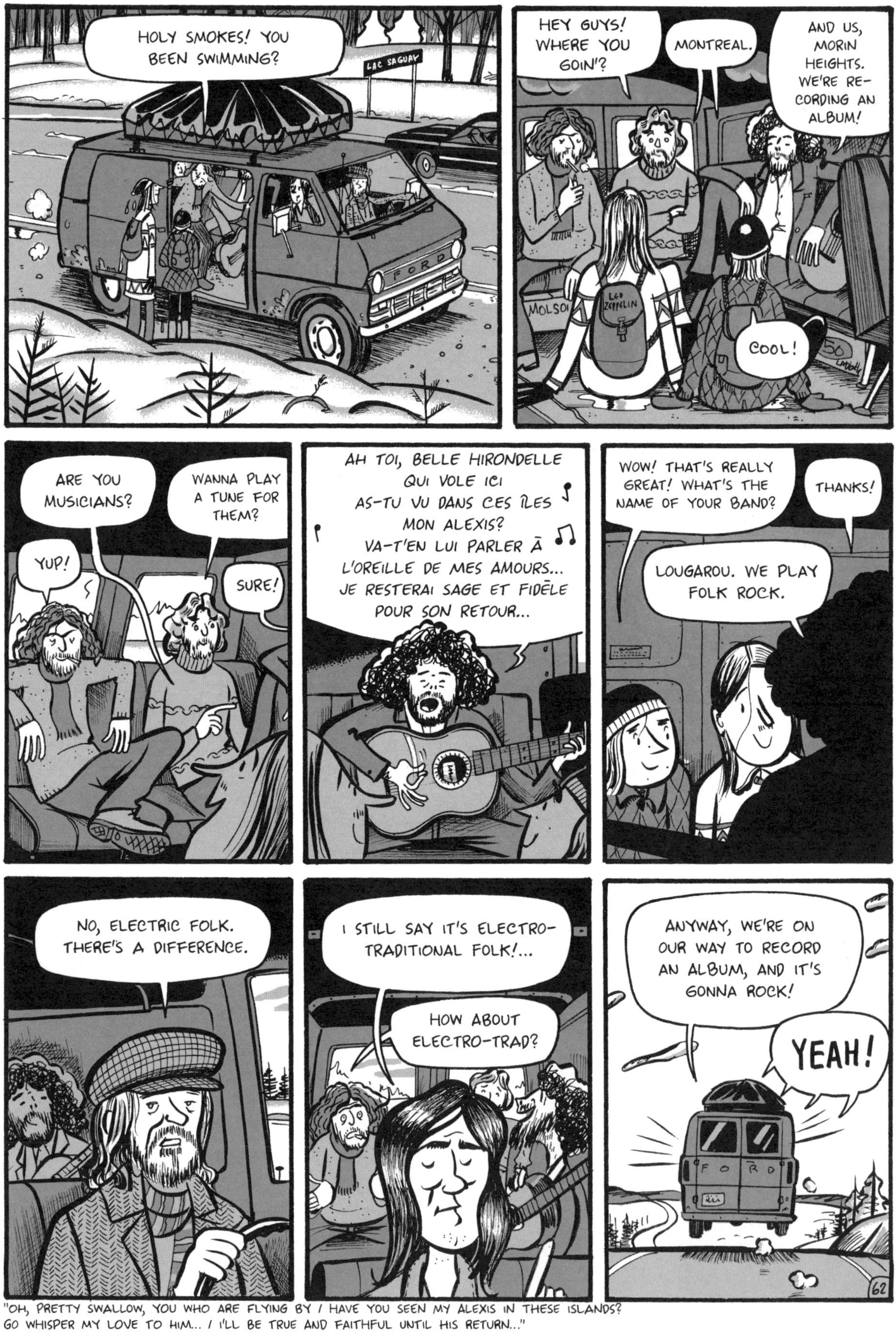

HOLY SMOKES! YOU BEEN SWIMMING?
LAC SAGUAY
HEY GUYS! WHERE YOU GOIN'?
MONTREAL.
AND US, MORIN HEIGHTS. WE'RE RECORDING AN ALBUM!
COOL!
ARE YOU MUSICIANS?
WANNA PLAY A TUNE FOR THEM?
YUP!
SURE!
AH TOI, BELLE HIRONDELLE
QUI VOLE ICI
AS-TU VU DANS CES ÎLES
MON ALEXIS?
VA-T'EN LUI PARLER À
L'OREILLE DE MES AMOURS...
JE RESTERAI SAGE ET FIDÈLE
POUR SON RETOUR...
WOW! THAT'S REALLY GREAT! WHAT'S THE NAME OF YOUR BAND?
THANKS!
LOUGAROU. WE PLAY FOLK ROCK.
NO, ELECTRIC FOLK. THERE'S A DIFFERENCE.
I STILL SAY IT'S ELECTRO-TRADITIONAL FOLK!...
HOW ABOUT ELECTRO-TRAD?
ANYWAY, WE'RE ON OUR WAY TO RECORD AN ALBUM, AND IT'S GONNA ROCK!
YEAH!
62

"OH, PRETTY SWALLOW, YOU WHO ARE FLYING BY / HAVE YOU SEEN MY ALEXIS IN THESE ISLANDS?
GO WHISPER MY LOVE TO HIM... / I'LL BE TRUE AND FAITHFUL UNTIL HIS RETURN..."

THE RETURN HOME WAS ABRUPT.

♪

THERE YOU ARE! WHERE THE HELL WERE YOU, GODDAMMIT?

UH, MONT-LAURIER... I TOLD YOU, REMEMBER?

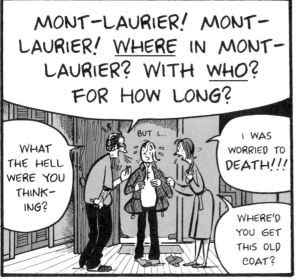

MONT-LAURIER! MONT-LAURIER! WHERE IN MONT-LAURIER? WITH WHO? FOR HOW LONG?

WHAT THE HELL WERE YOU THINKING?

BUT I...

I WAS WORRIED TO DEATH!!!

WHERE'D YOU GET THIS OLD COAT?

WE WERE ABOUT TO CALL THE POLICE KNUCKLEHEAD!

AND THAT BIG SNOWSTORM LAST NIGHT!

B...BUT I THOUGHT...

DID YOU EVEN THINK OF CALLING?

GO TO YOUR ROOM AND GET TO BED, NOW! WE'LL TALK TOMORROW!

GLP.

63

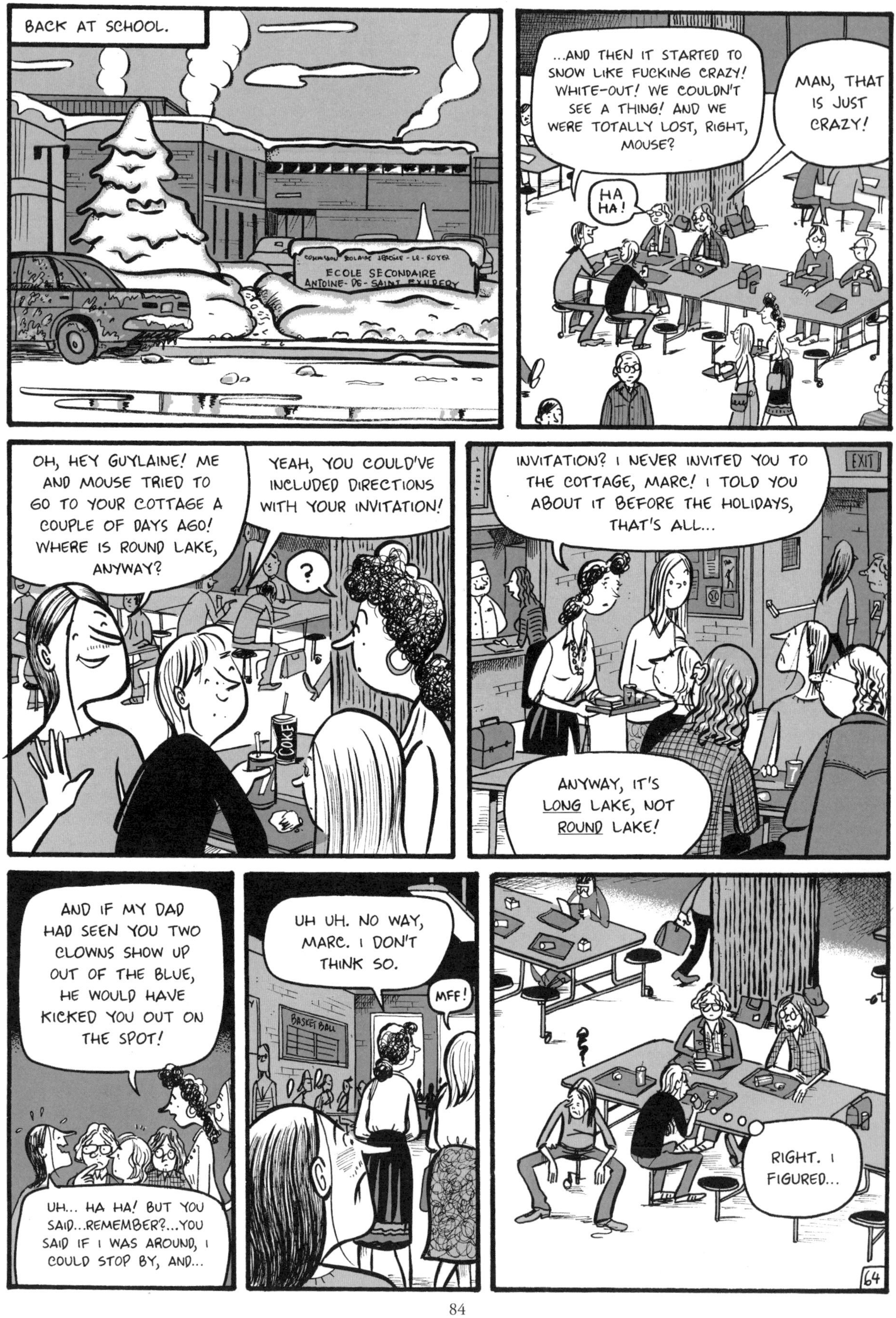
BACK AT SCHOOL.
COMMISSION SCOLAIRE JÉRÔME-LE-ROYER
ECOLE SECONDAIRE ANTOINE-DE-SAINT-EXUPERY
...AND THEN IT STARTED TO SNOW LIKE FUCKING CRAZY! WHITE-OUT! WE COULDN'T SEE A THING! AND WE WERE TOTALLY LOST, RIGHT, MOUSE?
HA HA!
MAN, THAT IS JUST CRAZY!
OH, HEY GUYLAINE! ME AND MOUSE TRIED TO GO TO YOUR COTTAGE A COUPLE OF DAYS AGO! WHERE IS ROUND LAKE, ANYWAY?
YEAH, YOU COULD'VE INCLUDED DIRECTIONS WITH YOUR INVITATION!
?
COKE
INVITATION? I NEVER INVITED YOU TO THE COTTAGE, MARC! I TOLD YOU ABOUT IT BEFORE THE HOLIDAYS, THAT'S ALL...
EXIT
ANYWAY, IT'S LONG LAKE, NOT ROUND LAKE!
AND IF MY DAD HAD SEEN YOU TWO CLOWNS SHOW UP OUT OF THE BLUE, HE WOULD HAVE KICKED YOU OUT ON THE SPOT!
UH... HA HA! BUT YOU SAID...REMEMBER?...YOU SAID IF I WAS AROUND, I COULD STOP BY, AND...
UH UH. NO WAY, MARC. I DON'T THINK SO.
MFF!
BASKETBALL
RIGHT. I FIGURED...
64

Puch Maxi

IN APRIL, I WENT BACK TO WORKING WITH UNCLE RAYNALD.

WE'RE NOT GONNA MOW TODAY. WE'LL JUST RAKE UP THE LEAVES AND THE GARBAGE THAT'S LYING AROUND...

OKAY.

BBC

SO, WHEN'RE YOU GONNA BUY THAT BIKE?

DUSTRIES

PERMA ON

I NEED TO SAVE UP ANOTHER HUNDRED BUCKS. BUT I THINK I'LL GET A MOPED INSTEAD...IT'S LESS EXPENSIVE, AND I WON'T NEED A PERMIT OR ANYTHING...

Deli

FORD

MONTREAL 1976

SMART MOVE! MOPEDS ARE FUN. YOU CAN GO ANYWHERE, AND THEY'RE CHEAP ON GAS!...

WOW!

CONSTRUCTION ON THE STADIUM IS COMING ALONG!...

YEAH, BUT NOT FAST ENOUGH! THE STRIKES AND SLOWDOWNS HAVE PUT EVERYTHING BEHIND SCHEDULE. THE TOWER WON'T BE FINISHED ON TIME! IT'S OFFICIAL!

THE TOWER?... N..NOT FINISHED?!? BUT THAT'S IMPOSSIBLE! IT'S THE MOST IMPORTANT PART! HOW'S THAT GONNA MAKE US LOOK?!

65

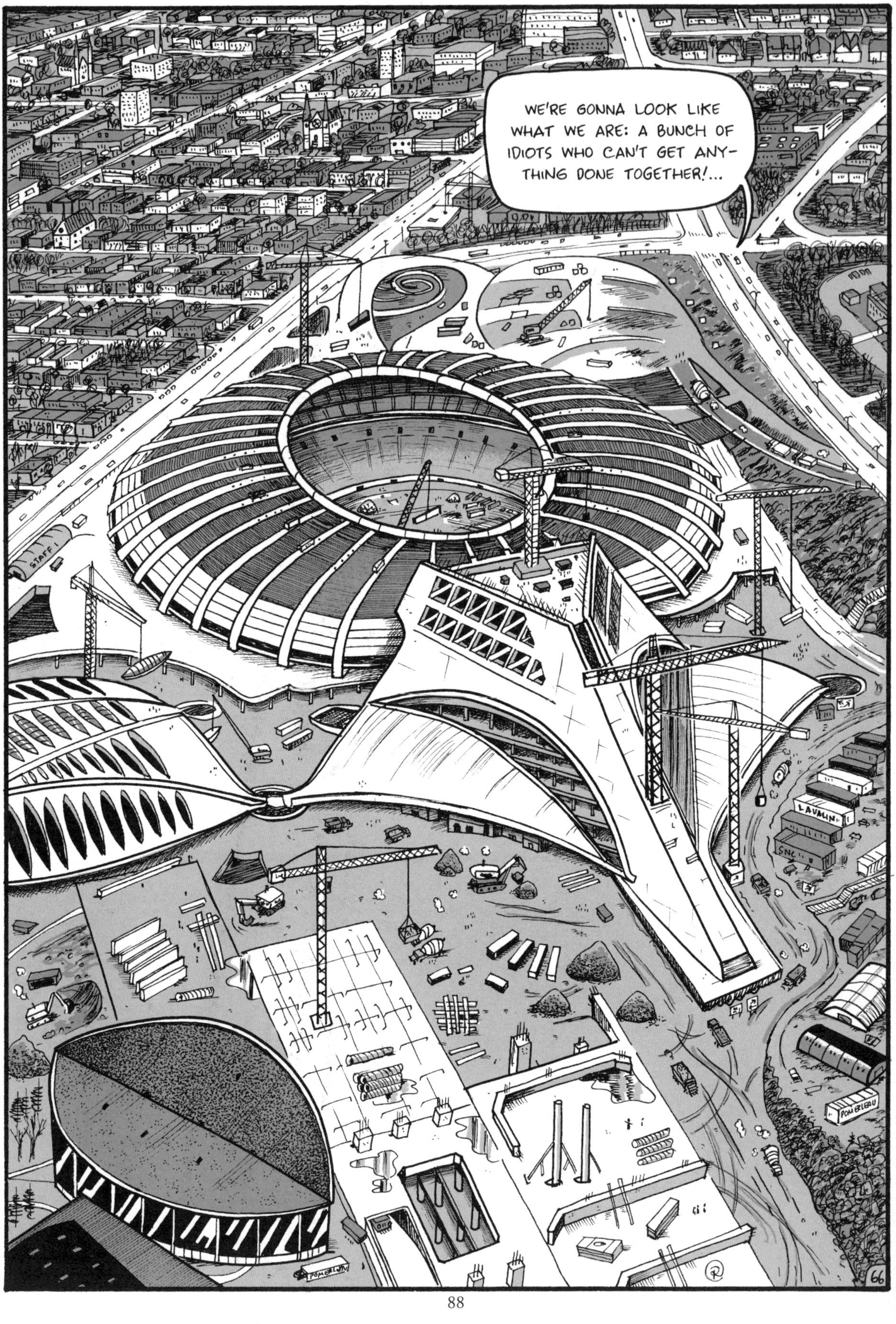
WE'RE GONNA LOOK LIKE WHAT WE ARE: A BUNCH OF IDIOTS WHO CAN'T GET ANY-THING DONE TOGETHER!...
STAFF
LAVALIN
SNC
POMERLEAU
66

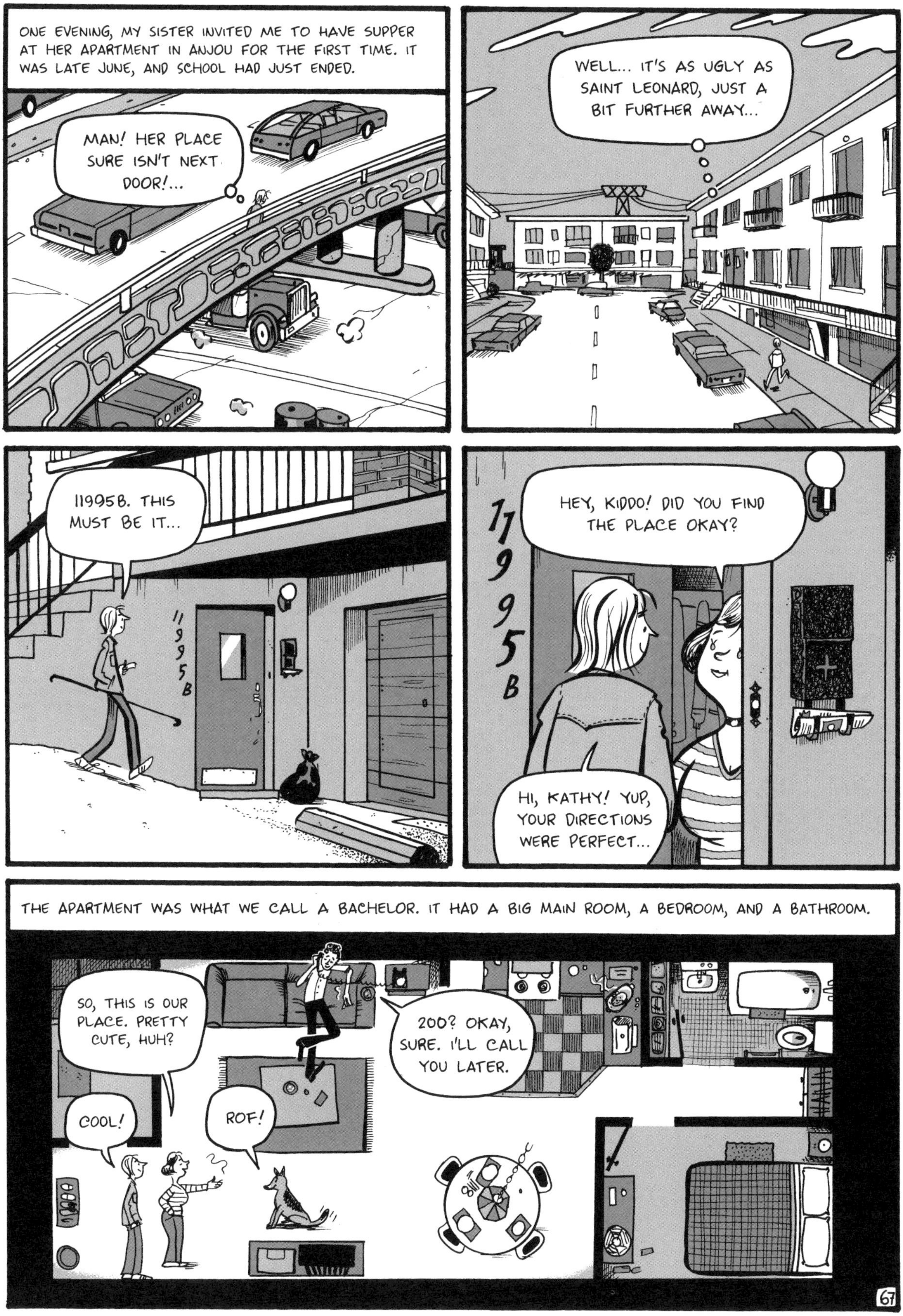

ONE EVENING, MY SISTER INVITED ME TO HAVE SUPPER AT HER APARTMENT IN ANJOU FOR THE FIRST TIME. IT WAS LATE JUNE, AND SCHOOL HAD JUST ENDED.
MAN! HER PLACE SURE ISN'T NEXT DOOR!...
WELL... IT'S AS UGLY AS SAINT LEONARD, JUST A BIT FURTHER AWAY...
11995B. THIS MUST BE IT...
11995B
HEY, KIDDO! DID YOU FIND THE PLACE OKAY?
11995B
HI, KATHY! YUP, YOUR DIRECTIONS WERE PERFECT...
THE APARTMENT WAS WHAT WE CALL A BACHELOR. IT HAD A BIG MAIN ROOM, A BEDROOM, AND A BATHROOM.
SO, THIS IS OUR PLACE. PRETTY CUTE, HUH?
200? OKAY, SURE. I'LL CALL YOU LATER.
COOL!
ROF!
67

CHECK THIS OUT, PAULY! IT'S CALLED A BETAMAX!

WHAT IS IT, A RADIO?

HA HA! WAY BETTER! THIS BABY LETS YOU RECORD ANY TV SHOW YOU WANT SO YOU CAN WATCH IT LATER! LOOK!...

WHOA! THAT'S CRAZY! IT MUST COST A FORTUNE!!

RCA

SONY

CLIC

WELL, AHEM... LET'S SAY I HAVE FRIENDS WHO KNOW HOW TO GET THEIR HANDS ON ALL KINDS OF STUFF...

SHUT UP, WOULD YOU, YVAN?

CLAK

ANYWAY, YOU JUST HIT PLAY, SEE? AND THERE'S YOUR SHOW.

HEY! I KNOW THOSE GUYS! THAT'S LOUGAROU!

DIS-MOI CHARLES C'EST UNE BAD LUCK, DIS MOI CHARLY J'SUIS BAD LUCKÉE

OH YEAH? NEVER HEARD OF 'EM. KATHY, DID YOU MESS UP THE BETAMAX?

RCA

SONY

"TELL ME, CHARLES, IT'S JUST BAD LUCK, TELL ME CHARLEY, I'M BAD LUCKY"

LADY! THE CHICKEN!

SCRUNCH GLOP GNAP!

ADY

RELAX, KATHY! YOUR SPAGHETTI'S GREAT!

I TOLD YOU TO KEEP AN EYE ON HER, YVAN! THAT'S NOT TOO COMPLICATED, IS IT? YOU KNOW HOW SHE IS WITH FOOD!

BAD DOG!

BAD!

Cuvée des PATRIOTES

Chef BOY-AR-DEE SPAGHETTI with MEATBALLS

68

90

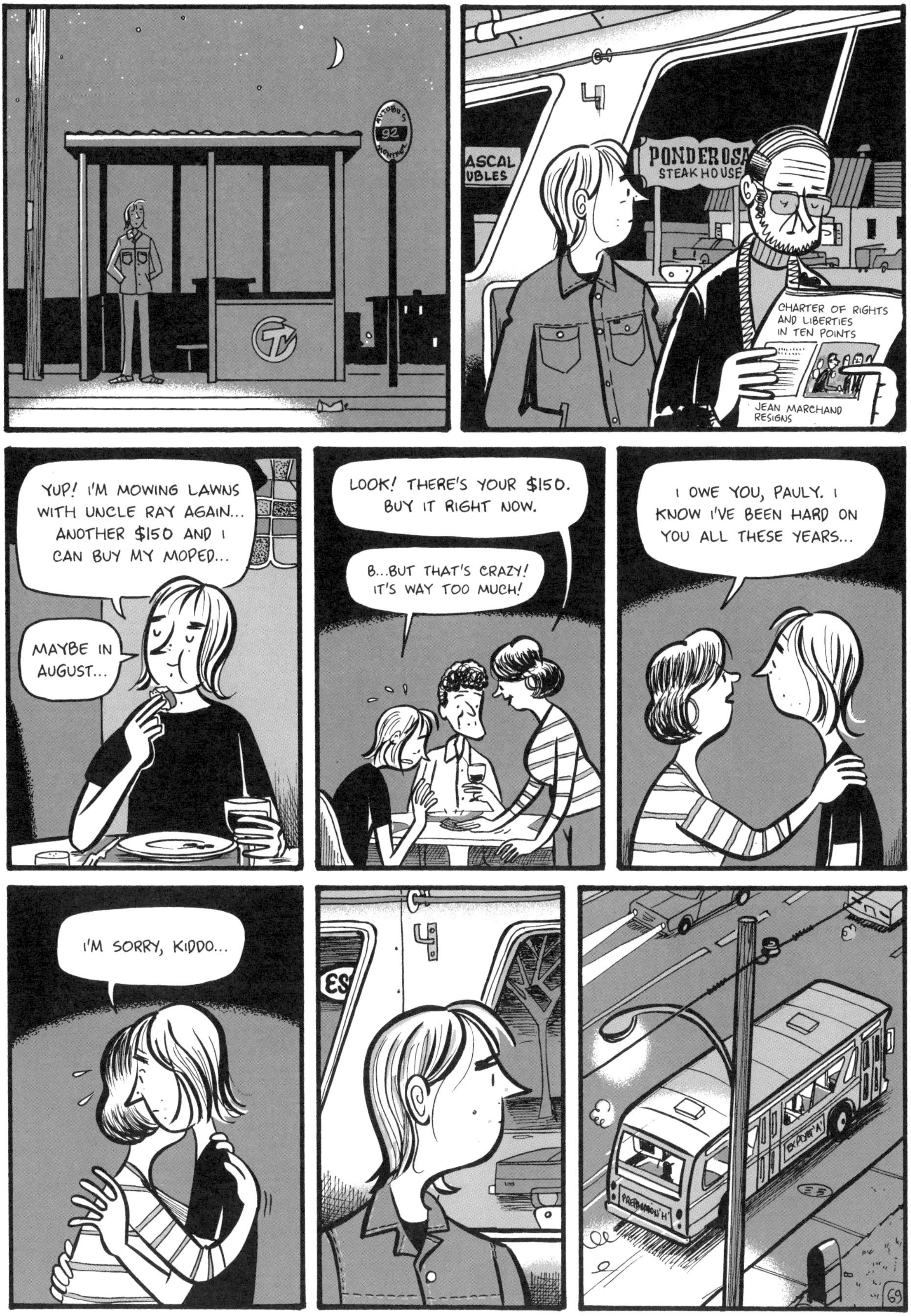
ASCAL
UBLES
PONDEROSA
STEAK HOUSE
CHARTER OF RIGHTS AND LIBERTIES IN TEN POINTS
JEAN MARCHAND RESIGNS
YUP! I'M MOWING LAWNS WITH UNCLE RAY AGAIN... ANOTHER $150 AND I CAN BUY MY MOPED...
MAYBE IN AUGUST...
LOOK! THERE'S YOUR $150. BUY IT RIGHT NOW.
B...BUT THAT'S CRAZY! IT'S WAY TOO MUCH!
I OWE YOU, PAULY. I KNOW I'VE BEEN HARD ON YOU ALL THESE YEARS...
I'M SORRY, KIDDO...

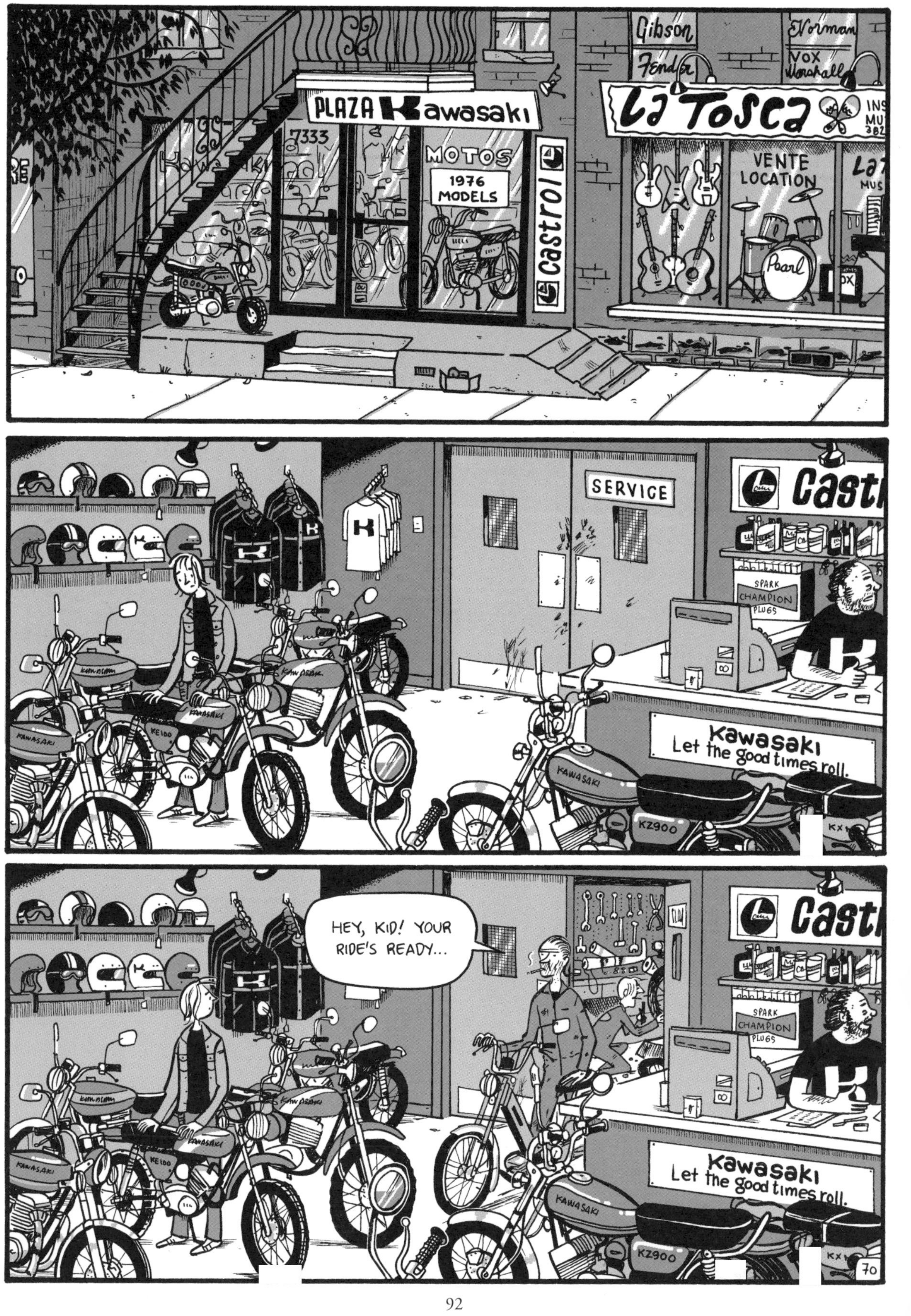
PLAZA Kawasaki
7333
MOTOS
1976 MODELS
castrol
Gibson
Fender
Norman
Vox
Marshall
La Tosca
VENTE
LOCATION
Pearl
SERVICE
Castr
SPARK CHAMPION PLUGS
KE100
KAWASAKI
Kawasaki
Let the good times roll.
KZ900
HEY, KID! YOUR RIDE'S READY...
70

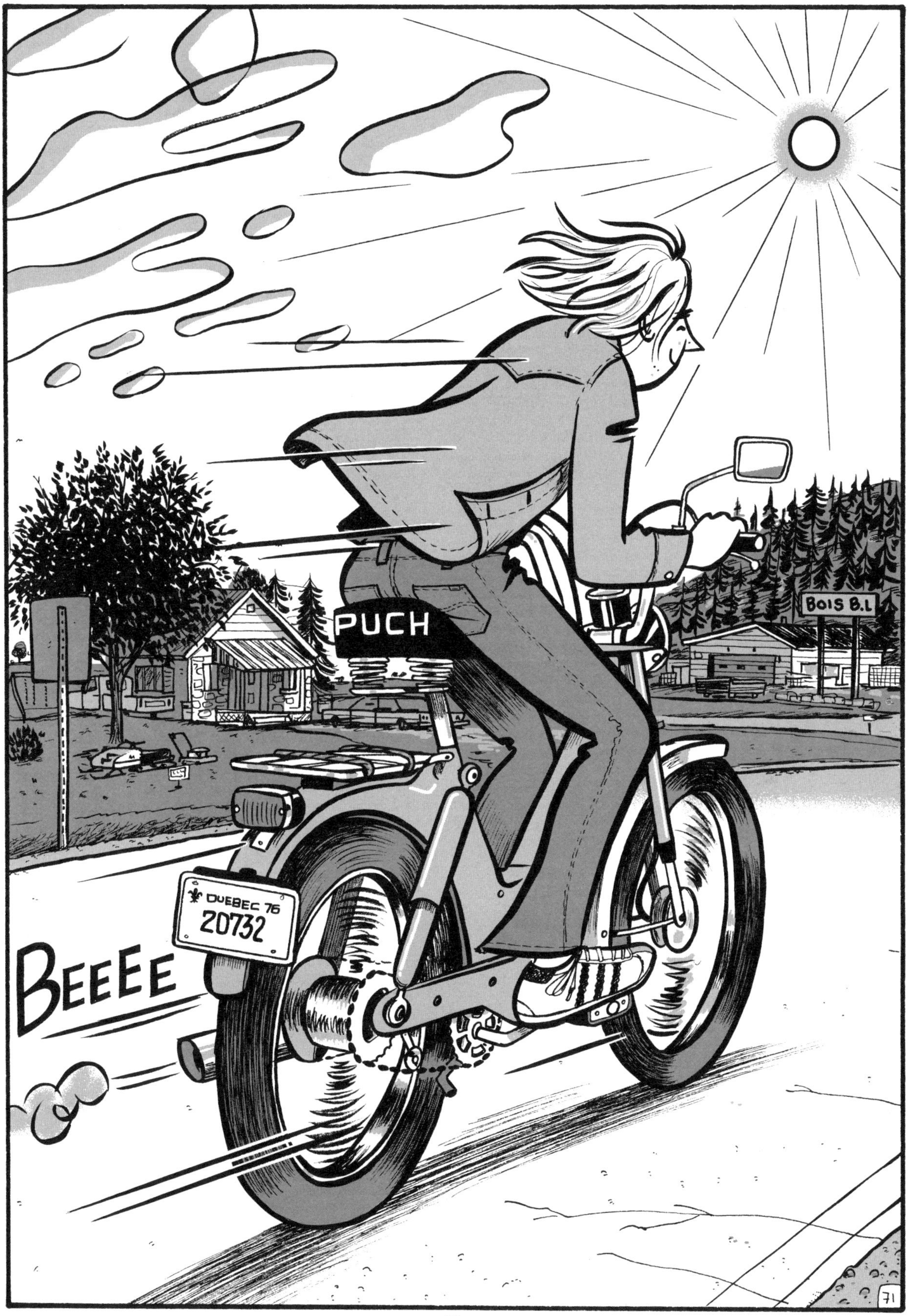
PUCH
BOIS B.L
QUEBEC 76
20732
BEEEE
71

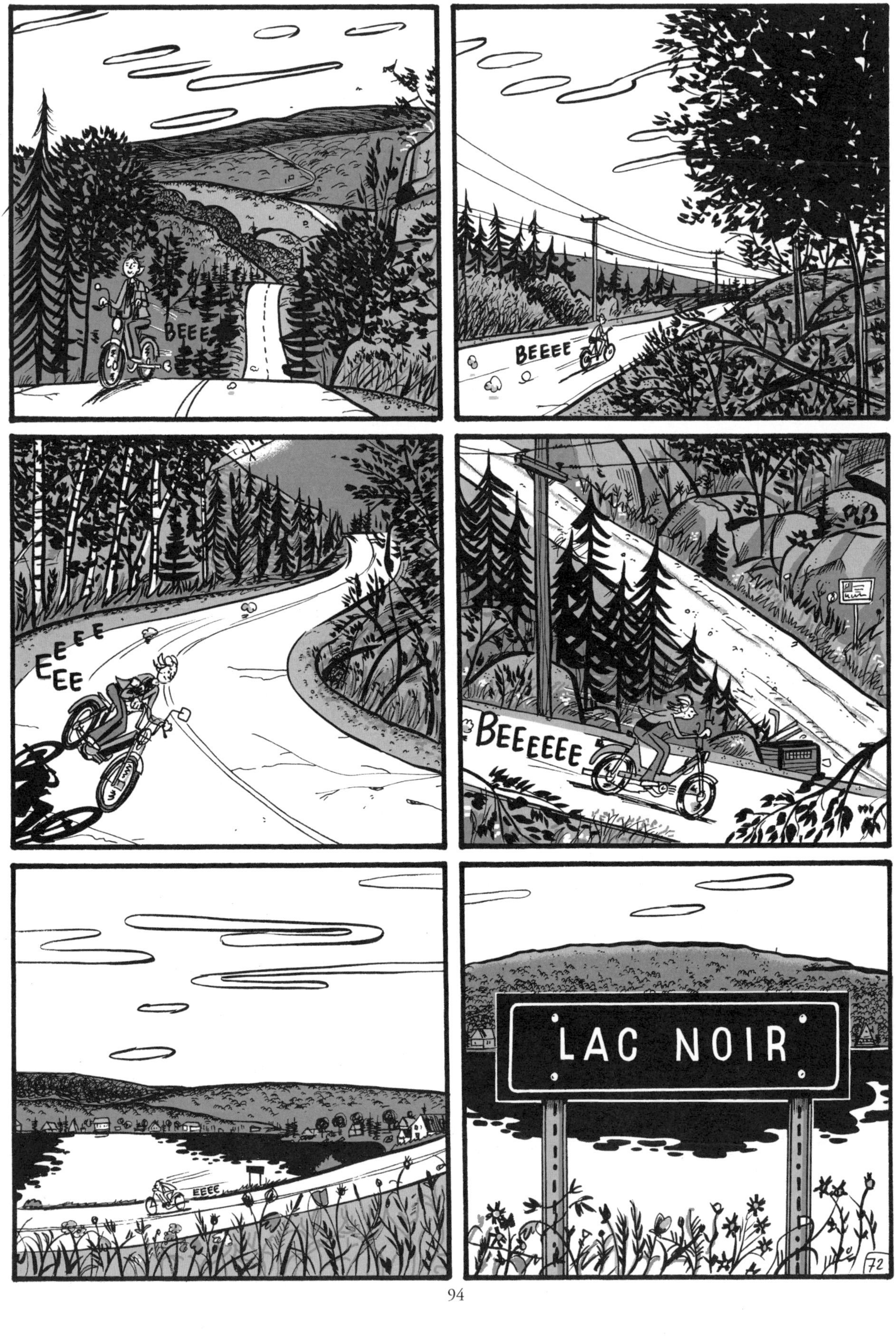
BEEE
BEEEE
EEE
EEE
BEEEEEE
EEEE
LAC NOIR
72

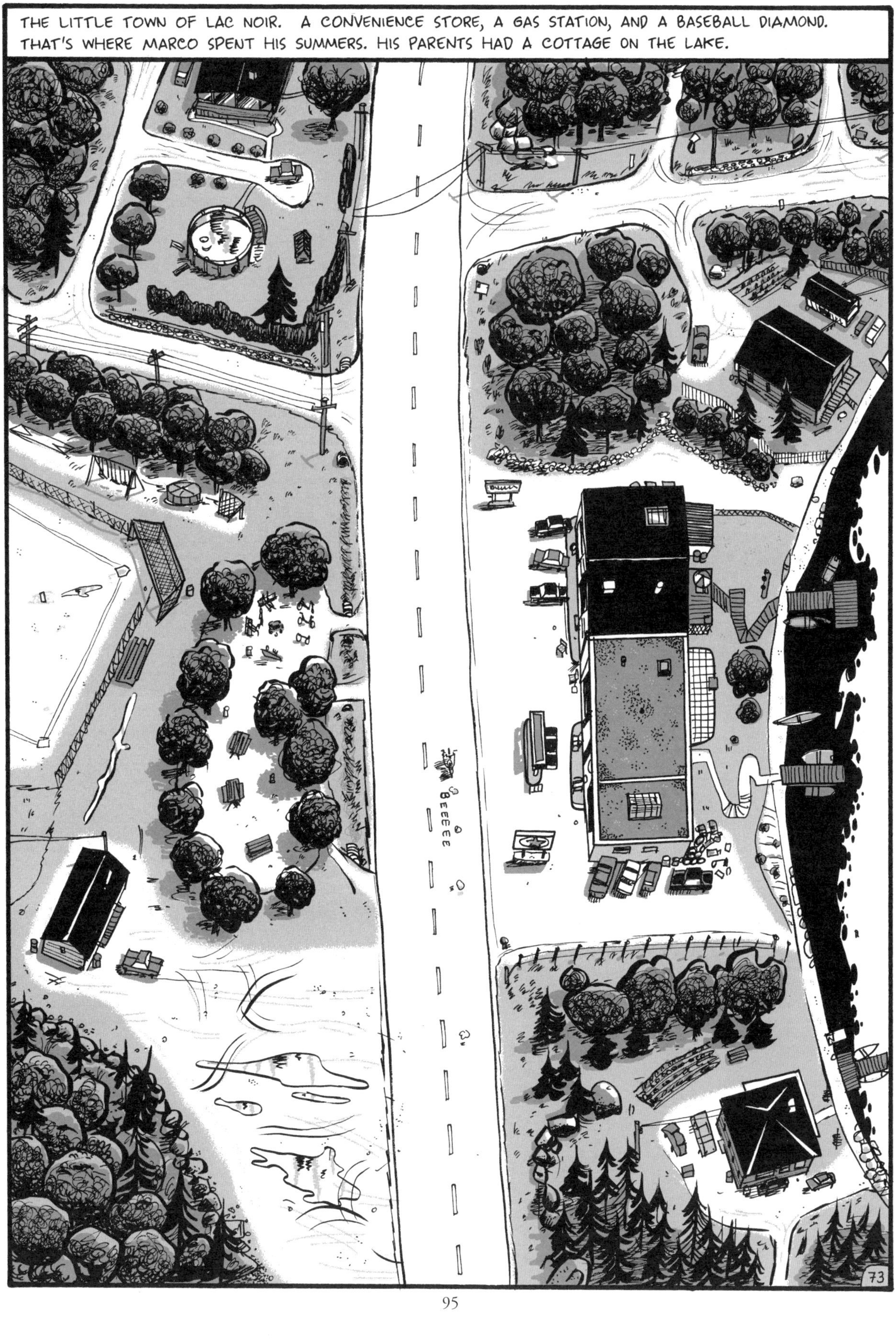
THE LITTLE TOWN OF LAC NOIR. A CONVENIENCE STORE, A GAS STATION, AND A BASEBALL DIAMOND. THAT'S WHERE MARCO SPENT HIS SUMMERS. HIS PARENTS HAD A COTTAGE ON THE LAKE.
BEEEEE
73

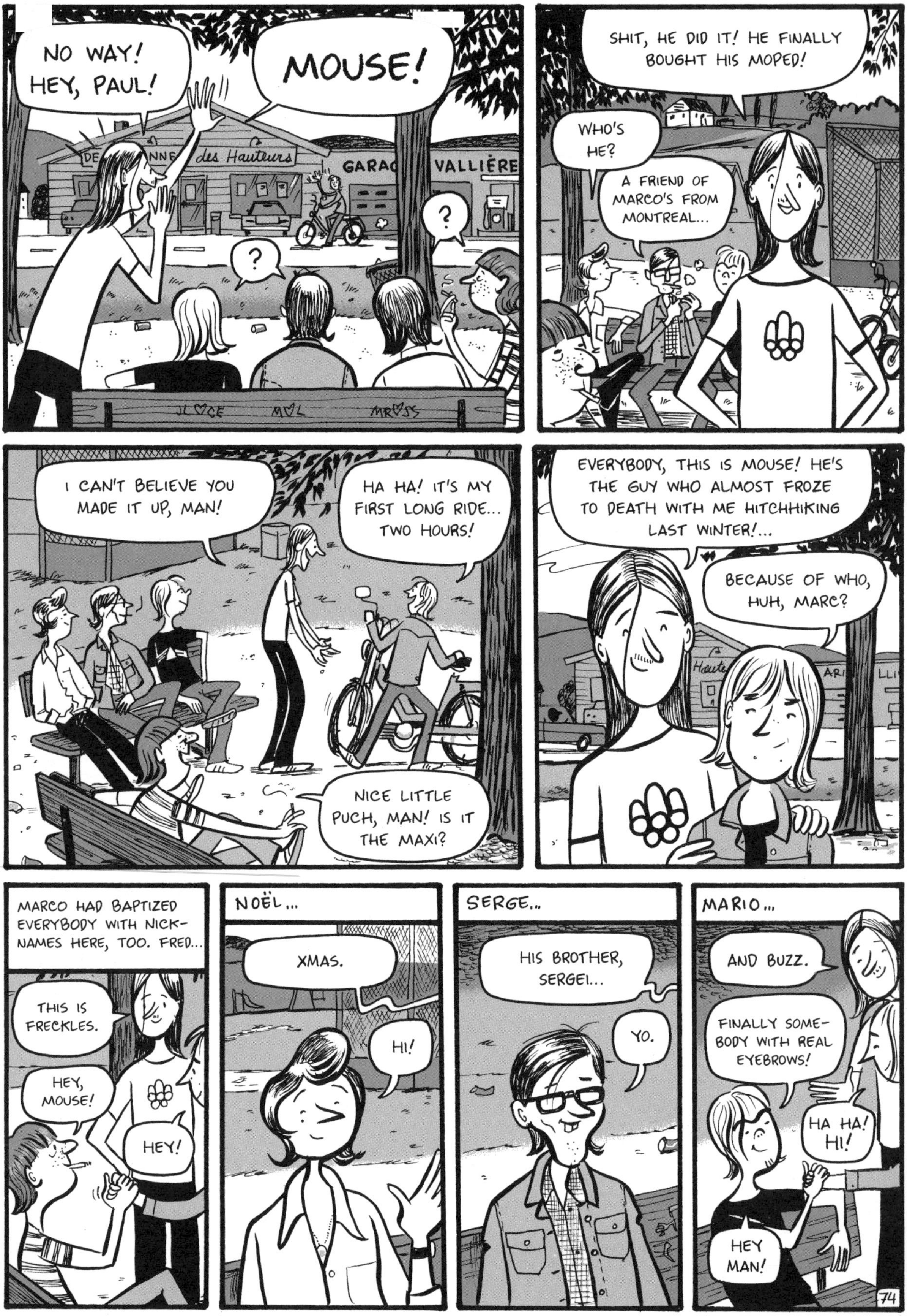
NO WAY! HEY, PAUL!
MOUSE!
des Hauteurs
GARAG VALLIÈRE
?
?
SHIT, HE DID IT! HE FINALLY BOUGHT HIS MOPED!
WHO'S HE?
A FRIEND OF MARCO'S FROM MONTREAL...
I CAN'T BELIEVE YOU MADE IT UP, MAN!
HA HA! IT'S MY FIRST LONG RIDE... TWO HOURS!
NICE LITTLE PUCH, MAN! IS IT THE MAXI?
EVERYBODY, THIS IS MOUSE! HE'S THE GUY WHO ALMOST FROZE TO DEATH WITH ME HITCHHIKING LAST WINTER!...
BECAUSE OF WHO, HUH, MARC?
MARCO HAD BAPTIZED EVERYBODY WITH NICK-NAMES HERE, TOO. FRED...
THIS IS FRECKLES.
HEY, MOUSE!
HEY!
NOËL...
XMAS.
HI!
SERGE...
HIS BROTHER, SERGEI...
YO.
MARIO...
AND BUZZ.
FINALLY SOME-BODY WITH REAL EYEBROWS!
HA HA! HI!
HEY MAN!
74

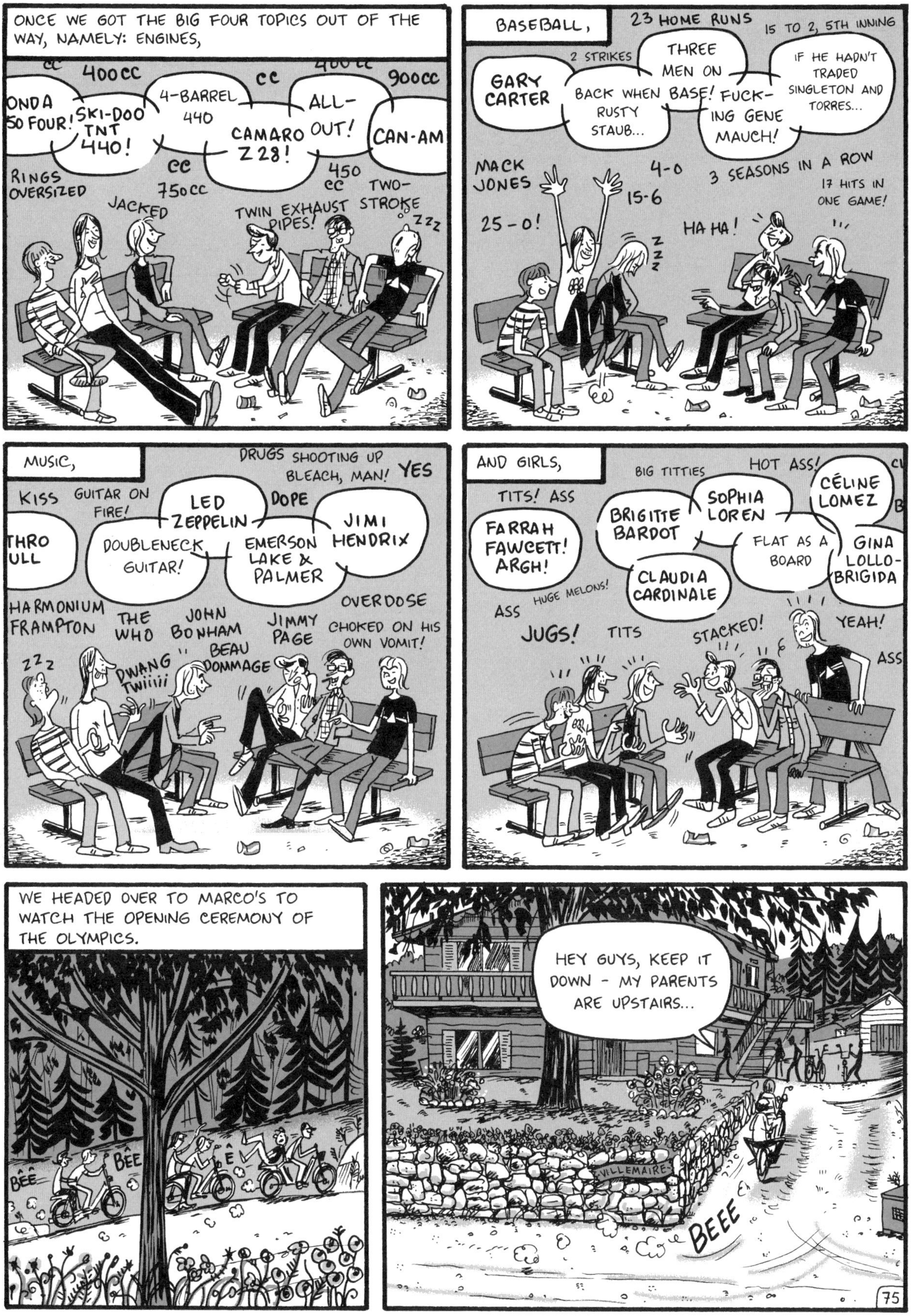
ONCE WE GOT THE BIG FOUR TOPICS OUT OF THE WAY, NAMELY: ENGINES,
400CC
CC
900CC
ONDA 50 FOUR!
SKI-DOO TNT 440!
4-BARREL 440
CAMARO Z28!
ALL-OUT!
CAN-AM
CC
750CC
450 CC
RINGS OVERSIZED
JACKED
TWIN EXHAUST PIPES!
TWO-STROKE
ZZZ
BASEBALL,
23 HOME RUNS
15 TO 2, 5TH INNING
2 STRIKES
GARY CARTER
BACK WHEN RUSTY STAUB...
THREE MEN ON BASE!
FUCK-ING GENE MAUCH!
IF HE HADN'T TRADED SINGLETON AND TORRES...
MACK JONES
4-0
3 SEASONS IN A ROW
15-6
17 HITS IN ONE GAME!
25-0!
HA HA!
ZZZ
MUSIC,
DRUGS
SHOOTING UP BLEACH, MAN!
YES
KISS
GUITAR ON FIRE!
LED ZEPPELIN
DOPE
THRO ULL
DOUBLENECK GUITAR!
EMERSON LAKE & PALMER
JIMI HENDRIX
HARMONIUM
FRAMPTON
THE WHO
JOHN BONHAM
JIMMY PAGE
OVERDOSE
CHOKED ON HIS OWN VOMIT!
BEAU DOMMAGE
ZZZ
DWANG TWIIIII
AND GIRLS,
BIG TITTIES
HOT ASS!
TITS! ASS
FARRAH FAWCETT! ARGH!
BRIGITTE BARDOT
SOPHIA LOREN
CÉLINE LOMEZ
FLAT AS A BOARD
GINA LOLLO-BRIGIDA
CLAUDIA CARDINALE
ASS
HUGE MELONS!
JUGS!
TITS
STACKED!
YEAH!
ASS
WE HEADED OVER TO MARCO'S TO WATCH THE OPENING CEREMONY OF THE OLYMPICS.
BÊÊ
BÊE
Ê
HEY GUYS, KEEP IT DOWN - MY PARENTS ARE UPSTAIRS...
VILLEMAIRE
BEEE
75

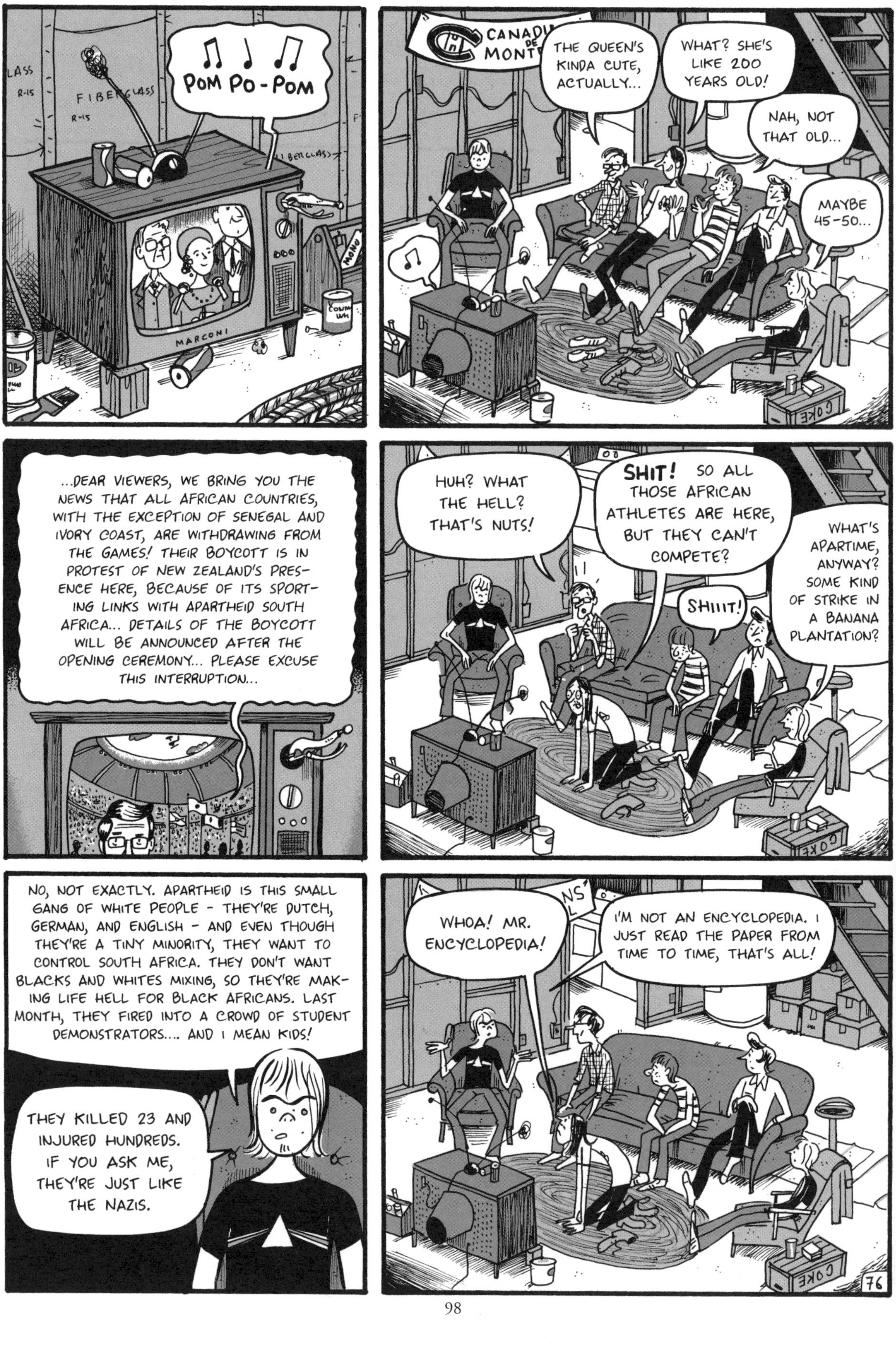

POM PO-POM
MARCONI
THE QUEEN'S KINDA CUTE, ACTUALLY...
WHAT? SHE'S LIKE 200 YEARS OLD!
NAH, NOT THAT OLD...
MAYBE 45-50...
...DEAR VIEWERS, WE BRING YOU THE NEWS THAT ALL AFRICAN COUNTRIES, WITH THE EXCEPTION OF SENEGAL AND IVORY COAST, ARE WITHDRAWING FROM THE GAMES! THEIR BOYCOTT IS IN PROTEST OF NEW ZEALAND'S PRESENCE HERE, BECAUSE OF ITS SPORTING LINKS WITH APARTHEID SOUTH AFRICA... DETAILS OF THE BOYCOTT WILL BE ANNOUNCED AFTER THE OPENING CEREMONY... PLEASE EXCUSE THIS INTERRUPTION...
HUH? WHAT THE HELL? THAT'S NUTS!
SHIT! SO ALL THOSE AFRICAN ATHLETES ARE HERE, BUT THEY CAN'T COMPETE?
SHIIIT!
WHAT'S APARTIME, ANYWAY? SOME KIND OF STRIKE IN A BANANA PLANTATION?
NO, NOT EXACTLY. APARTHEID IS THIS SMALL GANG OF WHITE PEOPLE - THEY'RE DUTCH, GERMAN, AND ENGLISH - AND EVEN THOUGH THEY'RE A TINY MINORITY, THEY WANT TO CONTROL SOUTH AFRICA. THEY DON'T WANT BLACKS AND WHITES MIXING, SO THEY'RE MAKING LIFE HELL FOR BLACK AFRICANS. LAST MONTH, THEY FIRED INTO A CROWD OF STUDENT DEMONSTRATORS.... AND I MEAN KIDS!
THEY KILLED 23 AND INJURED HUNDREDS. IF YOU ASK ME, THEY'RE JUST LIKE THE NAZIS.
WHOA! MR. ENCYCLOPEDIA!
I'M NOT AN ENCYCLOPEDIA. I JUST READ THE PAPER FROM TIME TO TIME, THAT'S ALL!
76

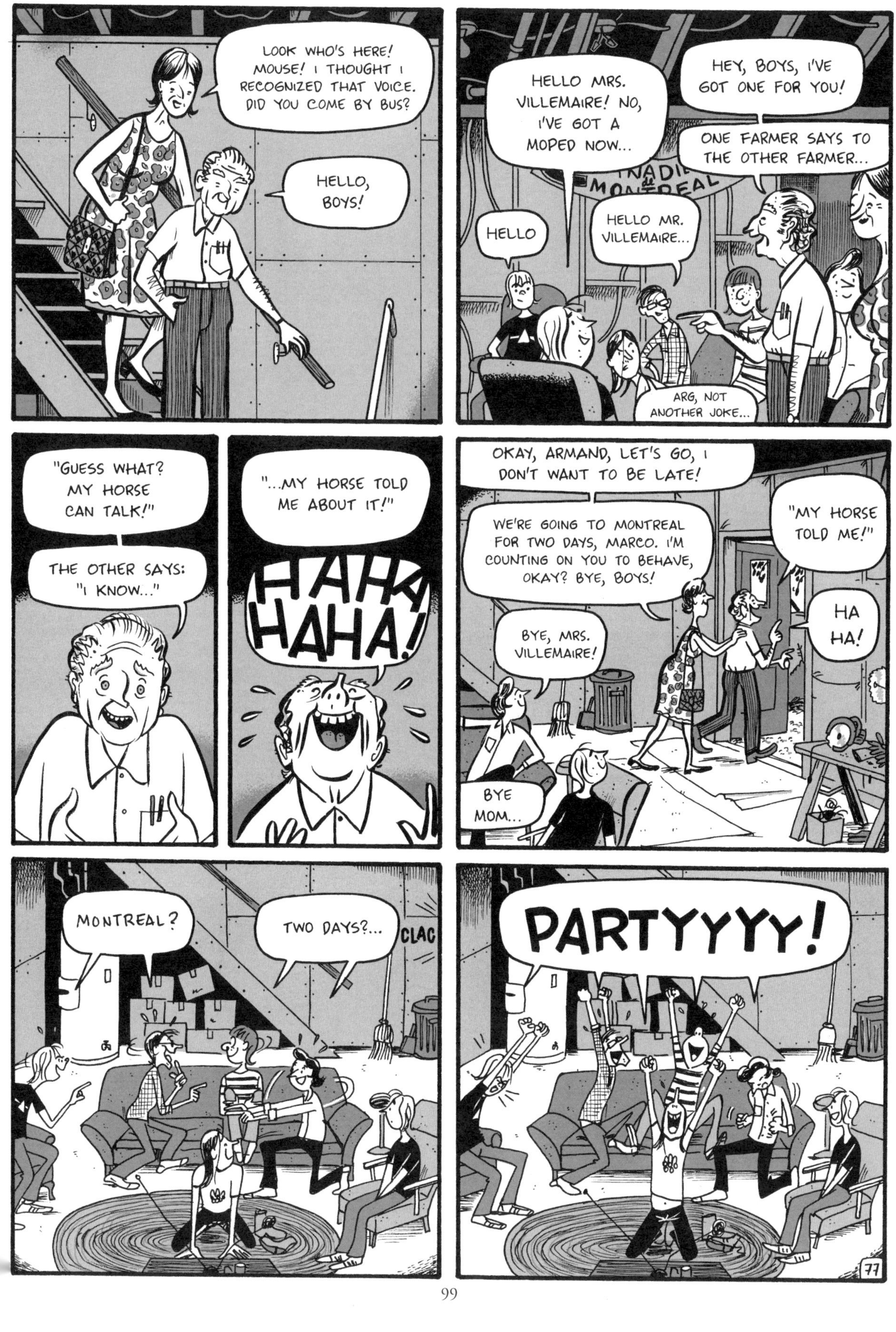
LOOK WHO'S HERE! MOUSE! I THOUGHT I RECOGNIZED THAT VOICE. DID YOU COME BY BUS?
HELLO, BOYS!
HELLO MRS. VILLEMAIRE! NO, I'VE GOT A MOPED NOW...
HEY, BOYS, I'VE GOT ONE FOR YOU!
ONE FARMER SAYS TO THE OTHER FARMER...
HELLO
HELLO MR. VILLEMAIRE...
ARG, NOT ANOTHER JOKE...
"GUESS WHAT? MY HORSE CAN TALK!"
THE OTHER SAYS: "I KNOW..."
"...MY HORSE TOLD ME ABOUT IT!"
HAHA HAHA!
OKAY, ARMAND, LET'S GO, I DON'T WANT TO BE LATE!
WE'RE GOING TO MONTREAL FOR TWO DAYS, MARCO. I'M COUNTING ON YOU TO BEHAVE, OKAY? BYE, BOYS!
"MY HORSE TOLD ME!"
HA HA!
BYE, MRS. VILLEMAIRE!
BYE MOM...
MONTREAL?
TWO DAYS?...
CLAC
PARTYYYY!
77

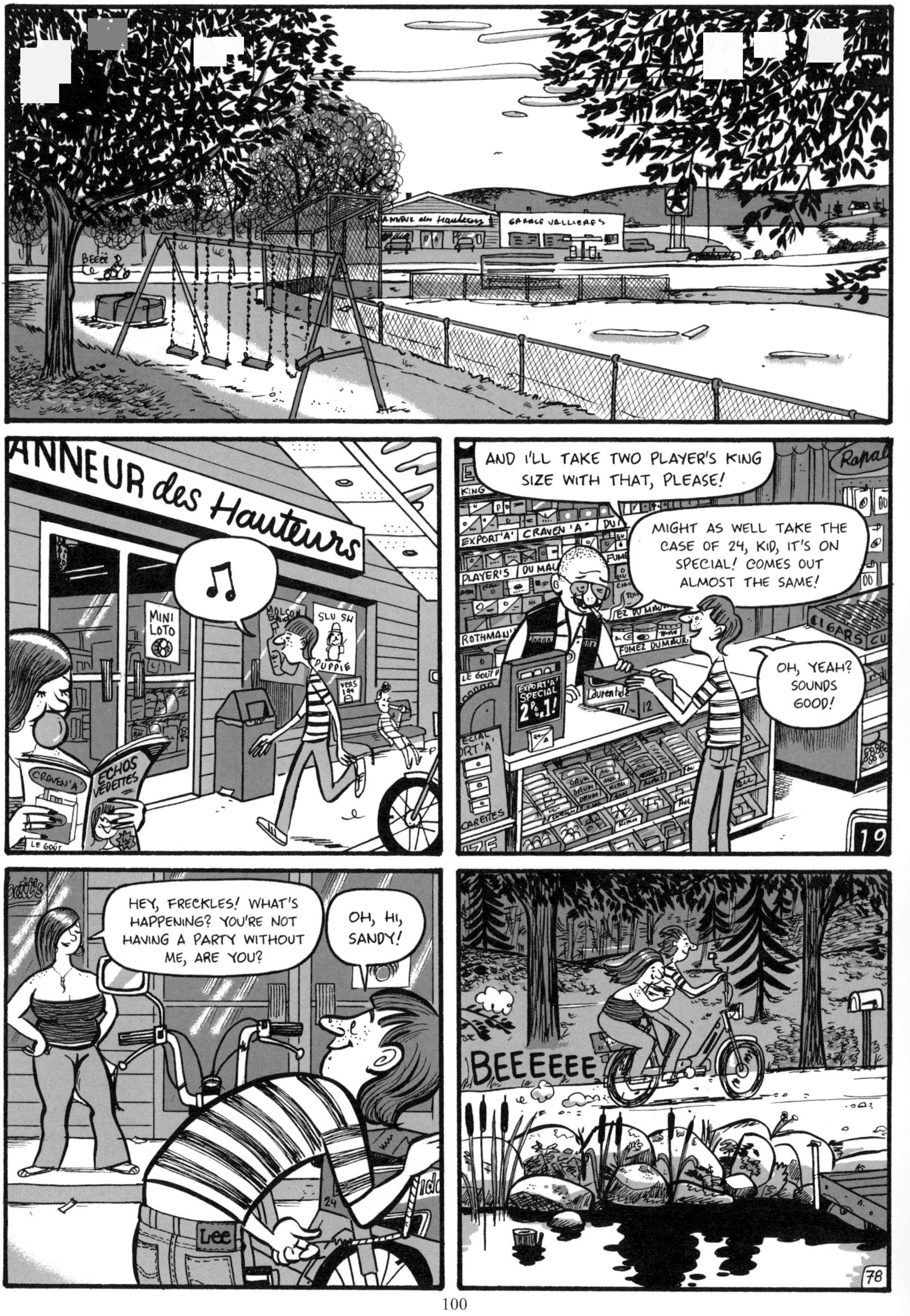
GARAGE VALLIERES
ANNEUR des Hauteurs
MINI LOTO
SLUSH PUPPIE
ECHOS VEDETTES
CRAVEN 'A'
AND I'LL TAKE TWO PLAYER'S KING SIZE WITH THAT, PLEASE!
MIGHT AS WELL TAKE THE CASE OF 24, KID, IT'S ON SPECIAL! COMES OUT ALMOST THE SAME!
OH, YEAH? SOUNDS GOOD!
HEY, FRECKLES! WHAT'S HAPPENING? YOU'RE NOT HAVING A PARTY WITHOUT ME, ARE YOU?
OH, HI, SANDY!
BEEEEEE
78

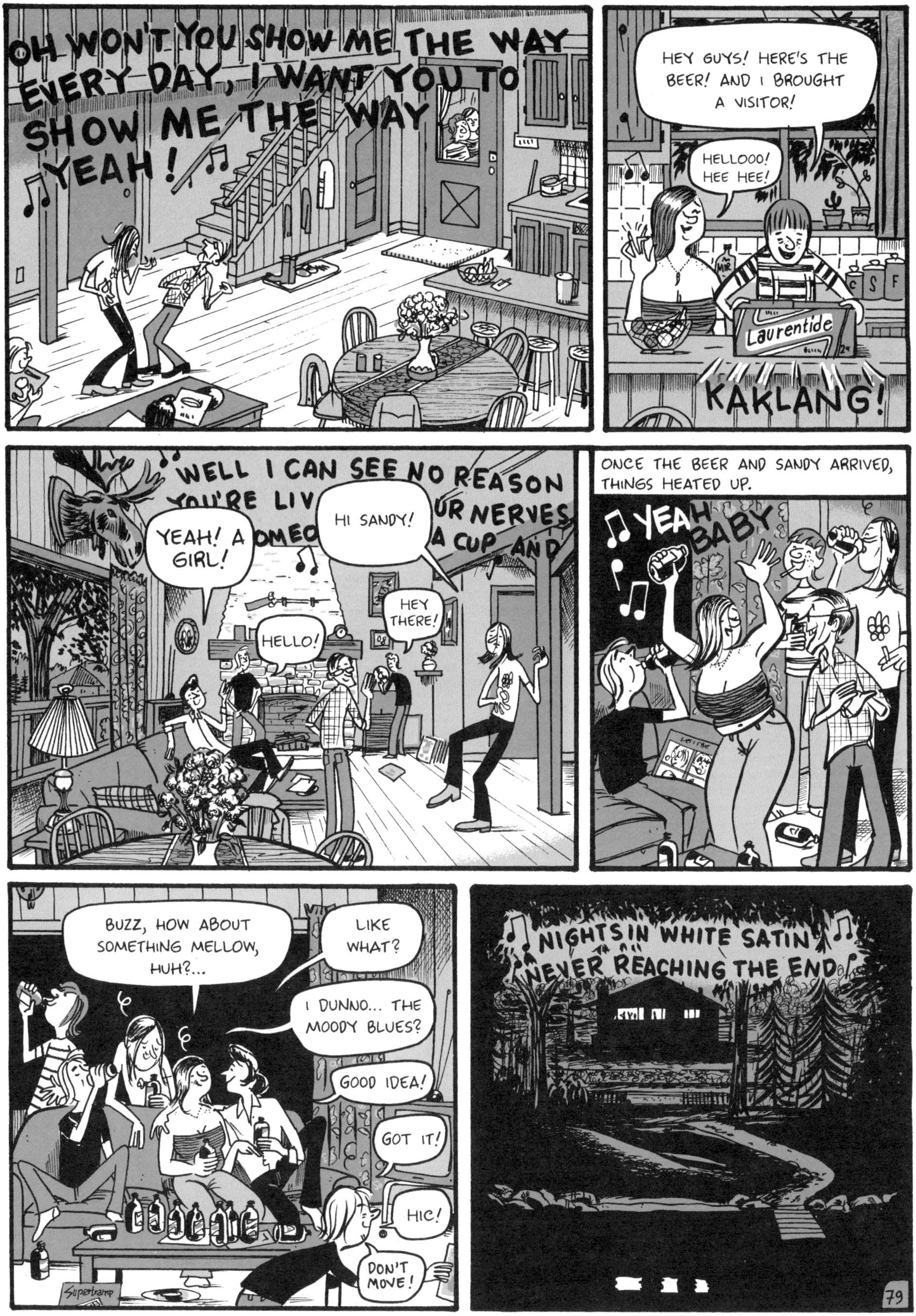

OH WON'T YOU SHOW ME THE WAY EVERY DAY, I WANT YOU TO SHOW ME THE WAY YEAH!
HEY GUYS! HERE'S THE BEER! AND I BROUGHT A VISITOR!
HELLOOO! HEE HEE!
Laurentide
KAKLANG!
WELL I CAN SEE NO REASON
YEAH! A GIRL!
HI SANDY!
HEY THERE!
HELLO!
ONCE THE BEER AND SANDY ARRIVED, THINGS HEATED UP.
YEAH BABY
BUZZ, HOW ABOUT SOMETHING MELLOW, HUH?...
LIKE WHAT?
I DUNNO... THE MOODY BLUES?
GOOD IDEA!
GOT IT!
HIC!
DON'T MOVE!
Supertramp
NIGHTS IN WHITE SATIN NEVER REACHING THE END
79

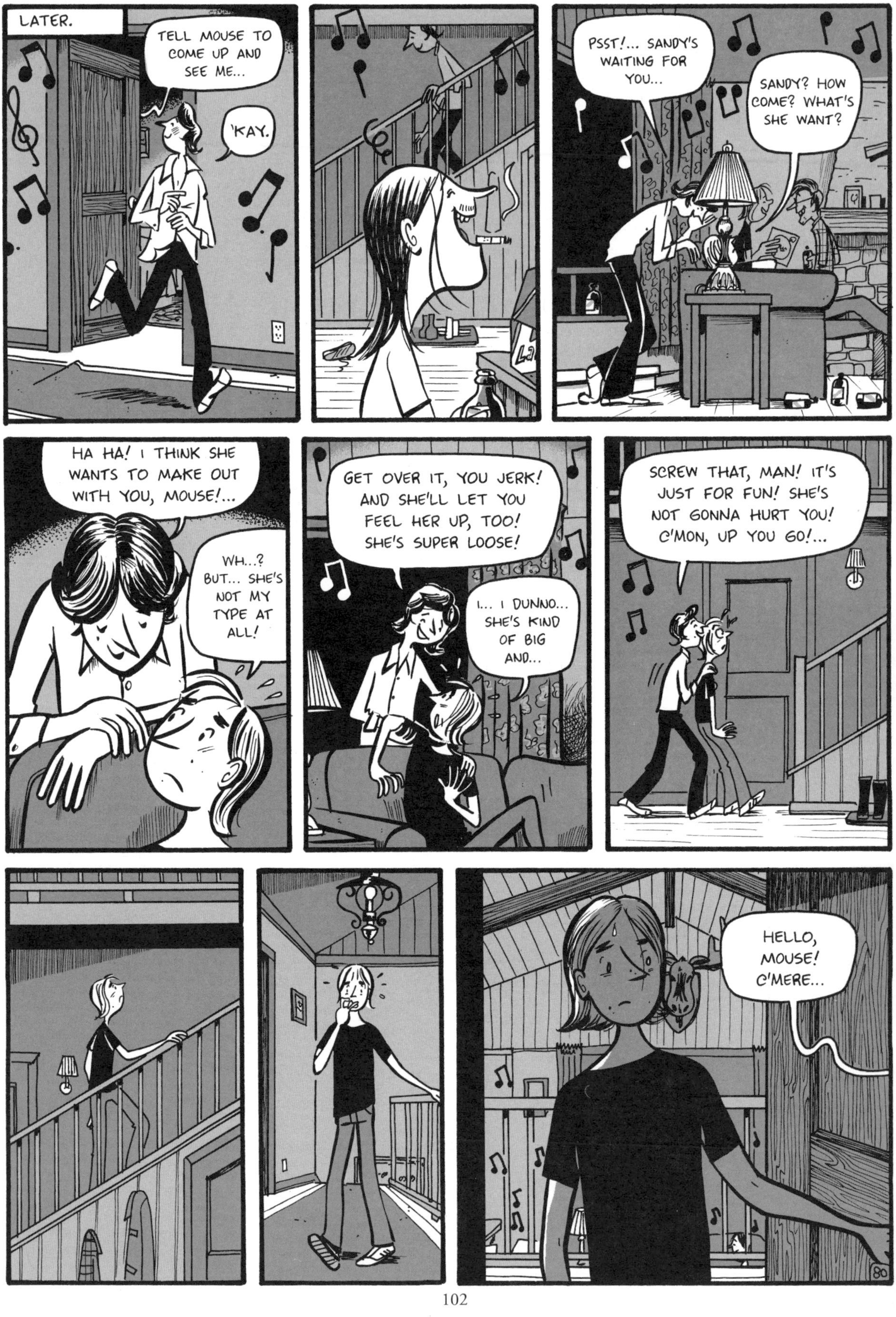
LATER.
TELL MOUSE TO COME UP AND SEE ME...
'KAY.
PSST!... SANDY'S WAITING FOR YOU...
SANDY? HOW COME? WHAT'S SHE WANT?
HA HA! I THINK SHE WANTS TO MAKE OUT WITH YOU, MOUSE!...
WH...? BUT... SHE'S NOT MY TYPE AT ALL!
GET OVER IT, YOU JERK! AND SHE'LL LET YOU FEEL HER UP, TOO! SHE'S SUPER LOOSE!
I... I DUNNO... SHE'S KIND OF BIG AND...
SCREW THAT, MAN! IT'S JUST FOR FUN! SHE'S NOT GONNA HURT YOU! C'MON, UP YOU GO!...
HELLO, MOUSE! C'MERE...
80

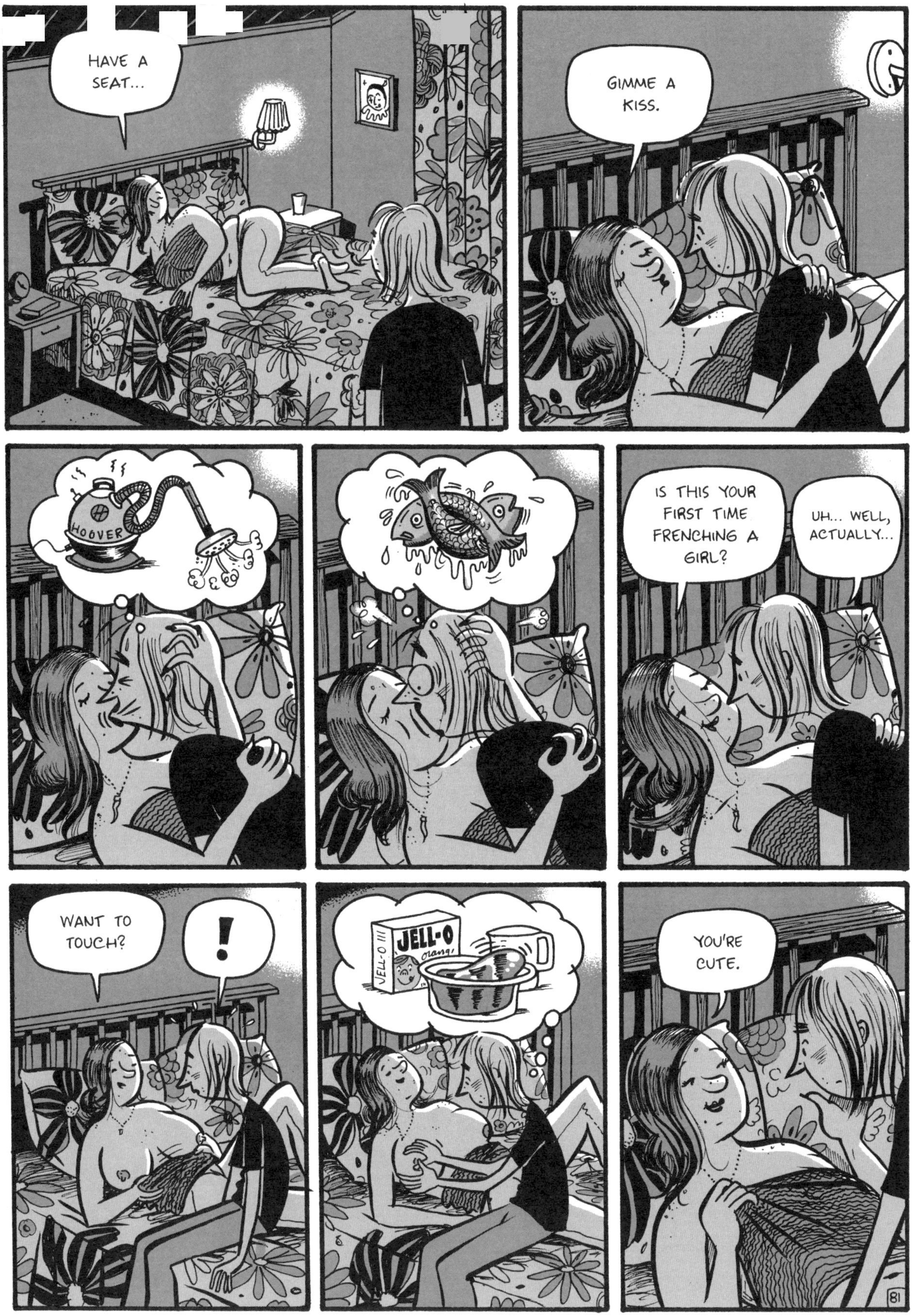
HAVE A SEAT...
GIMME A KISS.
HOOVER
IS THIS YOUR FIRST TIME FRENCHING A GIRL?
UH... WELL, ACTUALLY...
WANT TO TOUCH?
!
JELL-O
JELL-O
YOU'RE CUTE.
81

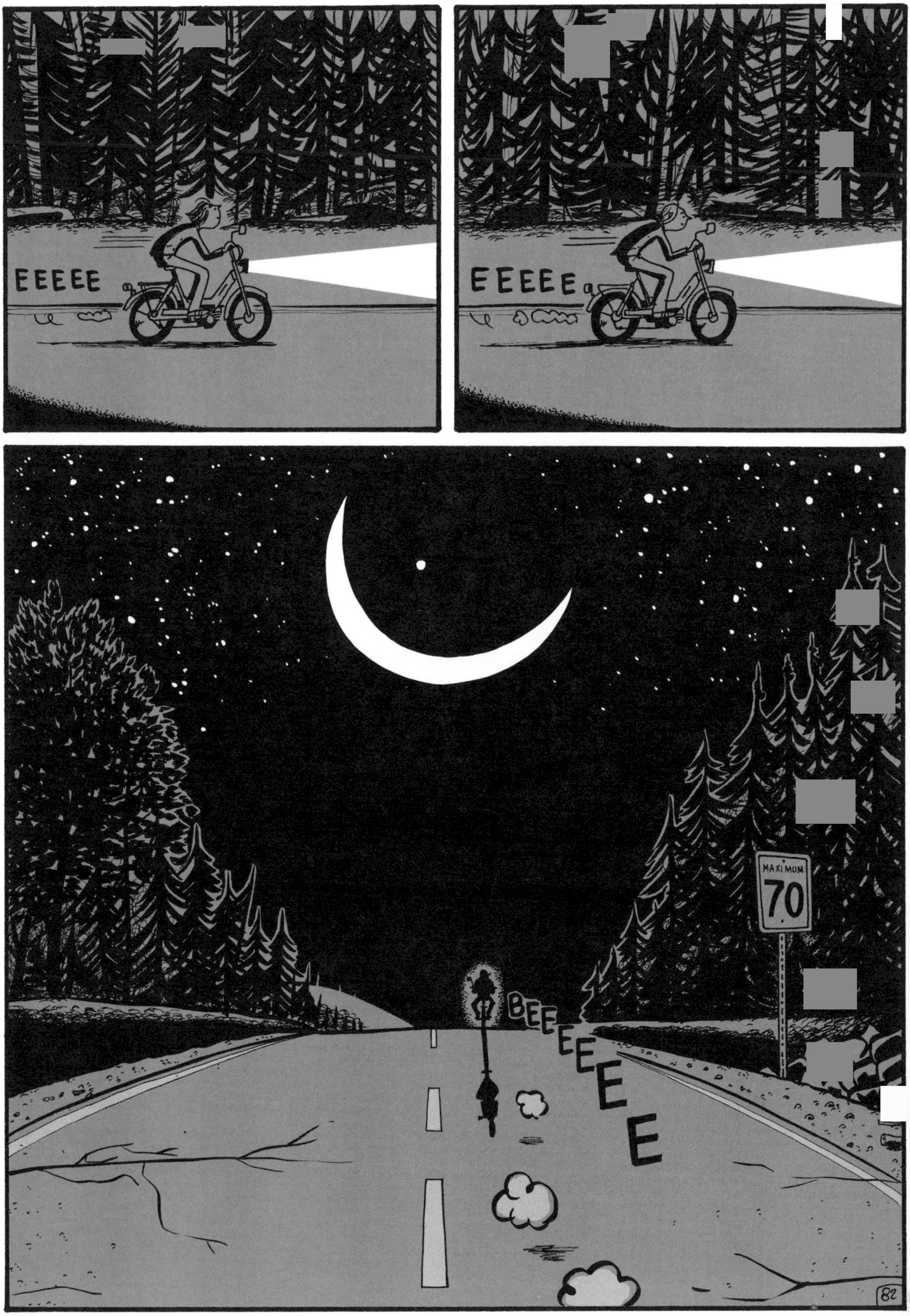
EEEEE
EEEEE
BEEEEEEE
MAXIMUM
70

Cardootch

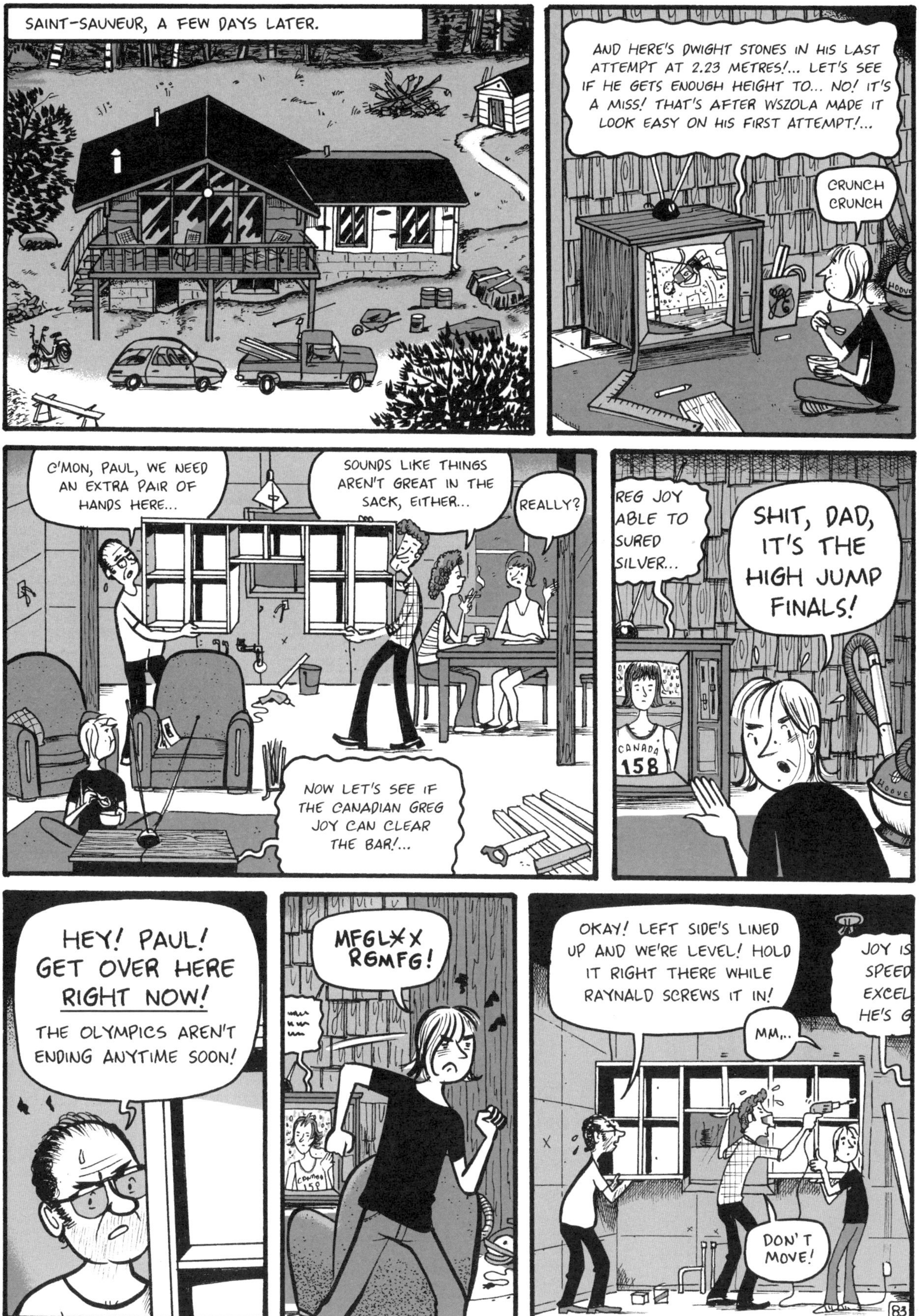
SAINT-SAUVEUR, A FEW DAYS LATER.
AND HERE'S DWIGHT STONES IN HIS LAST ATTEMPT AT 2.23 METRES!... LET'S SEE IF HE GETS ENOUGH HEIGHT TO... NO! IT'S A MISS! THAT'S AFTER WSZOLA MADE IT LOOK EASY ON HIS FIRST ATTEMPT!...
CRUNCH CRUNCH
C'MON, PAUL, WE NEED AN EXTRA PAIR OF HANDS HERE...
SOUNDS LIKE THINGS AREN'T GREAT IN THE SACK, EITHER...
REALLY?
NOW LET'S SEE IF THE CANADIAN GREG JOY CAN CLEAR THE BAR!...
REG JOY ABLE TO SURED SILVER...
SHIT, DAD, IT'S THE HIGH JUMP FINALS!
CANADA 158
HEY! PAUL! GET OVER HERE RIGHT NOW!
THE OLYMPICS AREN'T ENDING ANYTIME SOON!
MFGL✱X RGMFG!
OKAY! LEFT SIDE'S LINED UP AND WE'RE LEVEL! HOLD IT RIGHT THERE WHILE RAYNALD SCREWS IT IN!
MM...
JOY IS SPEED EXCEL HE'S G
DON'T MOVE!
83

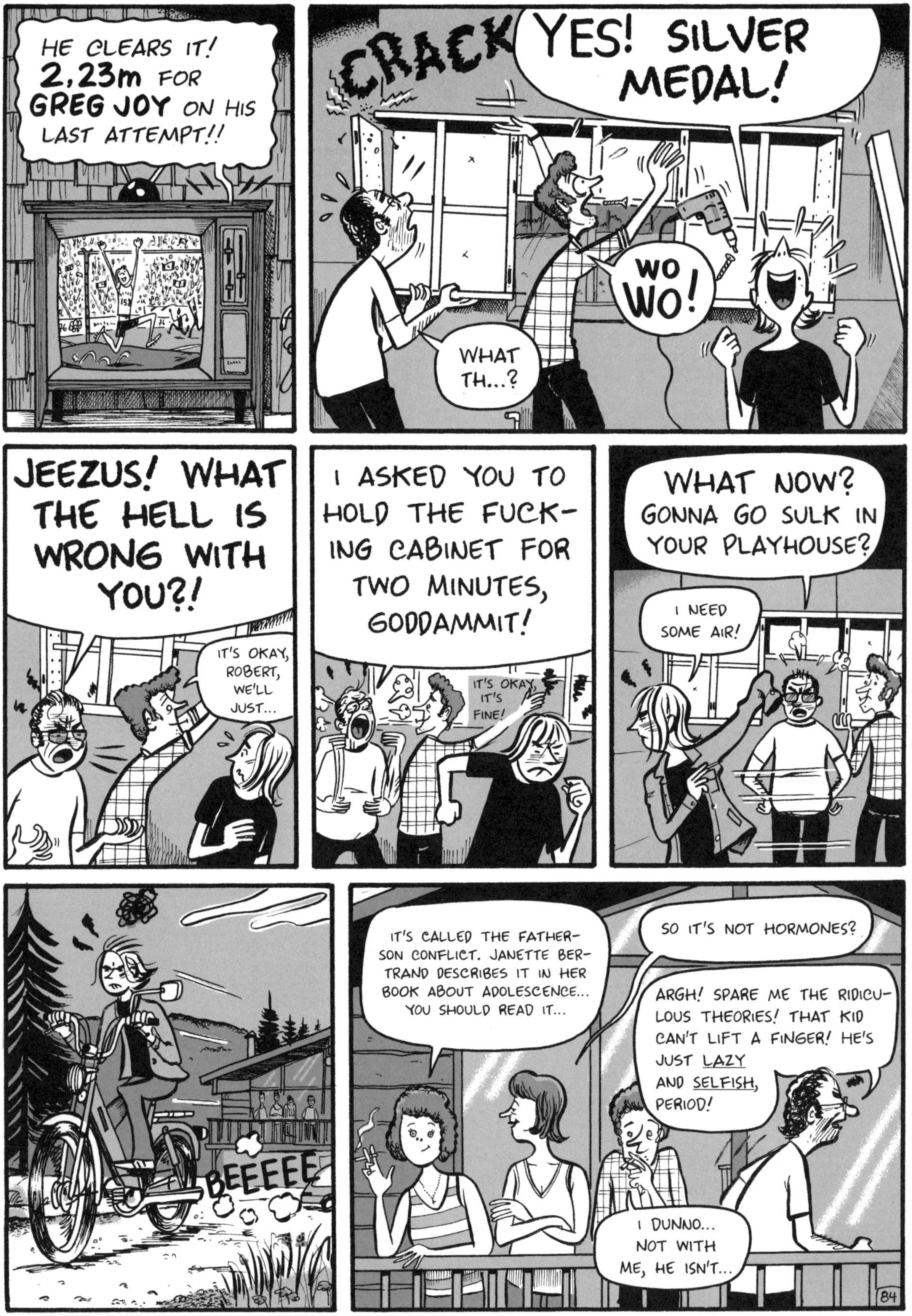
HE CLEARS IT! 2,23m FOR GREG JOY ON HIS LAST ATTEMPT!!
CRACK
YES! SILVER MEDAL!
WO WO!
WHAT TH...?
JEEZUS! WHAT THE HELL IS WRONG WITH YOU?!
IT'S OKAY, ROBERT, WE'LL JUST...
I ASKED YOU TO HOLD THE FUCKING CABINET FOR TWO MINUTES, GODDAMMIT!
IT'S OKAY, IT'S FINE!
WHAT NOW? GONNA GO SULK IN YOUR PLAYHOUSE?
I NEED SOME AIR!
BEEEEEE
IT'S CALLED THE FATHER-SON CONFLICT. JANETTE BERTRAND DESCRIBES IT IN HER BOOK ABOUT ADOLESCENCE... YOU SHOULD READ IT...
SO IT'S NOT HORMONES?
ARGH! SPARE ME THE RIDICULOUS THEORIES! THAT KID CAN'T LIFT A FINGER! HE'S JUST LAZY AND SELFISH, PERIOD!
I DUNNO... NOT WITH ME, HE ISN'T...
84

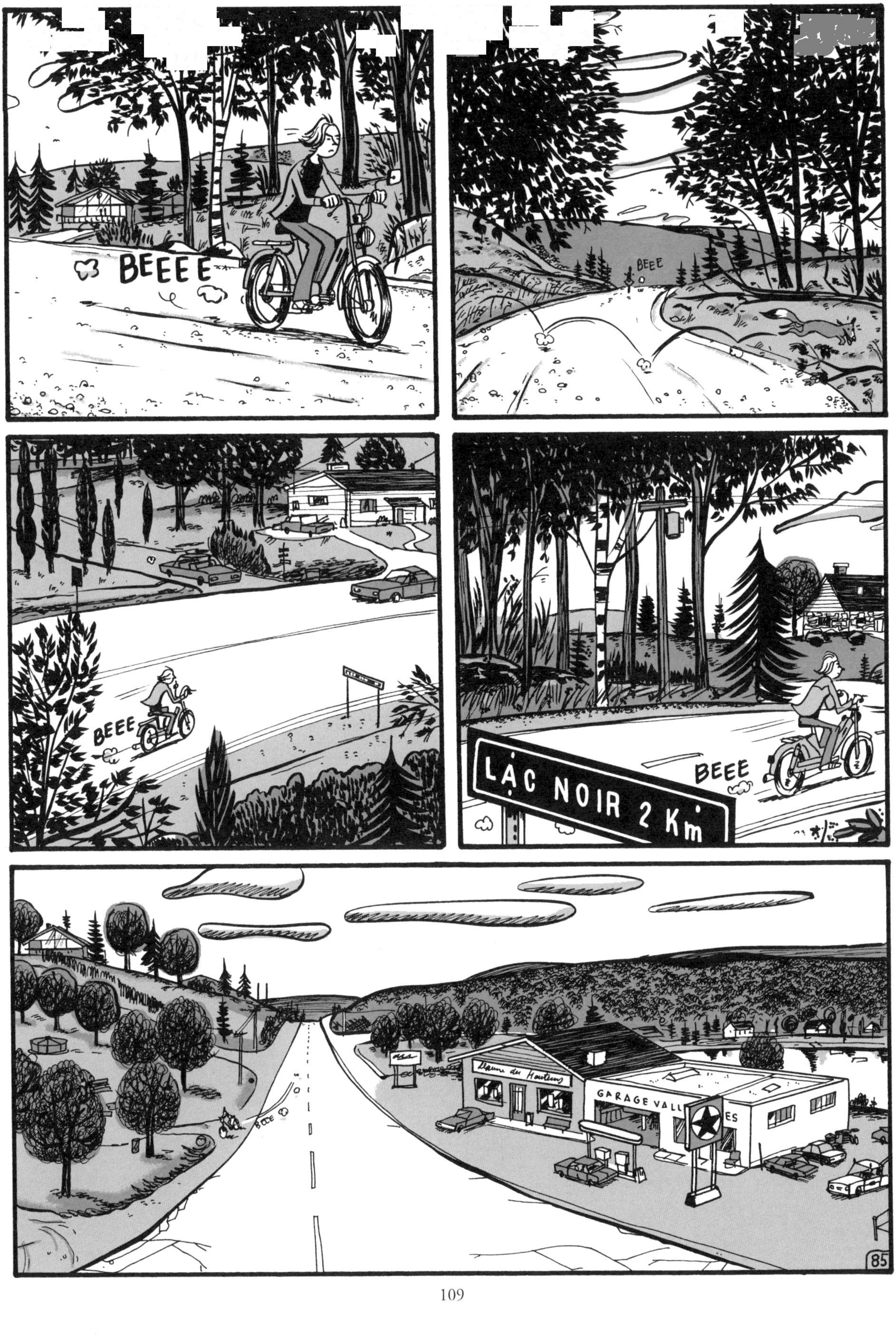
BEEEE
BEEE
BEEE
LAC NOIR 2 Km
BEEE
BEEE
GARAGE VALL
ES
85

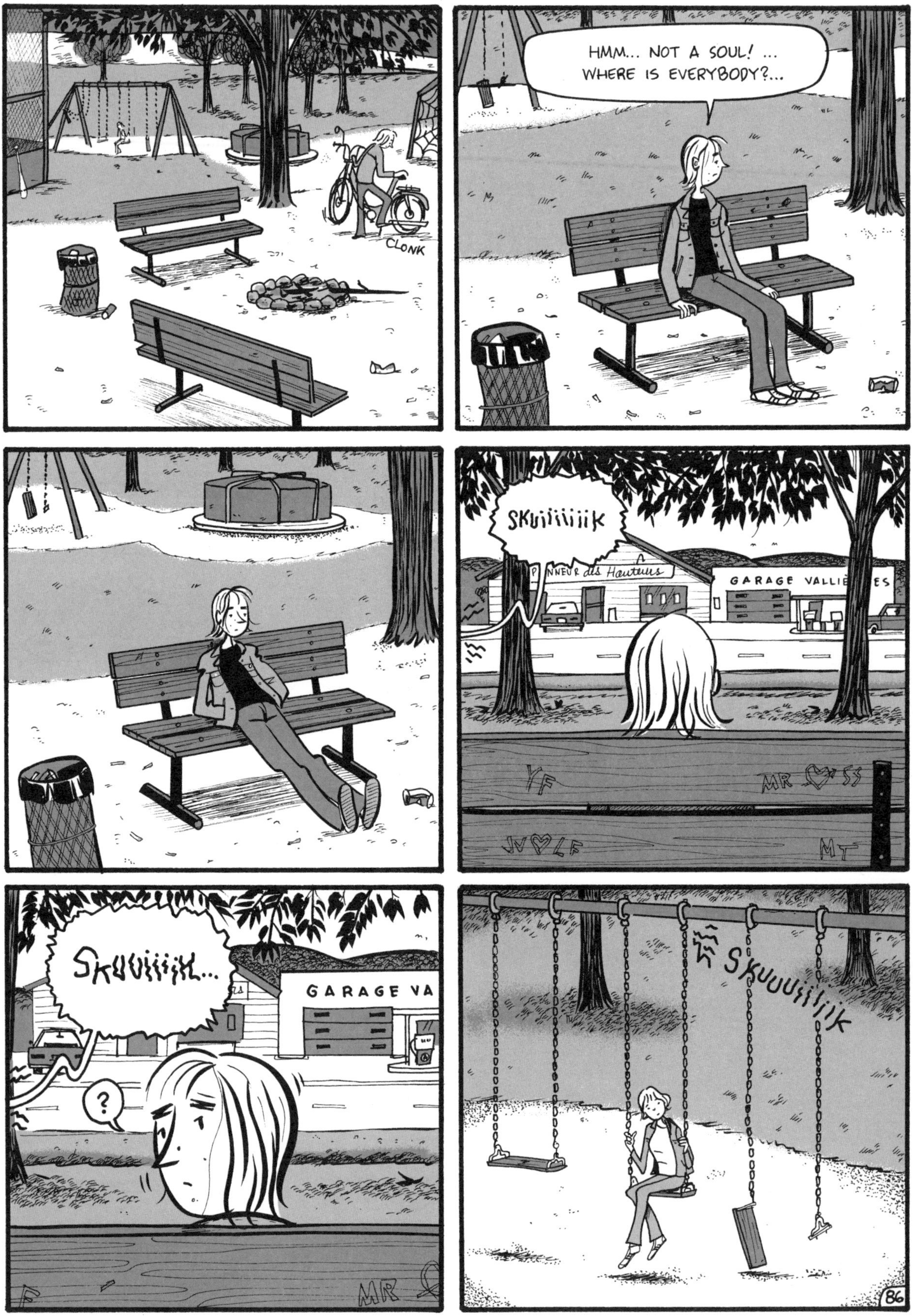
CLONK
HMM... NOT A SOUL! ... WHERE IS EVERYBODY?...
SKUiiiiiiiK
GARAGE VA
SKUUiiiiiK...
?
SKUUUiiiiiiK
86

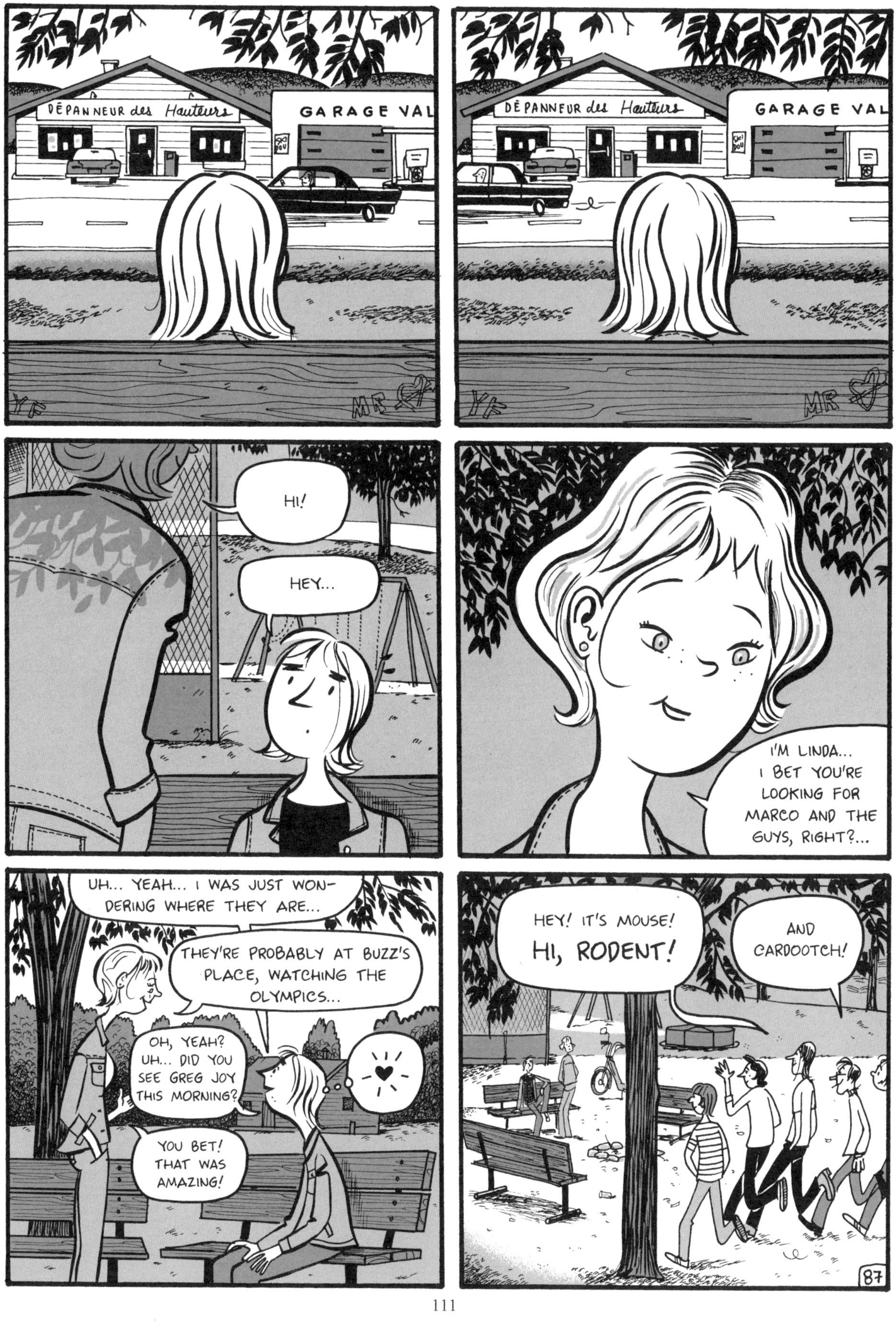
DÉPANNEUR des Hauteurs
GARAGE VAL
DÉPANNEUR des Hauteurs
GARAGE VAL
HI!
HEY...
I'M LINDA... I BET YOU'RE LOOKING FOR MARCO AND THE GUYS, RIGHT?...
UH... YEAH... I WAS JUST WONDERING WHERE THEY ARE...
THEY'RE PROBABLY AT BUZZ'S PLACE, WATCHING THE OLYMPICS...
OH, YEAH? UH... DID YOU SEE GREG JOY THIS MORNING?
YOU BET! THAT WAS AMAZING!
HEY! IT'S MOUSE! HI, RODENT!
AND CARDOOTCH!
87

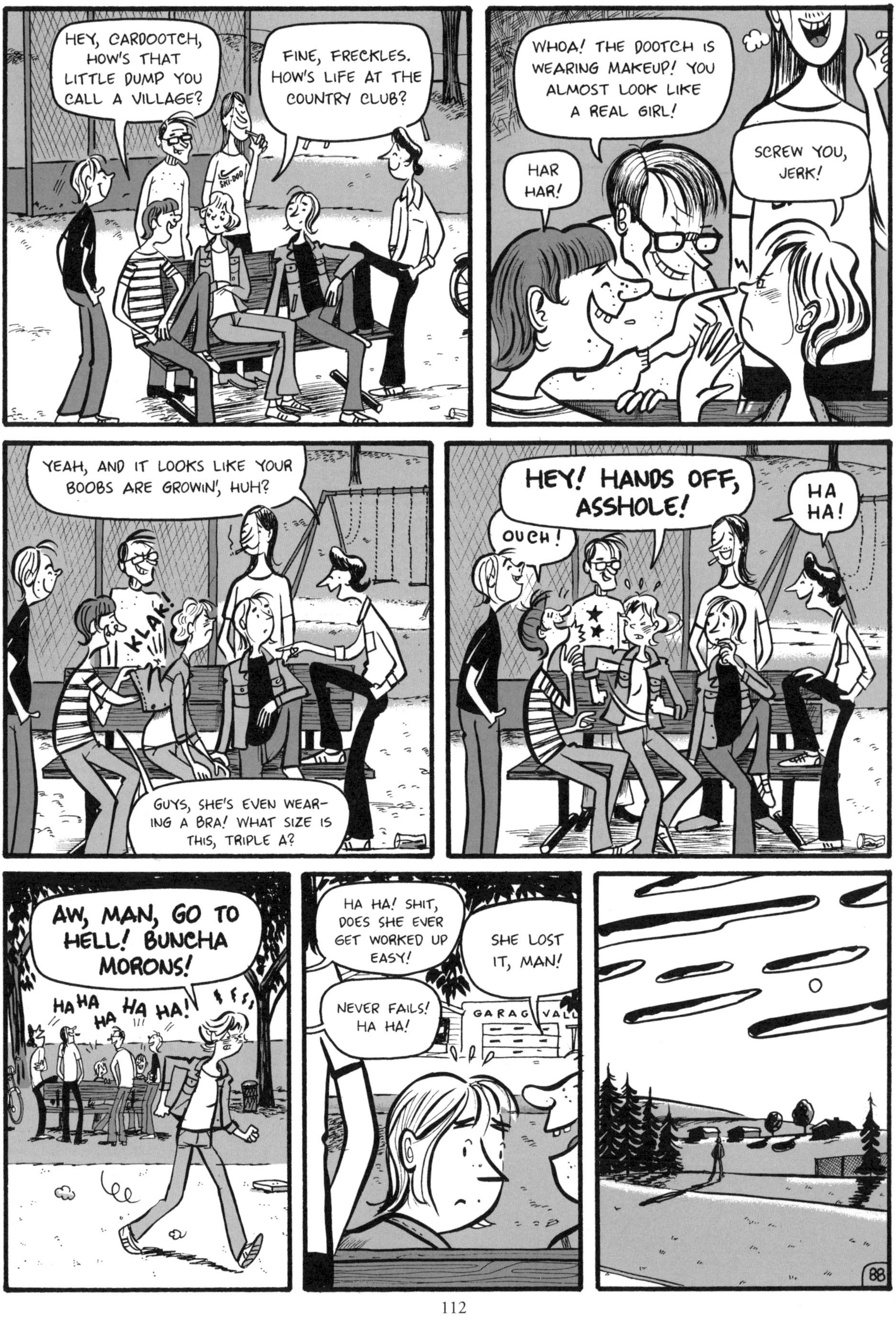
HEY, CARDOOTCH, HOW'S THAT LITTLE DUMP YOU CALL A VILLAGE?
FINE, FRECKLES. HOW'S LIFE AT THE COUNTRY CLUB?
SKI-DOO
WHOA! THE DOOTCH IS WEARING MAKEUP! YOU ALMOST LOOK LIKE A REAL GIRL!
HAR HAR!
SCREW YOU, JERK!
YEAH, AND IT LOOKS LIKE YOUR BOOBS ARE GROWIN', HUH?
KLAK!
GUYS, SHE'S EVEN WEAR-ING A BRA! WHAT SIZE IS THIS, TRIPLE A?
HEY! HANDS OFF, ASSHOLE!
OUCH!
HA HA!
AW, MAN, GO TO HELL! BUNCHA MORONS!
HA HA HA HA HA!
HA HA! SHIT, DOES SHE EVER GET WORKED UP EASY!
SHE LOST IT, MAN!
NEVER FAILS! HA HA!
GARAG VALL

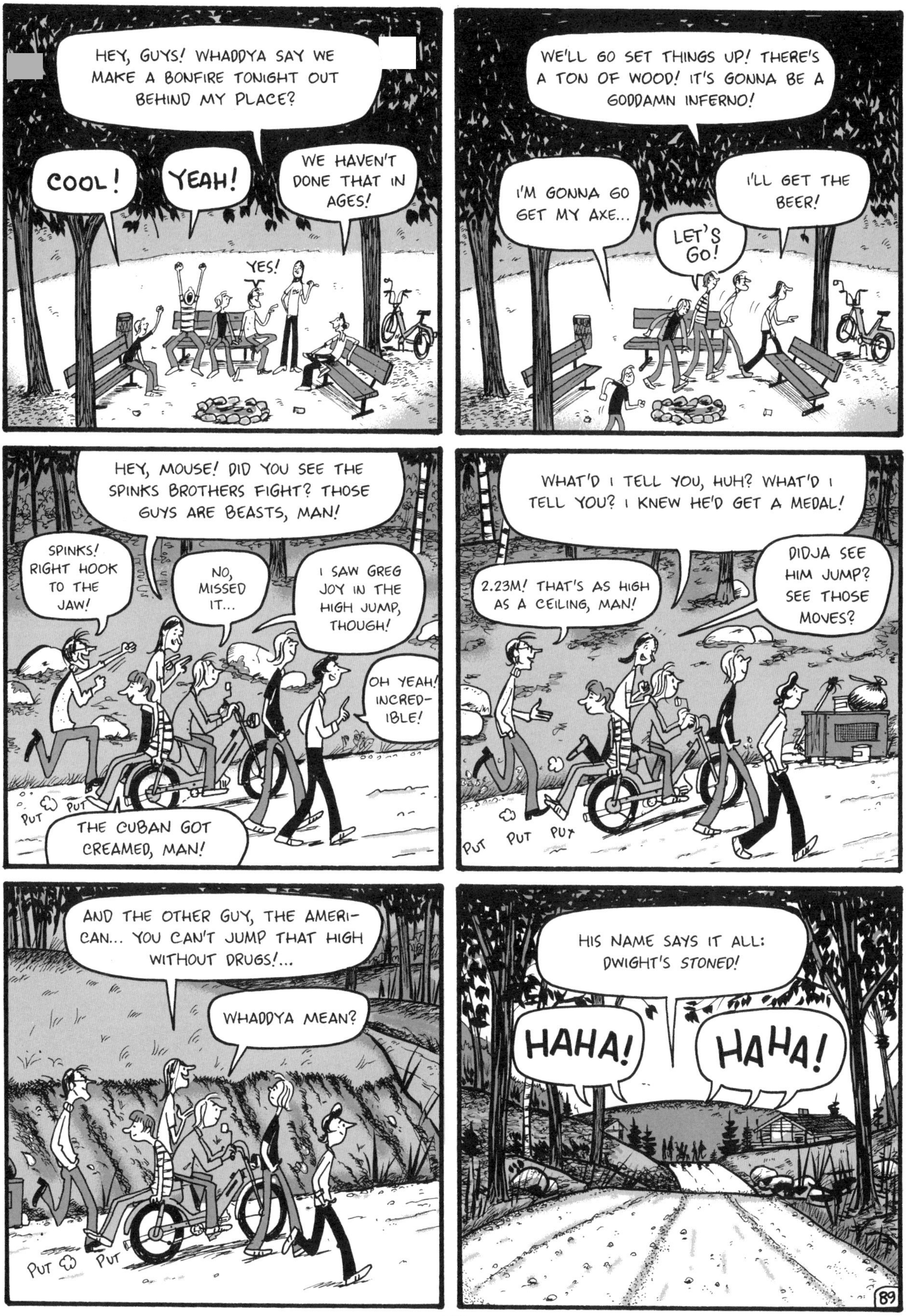
HEY, GUYS! WHADDYA SAY WE MAKE A BONFIRE TONIGHT OUT BEHIND MY PLACE?
COOL!
YEAH!
WE HAVEN'T DONE THAT IN AGES!
YES!
WE'LL GO SET THINGS UP! THERE'S A TON OF WOOD! IT'S GONNA BE A GODDAMN INFERNO!
I'M GONNA GO GET MY AXE...
LET'S GO!
I'LL GET THE BEER!
HEY, MOUSE! DID YOU SEE THE SPINKS BROTHERS FIGHT? THOSE GUYS ARE BEASTS, MAN!
SPINKS! RIGHT HOOK TO THE JAW!
NO, MISSED IT...
I SAW GREG JOY IN THE HIGH JUMP, THOUGH!
OH YEAH! INCRED-IBLE!
PUT PUT
THE CUBAN GOT CREAMED, MAN!
WHAT'D I TELL YOU, HUH? WHAT'D I TELL YOU? I KNEW HE'D GET A MEDAL!
2.23M! THAT'S AS HIGH AS A CEILING, MAN!
DIDJA SEE HIM JUMP? SEE THOSE MOVES?
PUT PUT PUT
AND THE OTHER GUY, THE AMERI-CAN... YOU CAN'T JUMP THAT HIGH WITHOUT DRUGS!...
WHADDYA MEAN?
PUT PUT
HIS NAME SAYS IT ALL: DWIGHT'S STONED!
HAHA!
HAHA!
89

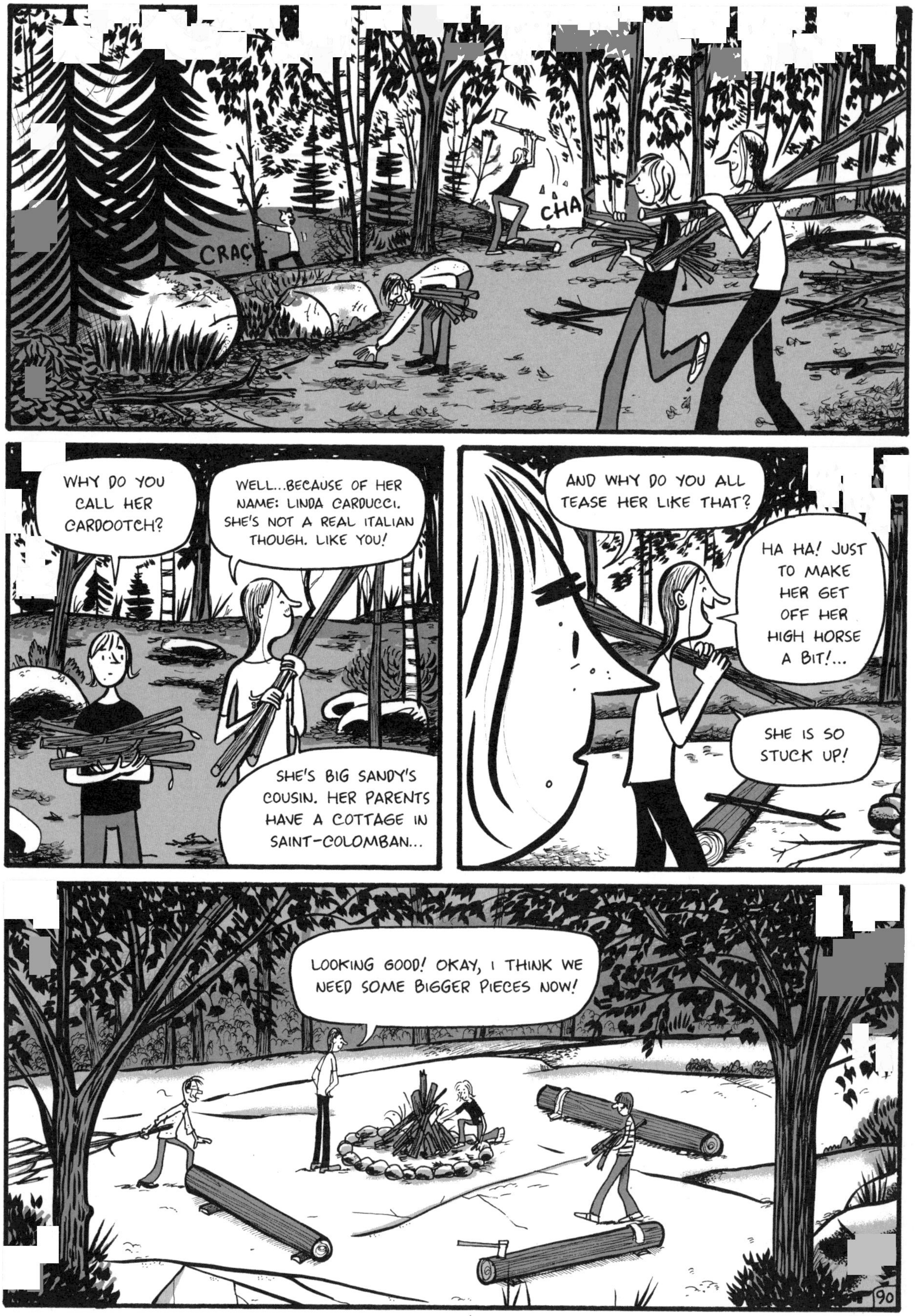
CRACK
CHA
WHY DO YOU CALL HER CARDOOTCH?
WELL...BECAUSE OF HER NAME: LINDA CARDUCCI. SHE'S NOT A REAL ITALIAN THOUGH. LIKE YOU!
SHE'S BIG SANDY'S COUSIN. HER PARENTS HAVE A COTTAGE IN SAINT-COLOMBAN...
AND WHY DO YOU ALL TEASE HER LIKE THAT?
HA HA! JUST TO MAKE HER GET OFF HER HIGH HORSE A BIT!...
SHE IS SO STUCK UP!
LOOKING GOOD! OKAY, I THINK WE NEED SOME BIGGER PIECES NOW!
90

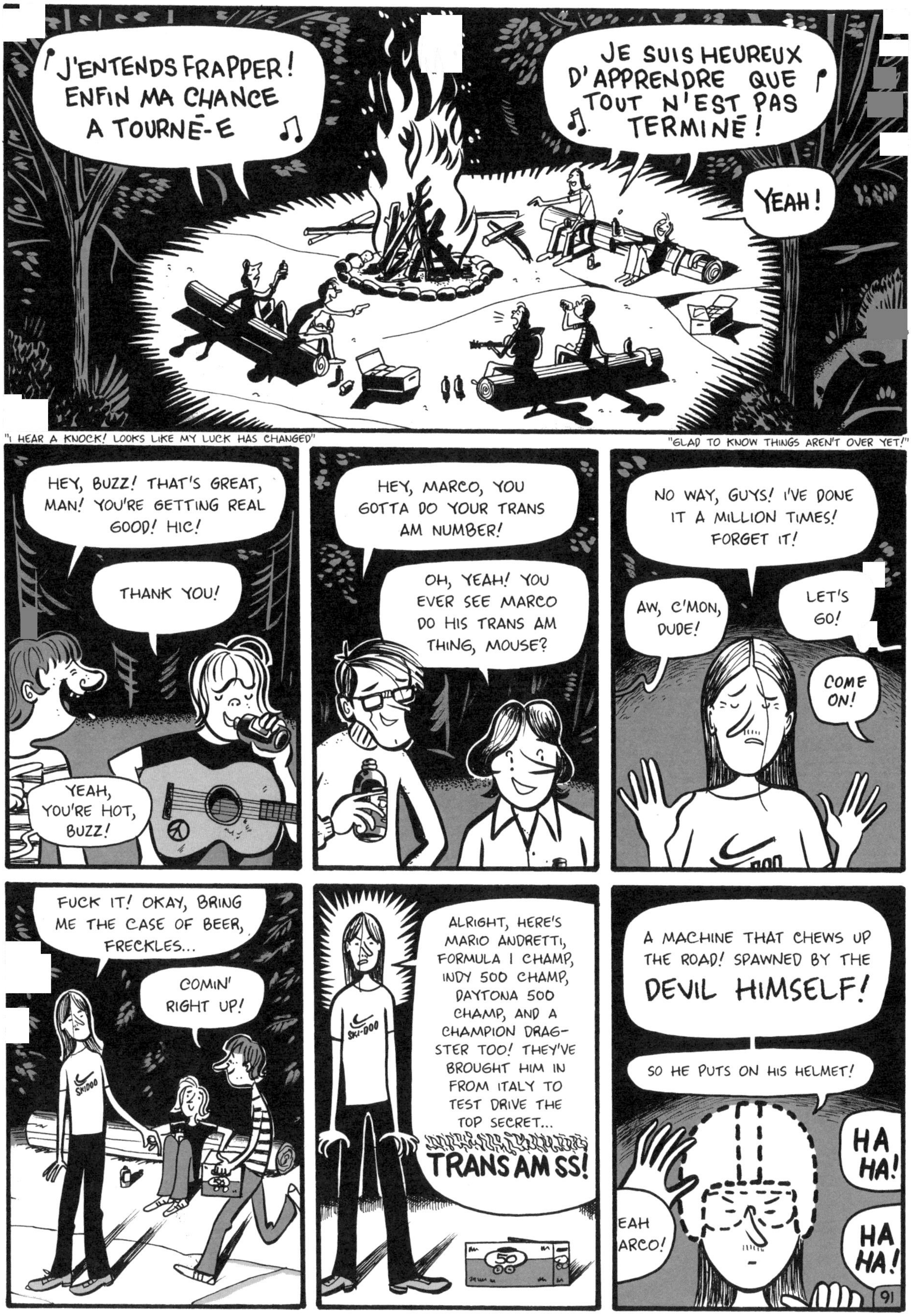
J'ENTENDS FRAPPER! ENFIN MA CHANCE A TOURNÉ-E
JE SUIS HEUREUX D'APPRENDRE QUE TOUT N'EST PAS TERMINÉ!
YEAH!
"I HEAR A KNOCK! LOOKS LIKE MY LUCK HAS CHANGED"
"GLAD TO KNOW THINGS AREN'T OVER YET!"
HEY, BUZZ! THAT'S GREAT, MAN! YOU'RE GETTING REAL GOOD! HIC!
THANK YOU!
YEAH, YOU'RE HOT, BUZZ!
HEY, MARCO, YOU GOTTA DO YOUR TRANS AM NUMBER!
OH, YEAH! YOU EVER SEE MARCO DO HIS TRANS AM THING, MOUSE?
NO WAY, GUYS! I'VE DONE IT A MILLION TIMES! FORGET IT!
AW, C'MON, DUDE!
LET'S GO!
COME ON!
FUCK IT! OKAY, BRING ME THE CASE OF BEER, FRECKLES...
COMIN' RIGHT UP!
SKIDOO
SKI-DOO
ALRIGHT, HERE'S MARIO ANDRETTI, FORMULA I CHAMP, INDY 500 CHAMP, DAYTONA 500 CHAMP, AND A CHAMPION DRAGSTER TOO! THEY'VE BROUGHT HIM IN FROM ITALY TO TEST DRIVE THE TOP SECRET...
TRANS AM SS!
50
A MACHINE THAT CHEWS UP THE ROAD! SPAWNED BY THE DEVIL HIMSELF!
SO HE PUTS ON HIS HELMET!
HA HA!
EAH ARCO!
HA HA!
91

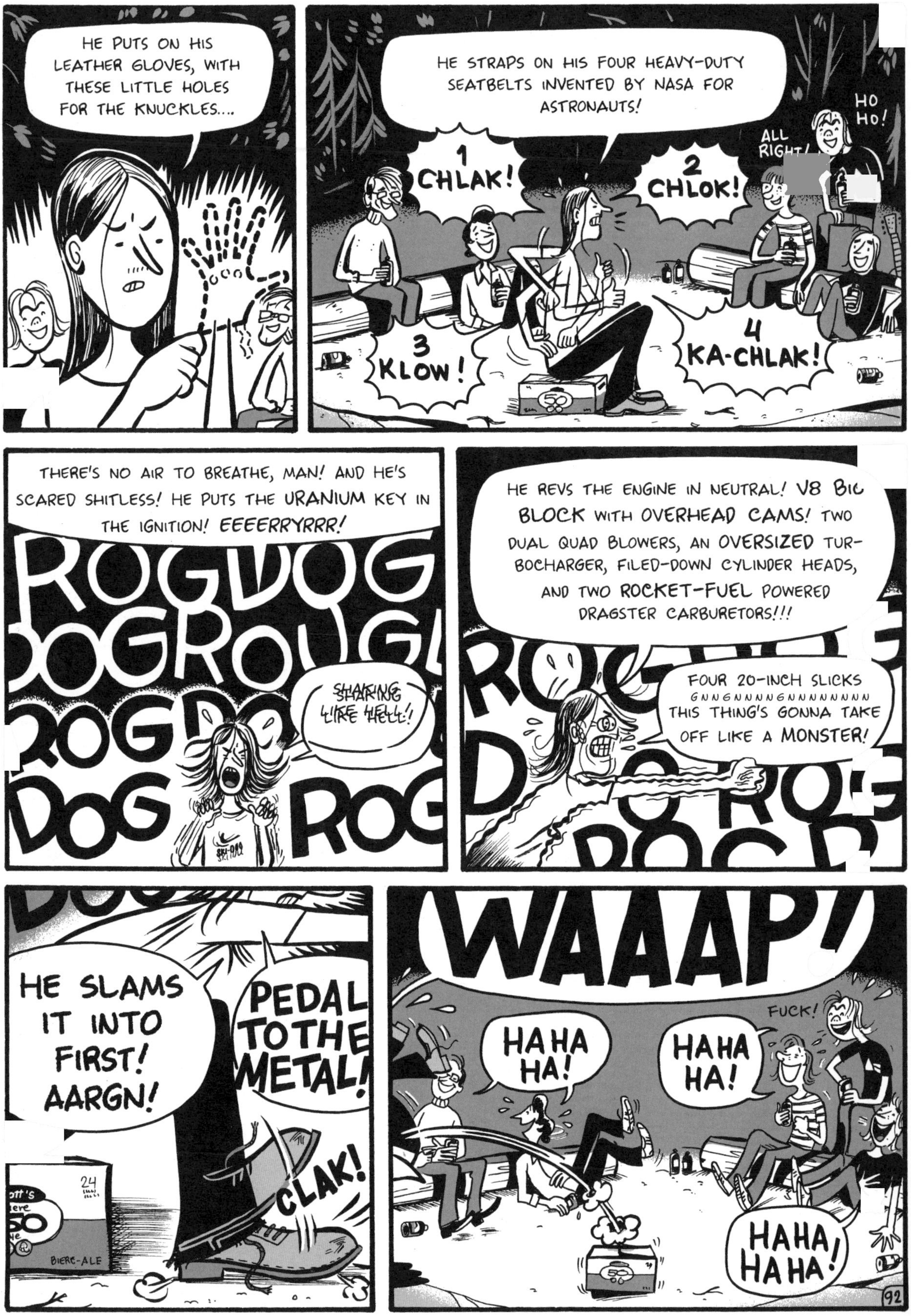

HE PUTS ON HIS LEATHER GLOVES, WITH THESE LITTLE HOLES FOR THE KNUCKLES....
HE STRAPS ON HIS FOUR HEAVY-DUTY SEATBELTS INVENTED BY NASA FOR ASTRONAUTS!
1 CHLAK!
2 CHLOK!
ALL RIGHT!
HO HO!
3 KLOW!
4 KA-CHLAK!
THERE'S NO AIR TO BREATHE, MAN! AND HE'S SCARED SHITLESS! HE PUTS THE URANIUM KEY IN THE IGNITION! EEEERRYRRR!
ROGDOG
DOG
ROG
SHAKING LIKE HELL!
HE REVS THE ENGINE IN NEUTRAL! V8 BIG BLOCK WITH OVERHEAD CAMS! TWO DUAL QUAD BLOWERS, AN OVERSIZED TURBOCHARGER, FILED-DOWN CYLINDER HEADS, AND TWO ROCKET-FUEL POWERED DRAGSTER CARBURETORS!!!
FOUR 20-INCH SLICKS GNNGNNNNGNNNNNNNN THIS THING'S GONNA TAKE OFF LIKE A MONSTER!
HE SLAMS IT INTO FIRST! AARGN!
PEDAL TO THE METAL!
CLAK!
24
BIERE-ALE
WAAAP!
FUCK!
HA HA HA!
HA HA HA!
HA HA HA HA!
92

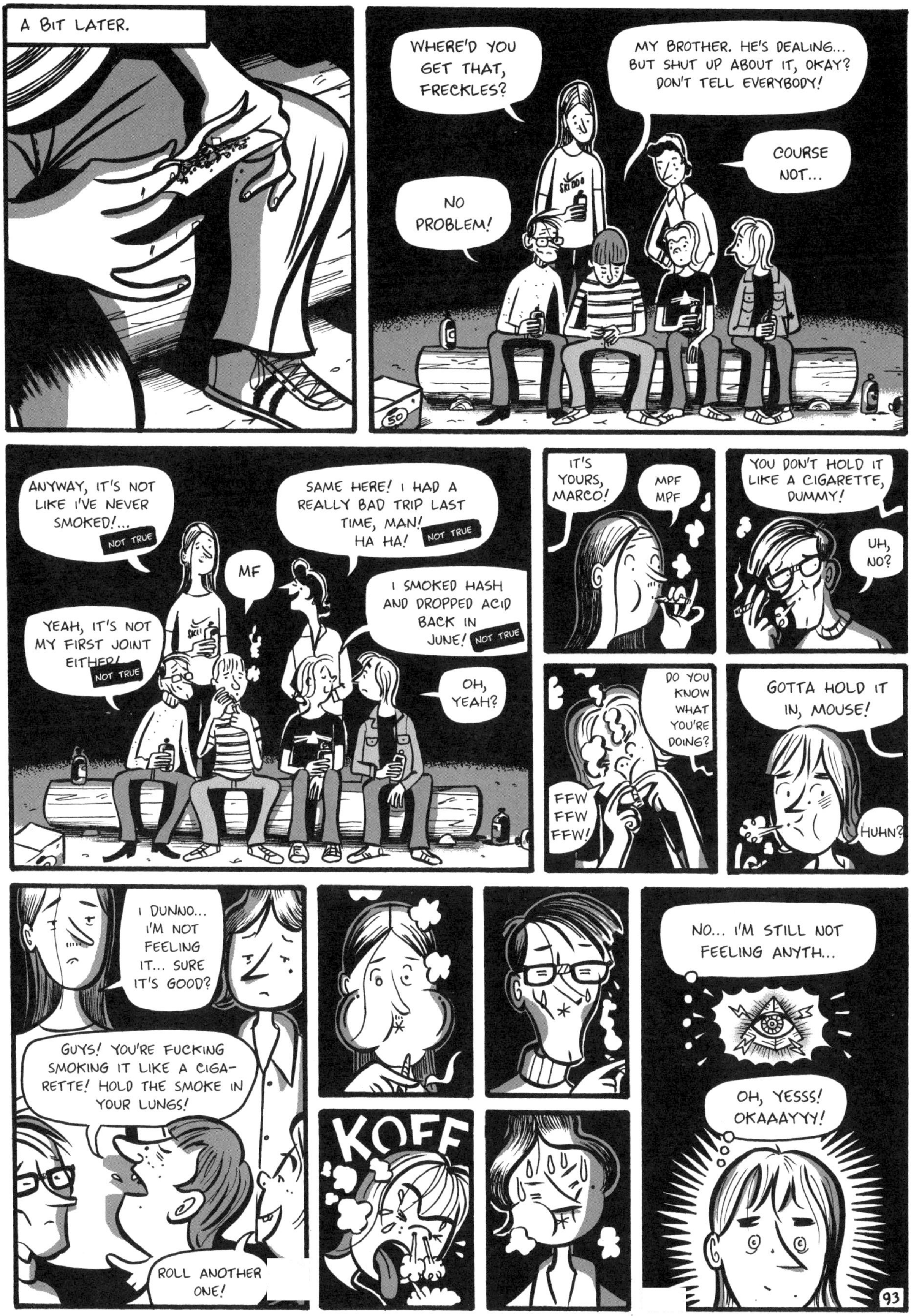
A BIT LATER.
WHERE'D YOU GET THAT, FRECKLES?
MY BROTHER. HE'S DEALING... BUT SHUT UP ABOUT IT, OKAY? DON'T TELL EVERYBODY!
COURSE NOT...
NO PROBLEM!
SKIDOO
50
ANYWAY, IT'S NOT LIKE I'VE NEVER SMOKED!...
NOT TRUE
SAME HERE! I HAD A REALLY BAD TRIP LAST TIME, MAN! HA HA!
NOT TRUE
MF
I SMOKED HASH AND DROPPED ACID BACK IN JUNE!
NOT TRUE
YEAH, IT'S NOT MY FIRST JOINT EITHER!
NOT TRUE
OH, YEAH?
IT'S YOURS, MARCO!
MPF MPF
YOU DON'T HOLD IT LIKE A CIGARETTE, DUMMY!
UH, NO?
DO YOU KNOW WHAT YOU'RE DOING?
FFW FFW FFW!
GOTTA HOLD IT IN, MOUSE!
HUHN?
I DUNNO... I'M NOT FEELING IT... SURE IT'S GOOD?
GUYS! YOU'RE FUCKING SMOKING IT LIKE A CIGA-RETTE! HOLD THE SMOKE IN YOUR LUNGS!
ROLL ANOTHER ONE!
KOFF
NO... I'M STILL NOT FEELING ANYTH...
OH, YESSS! OKAAAYYY!
93

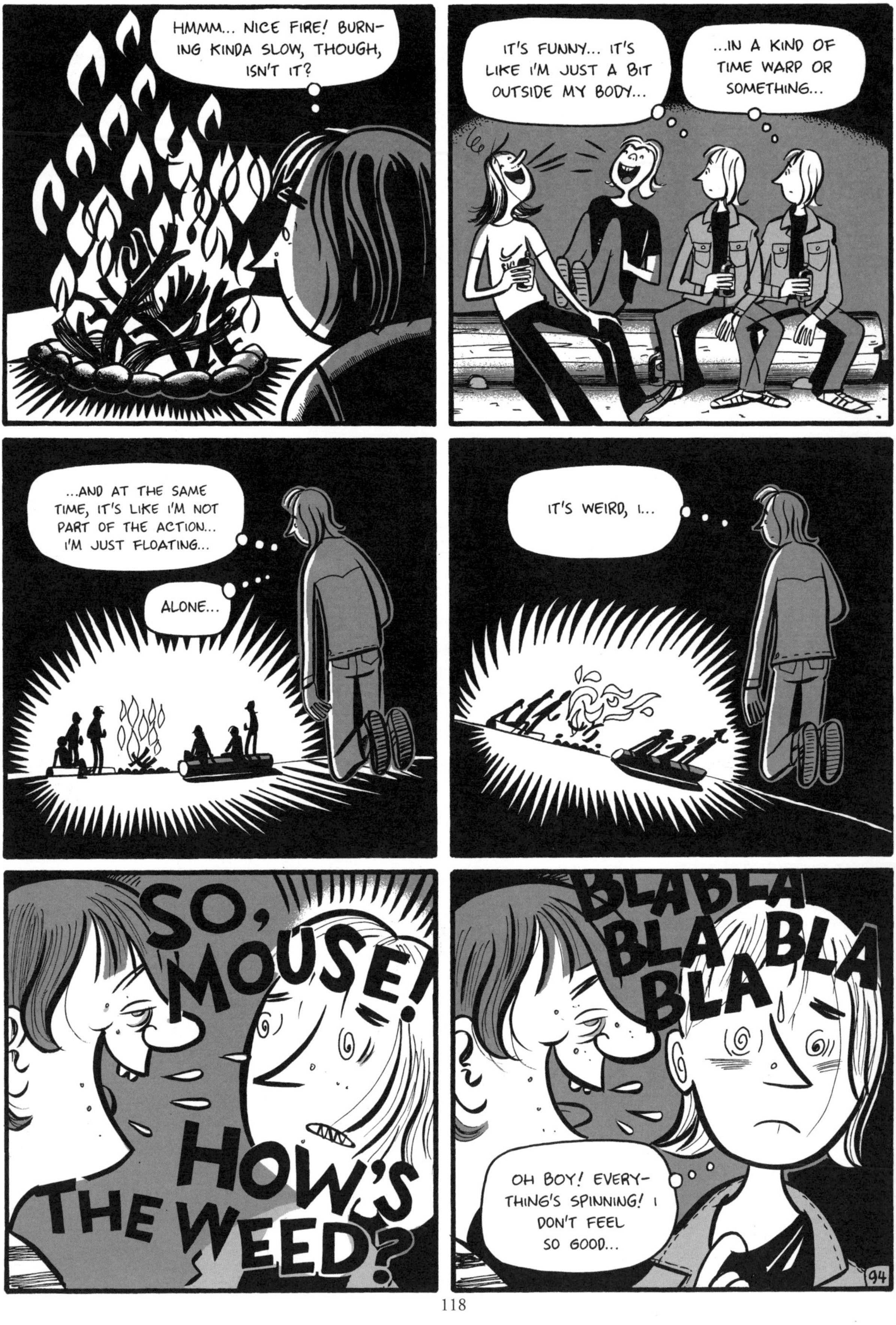
HMMM... NICE FIRE! BURNING KINDA SLOW, THOUGH, ISN'T IT?
IT'S FUNNY... IT'S LIKE I'M JUST A BIT OUTSIDE MY BODY...
...IN A KIND OF TIME WARP OR SOMETHING...
...AND AT THE SAME TIME, IT'S LIKE I'M NOT PART OF THE ACTION... I'M JUST FLOATING...
ALONE...
IT'S WEIRD, I...
SO, MOUSE! HOW'S THE WEED?
BLA BLA BLA BLA BLA
OH BOY! EVERYTHING'S SPINNING! I DON'T FEEL SO GOOD...
94

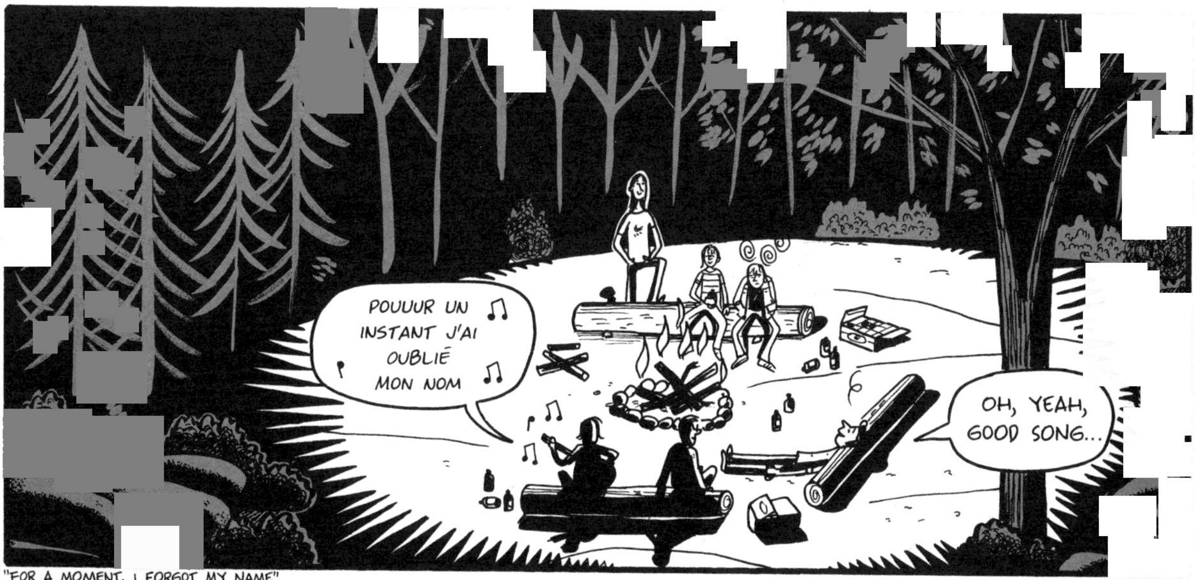
POUUUR UN INSTANT J'AI OUBLIÉ MON NOM
OH, YEAH, GOOD SONG...

"FOR A MOMENT, I FORGOT MY NAME"

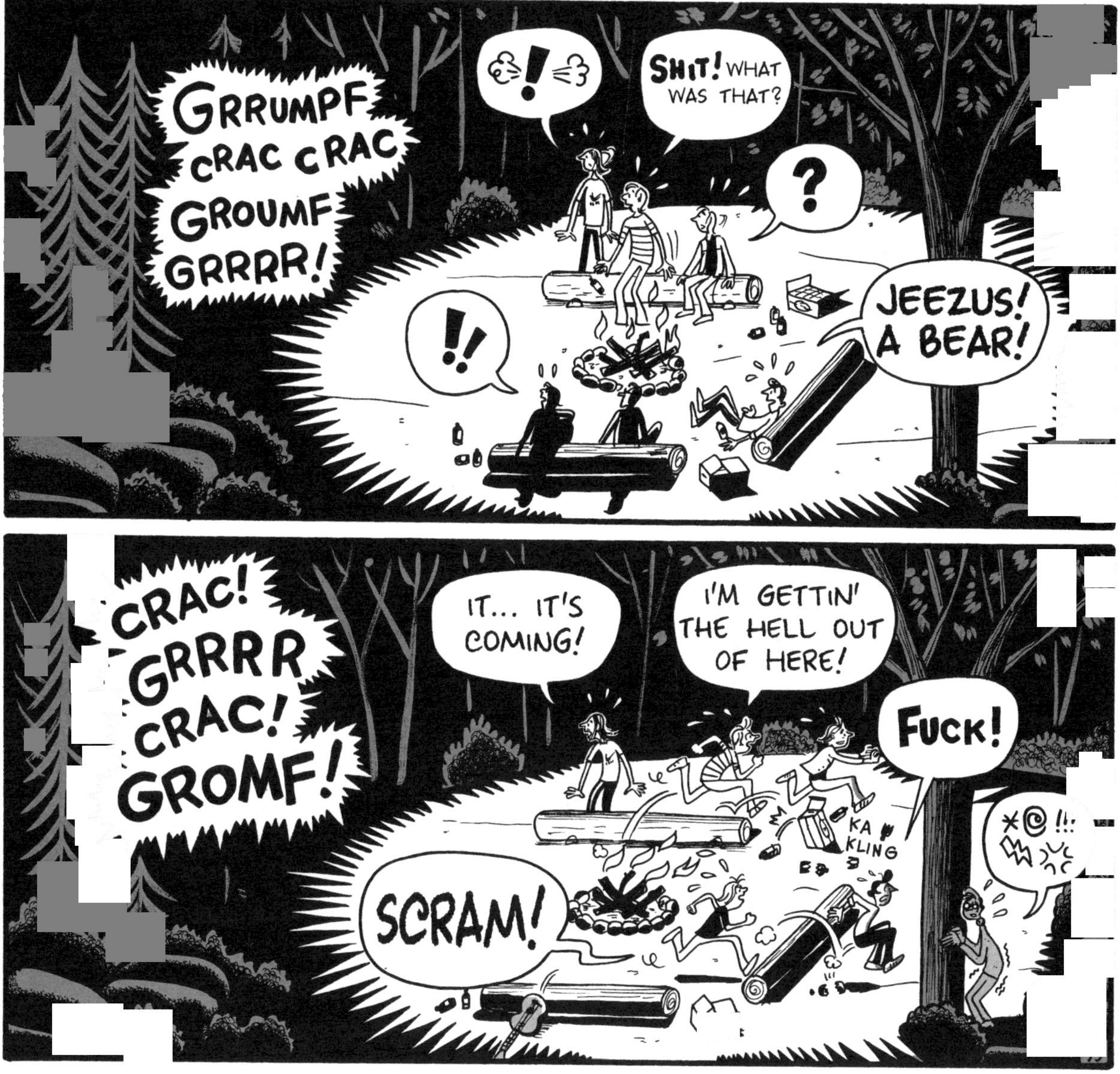
GRRUMPF CRAC CRAC GROUMF GRRRR!
!
SHIT! WHAT WAS THAT?
?
!!
JEEZUS! A BEAR!
CRAC! GRRRR CRAC! GROMF!
IT... IT'S COMING!
I'M GETTIN' THE HELL OUT OF HERE!
FUCK!
KA KLING
SCRAM!

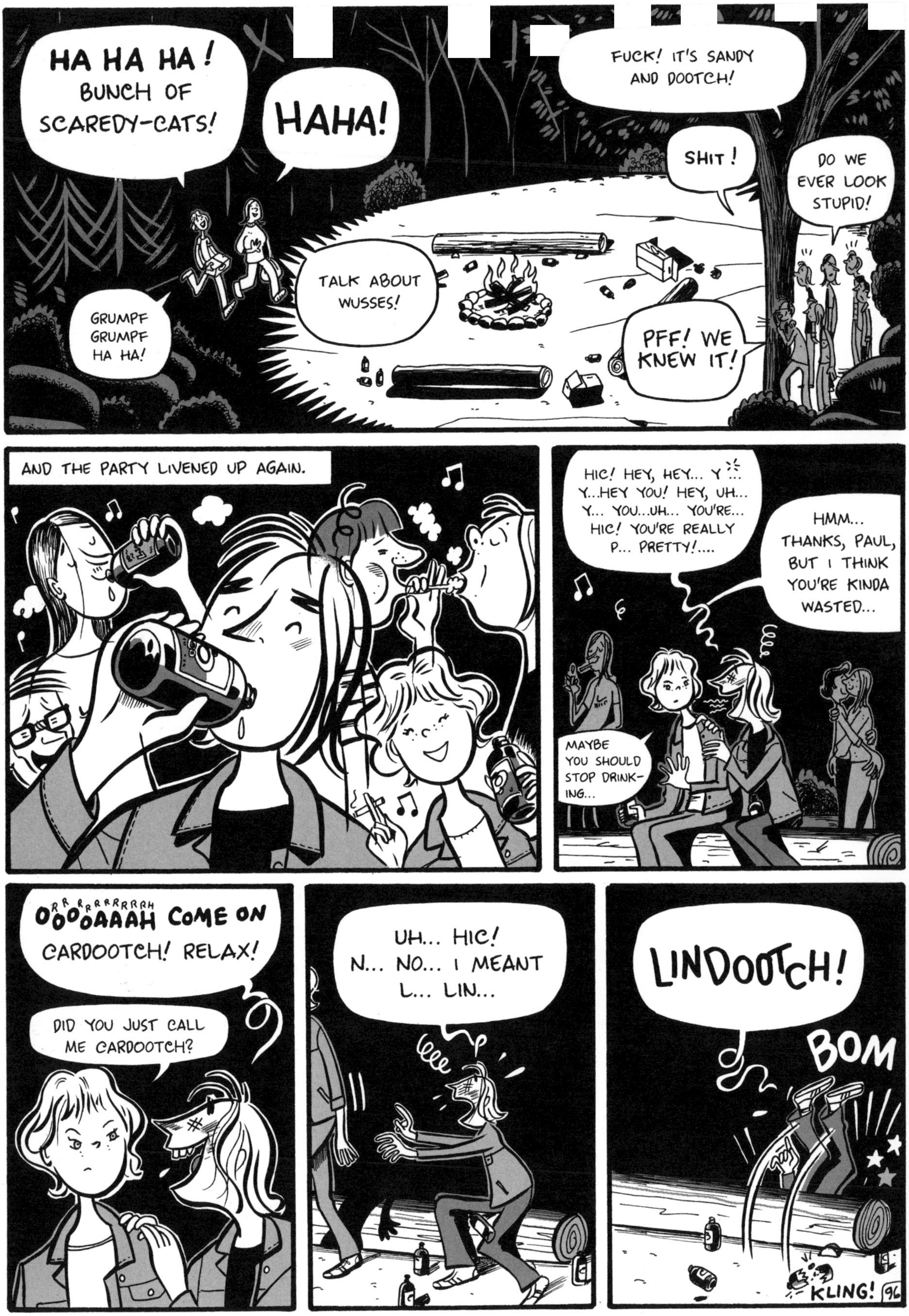
HA HA HA! BUNCH OF SCAREDY-CATS!
HAHA!
GRUMPF GRUMPF HA HA!
TALK ABOUT WUSSES!
FUCK! IT'S SANDY AND DOOTCH!
SHIT!
PFF! WE KNEW IT!
DO WE EVER LOOK STUPID!
AND THE PARTY LIVENED UP AGAIN.
HIC! HEY, HEY... Y... Y...HEY YOU! HEY, UH... Y... YOU...UH... YOU'RE... HIC! YOU'RE REALLY P... PRETTY!....
HMM... THANKS, PAUL, BUT I THINK YOU'RE KINDA WASTED...
MAYBE YOU SHOULD STOP DRINK-ING...
OOOOAAAH COME ON CARDOOTCH! RELAX!
DID YOU JUST CALL ME CARDOOTCH?
UH... HIC! N... NO... I MEANT L... LIN...
LINDOOTCH!
BOM
KLING!
96

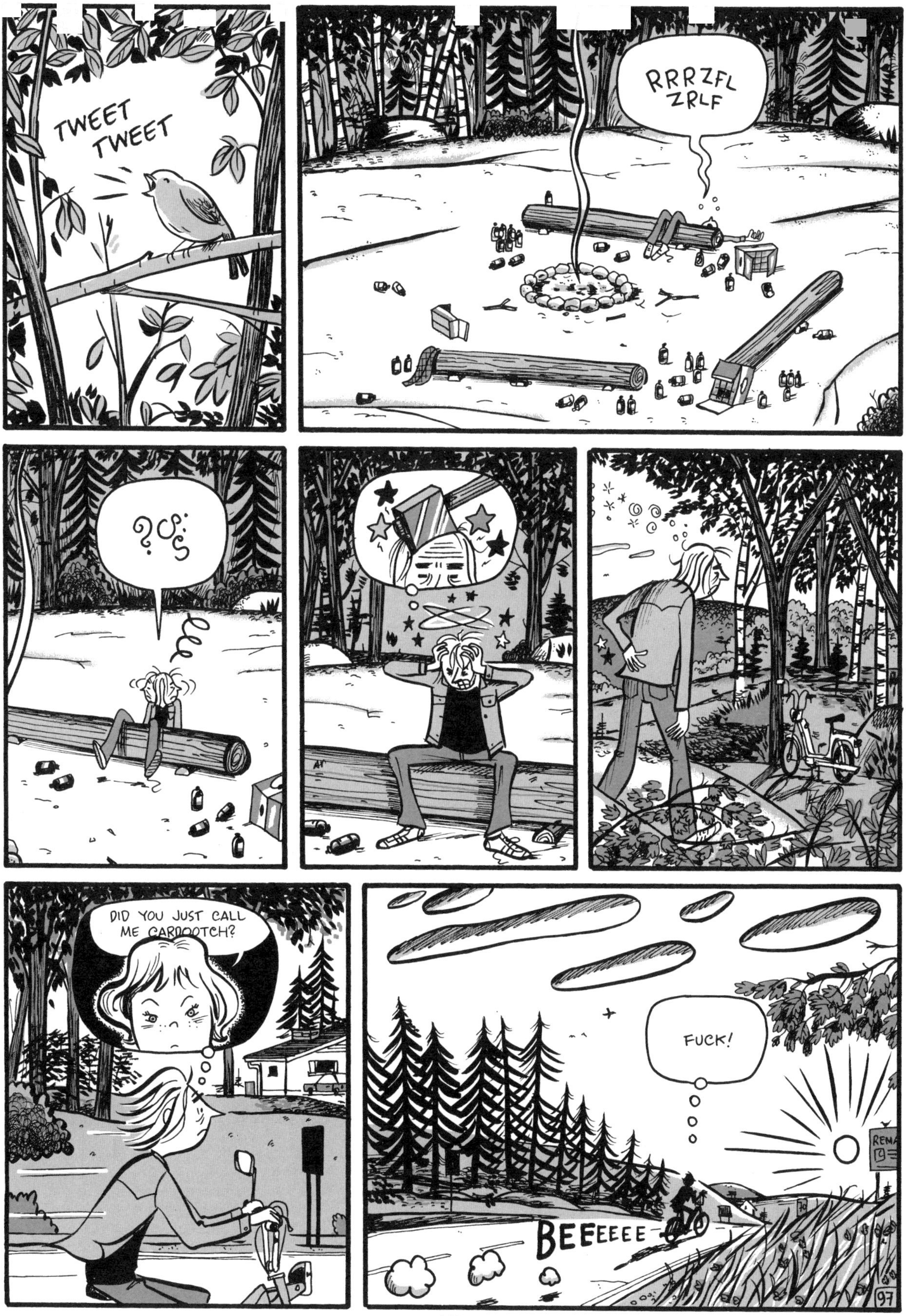
TWEET
TWEET
RRRZFL
ZRLF
DID YOU JUST CALL ME CARDOOTCH?
FUCK!
BEEEEEE

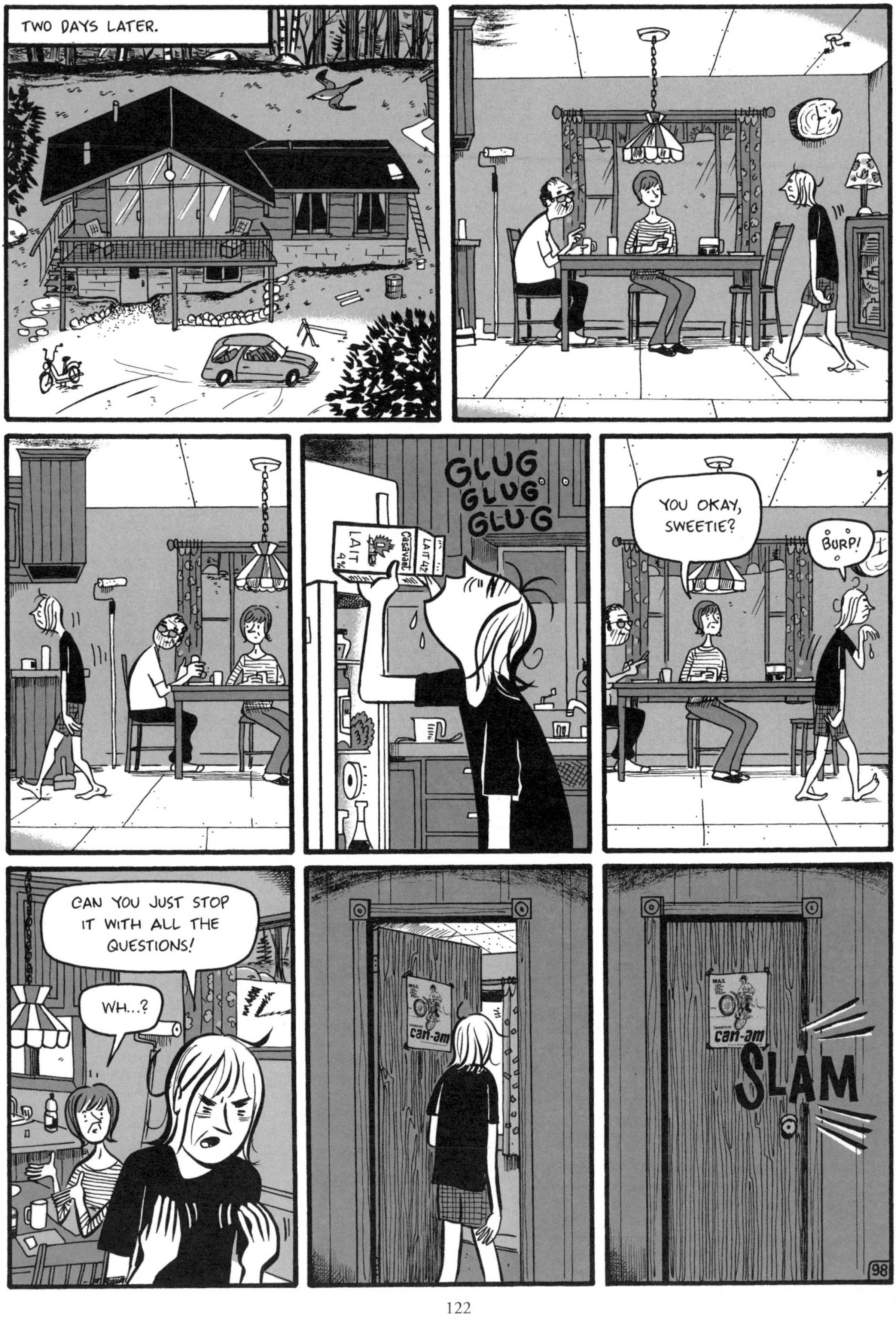
TWO DAYS LATER.
GLUG GLUG GLUG
YOU OKAY, SWEETIE?
BURP!
CAN YOU JUST STOP IT WITH ALL THE QUESTIONS!
WH...?
SLAM
98

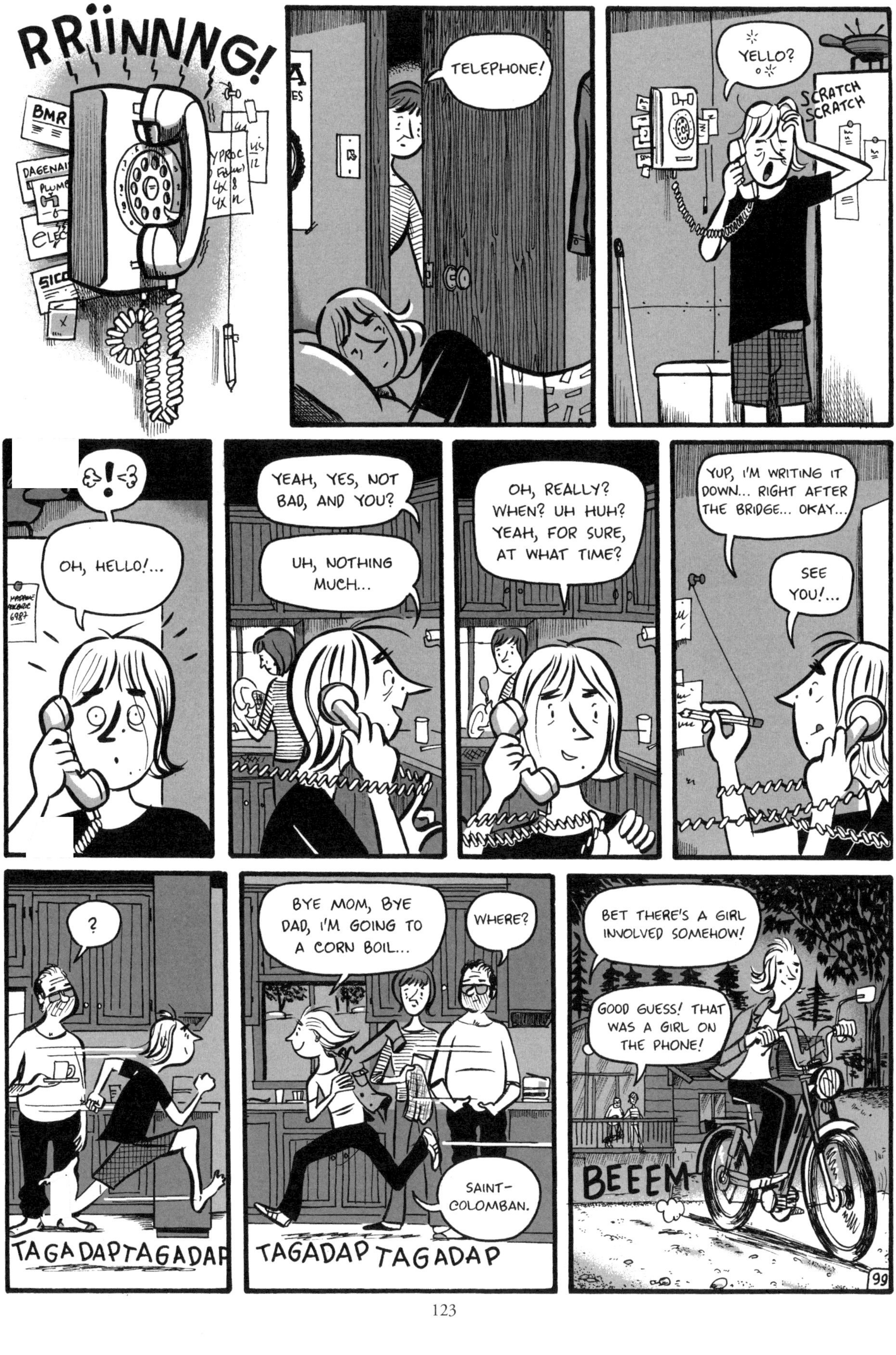
RRiiNNNG!
TELEPHONE!
YELLO?
SCRATCH
SCRATCH
!
OH, HELLO!...
YEAH, YES, NOT BAD, AND YOU?
UH, NOTHING MUCH...
OH, REALLY? WHEN? UH HUH? YEAH, FOR SURE, AT WHAT TIME?
YUP, I'M WRITING IT DOWN... RIGHT AFTER THE BRIDGE... OKAY...
SEE YOU!...
?
TAGADAPTAGADAP
BYE MOM, BYE DAD, I'M GOING TO A CORN BOIL...
WHERE?
SAINT-COLOMBAN.
TAGADAP TAGADAP
BET THERE'S A GIRL INVOLVED SOMEHOW!
GOOD GUESS! THAT WAS A GIRL ON THE PHONE!
BEEEM
99

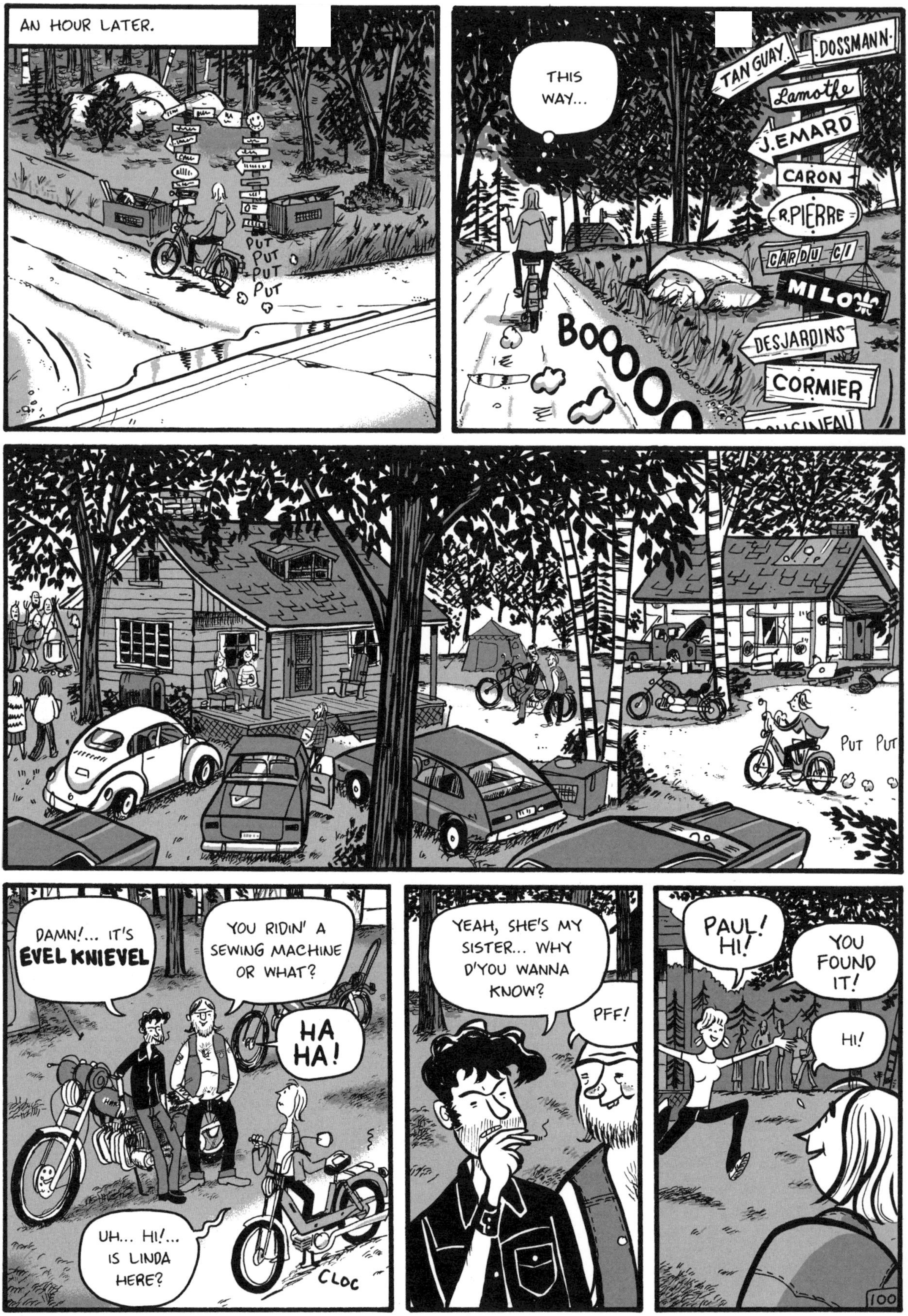
AN HOUR LATER.
PUT
PUT
PUT
PUT
PUT
THIS WAY...
TANGUAY
DOSSMANN
Lamothe
J.EMARD
CARON
R.PIERRE
CARDU CI
MILO
DESJARDINS
CORMIER
BOOOOO
PUT PUT
DAMN!... IT'S EVEL KNIEVEL
YOU RIDIN' A SEWING MACHINE OR WHAT?
HA HA!
UH... HI!... IS LINDA HERE?
CLOC
YEAH, SHE'S MY SISTER... WHY D'YOU WANNA KNOW?
PFF!
PAUL! HI!
YOU FOUND IT!
HI!
100

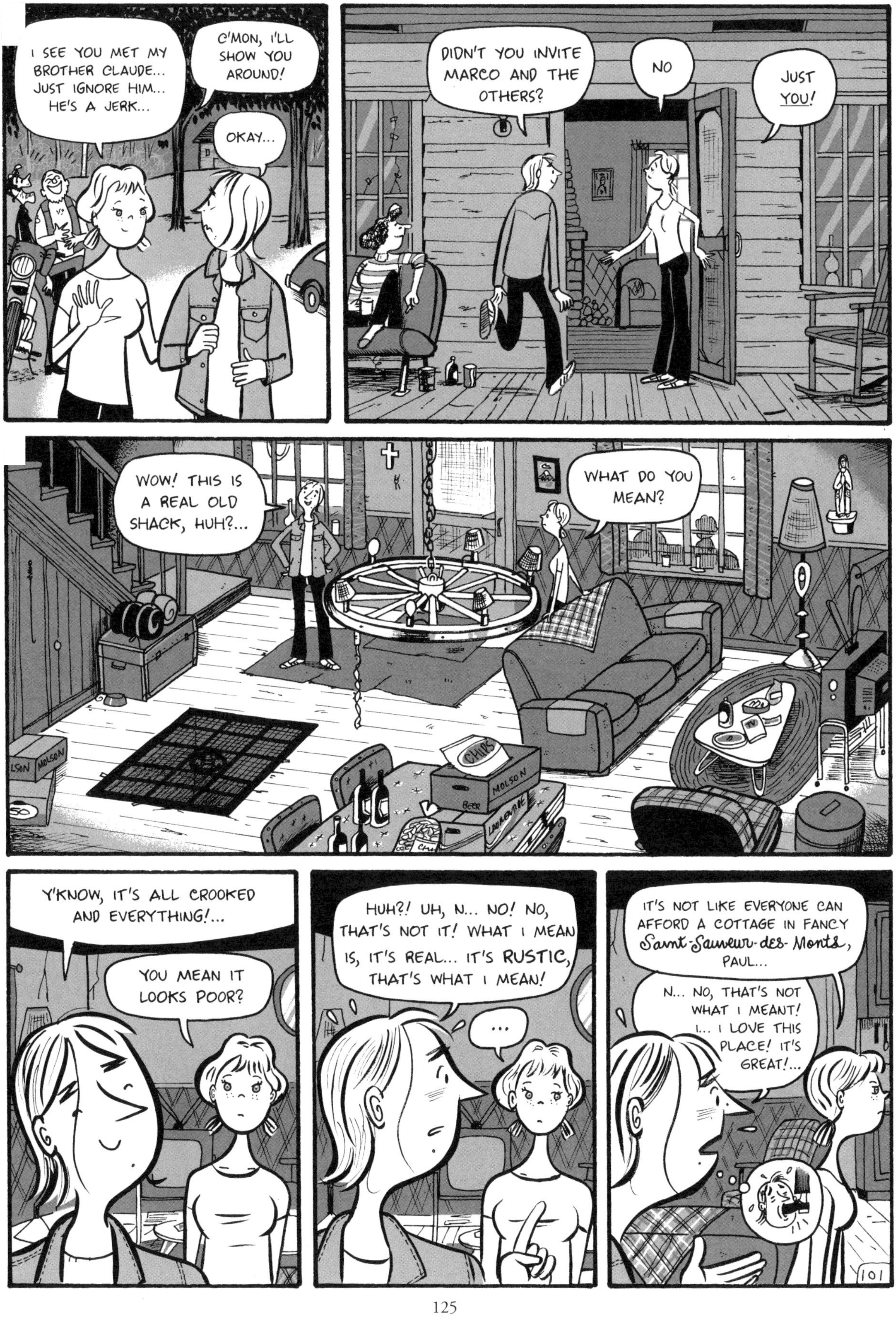
I SEE YOU MET MY BROTHER CLAUDE... JUST IGNORE HIM... HE'S A JERK...
C'MON, I'LL SHOW YOU AROUND!
OKAY...
DIDN'T YOU INVITE MARCO AND THE OTHERS?
NO
JUST YOU!
WOW! THIS IS A REAL OLD SHACK, HUH?...
WHAT DO YOU MEAN?
CHIPS
MOLSON
BEER
MOLSON
Y'KNOW, IT'S ALL CROOKED AND EVERYTHING!...
YOU MEAN IT LOOKS POOR?
HUH?! UH, N... NO! NO, THAT'S NOT IT! WHAT I MEAN IS, IT'S REAL... IT'S RUSTIC, THAT'S WHAT I MEAN!
...
IT'S NOT LIKE EVERYONE CAN AFFORD A COTTAGE IN FANCY Saint-Sauveur-des-Monts, PAUL...
N... NO, THAT'S NOT WHAT I MEANT! I... I LOVE THIS PLACE! IT'S GREAT!...
101

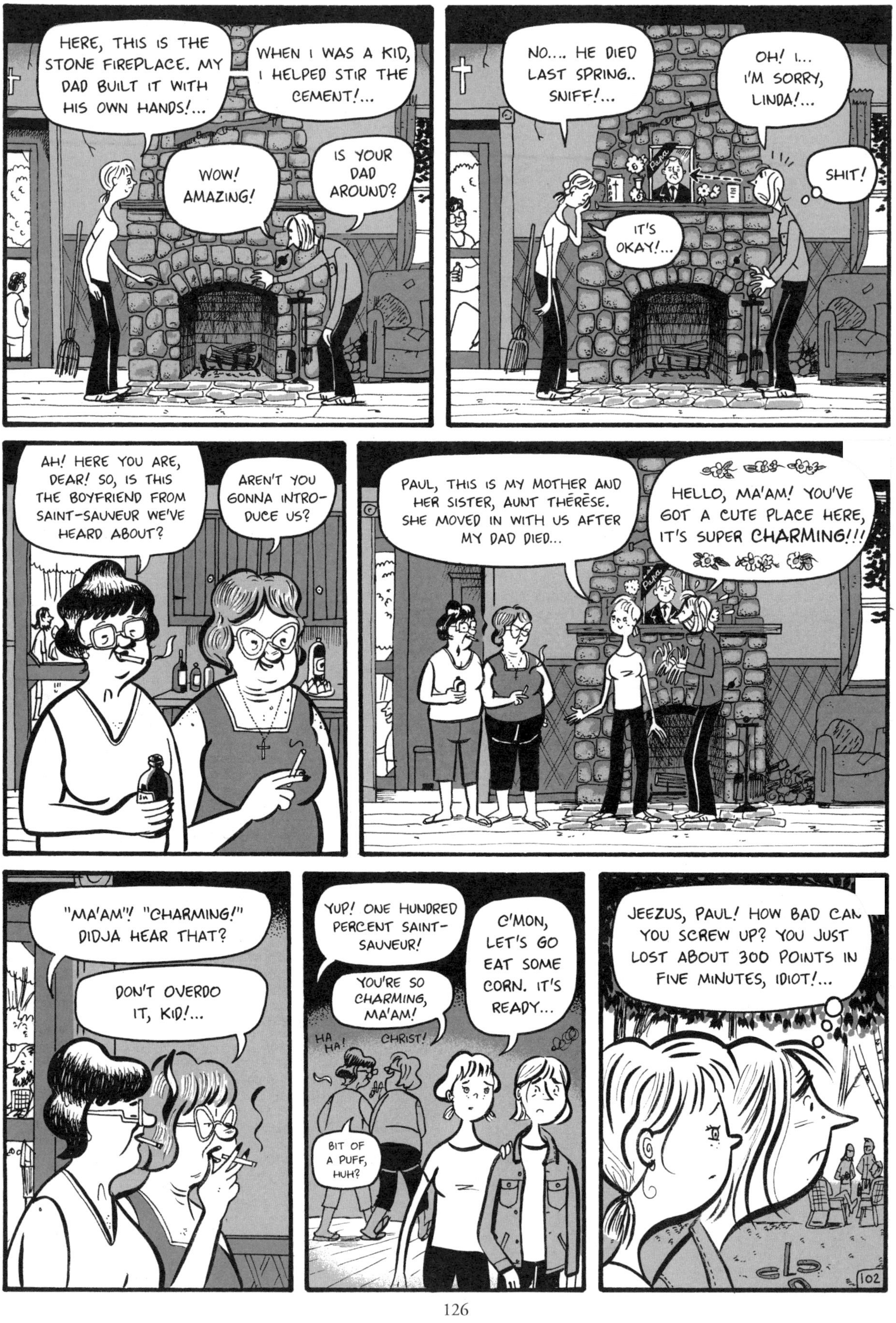
HERE, THIS IS THE STONE FIREPLACE. MY DAD BUILT IT WITH HIS OWN HANDS!...
WHEN I WAS A KID, I HELPED STIR THE CEMENT!...
WOW! AMAZING!
IS YOUR DAD AROUND?
NO.... HE DIED LAST SPRING.. SNIFF!...
OH! I... I'M SORRY, LINDA!...
SHIT!
IT'S OKAY!...
AH! HERE YOU ARE, DEAR! SO, IS THIS THE BOYFRIEND FROM SAINT-SAUVEUR WE'VE HEARD ABOUT?
AREN'T YOU GONNA INTRO-DUCE US?
PAUL, THIS IS MY MOTHER AND HER SISTER, AUNT THÉRÈSE. SHE MOVED IN WITH US AFTER MY DAD DIED...
HELLO, MA'AM! YOU'VE GOT A CUTE PLACE HERE, IT'S SUPER CHARMING!!!
"MA'AM"! "CHARMING!" DIDJA HEAR THAT?
DON'T OVERDO IT, KID!...
YUP! ONE HUNDRED PERCENT SAINT-SAUVEUR!
YOU'RE SO CHARMING, MA'AM!
HA HA!
CHRIST!
BIT OF A PUFF, HUH?
C'MON, LET'S GO EAT SOME CORN. IT'S READY...
JEEZUS, PAUL! HOW BAD CAN YOU SCREW UP? YOU JUST LOST ABOUT 300 POINTS IN FIVE MINUTES, IDIOT!...
102

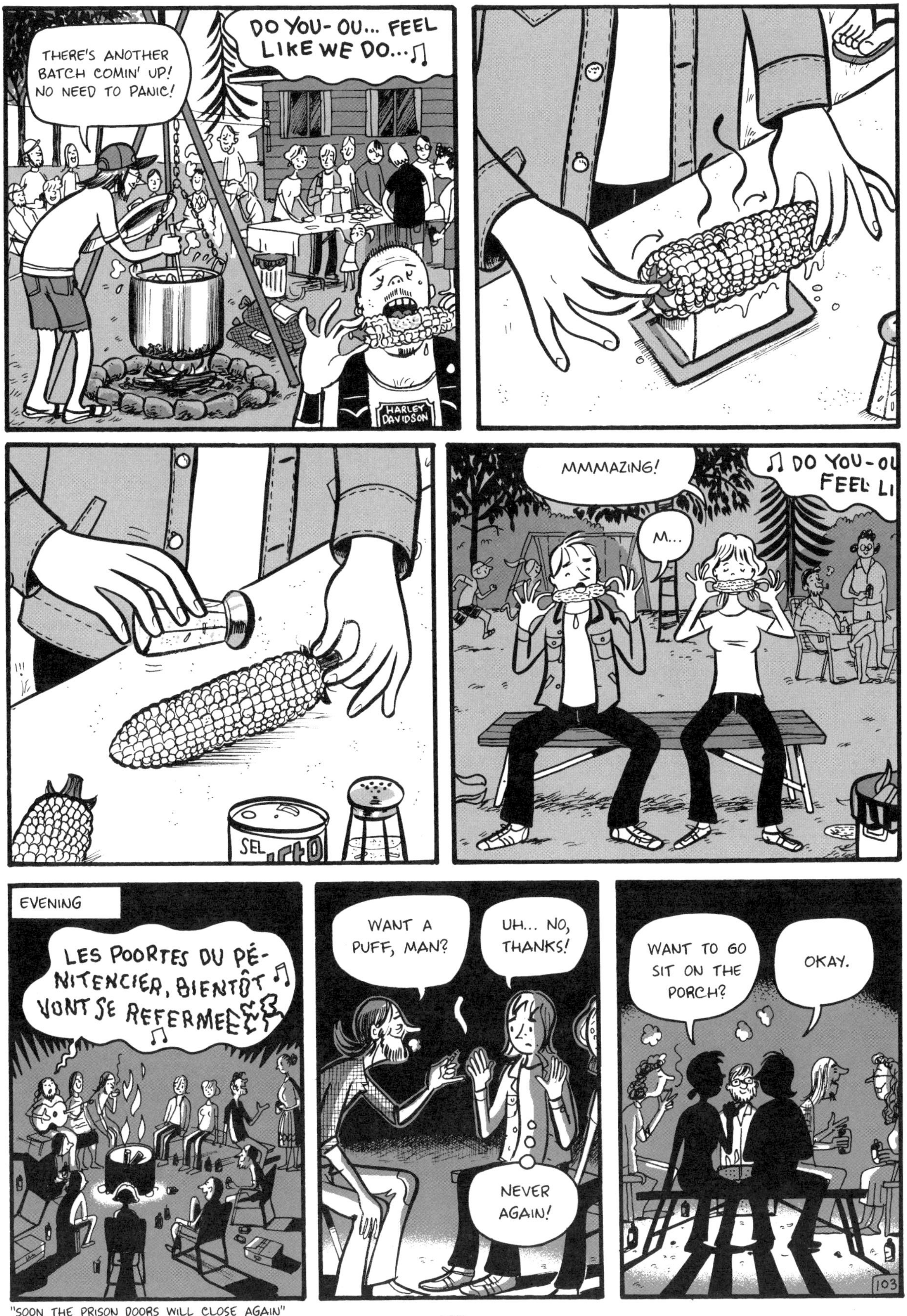
THERE'S ANOTHER BATCH COMIN' UP! NO NEED TO PANIC!
DO YOU-OU... FEEL LIKE WE DO...♫
HARLEY DAVIDSON
MMMAZING!
M...
♫ DO YOU-OU FEEL LI
SEL
EVENING
LES POORTES DU PÉNITENCIER, BIENTÔT VONT SE REFERMEEE ♫
WANT A PUFF, MAN?
UH... NO, THANKS!
NEVER AGAIN!
WANT TO GO SIT ON THE PORCH?
OKAY.
103
"SOON THE PRISON DOORS WILL CLOSE AGAIN"

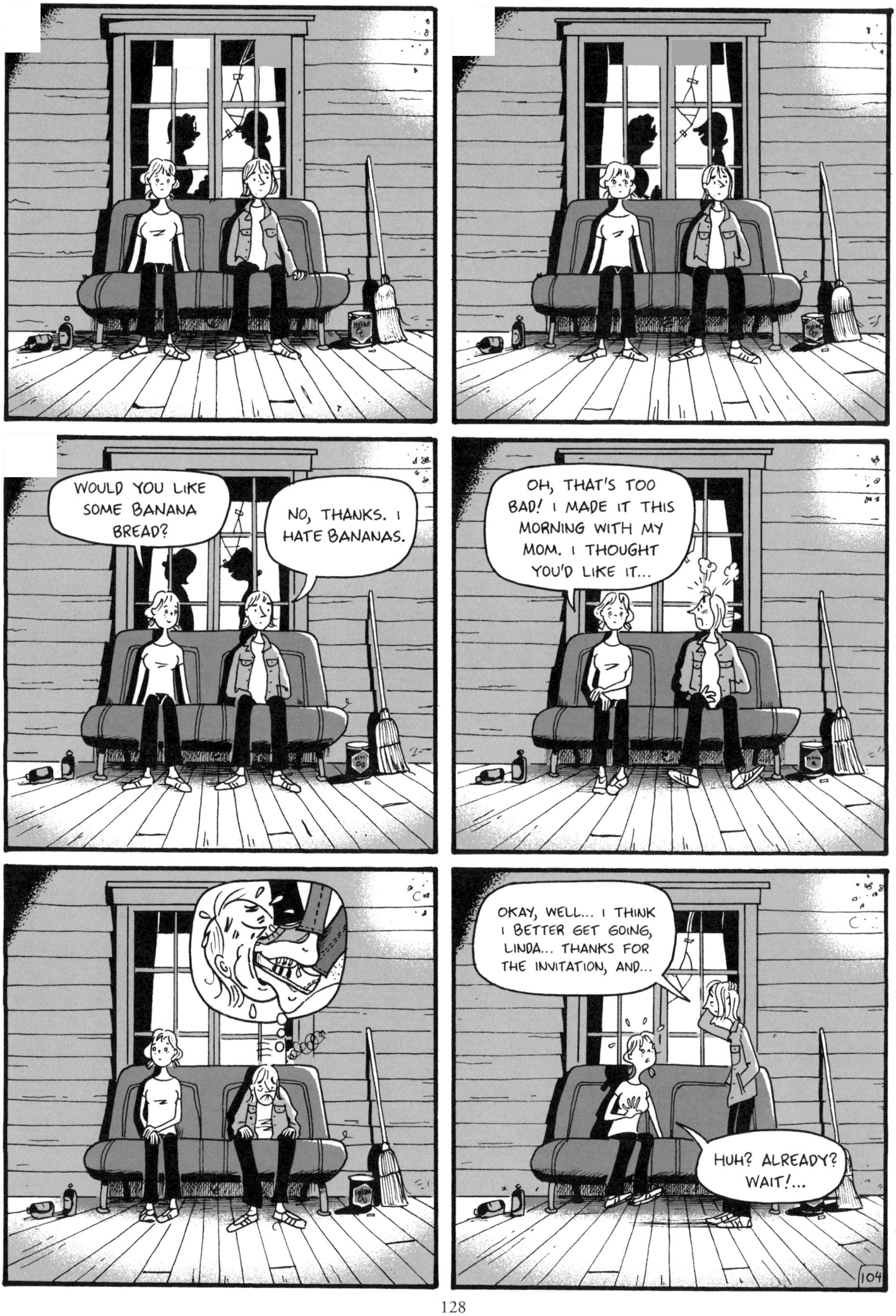
WOULD YOU LIKE SOME BANANA BREAD?
NO, THANKS. I HATE BANANAS.
OH, THAT'S TOO BAD! I MADE IT THIS MORNING WITH MY MOM. I THOUGHT YOU'D LIKE IT...
OKAY, WELL... I THINK I BETTER GET GOING, LINDA... THANKS FOR THE INVITATION, AND...
HUH? ALREADY? WAIT!...
104

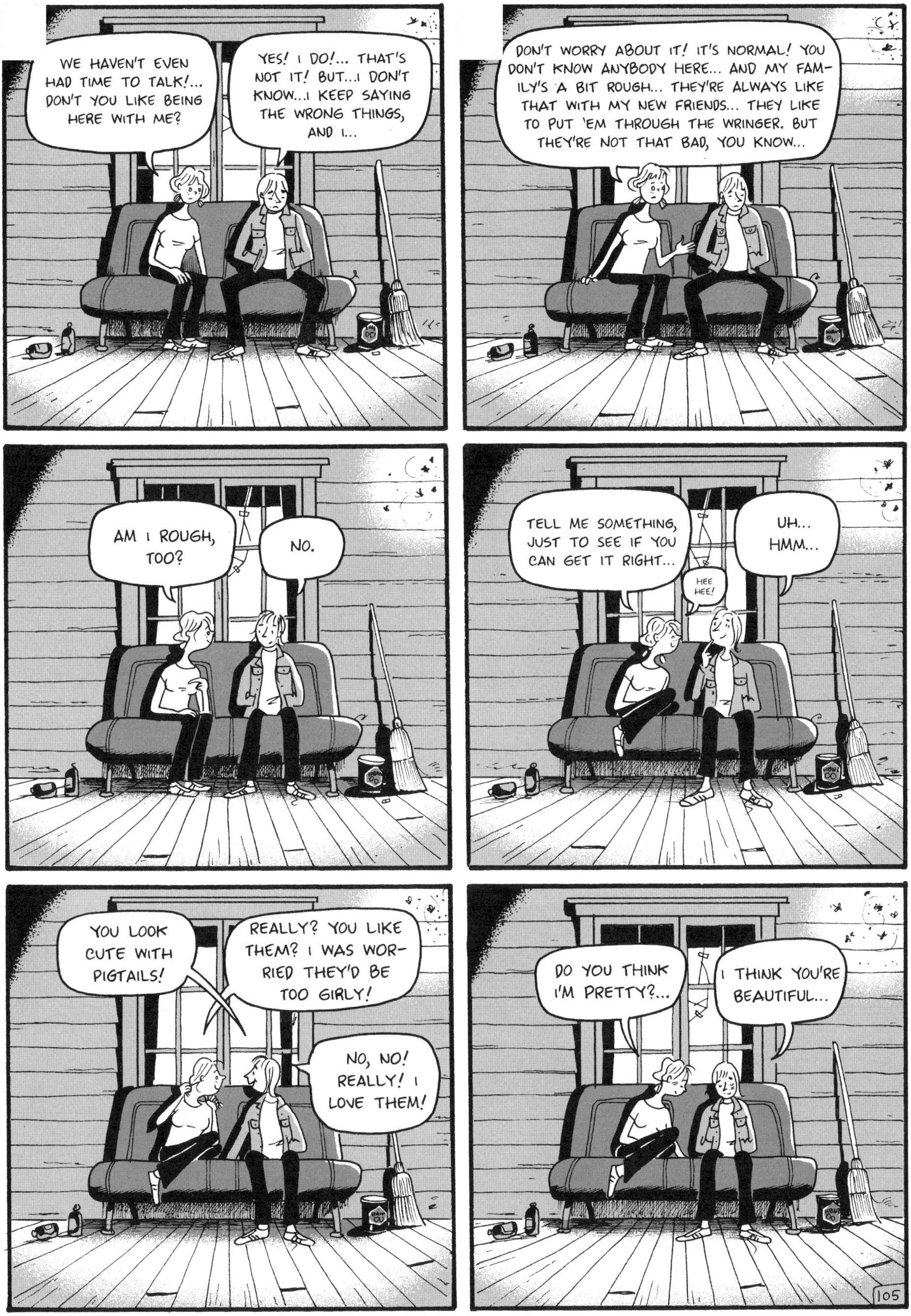
WE HAVEN'T EVEN HAD TIME TO TALK!... DON'T YOU LIKE BEING HERE WITH ME?
YES! I DO!... THAT'S NOT IT! BUT...I DON'T KNOW...I KEEP SAYING THE WRONG THINGS, AND I...
DON'T WORRY ABOUT IT! IT'S NORMAL! YOU DON'T KNOW ANYBODY HERE... AND MY FAMILY'S A BIT ROUGH... THEY'RE ALWAYS LIKE THAT WITH MY NEW FRIENDS... THEY LIKE TO PUT 'EM THROUGH THE WRINGER. BUT THEY'RE NOT THAT BAD, YOU KNOW...
AM I ROUGH, TOO?
NO.
TELL ME SOMETHING, JUST TO SEE IF YOU CAN GET IT RIGHT...
HEE HEE!
UH... HMM...
YOU LOOK CUTE WITH PIGTAILS!
REALLY? YOU LIKE THEM? I WAS WORRIED THEY'D BE TOO GIRLY!
NO, NO! REALLY! I LOVE THEM!
DO YOU THINK I'M PRETTY?...
I THINK YOU'RE BEAUTIFUL...
105

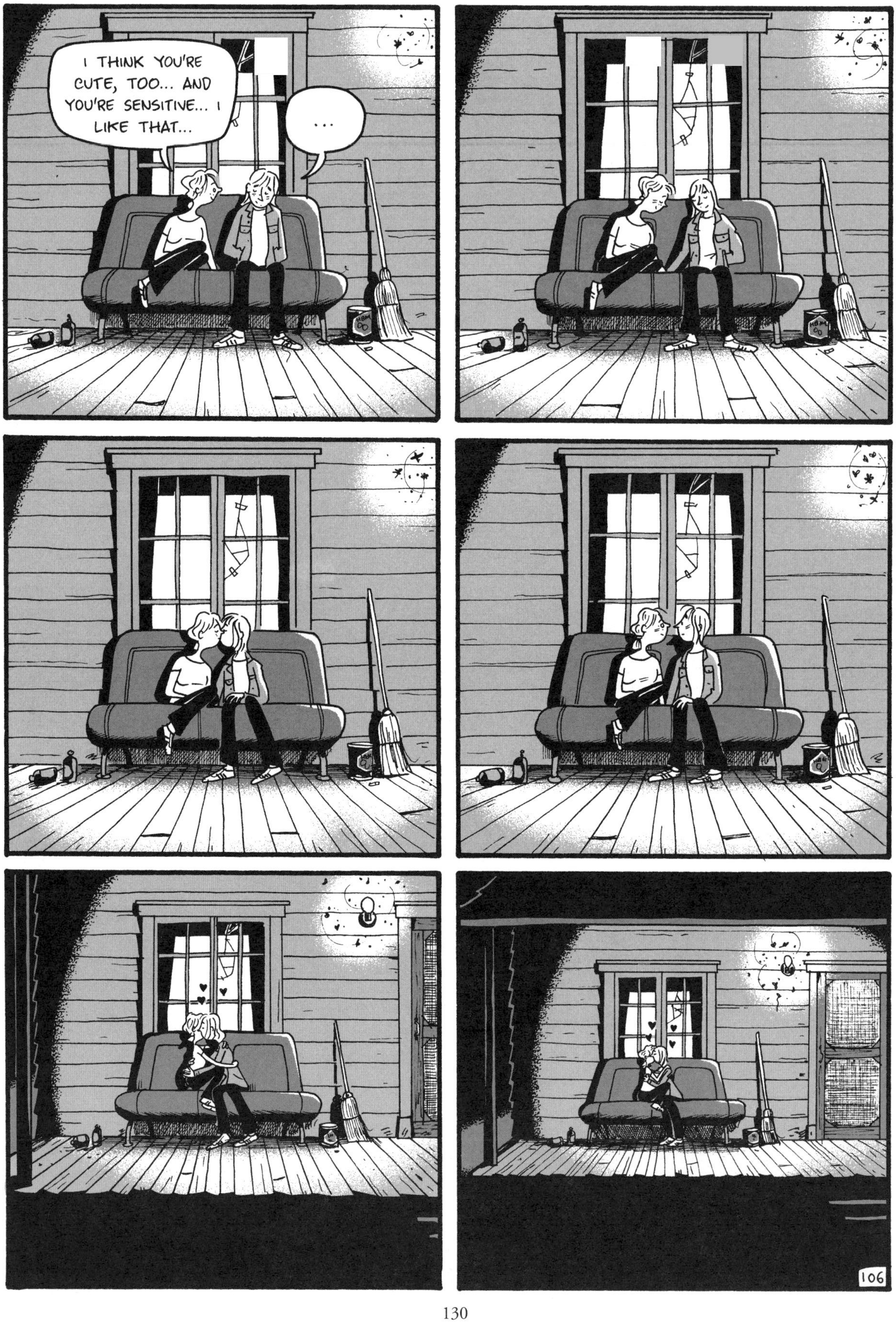
I THINK YOU'RE CUTE, TOO... AND YOU'RE SENSITIVE... I LIKE THAT...
...
106

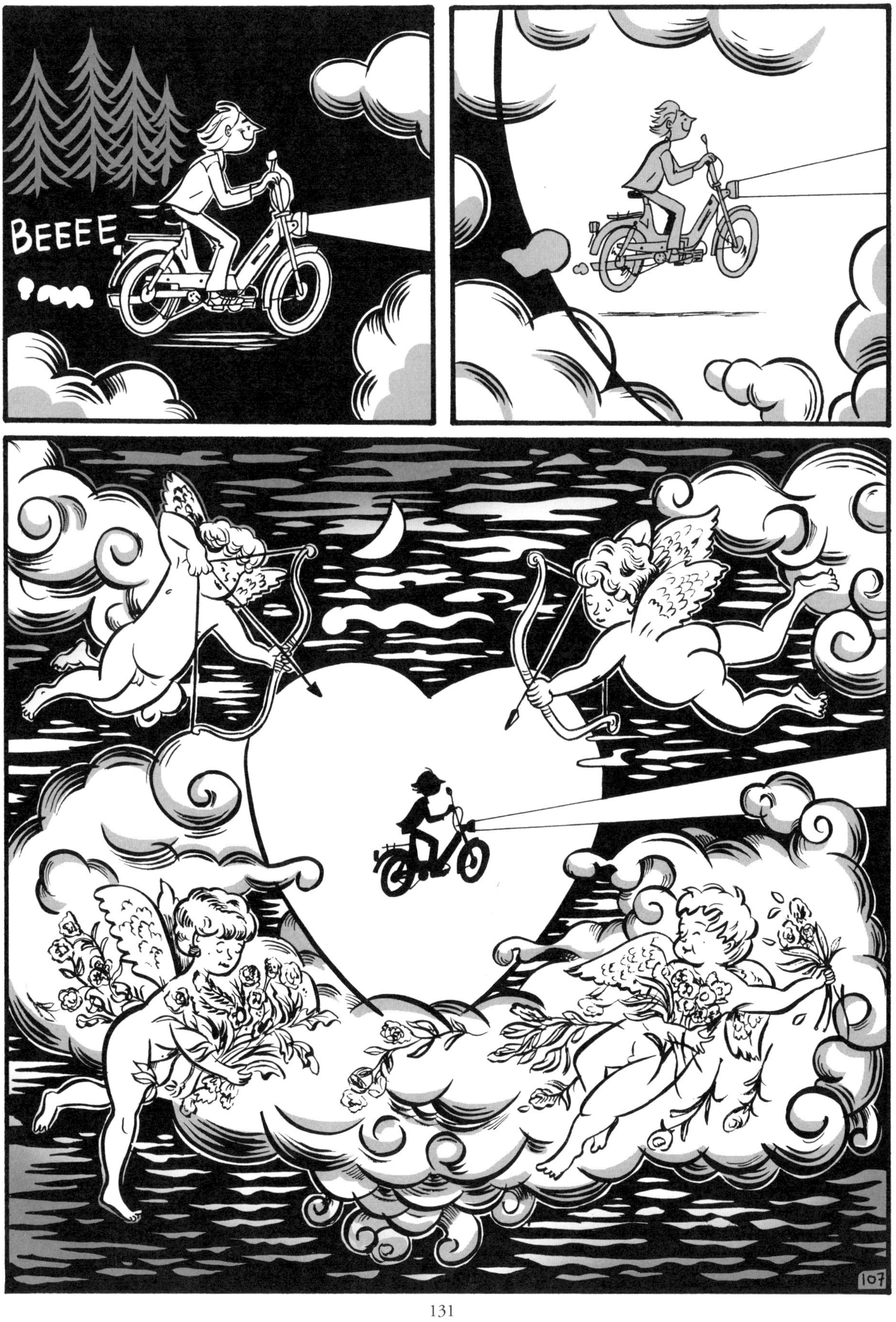
BEEEE
107

Nadia

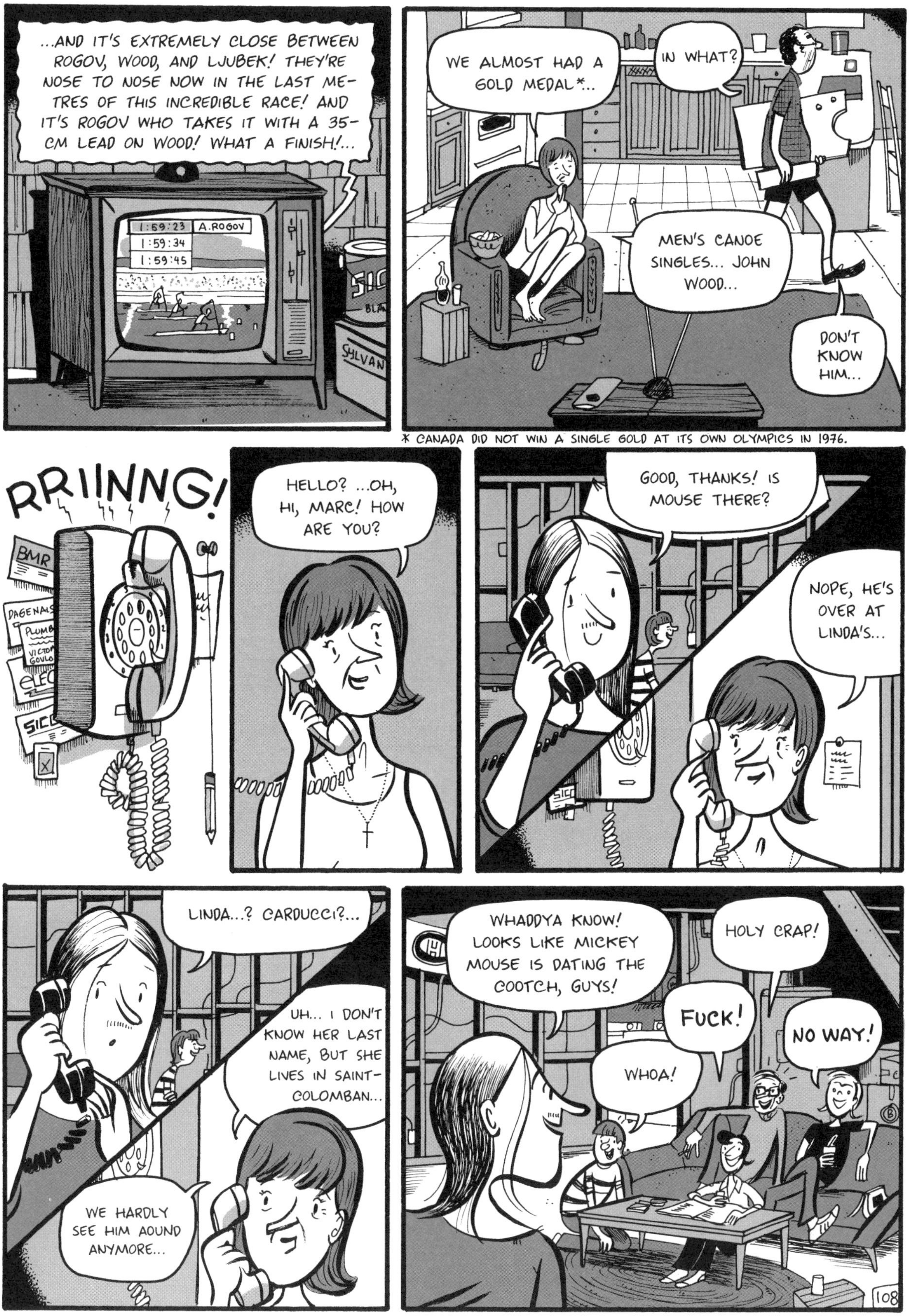
...AND IT'S EXTREMELY CLOSE BETWEEN ROGOV, WOOD, AND LJUBEK! THEY'RE NOSE TO NOSE NOW IN THE LAST METRES OF THIS INCREDIBLE RACE! AND IT'S ROGOV WHO TAKES IT WITH A 35-CM LEAD ON WOOD! WHAT A FINISH!...
1:59:23 A.ROGOV
1:59:34
1:59:45
WE ALMOST HAD A GOLD MEDAL*...
IN WHAT?
MEN'S CANOE SINGLES... JOHN WOOD...
DON'T KNOW HIM...
* CANADA DID NOT WIN A SINGLE GOLD AT ITS OWN OLYMPICS IN 1976.
RRIINNG!
HELLO? ...OH, HI, MARC! HOW ARE YOU?
GOOD, THANKS! IS MOUSE THERE?
NOPE, HE'S OVER AT LINDA'S...
LINDA...? CARDUCCI?...
UH... I DON'T KNOW HER LAST NAME, BUT SHE LIVES IN SAINT-COLOMBAN...
WE HARDLY SEE HIM AOUND ANYMORE...
WHADDYA KNOW! LOOKS LIKE MICKEY MOUSE IS DATING THE COOTCH, GUYS!
HOLY CRAP!
FUCK!
NO WAY!
WHOA!
108

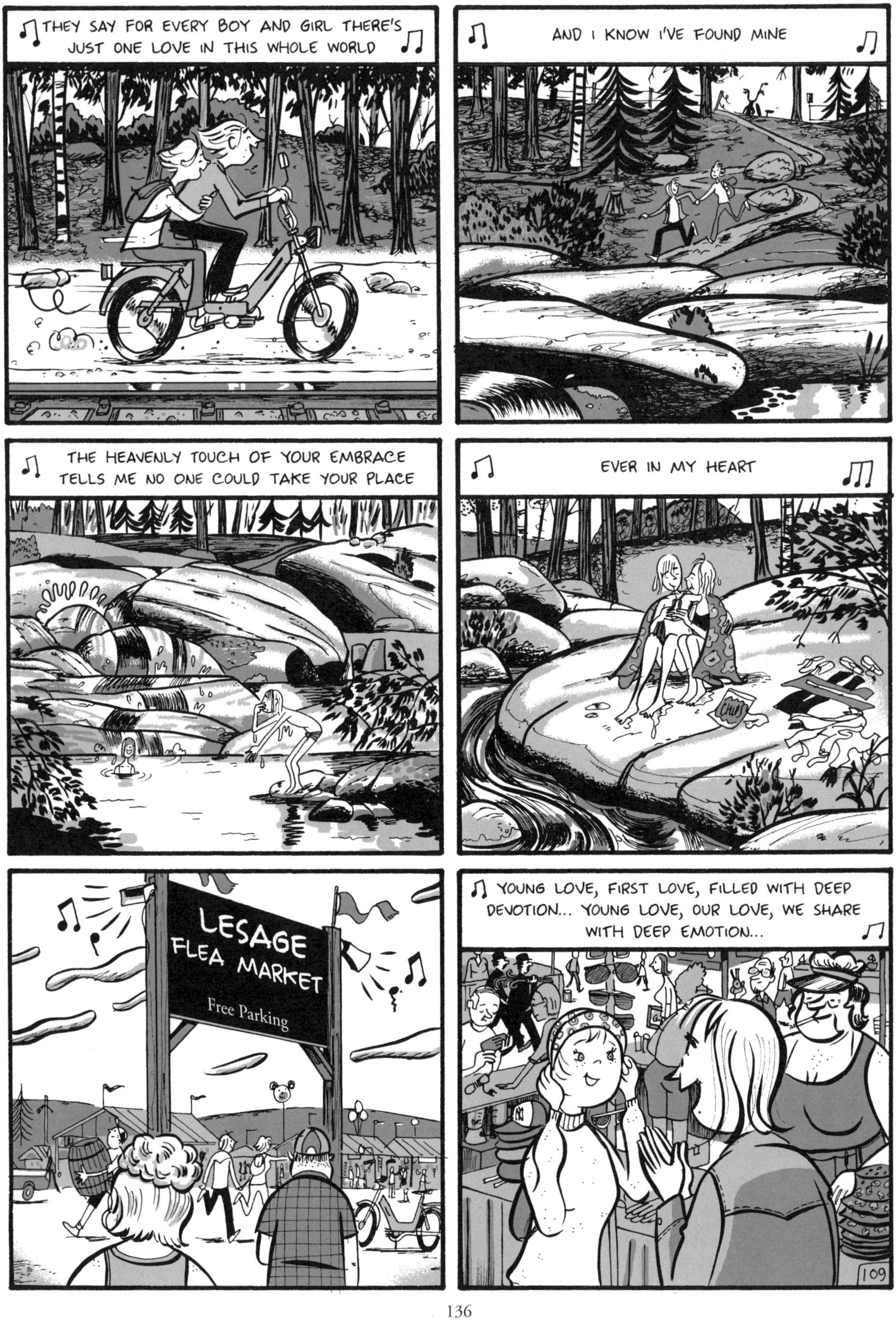
THEY SAY FOR EVERY BOY AND GIRL THERE'S JUST ONE LOVE IN THIS WHOLE WORLD
AND I KNOW I'VE FOUND MINE
THE HEAVENLY TOUCH OF YOUR EMBRACE TELLS ME NO ONE COULD TAKE YOUR PLACE
EVER IN MY HEART
CHIPS
LESAGE FLEA MARKET
Free Parking
YOUNG LOVE, FIRST LOVE, FILLED WITH DEEP DEVOTION... YOUNG LOVE, OUR LOVE, WE SHARE WITH DEEP EMOTION...
109

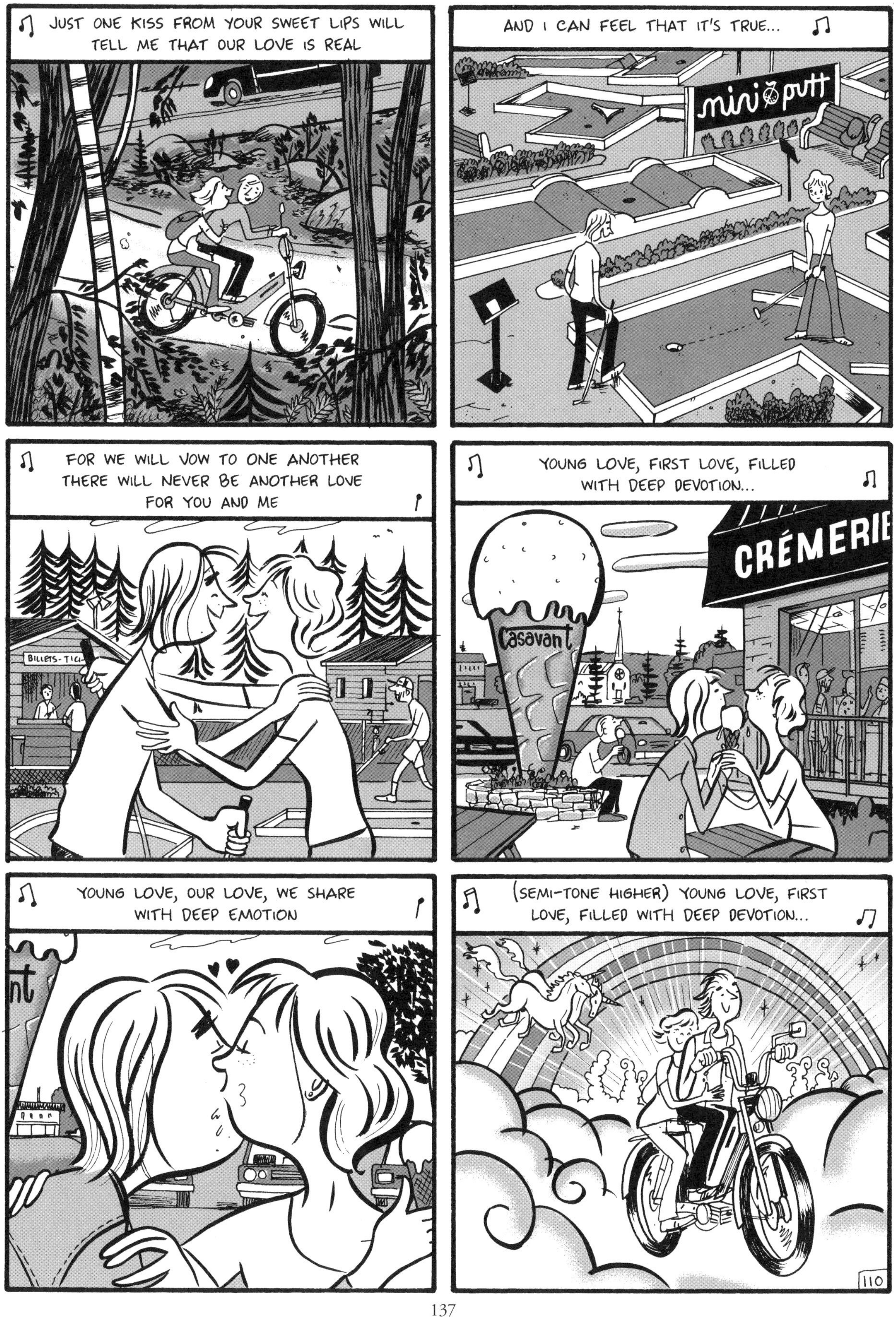
JUST ONE KISS FROM YOUR SWEET LIPS WILL TELL ME THAT OUR LOVE IS REAL
AND I CAN FEEL THAT IT'S TRUE...
mini putt
FOR WE WILL VOW TO ONE ANOTHER THERE WILL NEVER BE ANOTHER LOVE FOR YOU AND ME
BILLETS-TIC
YOUNG LOVE, FIRST LOVE, FILLED WITH DEEP DEVOTION...
CRÉMERIE
Casavant
YOUNG LOVE, OUR LOVE, WE SHARE WITH DEEP EMOTION
(SEMI-TONE HIGHER) YOUNG LOVE, FIRST LOVE, FILLED WITH DEEP DEVOTION...
110

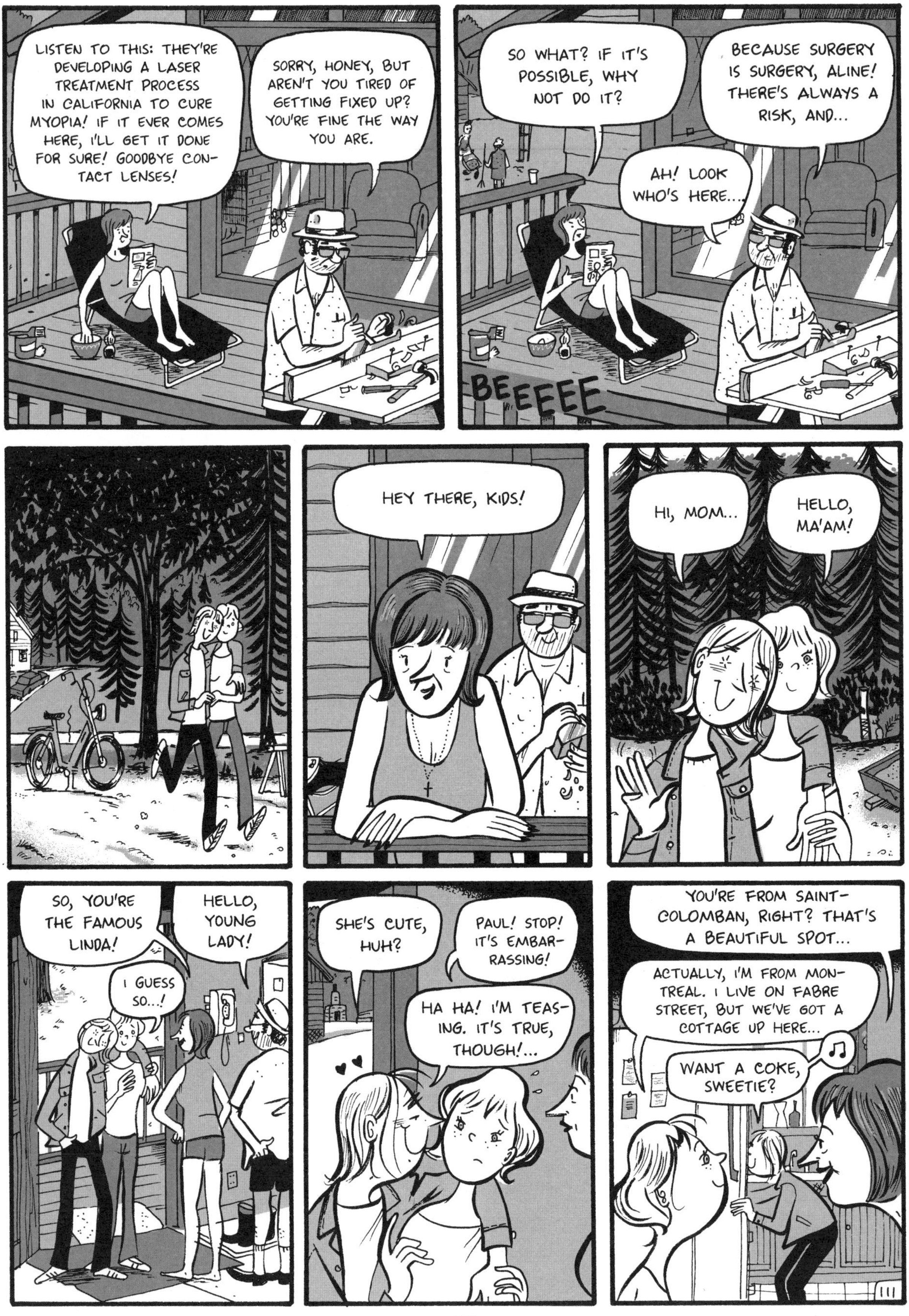
LISTEN TO THIS: THEY'RE DEVELOPING A LASER TREATMENT PROCESS IN CALIFORNIA TO CURE MYOPIA! IF IT EVER COMES HERE, I'LL GET IT DONE FOR SURE! GOODBYE CONTACT LENSES!
SORRY, HONEY, BUT AREN'T YOU TIRED OF GETTING FIXED UP? YOU'RE FINE THE WAY YOU ARE.
SO WHAT? IF IT'S POSSIBLE, WHY NOT DO IT?
BECAUSE SURGERY IS SURGERY, ALINE! THERE'S ALWAYS A RISK, AND...
AH! LOOK WHO'S HERE....
BEEEEE
HEY THERE, KIDS!
HI, MOM...
HELLO, MA'AM!
SO, YOU'RE THE FAMOUS LINDA!
HELLO, YOUNG LADY!
I GUESS SO...!
SHE'S CUTE, HUH?
PAUL! STOP! IT'S EMBARRASSING!
HA HA! I'M TEASING. IT'S TRUE, THOUGH!...
YOU'RE FROM SAINT-COLOMBAN, RIGHT? THAT'S A BEAUTIFUL SPOT...
ACTUALLY, I'M FROM MONTREAL. I LIVE ON FABRE STREET, BUT WE'VE GOT A COTTAGE UP HERE...
WANT A COKE, SWEETIE?

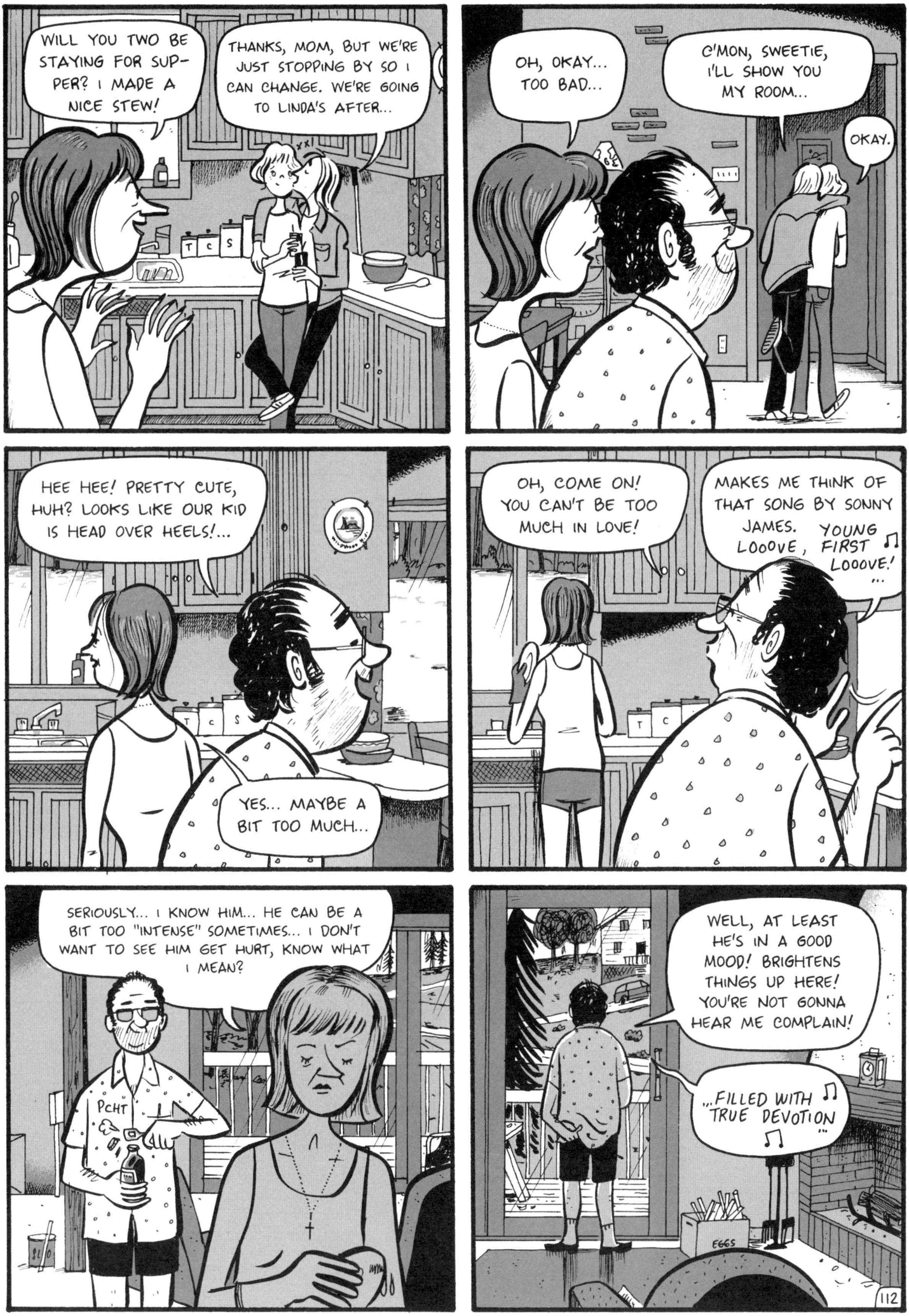
WILL YOU TWO BE STAYING FOR SUPPER? I MADE A NICE STEW!
THANKS, MOM, BUT WE'RE JUST STOPPING BY SO I CAN CHANGE. WE'RE GOING TO LINDA'S AFTER...
T C S
OH, OKAY... TOO BAD...
C'MON, SWEETIE, I'LL SHOW YOU MY ROOM...
OKAY.
HEE HEE! PRETTY CUTE, HUH? LOOKS LIKE OUR KID IS HEAD OVER HEELS!...
YES... MAYBE A BIT TOO MUCH...
OH, COME ON! YOU CAN'T BE TOO MUCH IN LOVE!
MAKES ME THINK OF THAT SONG BY SONNY JAMES. YOUNG LOOOVE, FIRST LOOOVE! ...
SERIOUSLY... I KNOW HIM... HE CAN BE A BIT TOO "INTENSE" SOMETIMES... I DON'T WANT TO SEE HIM GET HURT, KNOW WHAT I MEAN?
PCHT
WELL, AT LEAST HE'S IN A GOOD MOOD! BRIGHTENS THINGS UP HERE! YOU'RE NOT GONNA HEAR ME COMPLAIN!
...FILLED WITH TRUE DEVOTION ...
EGGS
112

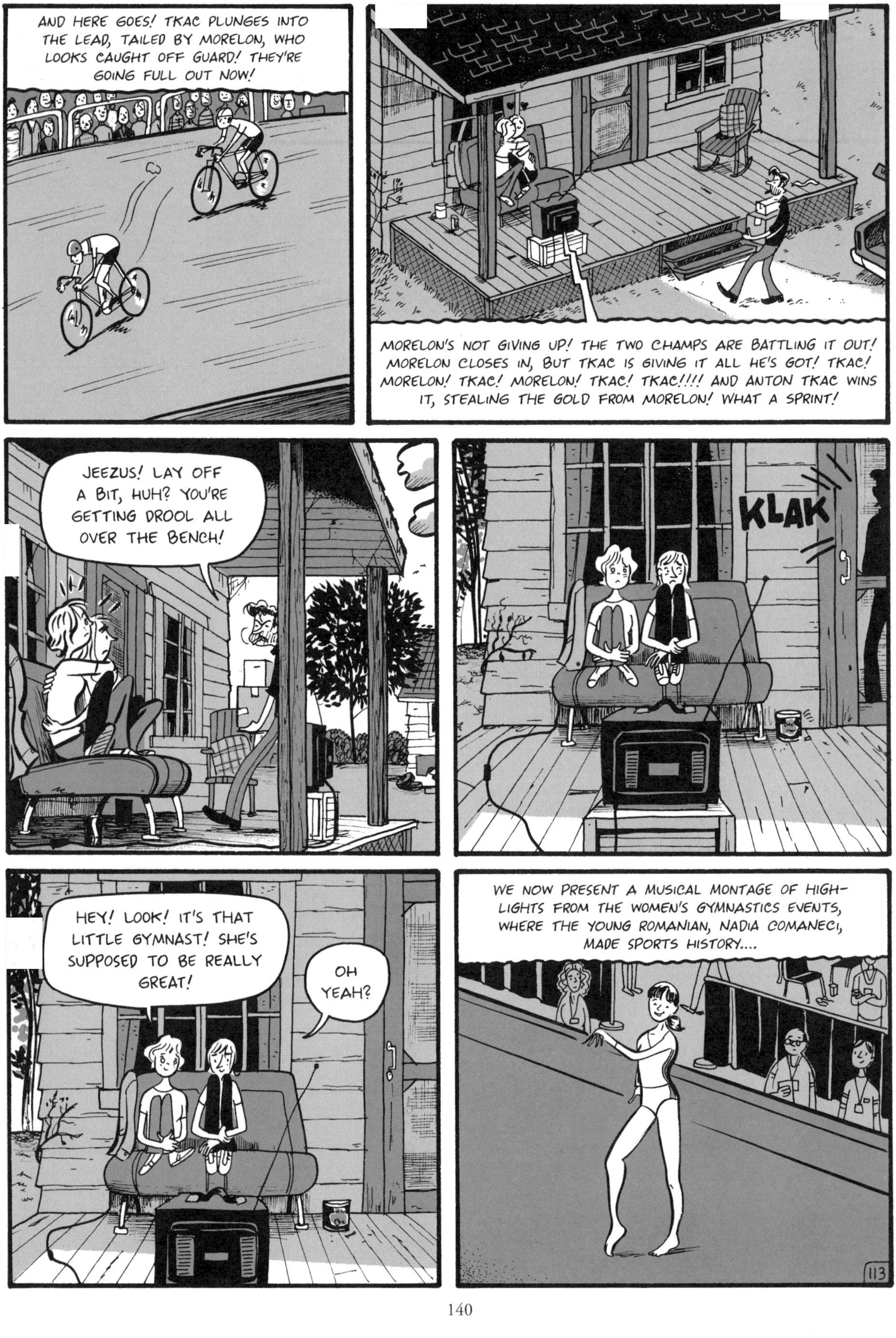
AND HERE GOES! TKAC PLUNGES INTO THE LEAD, TAILED BY MORELON, WHO LOOKS CAUGHT OFF GUARD! THEY'RE GOING FULL OUT NOW!
MORELON'S NOT GIVING UP! THE TWO CHAMPS ARE BATTLING IT OUT! MORELON CLOSES IN, BUT TKAC IS GIVING IT ALL HE'S GOT! TKAC! MORELON! TKAC! MORELON! TKAC! TKAC!!!! AND ANTON TKAC WINS IT, STEALING THE GOLD FROM MORELON! WHAT A SPRINT!
JEEZUS! LAY OFF A BIT, HUH? YOU'RE GETTING DROOL ALL OVER THE BENCH!
KLAK
HEY! LOOK! IT'S THAT LITTLE GYMNAST! SHE'S SUPPOSED TO BE REALLY GREAT!
OH YEAH?
WE NOW PRESENT A MUSICAL MONTAGE OF HIGHLIGHTS FROM THE WOMEN'S GYMNASTICS EVENTS, WHERE THE YOUNG ROMANIAN, NADIA COMANECI, MADE SPORTS HISTORY....
113

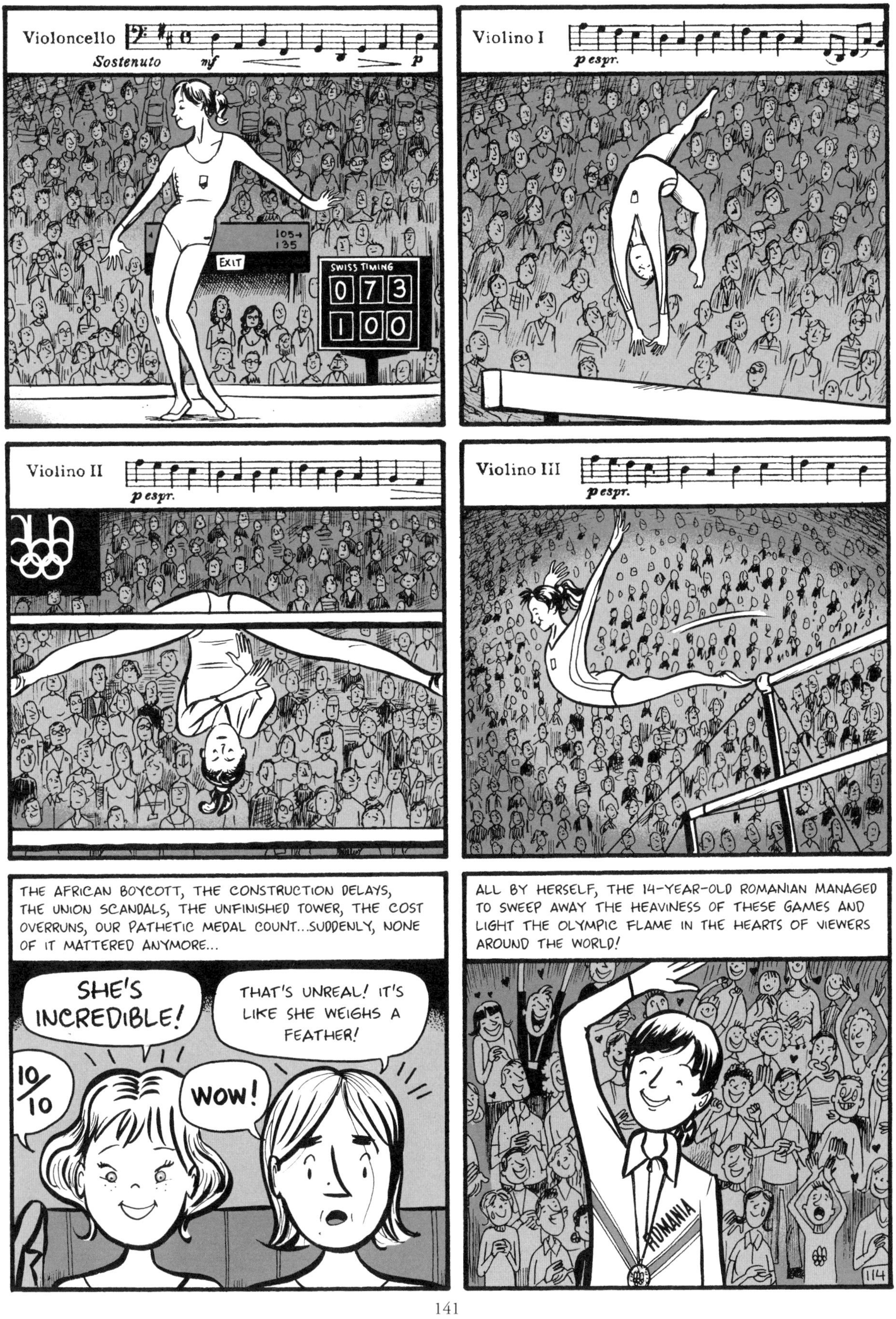

Violoncello
Sostenuto
mf
p
105
135
EXIT
SWISS TIMING
073
100
Violino I
p espr.
Violino II
p espr.
Violino III
p espr.
THE AFRICAN BOYCOTT, THE CONSTRUCTION DELAYS, THE UNION SCANDALS, THE UNFINISHED TOWER, THE COST OVERRUNS, OUR PATHETIC MEDAL COUNT...SUDDENLY, NONE OF IT MATTERED ANYMORE...
SHE'S INCREDIBLE!
THAT'S UNREAL! IT'S LIKE SHE WEIGHS A FEATHER!
10/10
WOW!
ALL BY HERSELF, THE 14-YEAR-OLD ROMANIAN MANAGED TO SWEEP AWAY THE HEAVINESS OF THESE GAMES AND LIGHT THE OLYMPIC FLAME IN THE HEARTS OF VIEWERS AROUND THE WORLD!
ROMANIA
114

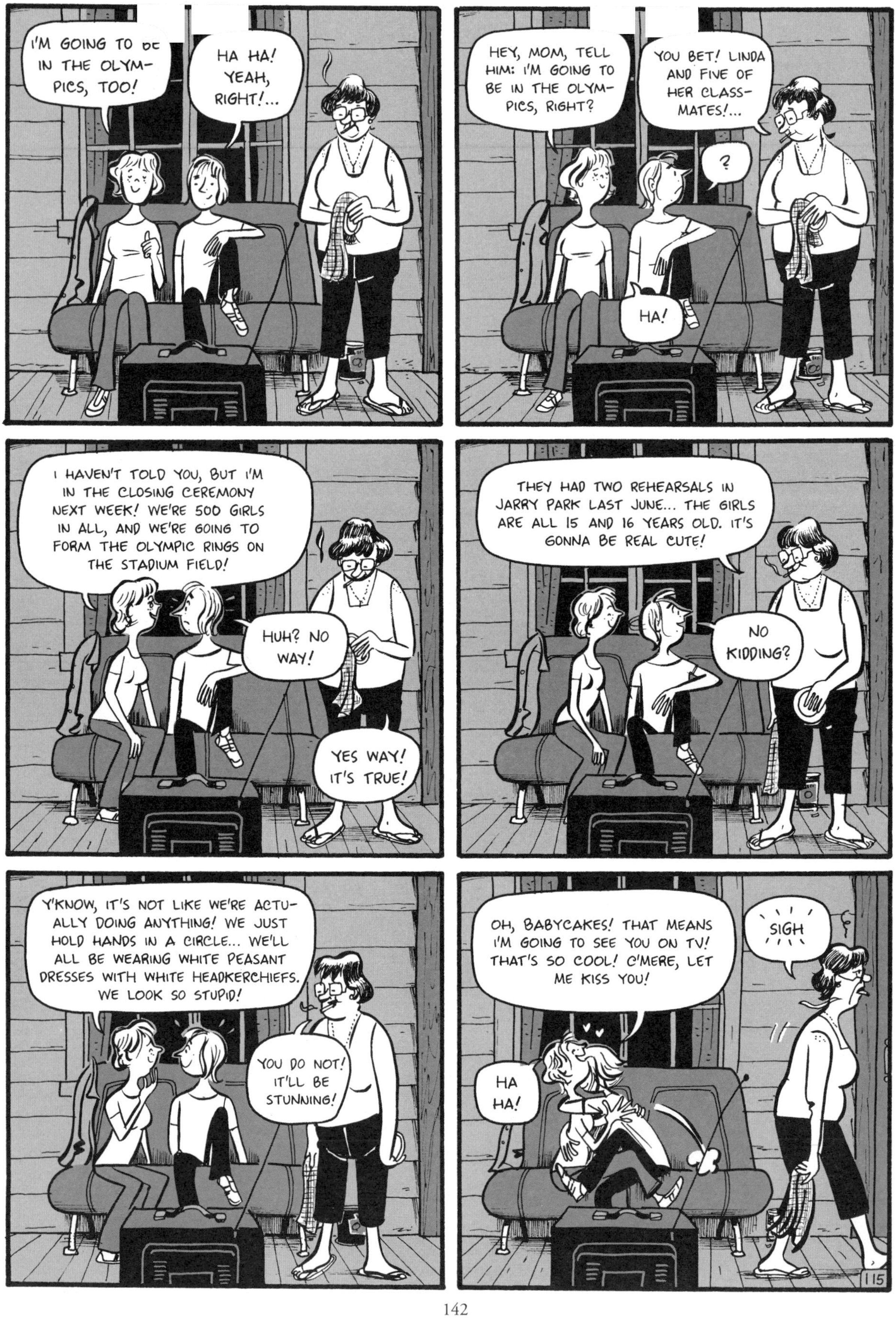
I'M GOING TO BE IN THE OLYMPICS, TOO!
HA HA! YEAH, RIGHT!...
HEY, MOM, TELL HIM: I'M GOING TO BE IN THE OLYMPICS, RIGHT?
YOU BET! LINDA AND FIVE OF HER CLASSMATES!...
?
HA!
I HAVEN'T TOLD YOU, BUT I'M IN THE CLOSING CEREMONY NEXT WEEK! WE'RE 500 GIRLS IN ALL, AND WE'RE GOING TO FORM THE OLYMPIC RINGS ON THE STADIUM FIELD!
HUH? NO WAY!
YES WAY! IT'S TRUE!
THEY HAD TWO REHEARSALS IN JARRY PARK LAST JUNE... THE GIRLS ARE ALL 15 AND 16 YEARS OLD. IT'S GONNA BE REAL CUTE!
NO KIDDING?
Y'KNOW, IT'S NOT LIKE WE'RE ACTUALLY DOING ANYTHING! WE JUST HOLD HANDS IN A CIRCLE... WE'LL ALL BE WEARING WHITE PEASANT DRESSES WITH WHITE HEADKERCHIEFS. WE LOOK SO STUPID!
YOU DO NOT! IT'LL BE STUNNING!
OH, BABYCAKES! THAT MEANS I'M GOING TO SEE YOU ON TV! THAT'S SO COOL! C'MERE, LET ME KISS YOU!
SIGH
HA HA!
115

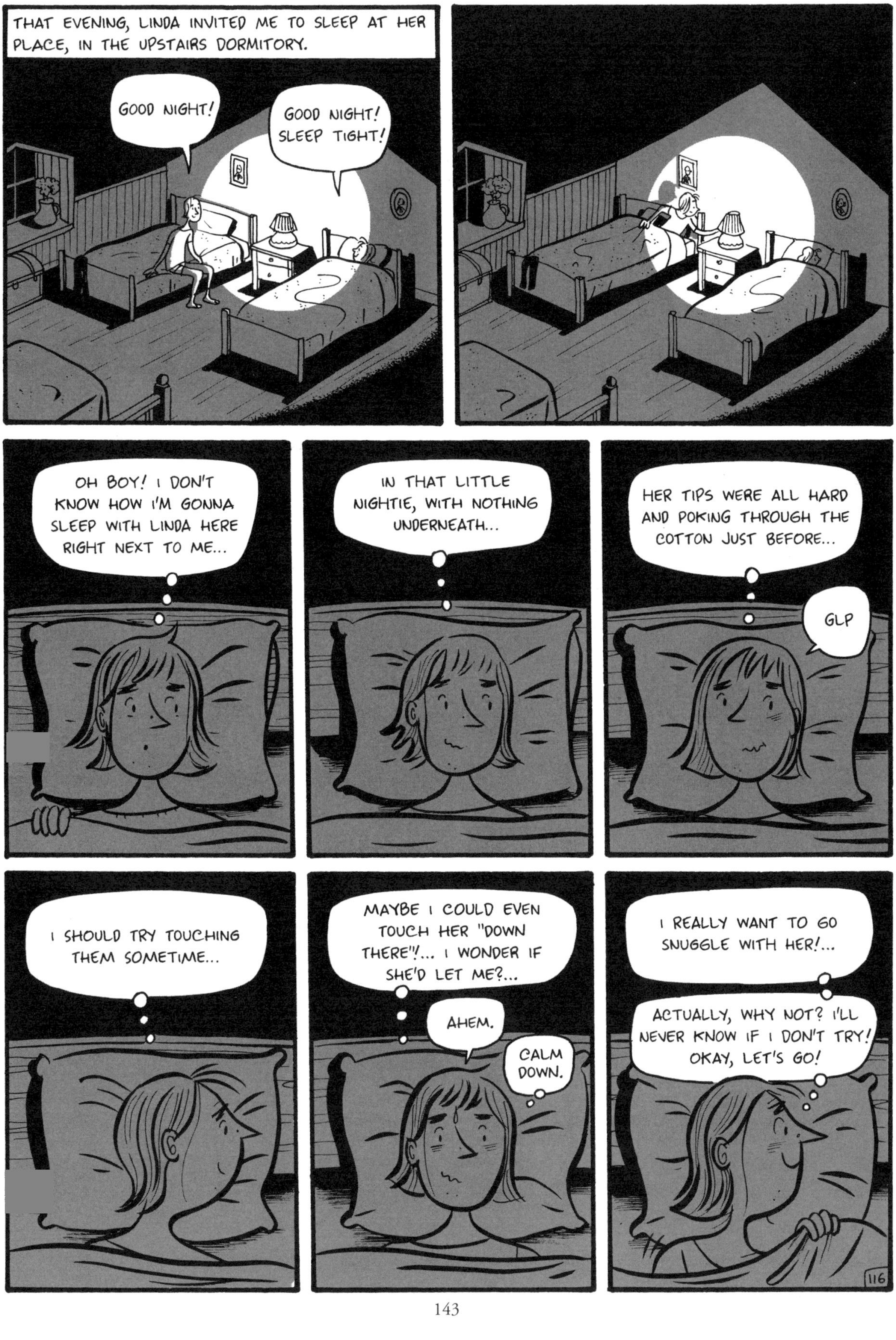
THAT EVENING, LINDA INVITED ME TO SLEEP AT HER PLACE, IN THE UPSTAIRS DORMITORY.
GOOD NIGHT!
GOOD NIGHT! SLEEP TIGHT!
OH BOY! I DON'T KNOW HOW I'M GONNA SLEEP WITH LINDA HERE RIGHT NEXT TO ME...
IN THAT LITTLE NIGHTIE, WITH NOTHING UNDERNEATH...
HER TIPS WERE ALL HARD AND POKING THROUGH THE COTTON JUST BEFORE...
GLP
I SHOULD TRY TOUCHING THEM SOMETIME...
MAYBE I COULD EVEN TOUCH HER "DOWN THERE"!... I WONDER IF SHE'D LET ME?...
AHEM.
CALM DOWN.
I REALLY WANT TO GO SNUGGLE WITH HER!...
ACTUALLY, WHY NOT? I'LL NEVER KNOW IF I DON'T TRY! OKAY, LET'S GO!
116

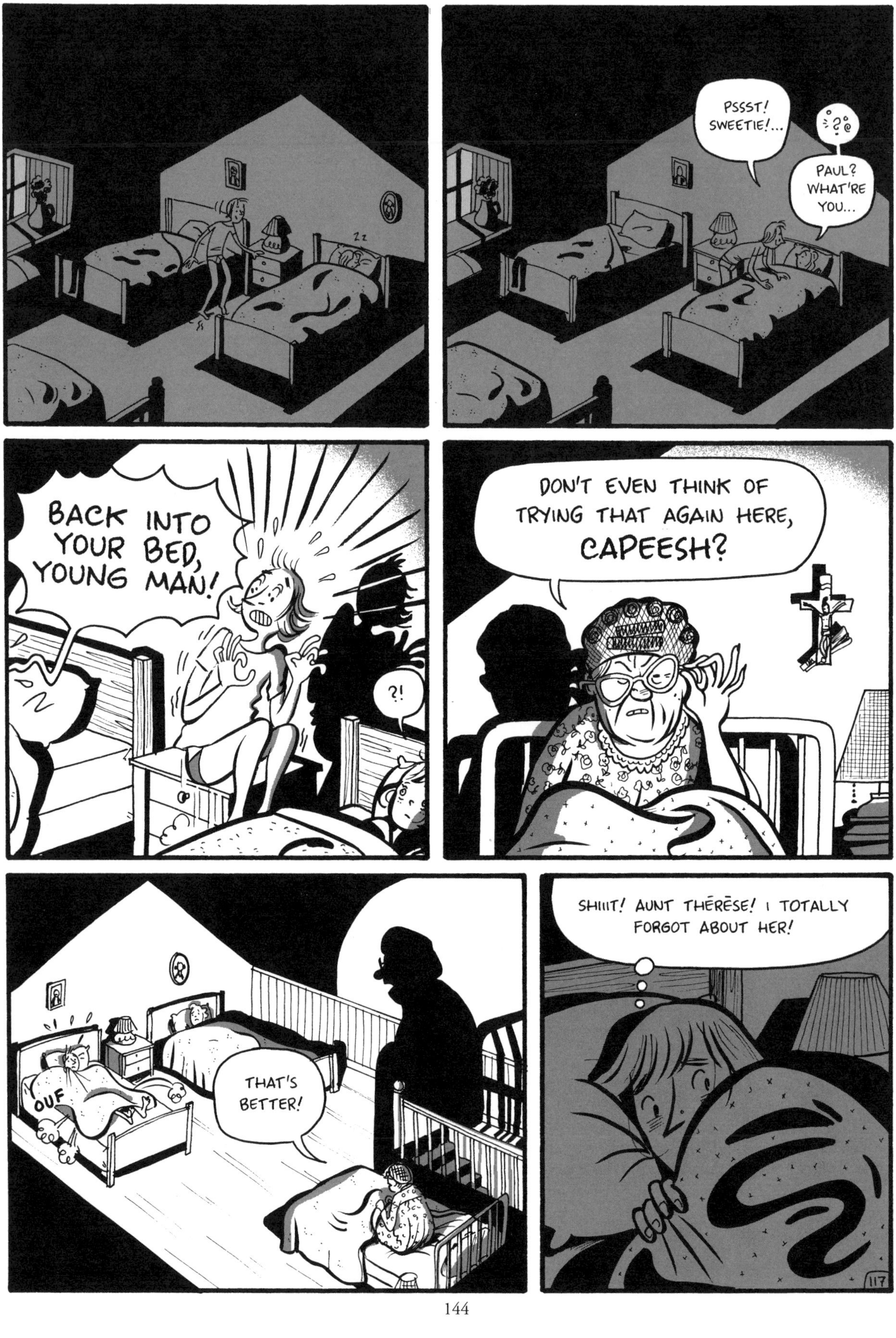

PSSST! SWEETIE!...
?
PAUL? WHAT'RE YOU...
BACK INTO YOUR BED, YOUNG MAN!
?!
DON'T EVEN THINK OF TRYING THAT AGAIN HERE, CAPEESH?
OUF
THAT'S BETTER!
SHIIIT! AUNT THÉRÈSE! I TOTALLY FORGOT ABOUT HER!
117

Closing Ceremony

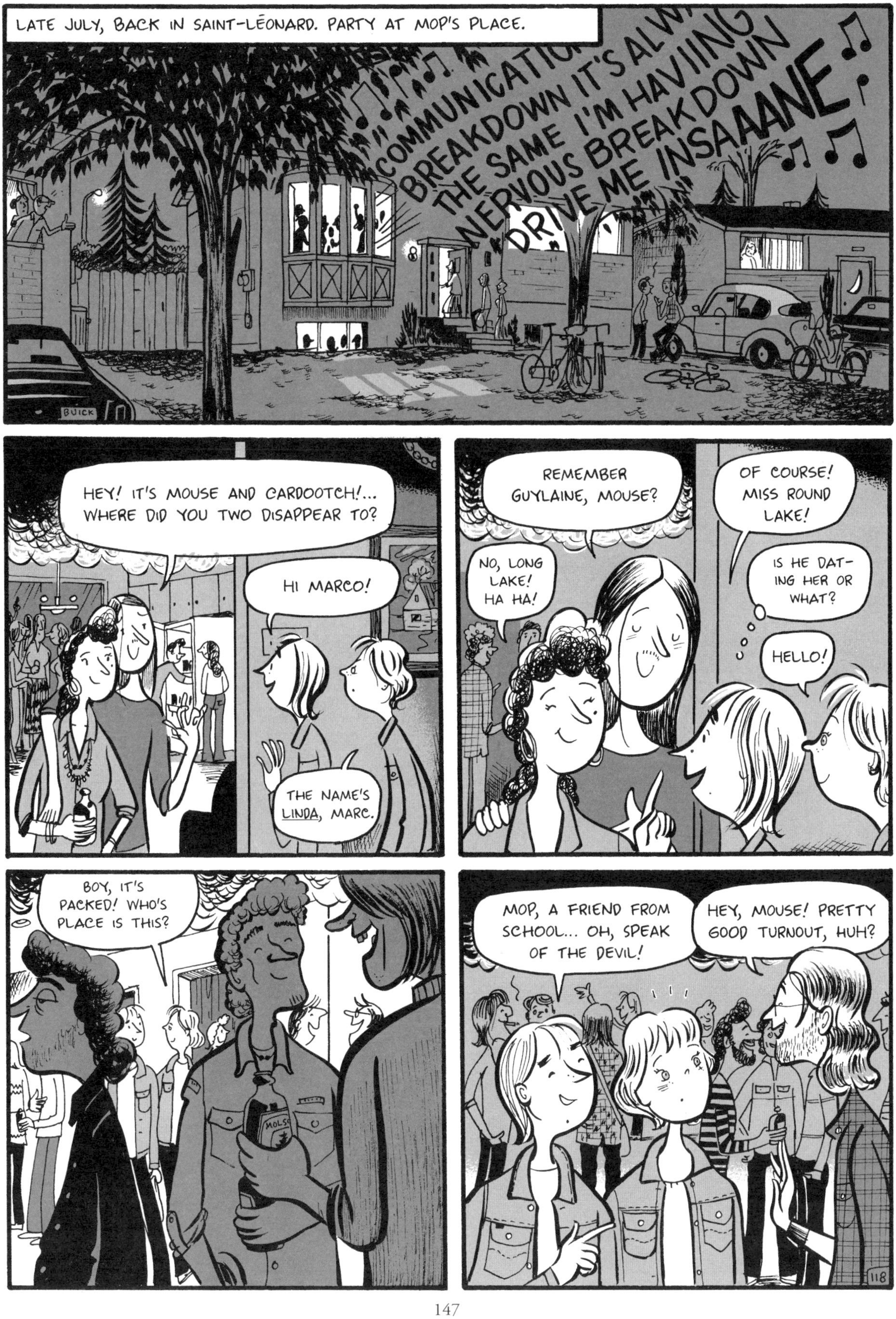
LATE JULY, BACK IN SAINT-LÉONARD. PARTY AT MOP'S PLACE.
BREAKDOWN
THE SAME I'M HAVIING
NERVOUS BREAKDOWN
DRIVE ME INSAAANE
BUICK
HEY! IT'S MOUSE AND CARDOOTCH!... WHERE DID YOU TWO DISAPPEAR TO?
HI MARCO!
THE NAME'S LINDA, MARC.
REMEMBER GUYLAINE, MOUSE?
OF COURSE! MISS ROUND LAKE!
NO, LONG LAKE! HA HA!
IS HE DATING HER OR WHAT?
HELLO!
BOY, IT'S PACKED! WHO'S PLACE IS THIS?
MOP, A FRIEND FROM SCHOOL... OH, SPEAK OF THE DEVIL!
HEY, MOUSE! PRETTY GOOD TURNOUT, HUH?
118

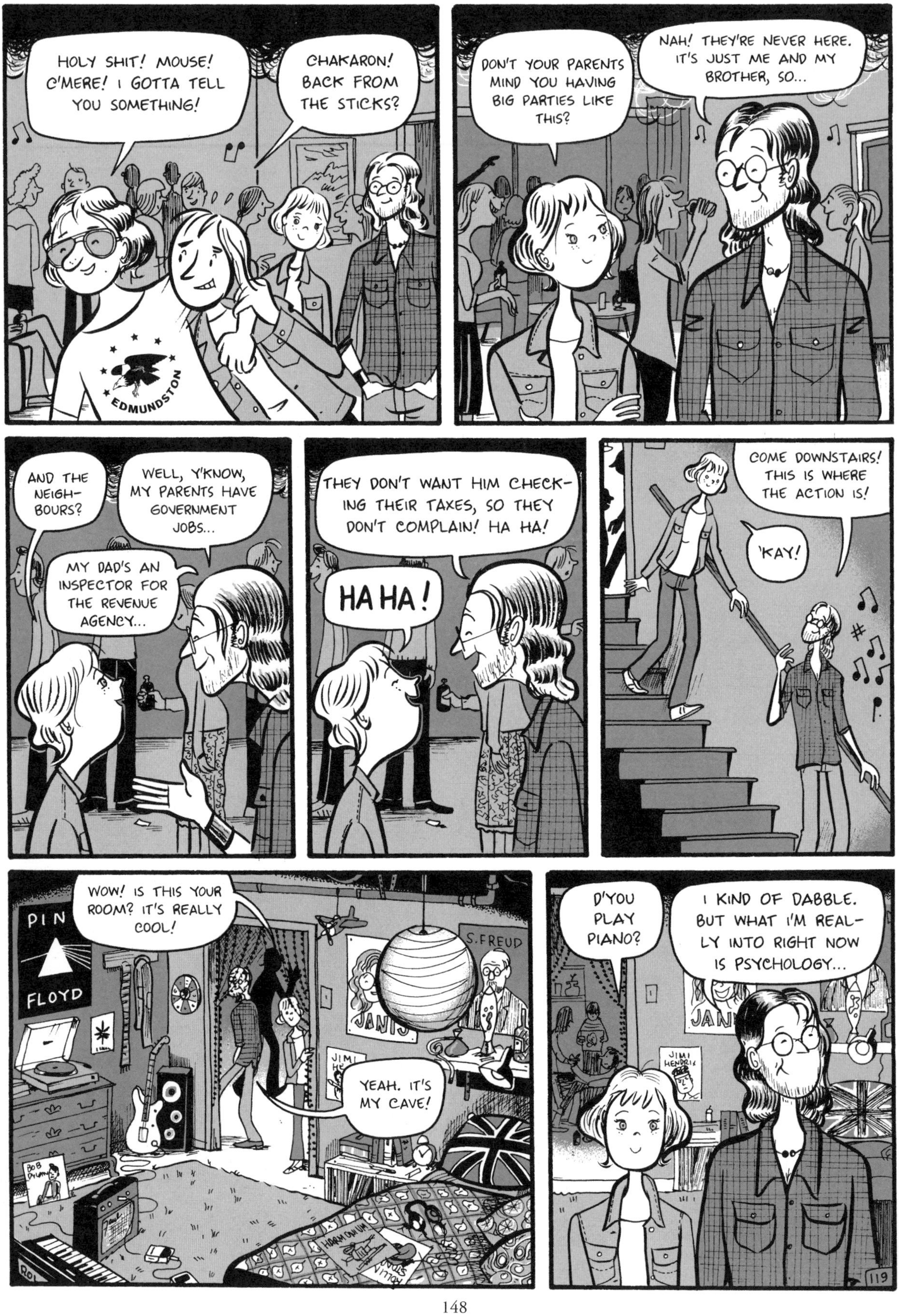
HOLY SHIT! MOUSE! C'MERE! I GOTTA TELL YOU SOMETHING!
CHAKARON! BACK FROM THE STICKS?
EDMUNDSTON
DON'T YOUR PARENTS MIND YOU HAVING BIG PARTIES LIKE THIS?
NAH! THEY'RE NEVER HERE. IT'S JUST ME AND MY BROTHER, SO...
AND THE NEIGH-BOURS?
WELL, Y'KNOW, MY PARENTS HAVE GOVERNMENT JOBS...
MY DAD'S AN INSPECTOR FOR THE REVENUE AGENCY...
THEY DON'T WANT HIM CHECK-ING THEIR TAXES, SO THEY DON'T COMPLAIN! HA HA!
HA HA!
COME DOWNSTAIRS! THIS IS WHERE THE ACTION IS!
'KAY!
WOW! IS THIS YOUR ROOM? IT'S REALLY COOL!
PIN
FLOYD
S.FREUD
JANIS
YEAH. IT'S MY CAVE!
D'YOU PLAY PIANO?
I KIND OF DABBLE. BUT WHAT I'M REAL-LY INTO RIGHT NOW IS PSYCHOLOGY...
119

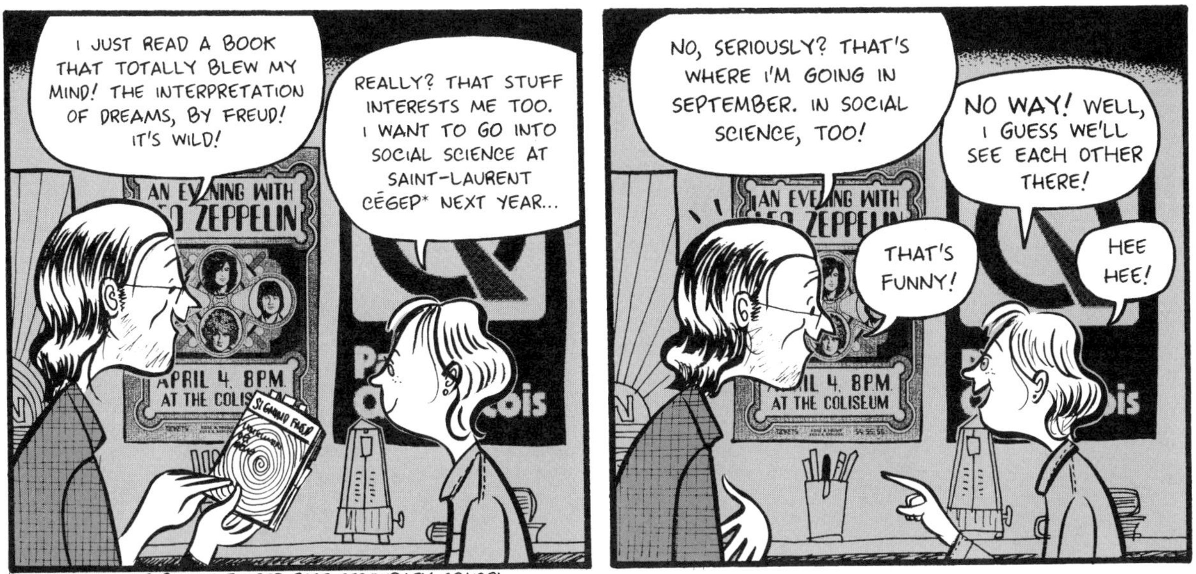
I JUST READ A BOOK THAT TOTALLY BLEW MY MIND! THE INTERPRETATION OF DREAMS, BY FREUD! IT'S WILD!
REALLY? THAT STUFF INTERESTS ME TOO. I WANT TO GO INTO SOCIAL SCIENCE AT SAINT-LAURENT CÉGEP* NEXT YEAR...
NO, SERIOUSLY? THAT'S WHERE I'M GOING IN SEPTEMBER. IN SOCIAL SCIENCE, TOO!
NO WAY! WELL, I GUESS WE'LL SEE EACH OTHER THERE!
THAT'S FUNNY!
HEE HEE!
APRIL 4, 8PM.
AT THE COLISEUM

* IN QUEBEC, A PUBLICLY FUNDED POST-SECONDARY SCHOOL

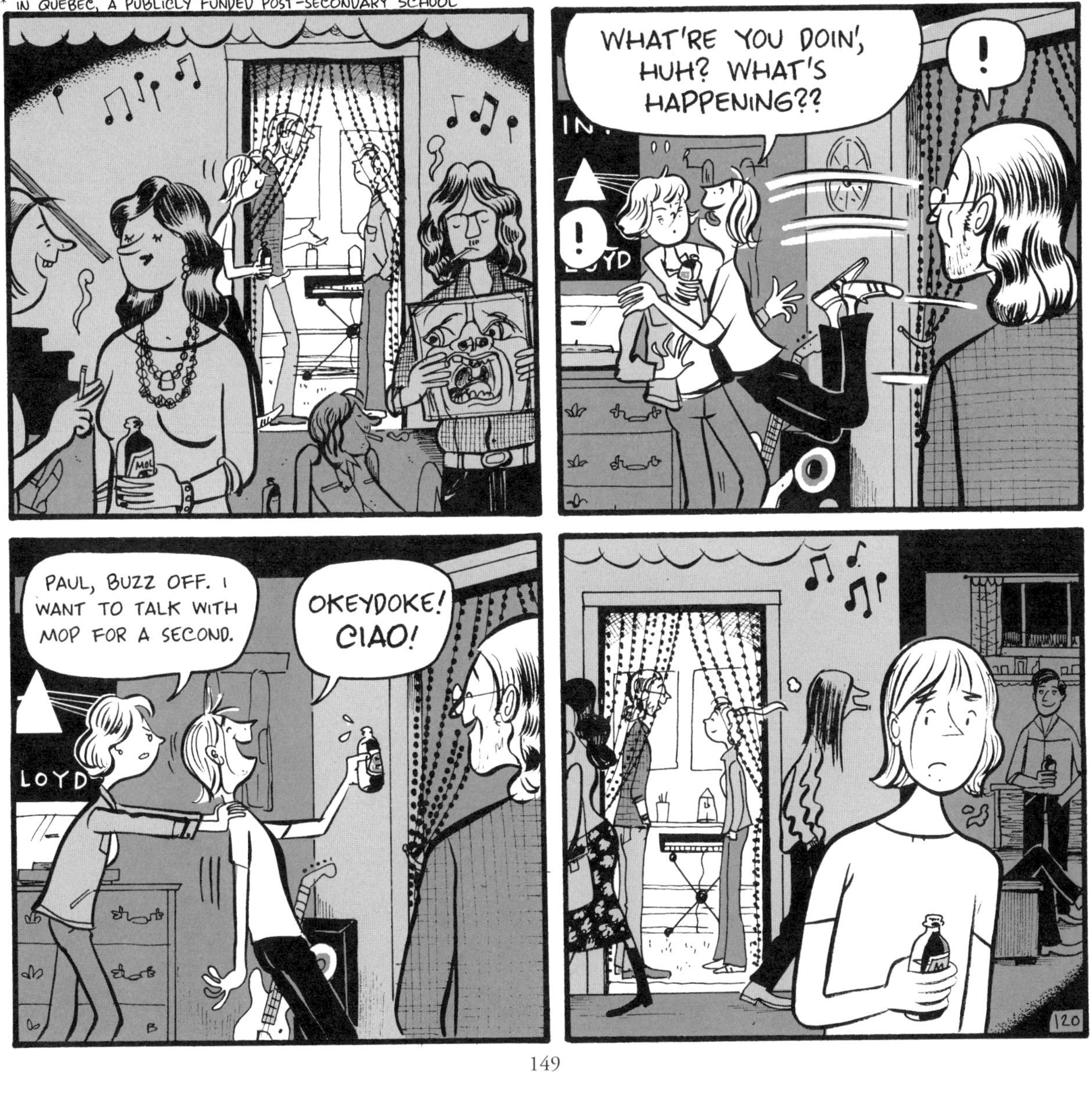
WHAT'RE YOU DOIN', HUH? WHAT'S HAPPENING??
!
PAUL, BUZZ OFF. I WANT TO TALK WITH MOP FOR A SECOND.
OKEYDOKE! CIAO!
120

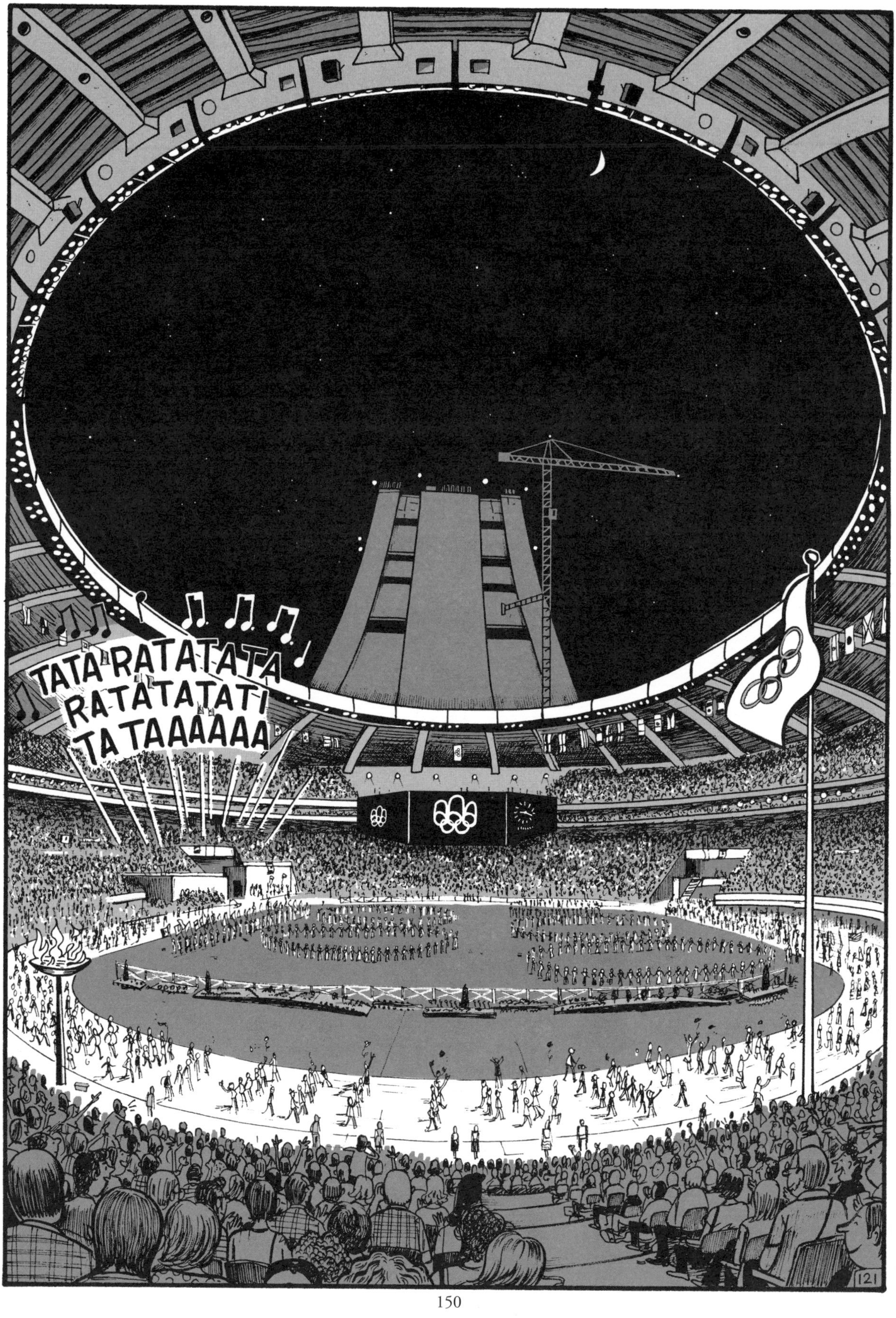
TATA RATATATA
RATATATATI
TA TAAAAAA
121

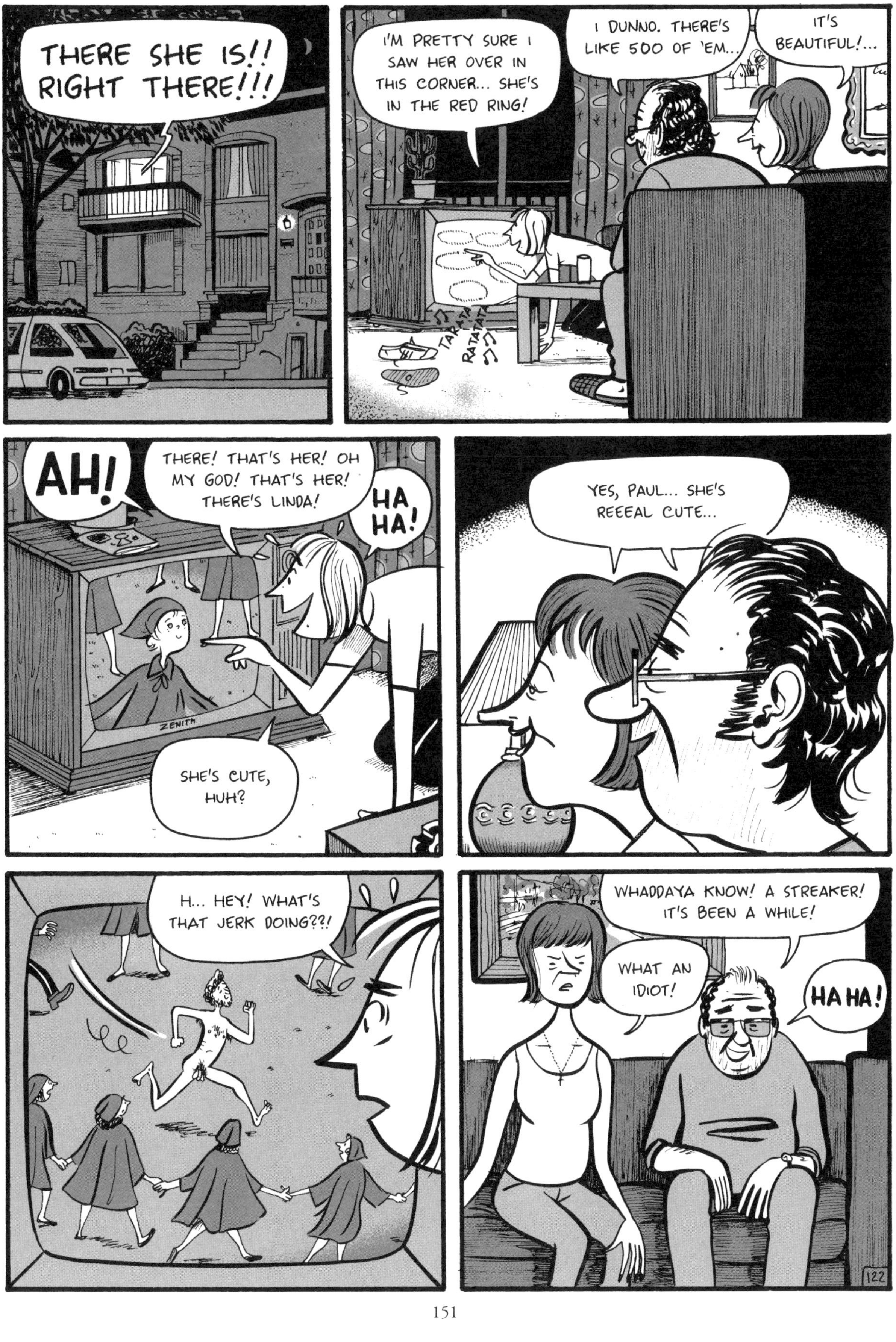
THERE SHE IS!! RIGHT THERE!!!
I'M PRETTY SURE I SAW HER OVER IN THIS CORNER... SHE'S IN THE RED RING!
I DUNNO. THERE'S LIKE 500 OF 'EM...
IT'S BEAUTIFUL!...
TARATATA
RATATATA
AH!
THERE! THAT'S HER! OH MY GOD! THAT'S HER! THERE'S LINDA!
HA HA!
ZENITH
SHE'S CUTE, HUH?
YES, PAUL... SHE'S REEEAL CUTE...
H... HEY! WHAT'S THAT JERK DOING??!
WHADDAYA KNOW! A STREAKER! IT'S BEEN A WHILE!
WHAT AN IDIOT!
HA HA!
122

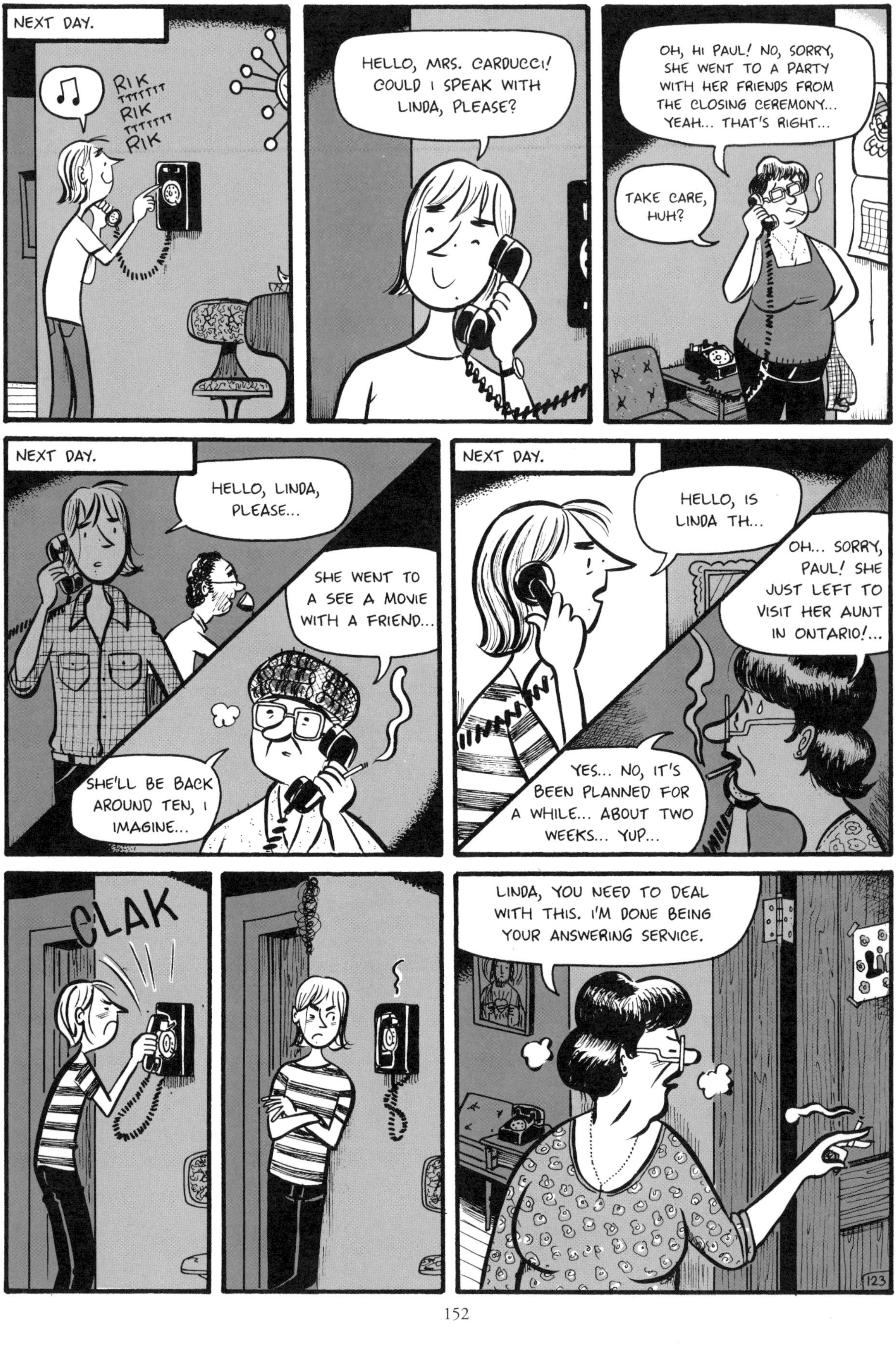
NEXT DAY.
RIK
TTTTTTT
RIK
TTTTTTT
RIK
HELLO, MRS. CARDUCCI! COULD I SPEAK WITH LINDA, PLEASE?
OH, HI PAUL! NO, SORRY, SHE WENT TO A PARTY WITH HER FRIENDS FROM THE CLOSING CEREMONY... YEAH... THAT'S RIGHT...
TAKE CARE, HUH?
NEXT DAY.
HELLO, LINDA, PLEASE...
SHE WENT TO A SEE A MOVIE WITH A FRIEND...
SHE'LL BE BACK AROUND TEN, I IMAGINE...
NEXT DAY.
HELLO, IS LINDA TH...
OH... SORRY, PAUL! SHE JUST LEFT TO VISIT HER AUNT IN ONTARIO!...
YES... NO, IT'S BEEN PLANNED FOR A WHILE... ABOUT TWO WEEKS... YUP...
CLAK
LINDA, YOU NEED TO DEAL WITH THIS. I'M DONE BEING YOUR ANSWERING SERVICE.
123

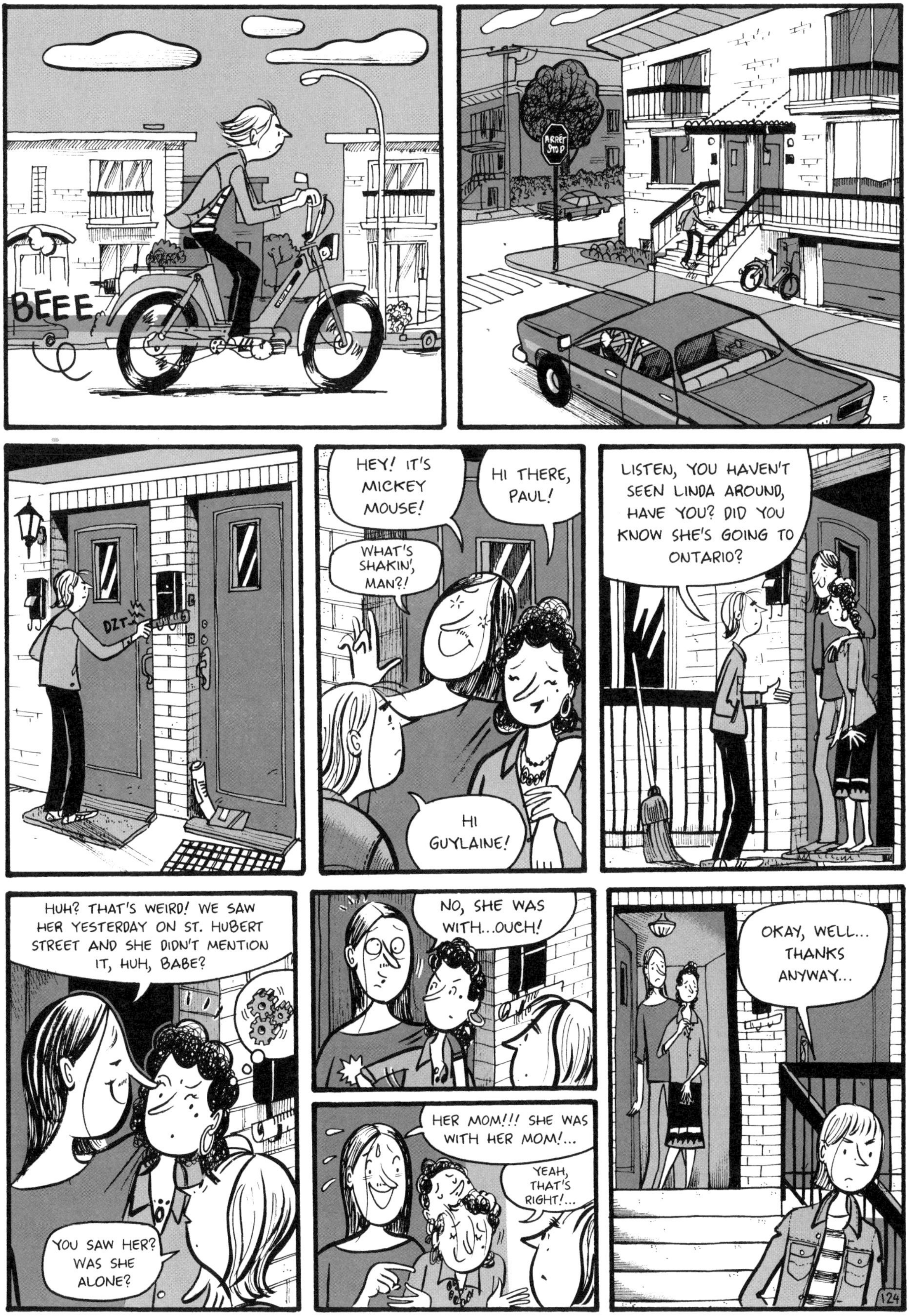
BEEE
ARRÊT STOP
DZT
HEY! IT'S MICKEY MOUSE!
HI THERE, PAUL!
WHAT'S SHAKIN', MAN?!
HI GUYLAINE!
LISTEN, YOU HAVEN'T SEEN LINDA AROUND, HAVE YOU? DID YOU KNOW SHE'S GOING TO ONTARIO?
HUH? THAT'S WEIRD! WE SAW HER YESTERDAY ON ST. HUBERT STREET AND SHE DIDN'T MENTION IT, HUH, BABE?
YOU SAW HER? WAS SHE ALONE?
NO, SHE WAS WITH...OUCH!
HER MOM!!! SHE WAS WITH HER MOM!...
YEAH, THAT'S RIGHT!...
OKAY, WELL... THANKS ANYWAY...
124

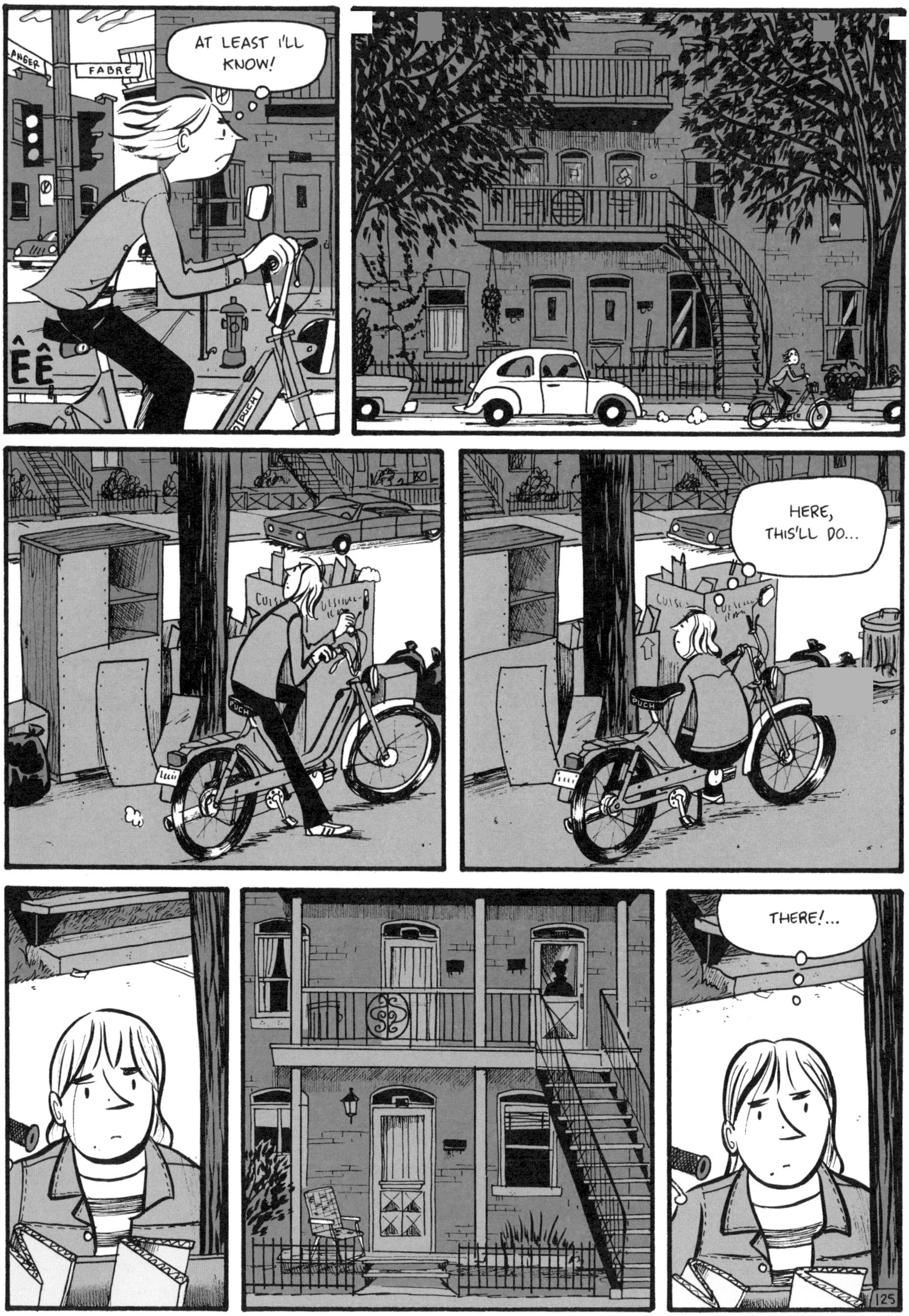
AT LEAST I'LL KNOW!
FABRE
PUCH
HERE, THIS'LL DO...
PUCH
THERE!...
125

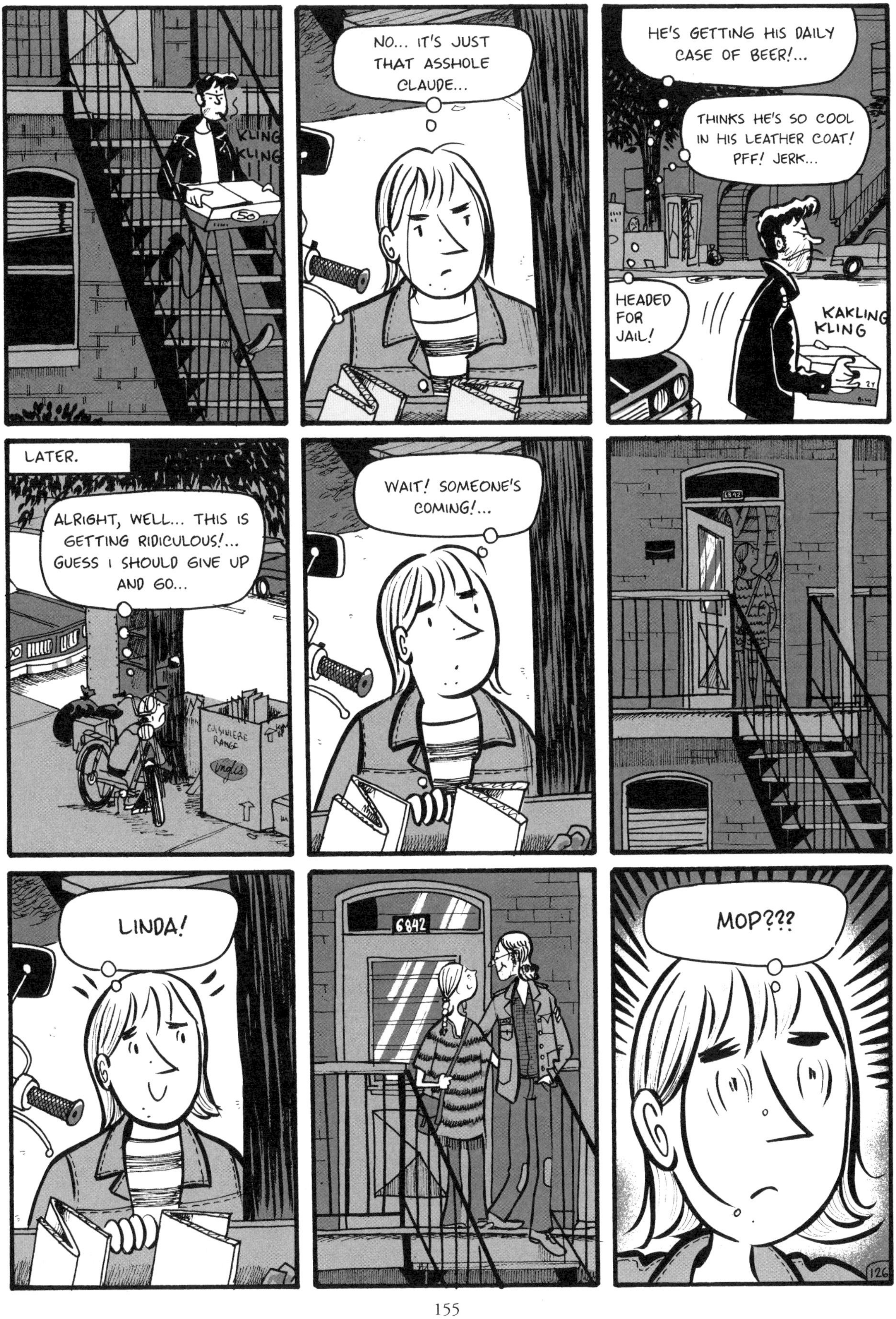
KLING
KLING
NO... IT'S JUST THAT ASSHOLE CLAUDE...
HE'S GETTING HIS DAILY CASE OF BEER!...
THINKS HE'S SO COOL IN HIS LEATHER COAT! PFF! JERK...
HEADED FOR JAIL!
KAKLING KLING
LATER.
ALRIGHT, WELL... THIS IS GETTING RIDICULOUS!... GUESS I SHOULD GIVE UP AND GO...
WAIT! SOMEONE'S COMING!...
6842
LINDA!
6842
MOP???
126

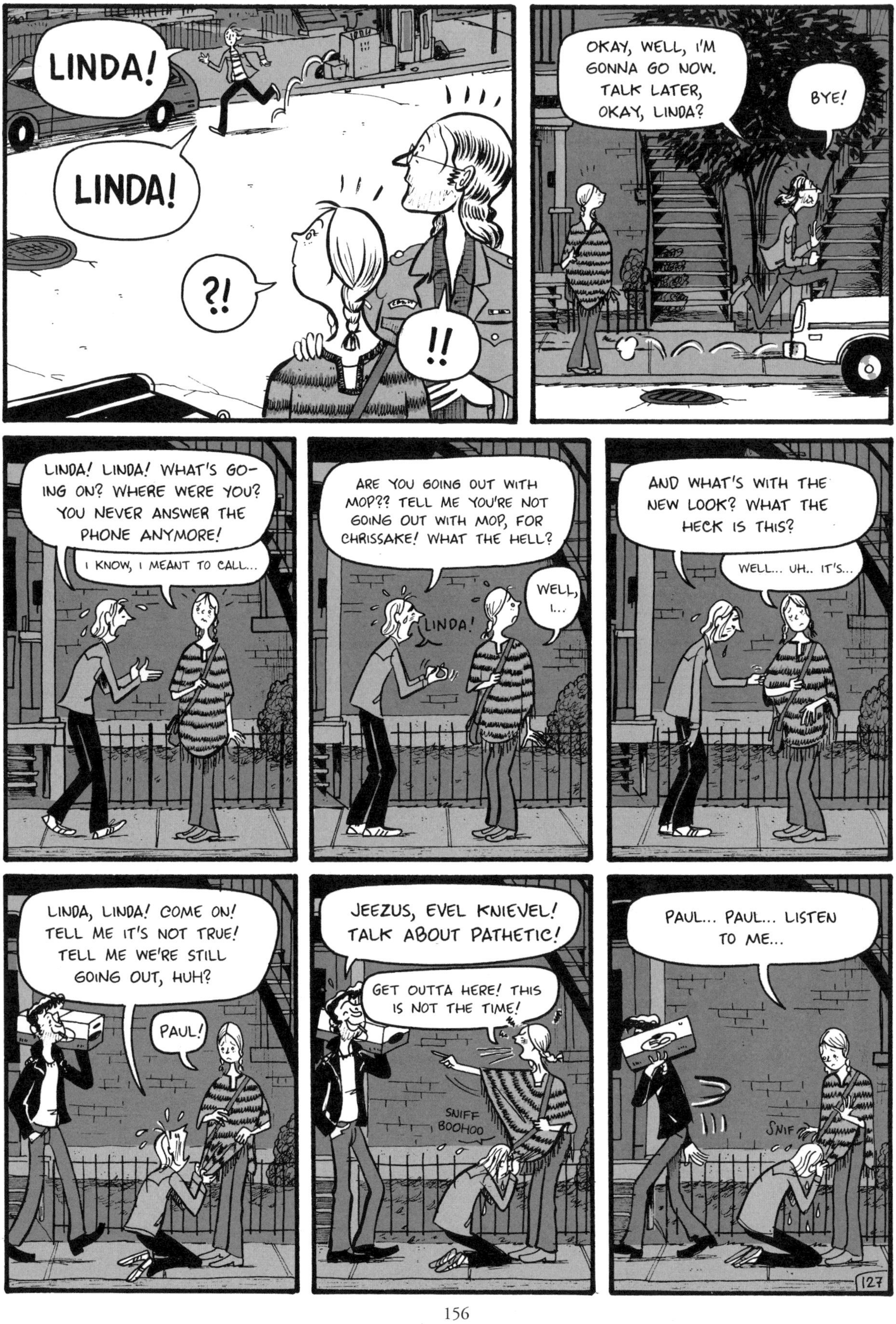
LINDA!
LINDA!
?!
!!
OKAY, WELL, I'M GONNA GO NOW. TALK LATER, OKAY, LINDA?
BYE!
LINDA! LINDA! WHAT'S GOING ON? WHERE WERE YOU? YOU NEVER ANSWER THE PHONE ANYMORE!
I KNOW, I MEANT TO CALL...
ARE YOU GOING OUT WITH MOP?? TELL ME YOU'RE NOT GOING OUT WITH MOP, FOR CHRISSAKE! WHAT THE HELL?
LINDA!
WELL, I...
AND WHAT'S WITH THE NEW LOOK? WHAT THE HECK IS THIS?
WELL... UH.. IT'S...
LINDA, LINDA! COME ON! TELL ME IT'S NOT TRUE! TELL ME WE'RE STILL GOING OUT, HUH?
PAUL!
JEEZUS, EVEL KNIEVEL! TALK ABOUT PATHETIC!
GET OUTTA HERE! THIS IS NOT THE TIME!
SNIFF BOOHOO
PAUL... PAUL... LISTEN TO ME...
SNIF
127

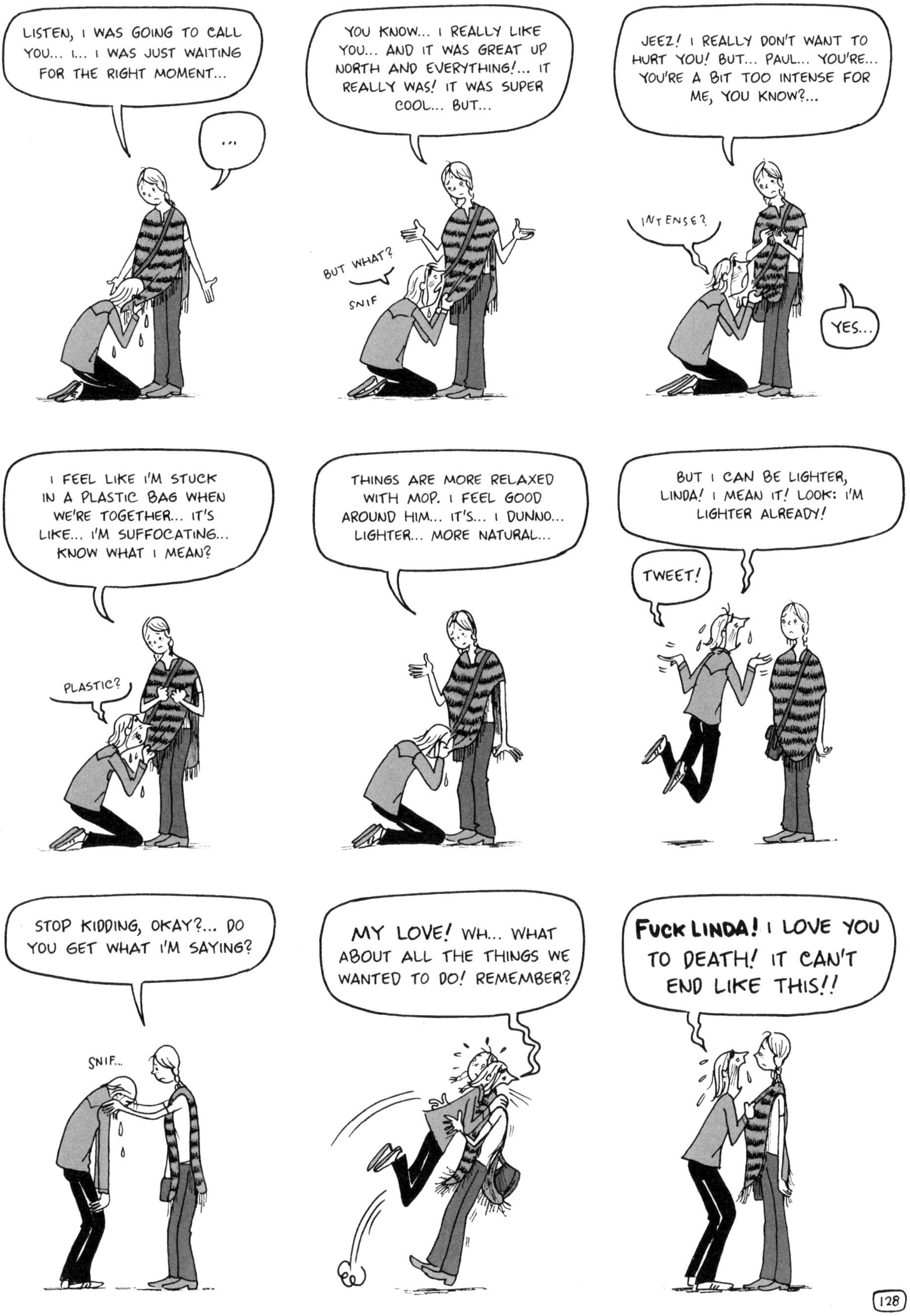
LISTEN, I WAS GOING TO CALL YOU... I... I WAS JUST WAITING FOR THE RIGHT MOMENT...
...
YOU KNOW... I REALLY LIKE YOU... AND IT WAS GREAT UP NORTH AND EVERYTHING!... IT REALLY WAS! IT WAS SUPER COOL... BUT...
BUT WHAT?
SNIF
JEEZ! I REALLY DON'T WANT TO HURT YOU! BUT... PAUL... YOU'RE... YOU'RE A BIT TOO INTENSE FOR ME, YOU KNOW?...
INTENSE?
YES...
I FEEL LIKE I'M STUCK IN A PLASTIC BAG WHEN WE'RE TOGETHER... IT'S LIKE... I'M SUFFOCATING... KNOW WHAT I MEAN?
PLASTIC?
THINGS ARE MORE RELAXED WITH MOP. I FEEL GOOD AROUND HIM... IT'S... I DUNNO... LIGHTER... MORE NATURAL...
BUT I CAN BE LIGHTER, LINDA! I MEAN IT! LOOK: I'M LIGHTER ALREADY!
TWEET!
STOP KIDDING, OKAY?... DO YOU GET WHAT I'M SAYING?
SNIF...
MY LOVE! WH... WHAT ABOUT ALL THE THINGS WE WANTED TO DO! REMEMBER?
FUCK LINDA! I LOVE YOU TO DEATH! IT CAN'T END LIKE THIS!!
128

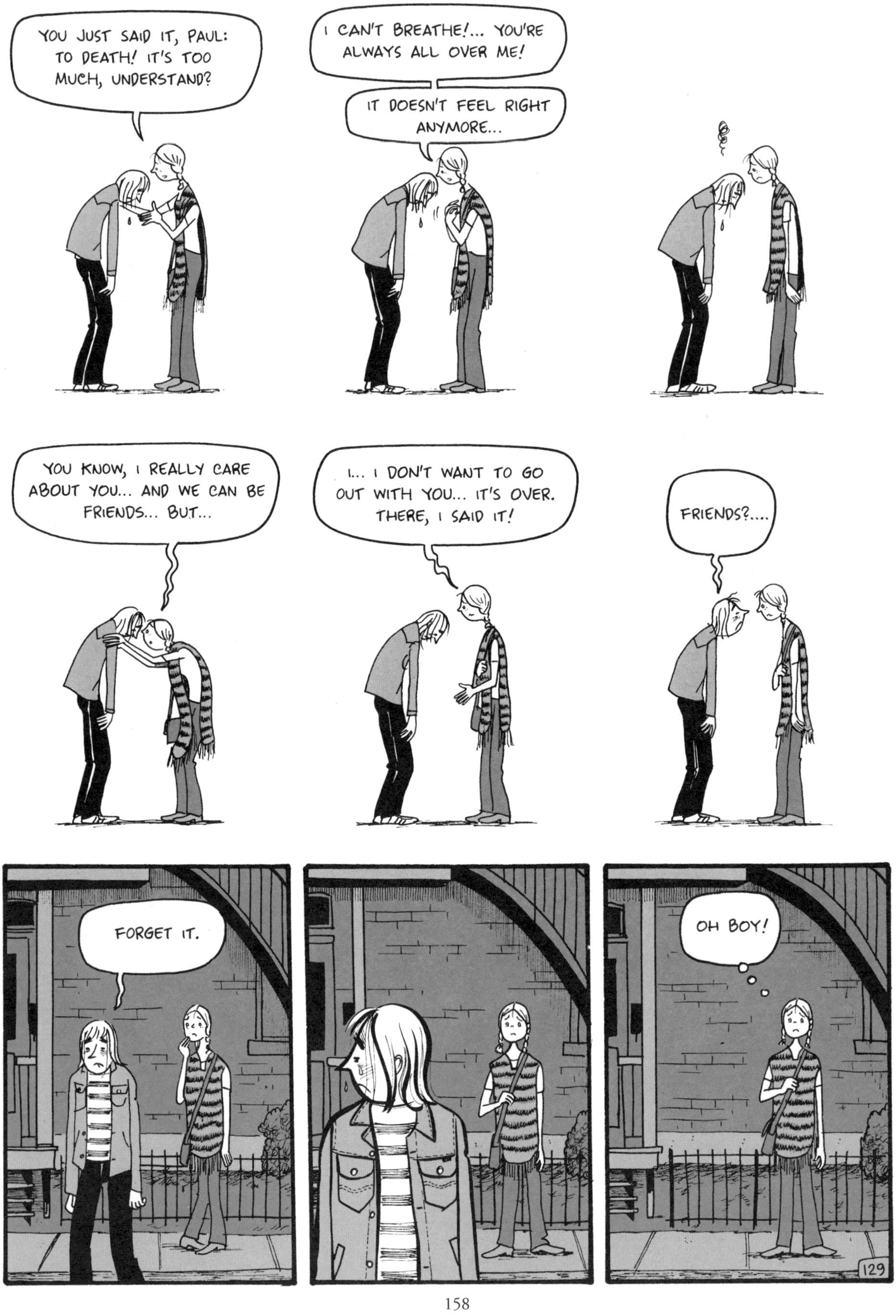
YOU JUST SAID IT, PAUL: TO DEATH! IT'S TOO MUCH, UNDERSTAND?
I CAN'T BREATHE!... YOU'RE ALWAYS ALL OVER ME!
IT DOESN'T FEEL RIGHT ANYMORE...
YOU KNOW, I REALLY CARE ABOUT YOU... AND WE CAN BE FRIENDS... BUT...
I... I DON'T WANT TO GO OUT WITH YOU... IT'S OVER. THERE, I SAID IT!
FRIENDS?....
FORGET IT.
OH BOY!
129

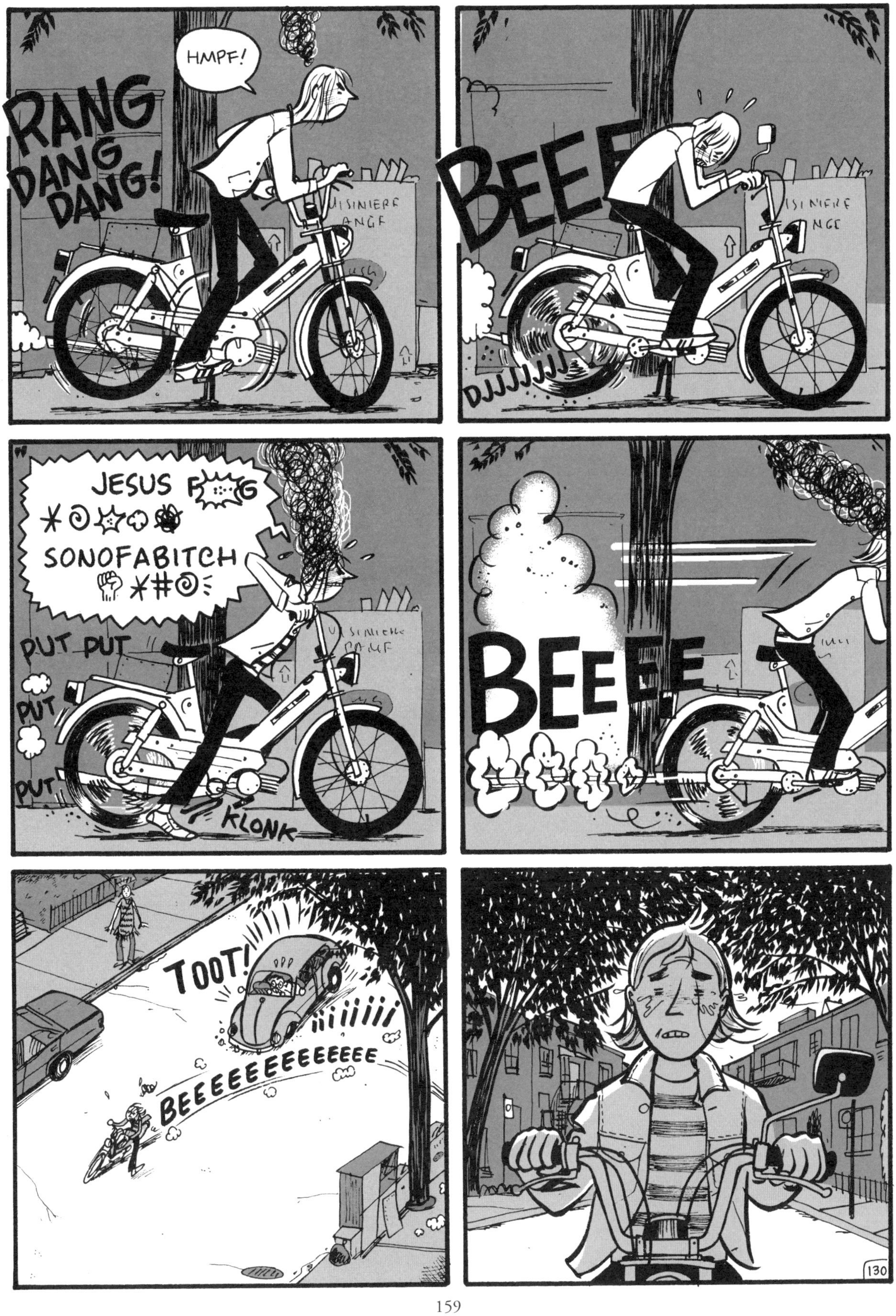
HMPF!
RANG DANG DANG!
BEEE
DJJJJJJ
JESUS F G
SONOFABITCH
PUT PUT
PUT
PUT
KLONK
BEEEE
TOOT!
BEEEEEEEEEEEEE
130

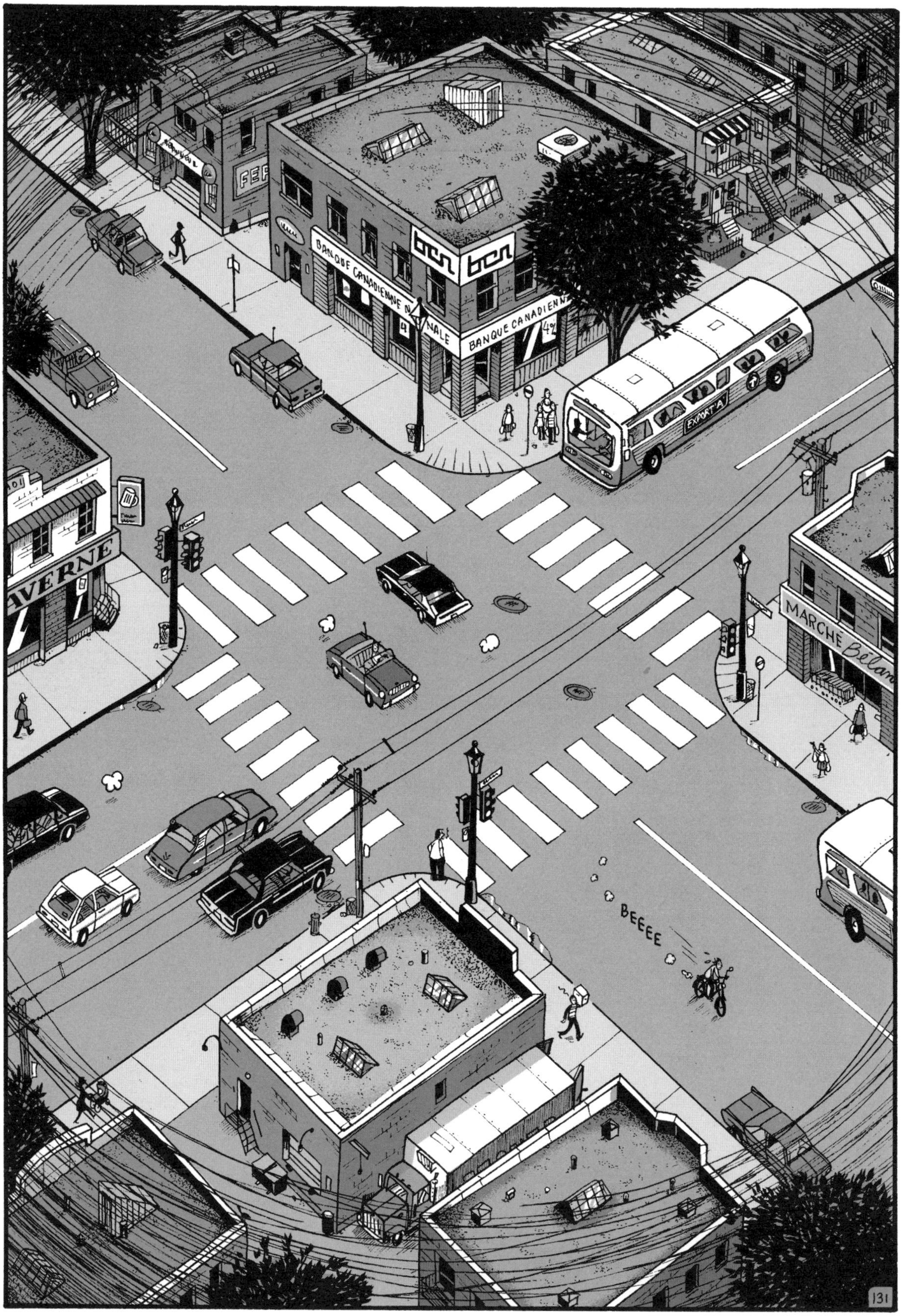
bcn
bcn
BANQUE CANADIENNE
EXPORT'A
MARCHÉ
BEEEE
131

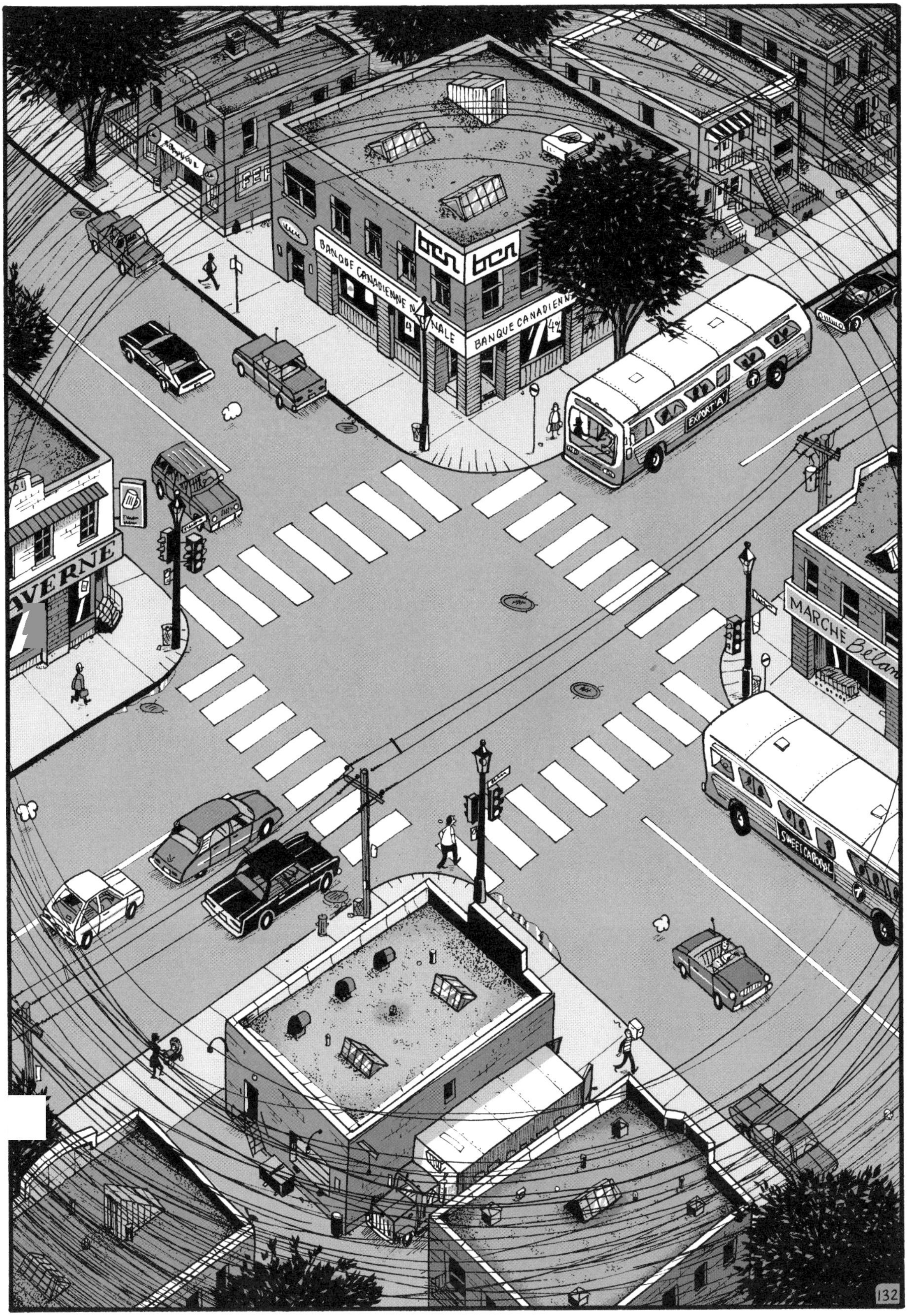
bcn
bcn
BANQUE CANADIENNE
NALE
EXPORT 'A'
AVERNE
MARCHE
SWEET CAPORAL
132

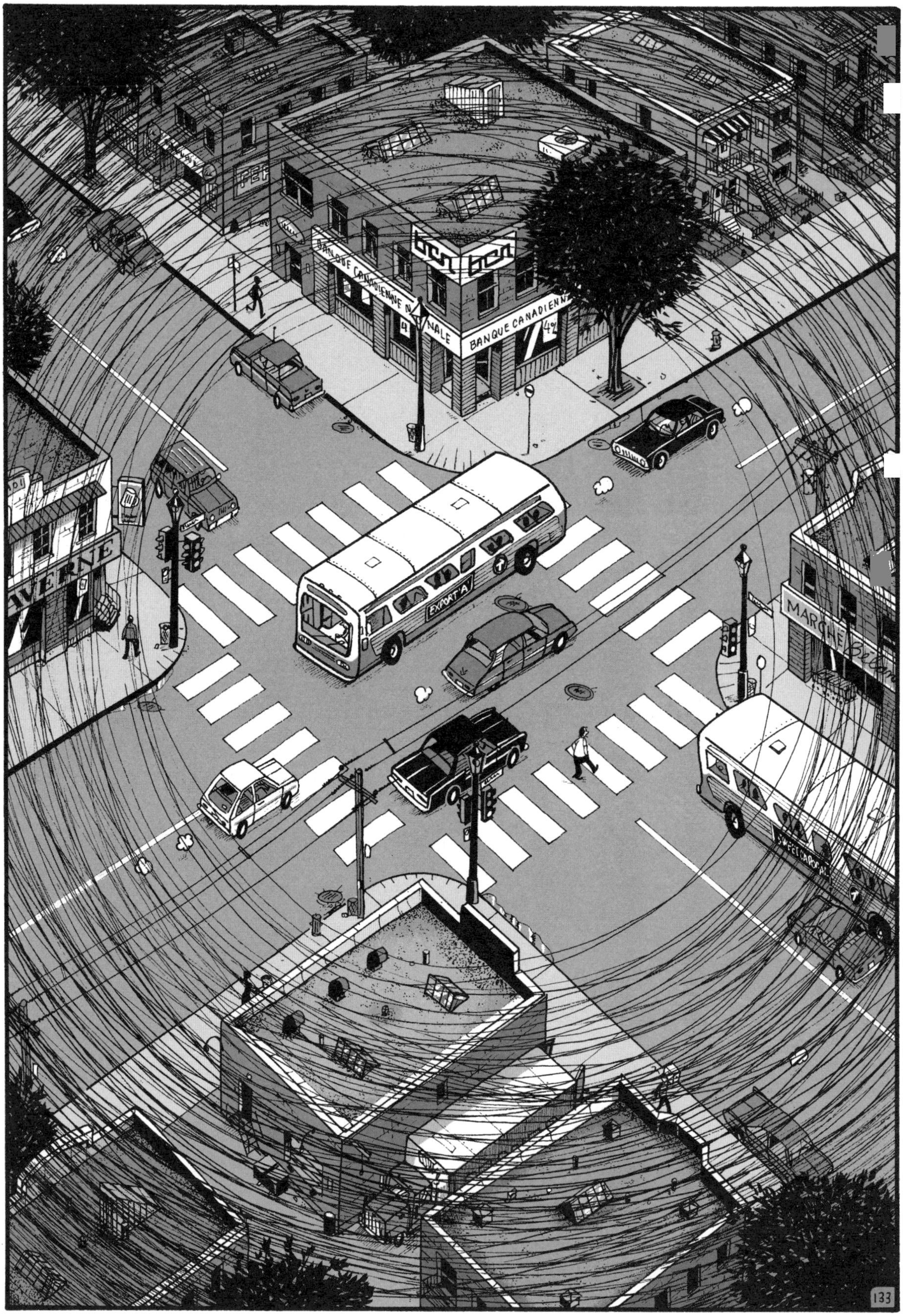
BANQUE CANADIENNE
EXPORT 'A'
MARCHÉ
133

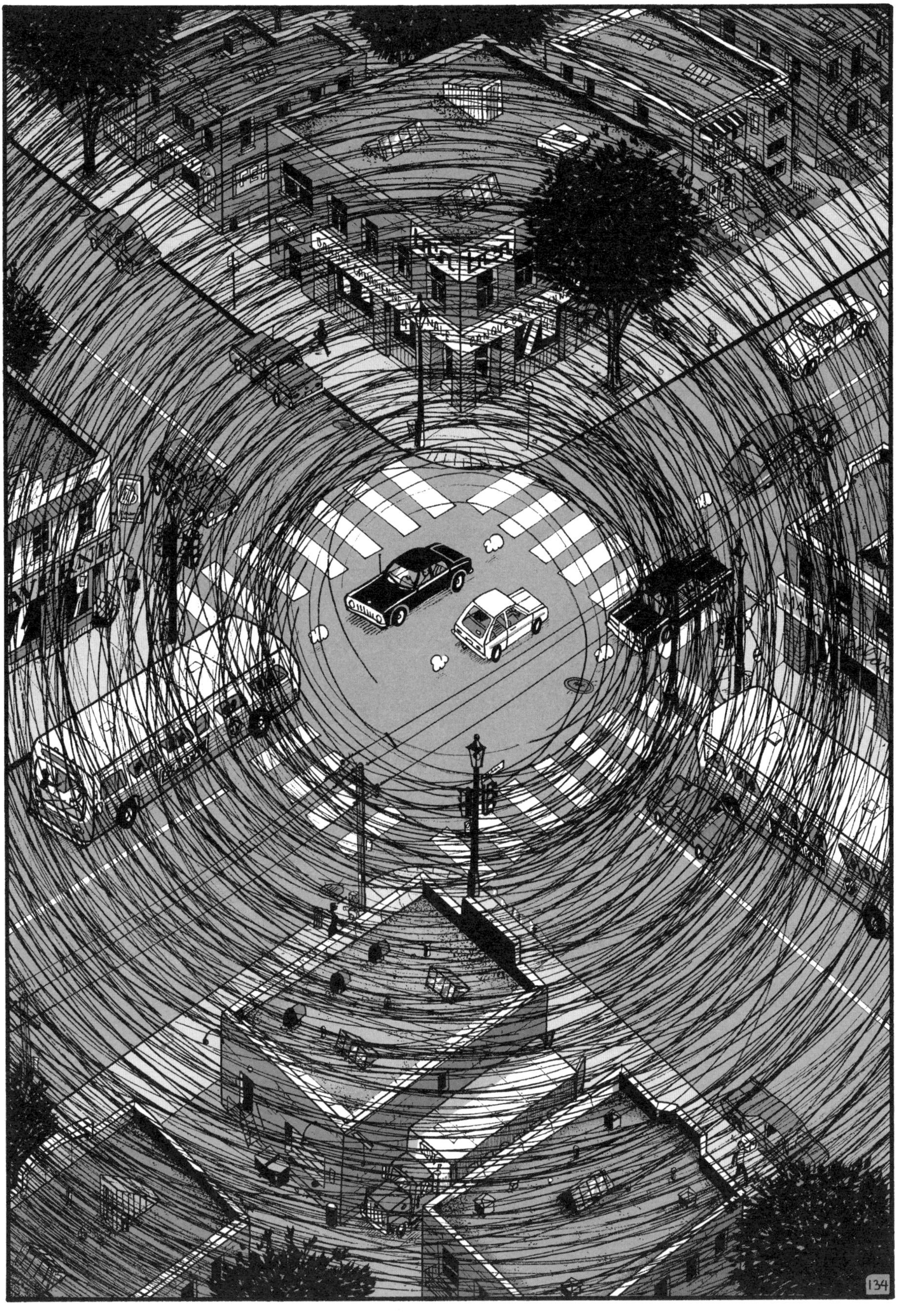
134

Montreal

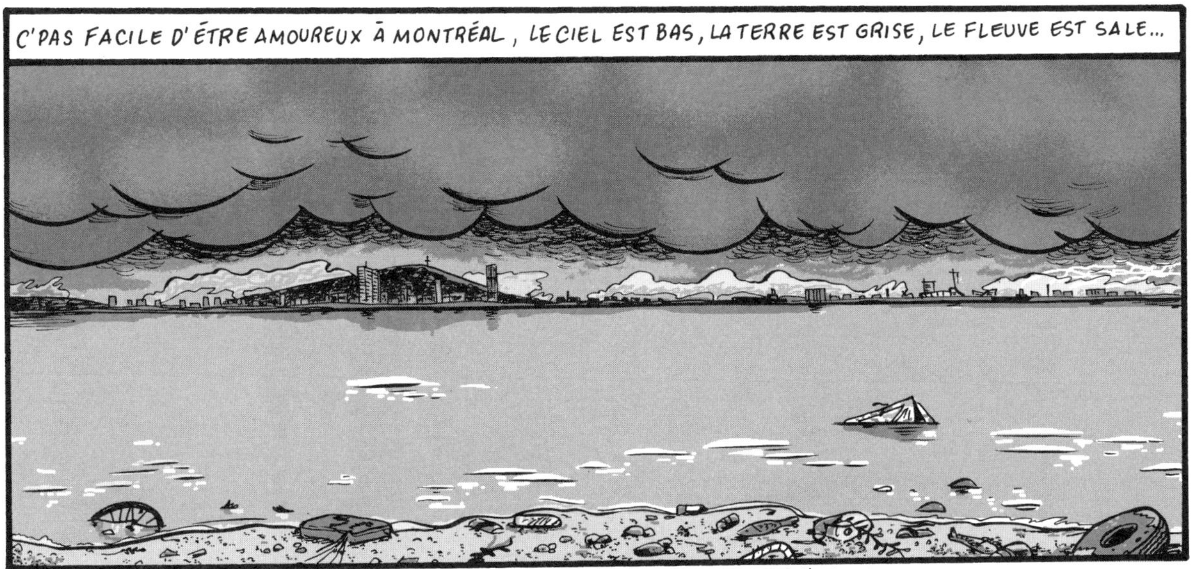
C'PAS FACILE D'ÊTRE AMOUREUX À MONTRÉAL, LE CIEL EST BAS, LA TERRE EST GRISE, LE FLEUVE EST SALE...

"IT'S NOT EASY TO BE IN LOVE IN MONTREAL, THE SKY IS LOW, THE EARTH IS GREY, THE RIVER'S DIRTY...

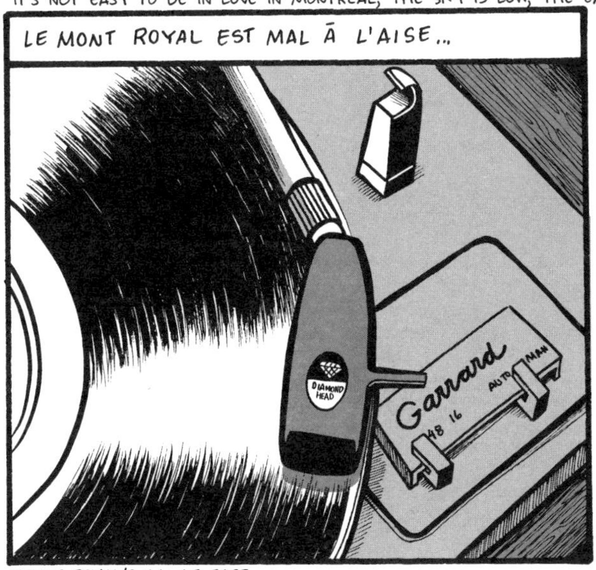
LE MONT ROYAL EST MAL À L'AISE...
DIAMOND HEAD
Garrard
AUTO MAN

MOUNT ROYAL'S ILL AT EASE...

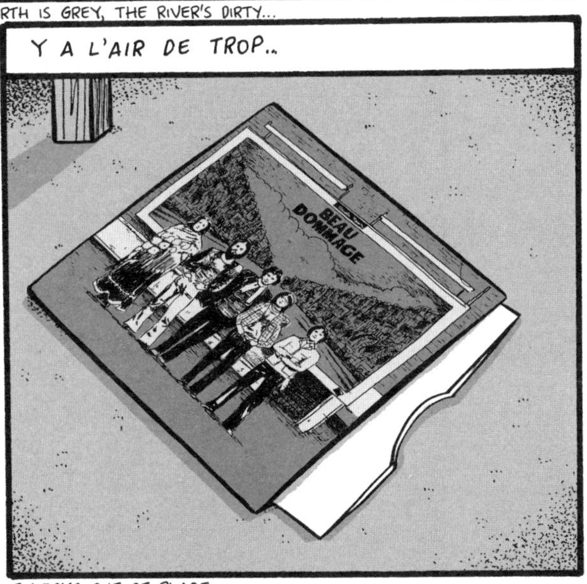
Y A L'AIR DE TROP..
BEAU DOMMAGE

IT LOOKS OUT OF PLACE...

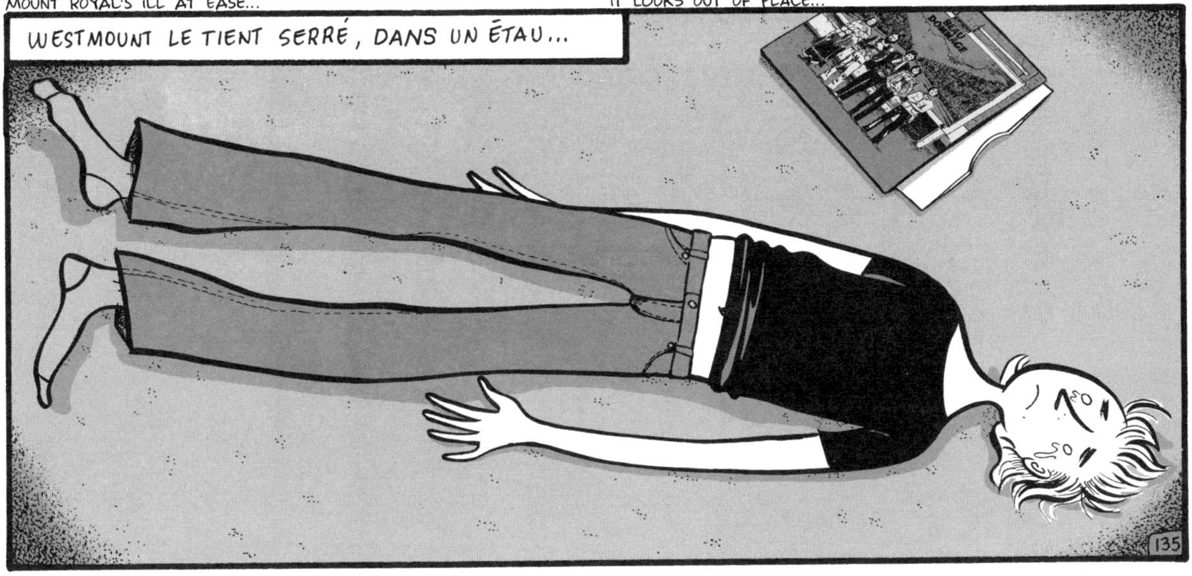
WESTMOUNT LE TIENT SERRÉ, DANS UN ÉTAU...
BEAU DOMMAGE
135

WESTMOUNT'S GOT IT IN A STRANGLEHOLD..."

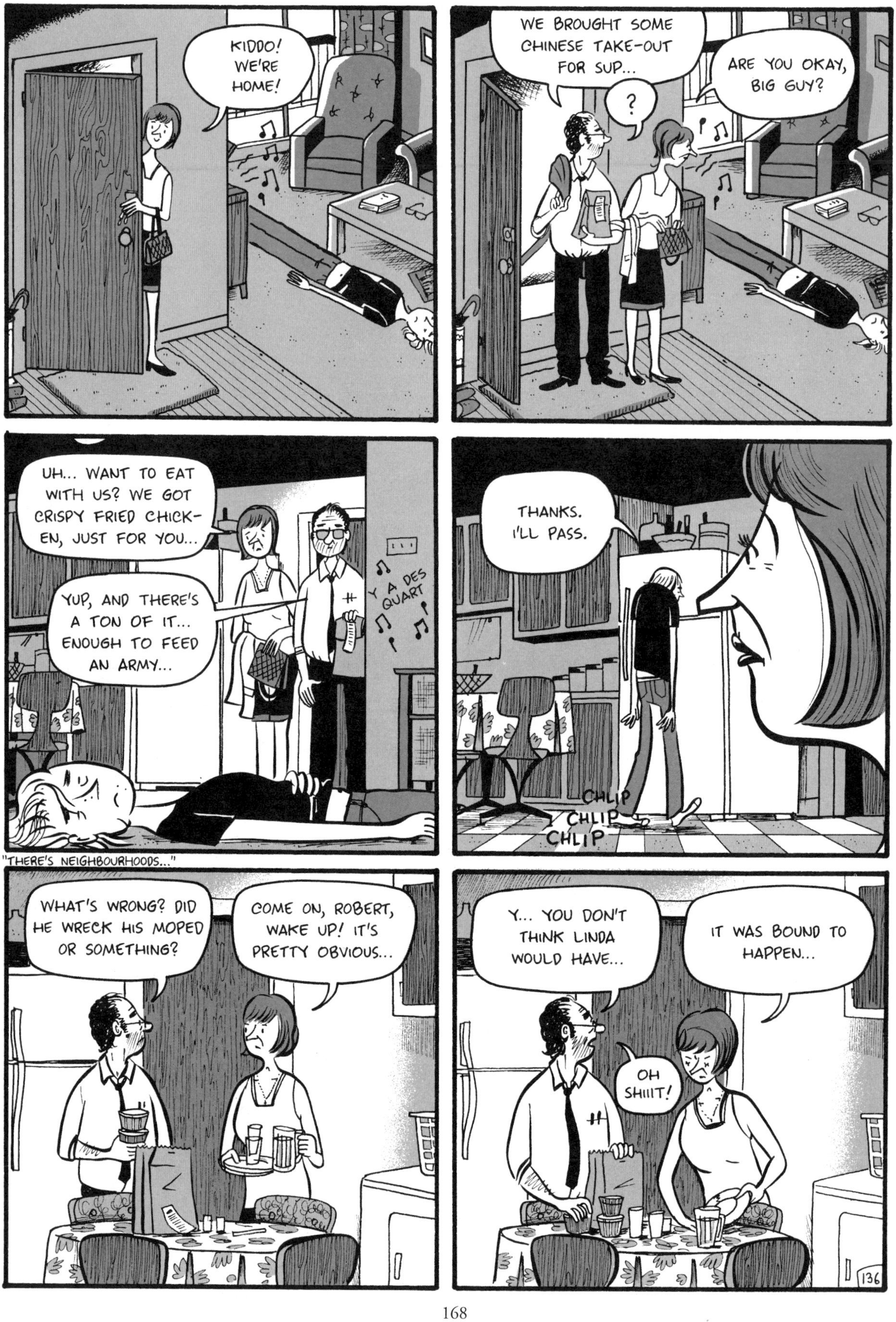
KIDDO! WE'RE HOME!
WE BROUGHT SOME CHINESE TAKE-OUT FOR SUP...
?
ARE YOU OKAY, BIG GUY?
UH... WANT TO EAT WITH US? WE GOT CRISPY FRIED CHICK-EN, JUST FOR YOU...
YUP, AND THERE'S A TON OF IT... ENOUGH TO FEED AN ARMY...
Y A DES QUART
"THERE'S NEIGHBOURHOODS..."
THANKS. I'LL PASS.
CHLIP
CHLIP
CHLIP
WHAT'S WRONG? DID HE WRECK HIS MOPED OR SOMETHING?
COME ON, ROBERT, WAKE UP! IT'S PRETTY OBVIOUS...
Y... YOU DON'T THINK LINDA WOULD HAVE...
IT WAS BOUND TO HAPPEN...
OH SHIIIT!
136

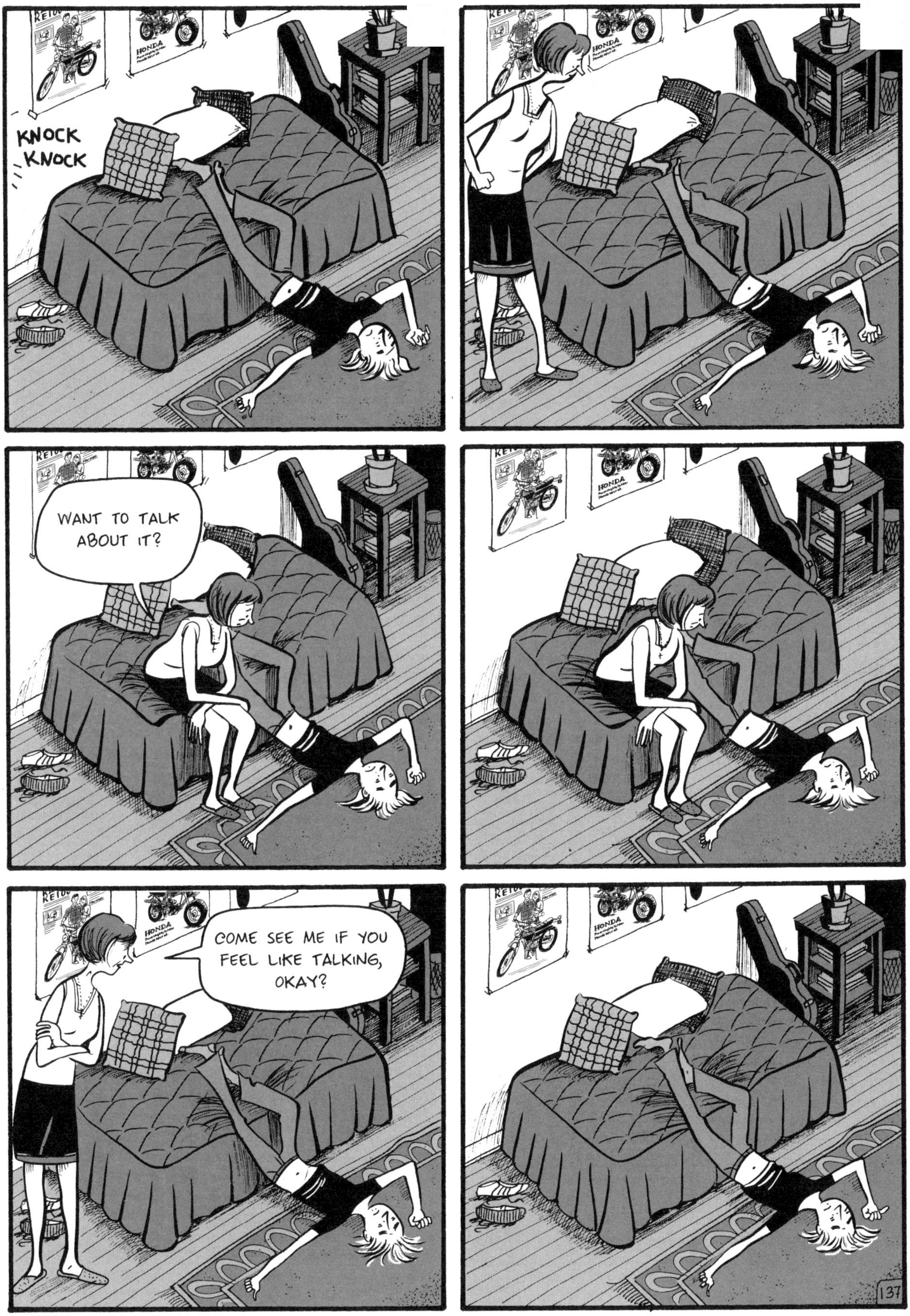
KNOCK KNOCK
WANT TO TALK ABOUT IT?
COME SEE ME IF YOU FEEL LIKE TALKING, OKAY?
137

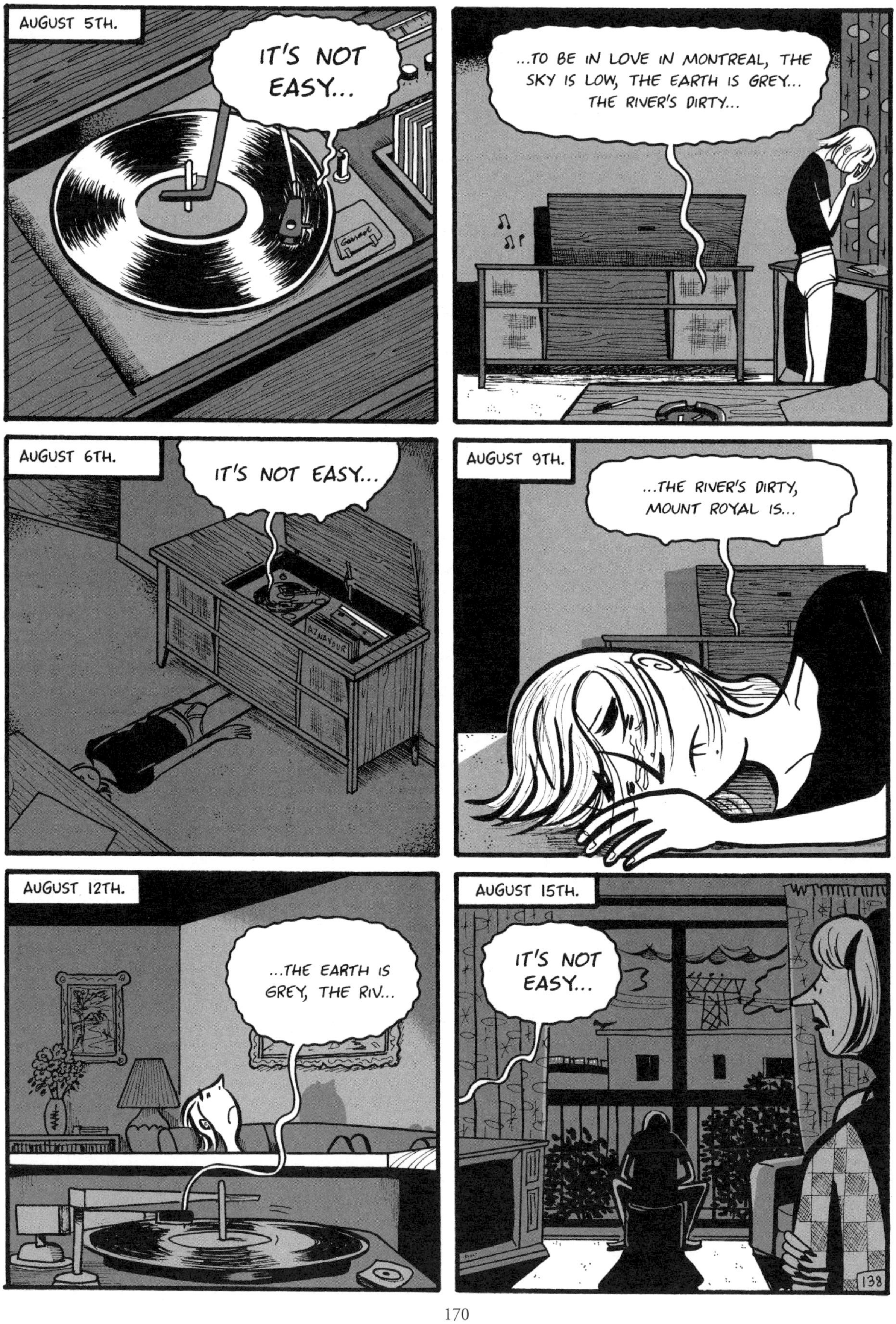
AUGUST 5TH.
IT'S NOT EASY...
...TO BE IN LOVE IN MONTREAL, THE SKY IS LOW, THE EARTH IS GREY... THE RIVER'S DIRTY...
AUGUST 6TH.
IT'S NOT EASY...
AZNAVOUR
AUGUST 9TH.
...THE RIVER'S DIRTY, MOUNT ROYAL IS...
AUGUST 12TH.
...THE EARTH IS GREY, THE RIV...
AUGUST 15TH.
IT'S NOT EASY...
138

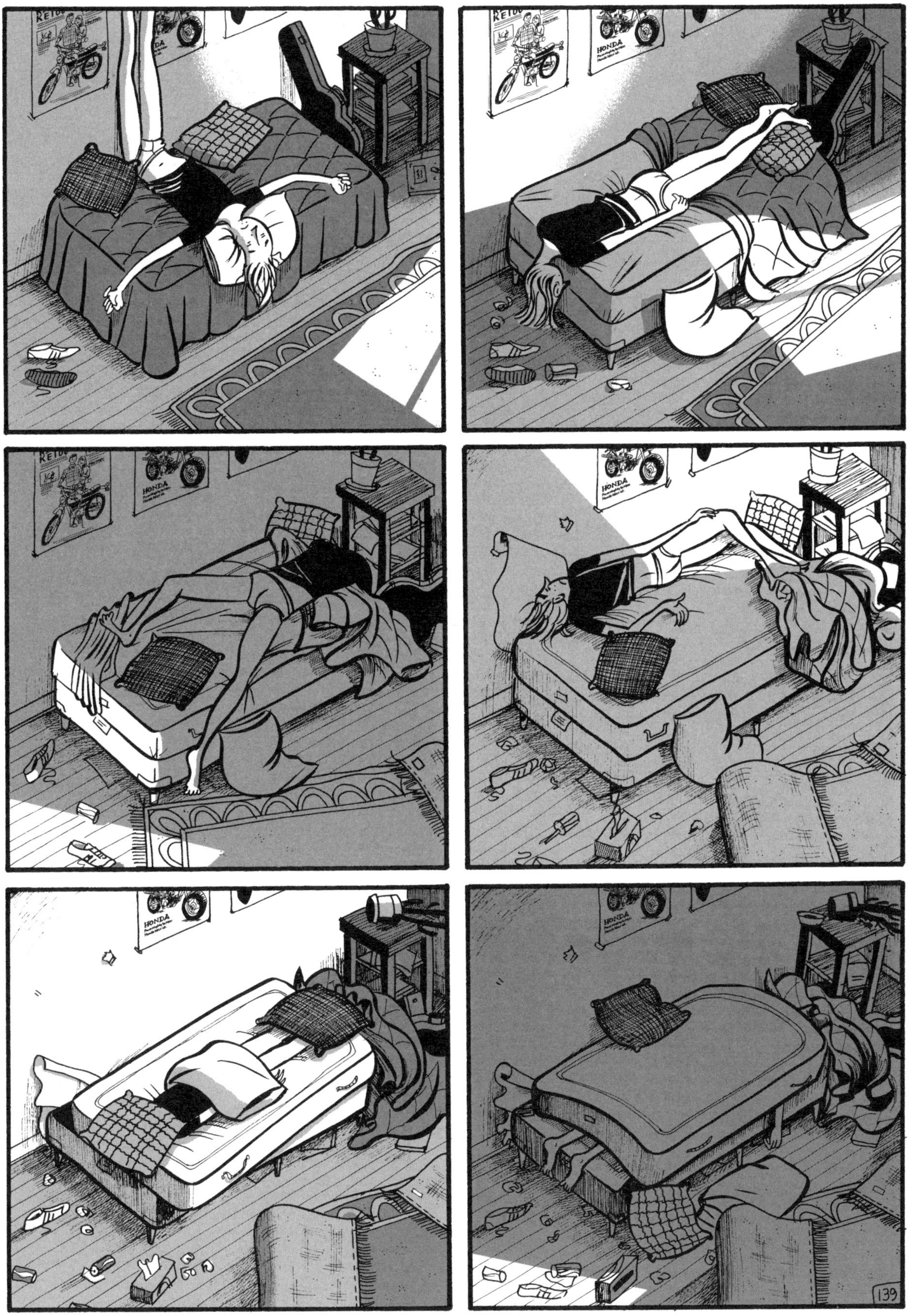
HONDA

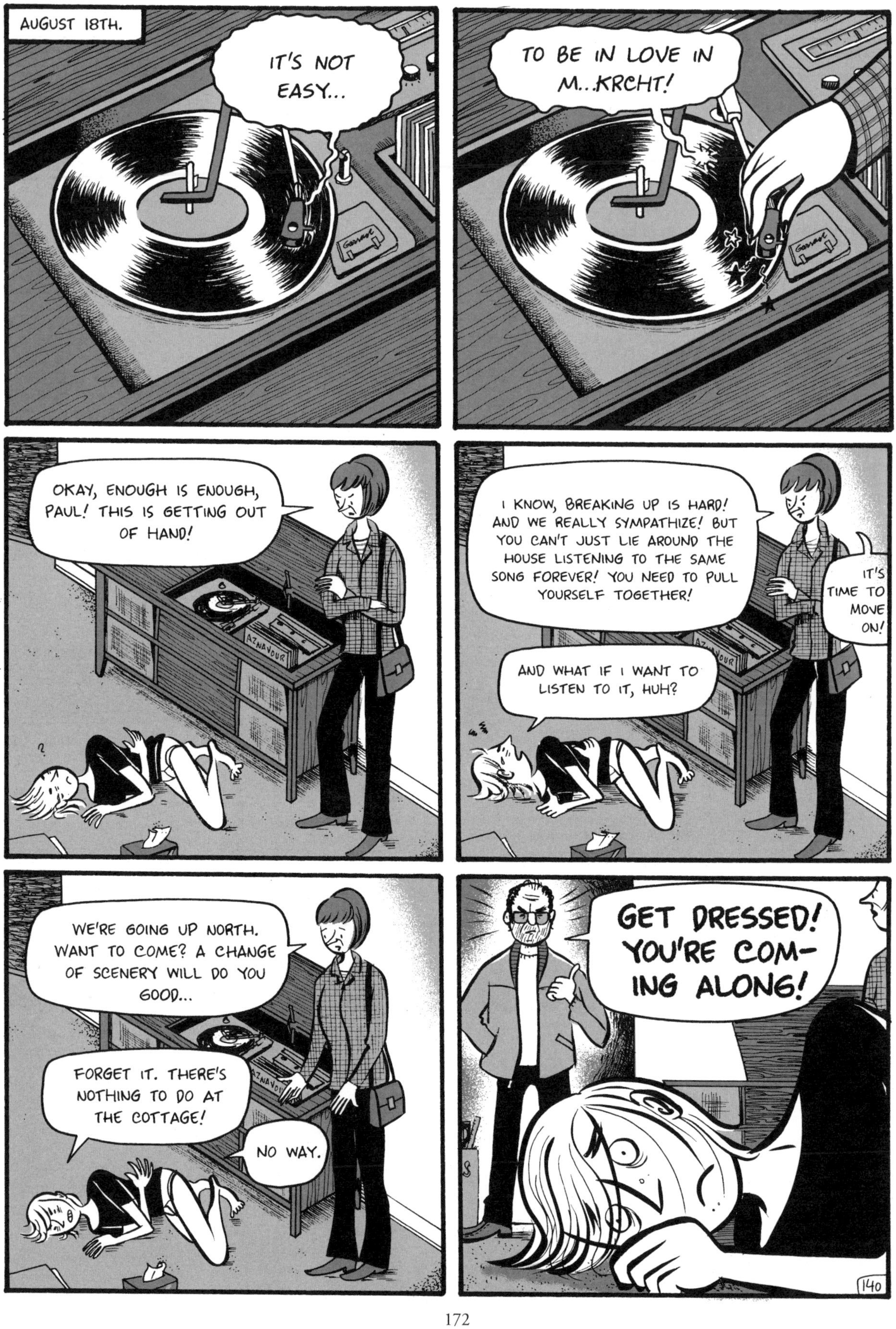
AUGUST 18TH.
IT'S NOT EASY...
TO BE IN LOVE IN M...KRCHT!
OKAY, ENOUGH IS ENOUGH, PAUL! THIS IS GETTING OUT OF HAND!
I KNOW, BREAKING UP IS HARD! AND WE REALLY SYMPATHIZE! BUT YOU CAN'T JUST LIE AROUND THE HOUSE LISTENING TO THE SAME SONG FOREVER! YOU NEED TO PULL YOURSELF TOGETHER!
IT'S TIME TO MOVE ON!
AND WHAT IF I WANT TO LISTEN TO IT, HUH?
WE'RE GOING UP NORTH. WANT TO COME? A CHANGE OF SCENERY WILL DO YOU GOOD...
FORGET IT. THERE'S NOTHING TO DO AT THE COTTAGE!
NO WAY.
GET DRESSED! YOU'RE COMING ALONG!
140

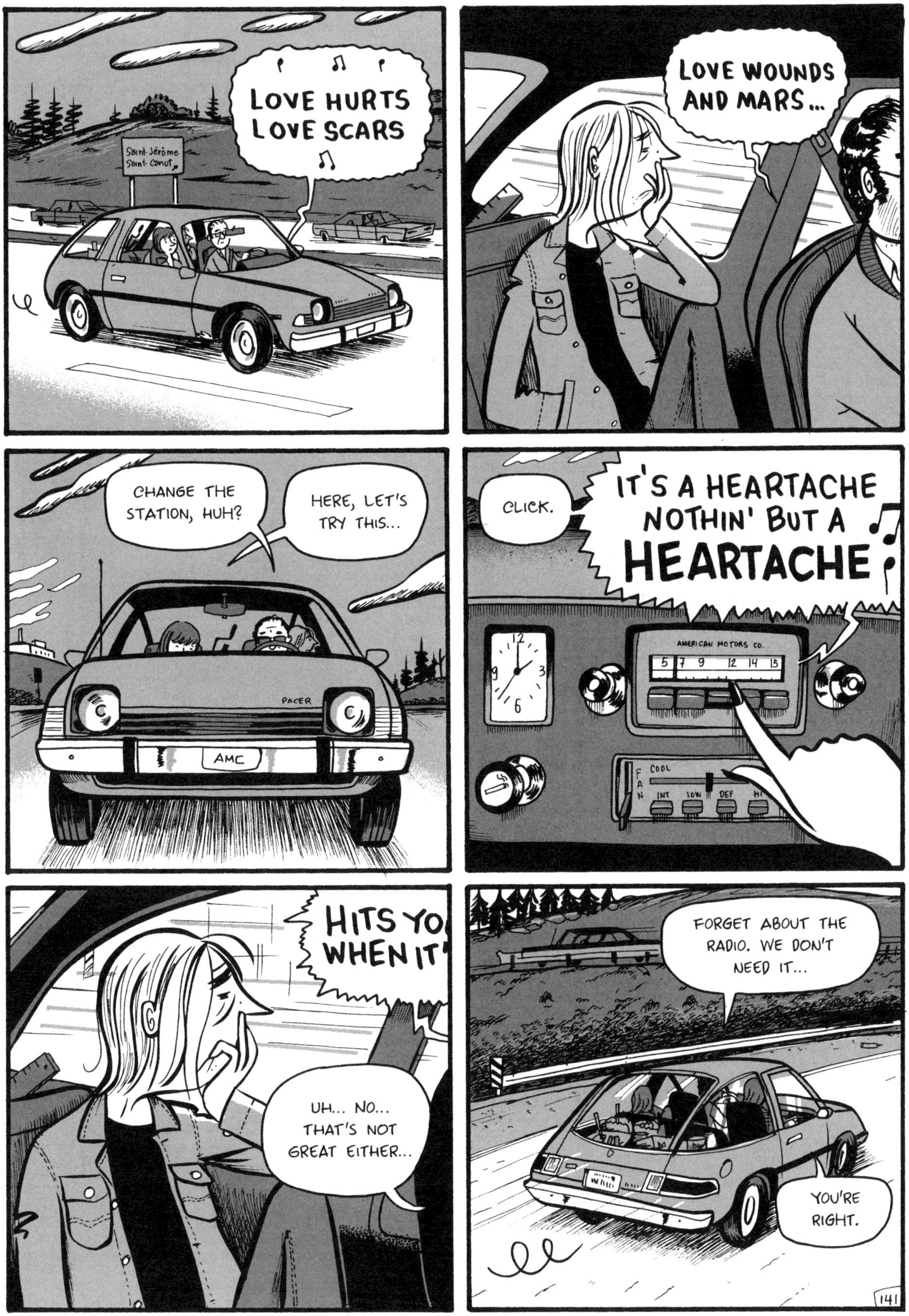
Saint-Jérôme
Saint-Canut
LOVE HURTS
LOVE SCARS
LOVE WOUNDS
AND MARS...
CHANGE THE STATION, HUH?
HERE, LET'S TRY THIS...
PACER
AMC
CLICK.
IT'S A HEARTACHE
NOTHIN' BUT A
HEARTACHE
AMERICAN MOTORS CO.
COOL
FAN
INT LOW DEF
HITS YO
WHEN IT
UH... NO... THAT'S NOT GREAT EITHER...
FORGET ABOUT THE RADIO. WE DON'T NEED IT...
YOU'RE RIGHT.
141

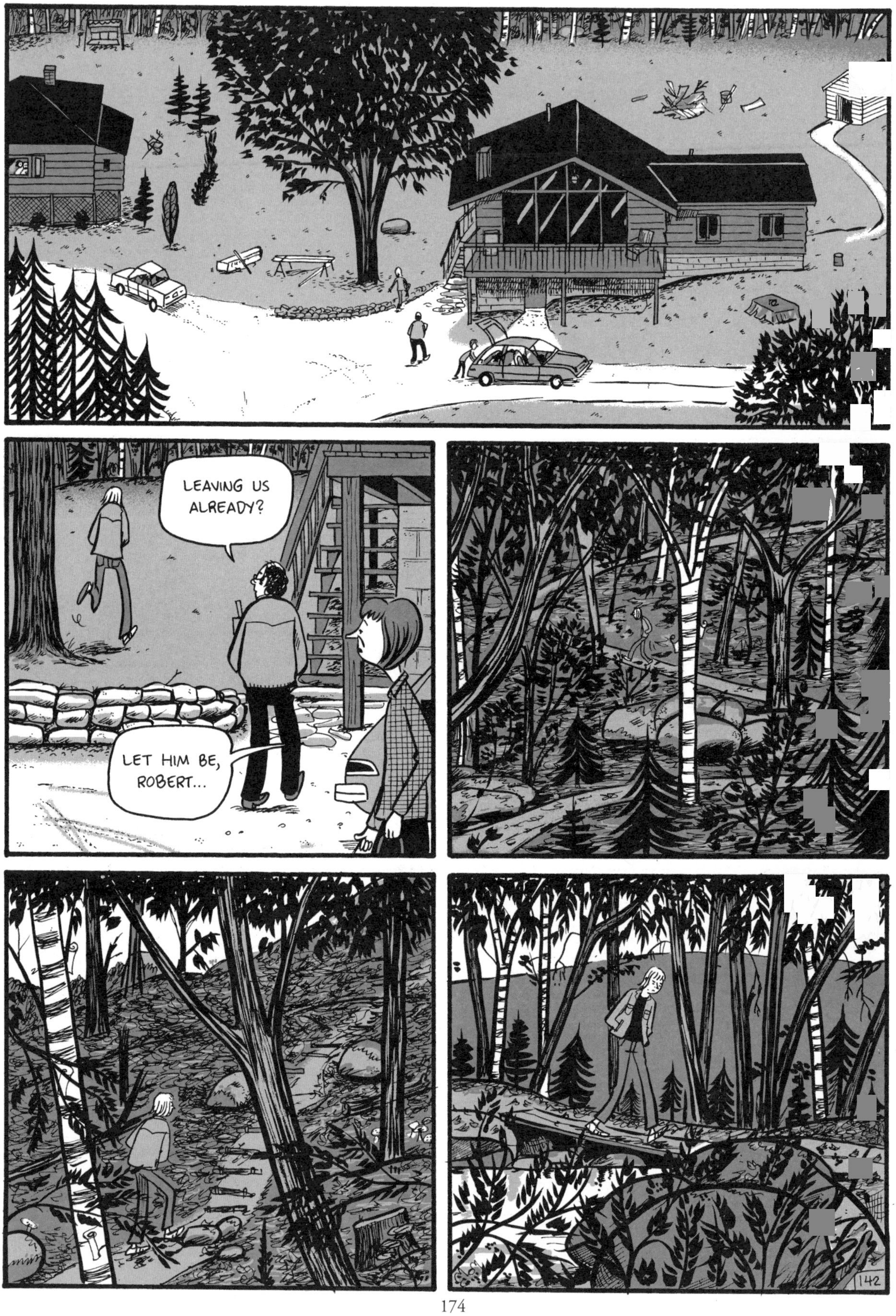
LEAVING US ALREADY?
LET HIM BE, ROBERT...
142

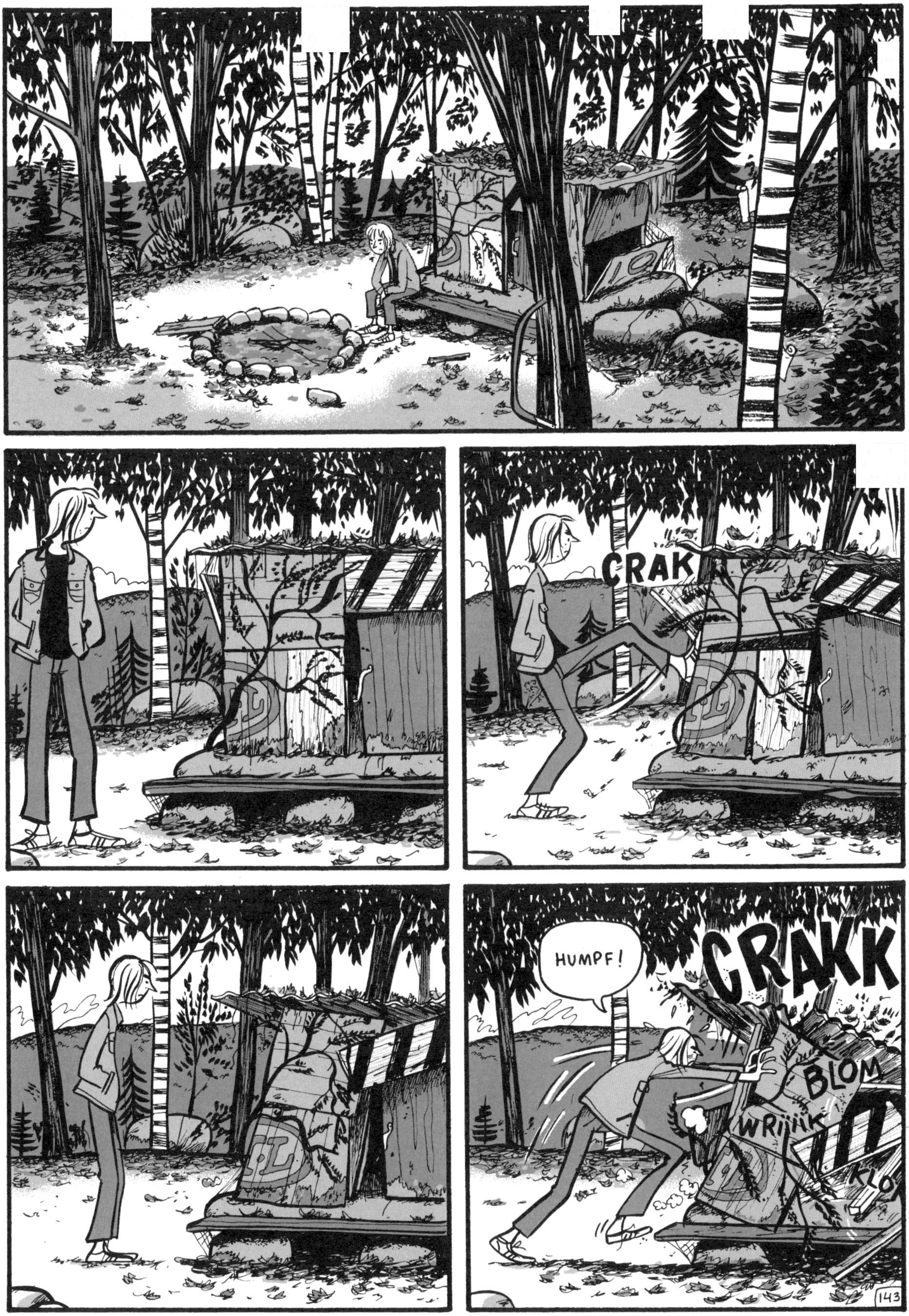
CRAK
HUMPF!
CRAKK
BLOM
WRIIIK
KLO
143

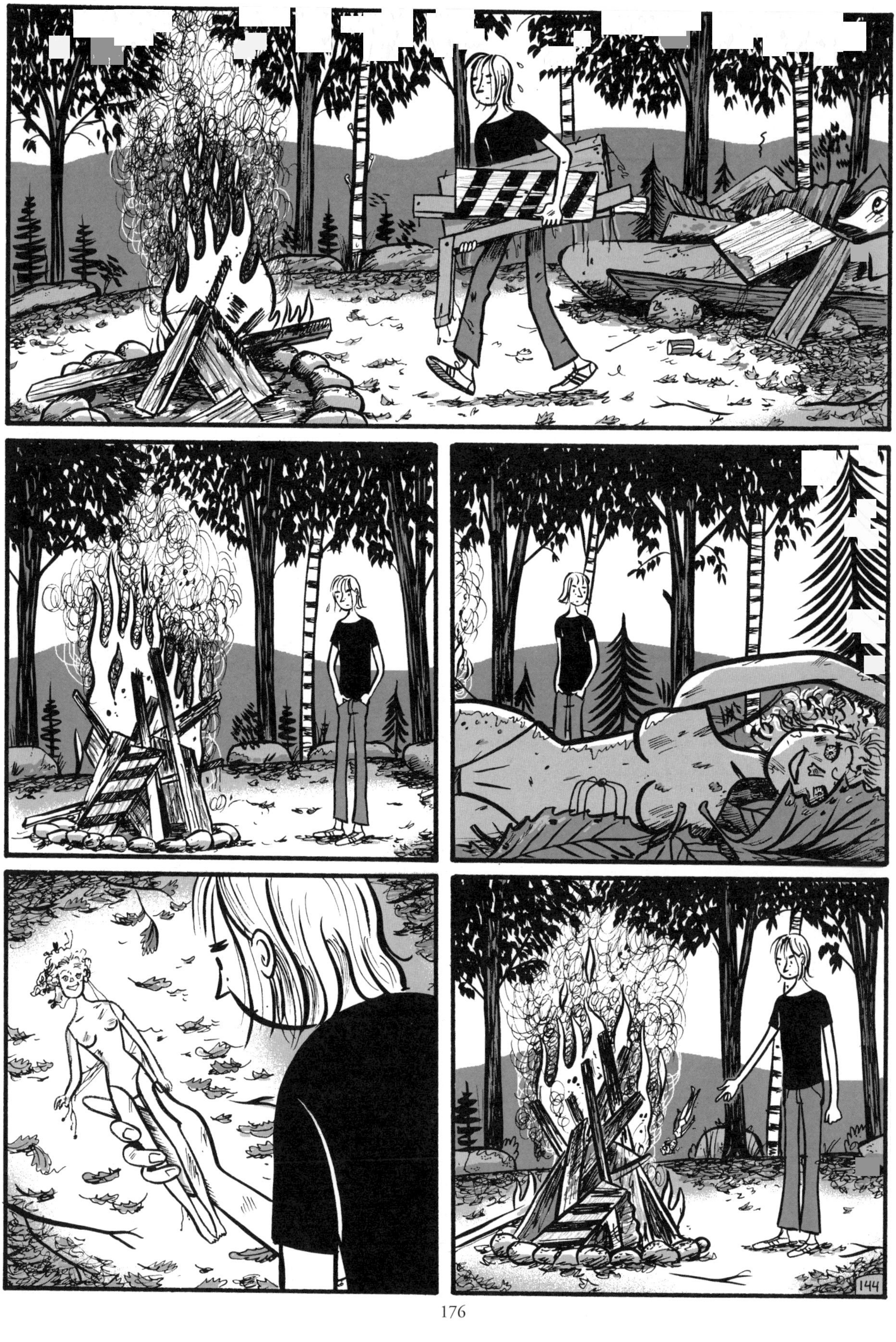
144

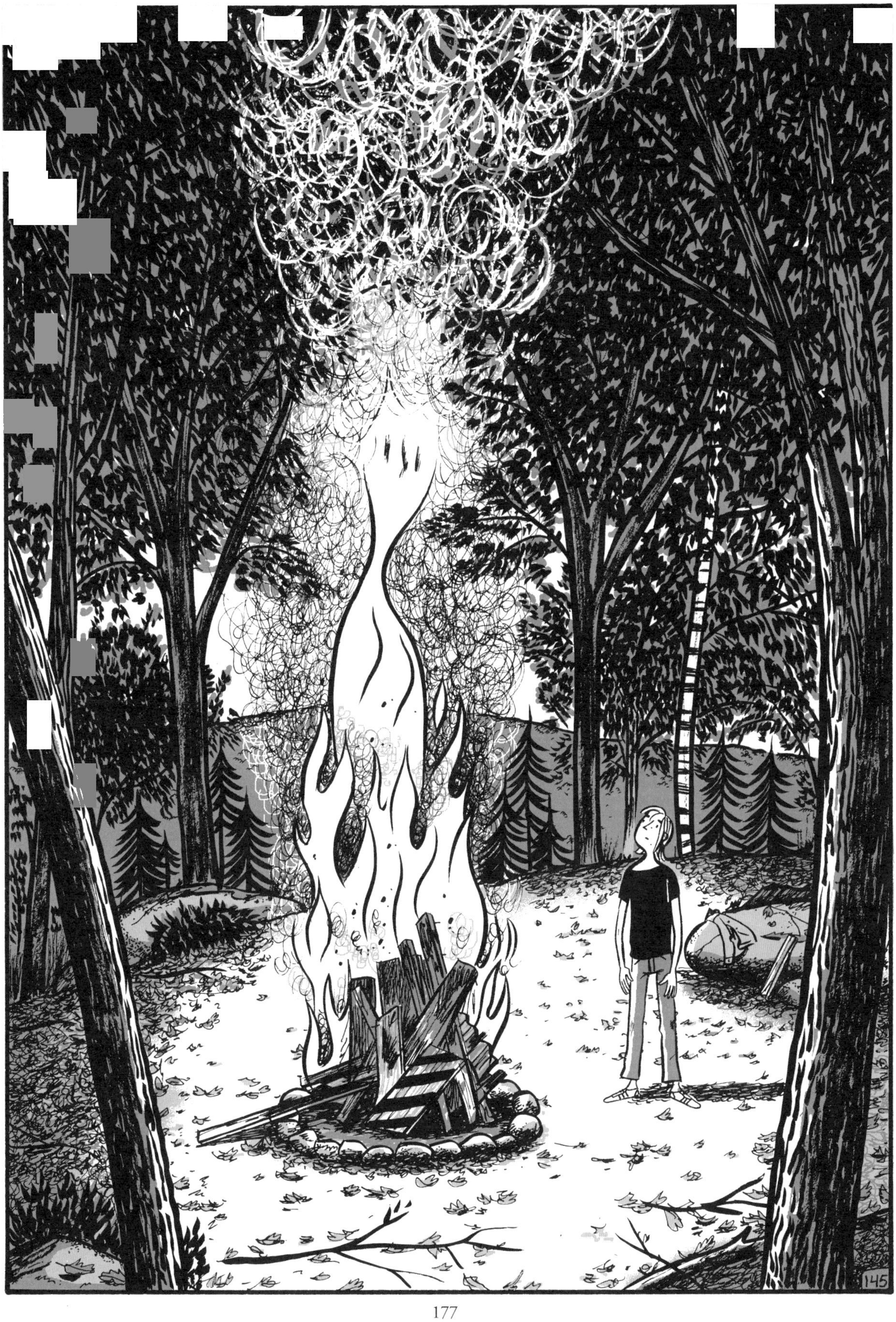
145

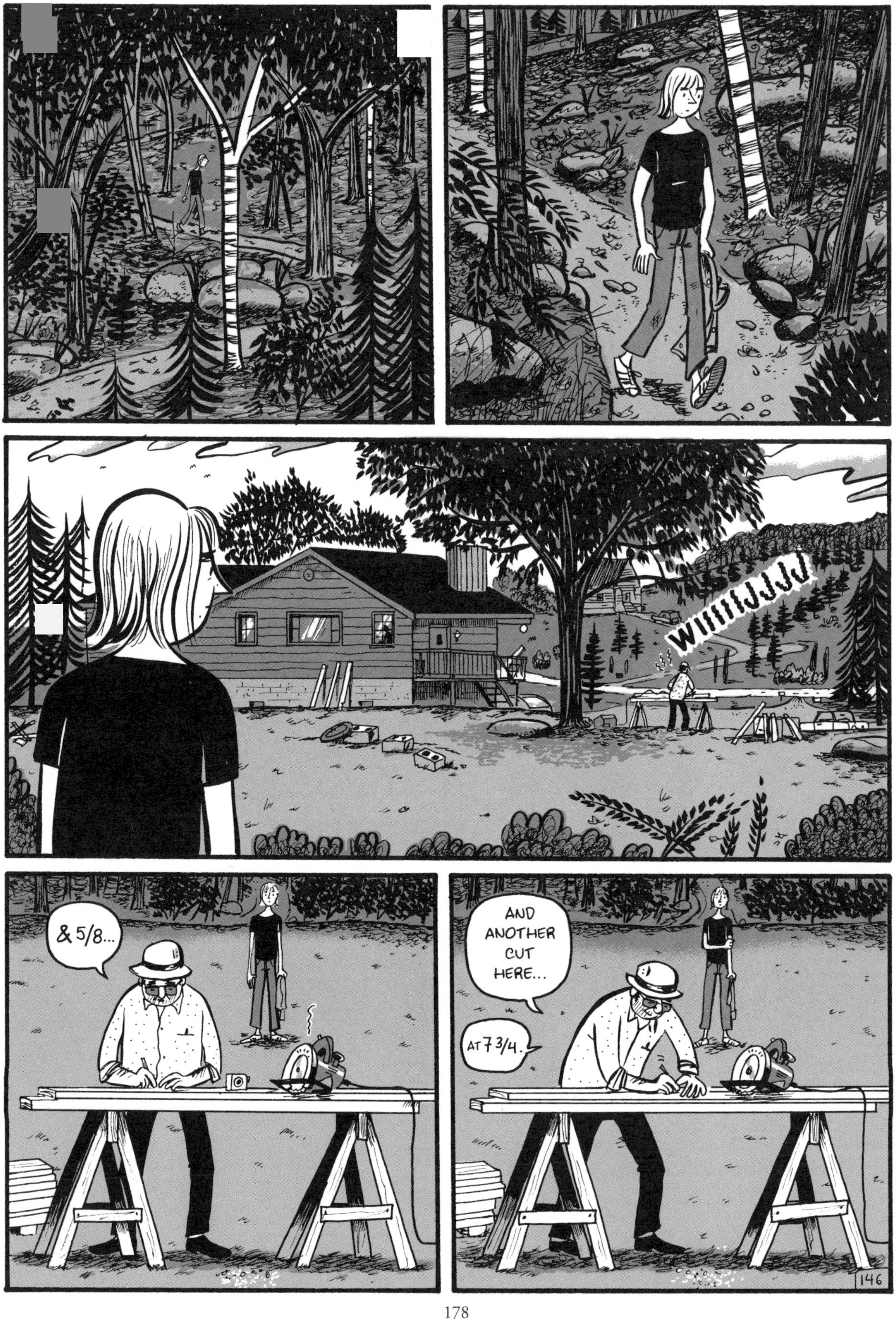
WIIIIIJJJJ
& 5/8...
AND ANOTHER CUT HERE...
AT 7 3/4.
146

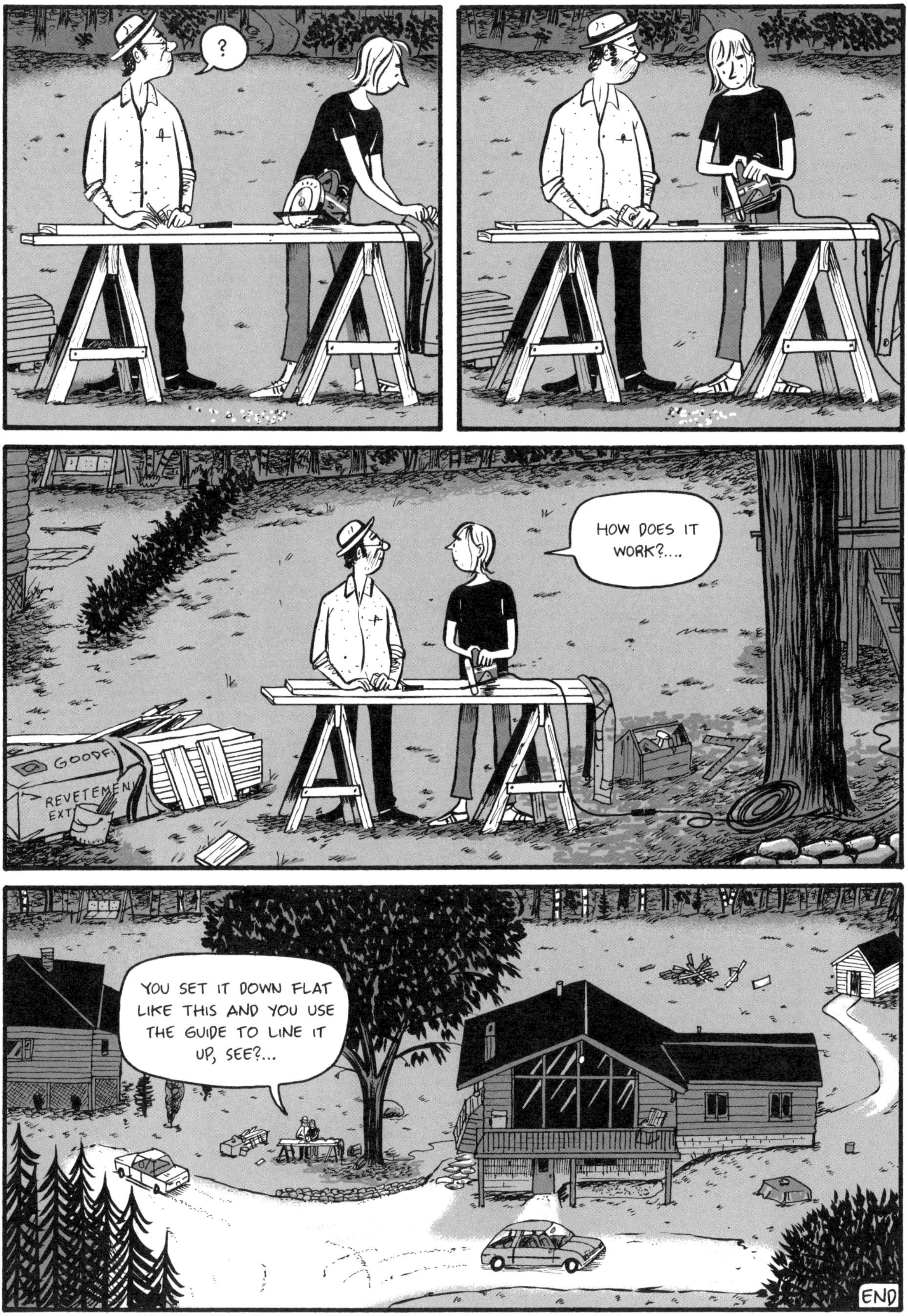
?
HOW DOES IT WORK?....
YOU SET IT DOWN FLAT LIKE THIS AND YOU USE THE GUIDE TO LINE IT UP, SEE?...
END

MICHEL RABAGLIATI JUNE 2015

Music

Put Your Hand in the Hand
Joan Baez

Get Down Tonight
KC & the Sunshine Band

Lady Marmalade
B. Crewe, K. Nolan — P. LaBelle

Never Never Gonna Give You Up
Barry White

Kung Fu Fighting
Carl Douglas

Ma patrie est à terre
P. Harel — Offenbach

La vie en rose
E. Piaf, R. Chauvigny — Offenbach

La maudite machine
P. Flynn — Octobre

Nancy Beaudoin
L. Francoeur — Aut'Chose

Welcome to the Machine
R. Waters — Pink Floyd

Whole Lotta Love
W. Dixon, R. Plant — Led Zeppelin

Ginette
P. Huet, M. Rivard — Beau Dommage

My Eyes Adored You
B. Crewe, K. Nolan — Frankie Valli

Ah toi, belle hirondelle! et *Dis-moi Charles*
Traditional — Lougarou

Do You Feel Like We Do
Peter Frampton

Nights in White Satin
J. Hayward — The Moody Blues

J'entends frapper
Michel Pagliaro

Pour un instant
S. Fiori, M. Normandeau — Harmonium

Show Me The Way
Peter Frampton

Le pénitencier
The Animals — H. Aufray, J. Hallyday

Young Love
Sonny James

Canon en ré majeur
Johann Pachelbel

Communication Breakdown
J. Page, J. Bonham, J.P. Jones — Led Zeppelin

Montréal
P. Huet, R. Léger — Beau Dommage

Love Hurts
B. Bryant — Nazareth

It's a Heartache
R. Scott, S. Wolfe — Bonnie Tyler

Also by Michel Rabagliati from Conundrum Press

The Song of Roland

Winner of the Doug Wright Award for Best Book 2012
ISBN 978-1-894994-61-3

Paul Joins the Scouts

Winner of the Doug Wright Award for Best Book 2013
Nominated for the Slate Cartoonists Studio Prize
Listed by YALSA as a Great Graphic Novel for Teens
ISBN 987-1-894994-69-9